CW01346812

Reservations for Women

ISSUES IN CONTEMPORARY INDIAN FEMINISM

Reservations for Women

Edited by
MEENA DHANDA

Series Editor
RAJESWARI SUNDER RAJAN

women
UNLIMITED
an associate of
kali for women

kali for women

Reservations for Women
was first published in India in 2008 by

Women Unlimited
(an associate of Kali for Women)
K-36, Hauz Khas Enclave, Ground Floor
New Delhi 110016

© 2008 this collection, Women Unlimited
© 2008 individual essays with the authors

All rights reserved

ISBN: 81-88965-41-3

Cover design: peali@pealistudio.com

Typeset at Tulika Print Communication Services,
35A/1, Shahpur Jat, New Delhi 110049
and printed at Raj Press,
R-3, Inderpuri, New Delhi 110012

Contents

Series Note
    Rajeswari Sunder Rajan   ix

Acknowledgements   xi

Introduction
    Meena Dhanda   xiii

I. Historical Background

Women's Challenges to Reservations in Pre-Independence India
    Sarojini Naidu, Begum Shah Nawaz & others   3

Dissenting Voices
    Lotika Sarkar & Vina Mazumdar   11

Historical Soundings
    Vina Mazumdar   17

Reservations and the Women's Movement in Twentieth Century India
    Mary E. John   29

II. Theoretical Issues

The Quota Question: Women and Electoral Seats
    Nandita Shah & Nandita Gandhi   61

Quotas for Women
    Anne Phillips   82

Democratic Institutions, Political Representation and
Women's Empowerment
    SHIRIN M. RAI   111

Representation for Women:
Should Feminists Support Quotas?
    MEENA DHANDA   132

Elusive 'Woman':
Feminism and Women's Reservation Bill
    NIVEDITA MENON   158

III. Women as Policy Makers

Women, Zilla Parishads and Panchayat Raj
    GAIL OMVEDT   189

Women in the Calcutta Municipal Corporation
    STÉPHANIE TAWA LAMA-REWAL   197

The Impact of Reservation in the Panchayati Raj
    RAGHABENDRA CHATTOPADHYAY & ESTHER DUFLO   245

Panchayat Raj Institution (PRI) and Women's Reservation
    R. GEETHA   270

IV. Alternatives to the Women's Reservation Bill

Women and Politics: Beyond Quotas
    MADHU KISHWAR   299

Women's Reservation and Democratisation:
An Alternative Perspective
    VASANTHI RAMAN   327

Enhancing Women's Representation in Legislatures
    JAYAPRAKASH NARAYAN, DHIRUBHAI SHETH,
    YOGENDRA YADAV & MADHU KISHWAR
    (Forum for Democratic Reforms)   332

Women and PR
  GAIL OMVEDT   351

Dual-member Constituencies:
  Resolving Deadlock on Women's Reservation
  MEDHA NANIVADEKAR   355

Appendix 1: The Constitution (Eighty-first
  Amendment) Bill, 1996   371

Appendix 2a: Women and National Parliaments
  as of 31 January 2007   374

Appendix 2b: Women and National Parliaments
  as of 31 January 2007   376

Contributors   383

Series Note

Issues in Contemporary Indian Feminism is a series that is premised on the need for an overview of the substantial writing available on a variety of issues in Indian feminism. Each individual volume will relate to an issue of some moment, specifically one on which there has been a wide variety of views and positions. The mapping of these complex and often contentious issues—around 'feminism' itself, gender and caste, dowry and inheritance, gender and censorship, and sexualities, to name the topics of the first few volumes—is intended to serve as a point of entry and guide to what might be unfamiliar territory to some; to those closer home, themselves perhaps participants in these debates, they would indicate some of the shifts in the direction various feminist debates have undergone.

With these volumes we hope to construct a long overdue archive of writings relating to gender issues in India. The materials have been selected from a large mass of several decades of feminist writing scattered in journals and books, pamphlets, manifestoes, speeches and official documents. By bringing them within the covers of a single volume, we hope to provide handy reference to otherwise hard-to-access resources. The series is therefore particularly intended to serve the needs of research scholars, teachers in Women's Studies courses, and activists. These collections will at the same time, we hope, bring to prominence a substantial, complex and important body of feminist writing that is closely related to the issues tackled by the women's movement in India. Viewed in this way, it becomes evident that these engagements, at once topical and far-sighted, make a major contribution to global feminist theory.

The editors of the individual volumes are experts in their areas. Their introductory essays will provide an overview of the debate/discourse on each topic, identify its landmarks, and offer a distinctive perspective on the theoretical tendencies that determine its frames of reference. The selections are based on implicit criteria, such as the influence a work may have exerted on subsequent thought or policy, its representation of a prominent trend, the contribution it makes to a particular debate, or its intrinsic 'merit'.

Rajeswari Sunder Rajan
Series Editor
(Global Distinguished Professor of English,
New York University)

Acknowledgements

My ideas on the subject of gender quotas for women were first discussed in the public domain at a conference of the British Association of South Asian Studies held at Bath Spa University in 1997. I thank the participants of that conference for their interrogations, which made me appreciate the complexities of the issue. Later, *Women's Philosophy Review* carried my article in a special issue on Feminist Political Philosophy in 1998; I thank the editors and the anonymous referees for their rigorous questioning and constructive advice. The stalwart editor of *Economic and Political Weekly*, the late Krishna Raj, made space for my revised article on the theme in 2000. I remember him with gratitude.

The present volume was the brainchild of Rajeswari Sunder Rajan who reposed her trust in my ability to give this fraught issue of reservations for women in the Parliament and legislative assemblies, a thought-provoking, fair and balanced handling. I thank her and hope to have lived up to her expectations.

I am very grateful to Mallarika Sinha for her research assistance; she used her access to facilities at Oxford University to get me printouts of news reports and several other writings on the subject. My daughter, Tanya Singh, edited my introductory essay and provided help in collating various materials accumulated over a period of almost 10 years. As always, she's been there for me.

Ritu Menon continued to patiently wait for the completion of the project even when it was inching forward slowly. Ratna Sahai has been an expert editor, firm and considerate.

ACKNOWLEDGEMENTS

Above all, I thank Pritam Singh, for believing in me and supporting me throughout the project by feeding bites of crucial information at the right time. I am grateful for his intellectual friendship.

My faith in formerly apolitical women to acquire quickly the ability to prioritise objectives, streamline decision-making and govern in a democratic and accountable manner, stems from watching my mother grow into the role of President of her local ladies club in Ludhiana many years ago in the 1970s. After years of managing a house and providing a loving home for our family, she has returned to having a role in organising a public institution as an honorary warden at a women's hostel in Dayalbagh. I dedicate this volume to my energetic mother, Sushila Dhanda.

Meena Dhanda
University of Wolverhampton

Introduction

MEENA DHANDA

The problem of representation has a long-standing history in Indian political thinking. The constitution makers had struggled with designing a structure of representation capable of doing justice to the qualitatively different perspectives of the diverse collectives that made up the Indian political scene in the early part of the 20th century. Foremost amongst these pathfinders was Babasaheb Ambedkar, a passionate advocate of 'personal representation' beyond merely representing interests of different groups.[1] At a session of the Round Table Conferences (1930-32) convened to widen the scope of representative government in what was then called Dominion India, Ambedkar had said:

> ... the Depressed Classes have been systematically left out. No thought has been given to their claim for political power. I protest with all the emphasis I can that we will not stand this any longer. The settlement of our problem must be part of the general political settlement and must not be left over to the shifting sands of sympathy and goodwill of the rulers of the future.
>
> (cited by Tejani 2007: 55)

It is uncanny that a mere substitution of the term 'depressed classes' with 'women' would capture the spirit of many arguments put forward by feminists,[2] in support of greater presence of women in legislative bodies. The suggested substitution also signals an affinity; women's lack of adequate representation is *like* the lack suffered by the 'Depressed Classes'. In the present juncture, the Women's Reservation Bill has met with objections coined in a language in which the political stakes of women and backward classes are pitted *as if* they are opposed to each other. But are they? We need to pause and ask: Is there a clash between enhanced democratisation in the political participation of caste-based collectives and that of women through their presence in legislative bodies?

It is my suggestion that a greater awareness of caste fissures and of their modulation of patriarchal relations is essential in recommending imaginative long-term measures for sustainable democratisation in India. As in the early part of the 20th century with respect to the 'depressed classes', political thinkers now agree on the need for greater political participation of women. The disagreements now, as then, are about how to bring about the desired change. This volume presents the different positions taken on the issue of instituting the Women's Reservation Bill, or an alternative mechanism for increasing the presence of women in the Lok Sabha and state legislative assemblies, with a view to fostering an informed and constructive debate and consolidating current thinking on the subject. The material offered here is wide-ranging, from historical antecedents of current demands for increased presence of women in legislative bodies in India, to alternative strategies for political reforms in this area.

This introduction will locate the Indian contributions emerging from different historical, theoretical, practical and political contexts within a global context to help identify the general features that underpin problems of enhancing women's political participation in government decision-making bodies.

Globally speaking, after the suffragette movement and its victory, the most remarkable positive development of modern political times is a surge in the attempt to increase the participation of women in the arena of political representation. This surge is not a part of a consolidated movement, and may never become one. However, the half-heard stories of the successes of increased participation of women in parliaments across the world have prepared the ground in many parts of the world for a willingness to consider seriously, and, if conditions permit, to attempt experimentation in this area.[3]

It is heartening to note too that on the issue of gender quotas, activists, political theorists and governments of different countries are looking across national borders for models and inspiration. The complaint that 'western' models of political thinking exercise a menacing influence on the minds of indigenous designers of political reform has passed its 'use by' date. The traffic of ideas does not obey border policing or immigration controls. Whether we like it or not, our actions have an influence on those taking decisions elsewhere.[4] It is also important to learn from experiments already taking place elsewhere in the world when there is a wealth of information awaiting scrutiny and analysis.

A cursory glance at published data on women in Parliament worldwide raises several questions about many of the usual generalisations made about factors affecting women's presence. The relative positions of different countries in the league table are worth reflecting upon. The oft-cited regional experience of Nordic countries needs to be compared with recent institutional changes in countries such as South Africa and Mexico. The experience of Nordic countries also needs to be more thoroughly investigated in its local European context before lessons from it are drawn for use or rejected in the Indian context.[5] It should be noted that on average, women account for 16 per cent of the world's parliamentary representatives. Many highly industrialised countries fall well *below* this average. Japan and Russia are stark examples, with United States barely hitting the mark. If economic development is the key to women's greater participation in Parliament then what has prevented women in these countries from taking their rightful place?

Similarly the data do not show the North in the lead or a North-South divide in women's achievement in this area either. Britain, teetering just above the world average, is way behind Cuba, Argentina and South Africa. Does this mean then that the level of poverty, typically associated with the North-South divide, may not be directly connected to women's enhanced participation?

India happens to be in the lowest rungs. It is admirably surpassed by its much maligned neighbours Pakistan[6] (with twice the percentage of total seats held by women than in India) and China, just below Pakistan, but both higher than the world average. One is forced to ask: is greater democratisation not directly linked to women's better presence?

Finally, if one was to propose multicultural complexity of the polity as a reason for a country's laggard performance, it is hard to answer the obvious question: why has Indonesia done better than India, both equally complex in their multiculturalness?

We need to take into account a combination of the factors hinted at above while making comparisons between countries—economic development, poverty, democratisation, multicultural complexity—and some more, such as the presence or absence of an egalitarian culture, the extent of women's education and professional achievements and the range of the inequality gap. All of these are implicated in the causes for women's low average in parliament.

Different factors predominate at different historical junctures, but in my view, the particular environment within a country is susceptible to changes in the global situation. The local context with its particularities and exigencies determines which global influence will take root. In India, the relevant particular context includes the restructuring of the Panchayati Raj Institutions and the local municipal corporations, the deeply caste divided polity and the 'personalised, patronage- and status-oriented' (Fleschenberg 2005) features of politics common to South and South-east Asia.

But it may be too soon to draw any lessons for the whole country based on reports of the experience of women in Panchayati Raj Institutes. More research needs to be done in all states. The effect of linkages should also be studied. In time, can we expect women sarpanches, panches and municipal corporators to edge their way into legislative assemblies and eventually the central government? Comprehensive data on the re-election of women and on their upward mobility from local to central political arenas would be needed.

The research findings included in this volume present an optimistic picture of women *wanting* to move to state

INTRODUCTION

legislatures, despite hurdles obstructing their progress at every step. Many have faced the hostility of male panches in the shape of no-confidence motions, adverse caste sentiments, trickery and non-cooperation (Pegu 1999). Yet, the number of women contesting for every seat in the second round of elections has on average doubled. There is no doubt that women have stood up to the challenge and begun to make a dent in this male stronghold. Should things be left as they are? Should one wait to see the osmotic effect of this enthusiasm of the new women policy-makers and hope that further legislative steps are rendered redundant? To make any credible judgement one would need data mapping the usual trajectory or 'career progression' of people's representatives in general and compare it to the progress of women candidates in particular.

Much remains to be done and said; this book brings together what has already been said. Section One on 'Historical Background' provides the divergent views of the leaders of pre-independence India on women's effective political participation. It also addresses specifically the recalcitrant divide of caste within the Indian polity that has posed a challenge to the use of political measures on behalf of women, regardless of caste or religion. Section Two on 'Theoretical Issues', collects a selection of articles and extracts from contemporary publications on the legitimacy of representation of women as a group, the problems of defining inclusiveness in a democracy, and of reliance on 'top-down' state support for bringing about political reform and the general difficulty in assessing the efficacy of political measures, institutional or otherwise. Section Three on 'Women as Policy Makers' draws upon research on women's active contribution in panchayats following the 73rd and 74th Constitutional Amendments for one-third reservation for women. This aims to provide a realistic portrayal of the likely outcome if women are present in significantly large numbers in legislative bodies, by highlighting what women have done 'as women' when in power at the local level. Section Four on 'Alternatives to the Women's Reservation Bill' brings together sceptical perspectives on the use of quotas. The alternatives espoused vary from the use of party lists or proportional representation, to electoral reforms and the use of non-state measures of democratisation. An extract from a comprehensive 'alternative' proposal arguably claims to be free from the 'flaws' of the Women's Reservation Bill but has not yet been given significant support for its proposals (for candidate quotas in party lists) by feminists thinkers or politicians.[7]

A criticism of the use of quotas in closed party lists comes from Louise Vincent reporting on the experience of South Africa. Vincent points out that the demand of the African National Congress's Women's League for 30 per cent women's representation in elected positions within the ANC was not put to vote at its conference in 1991 but 'pushed through by the ANC's National Executive Committee just prior to the first democratic elections in 1994' (Vincent 2004: 76). Vincent adds: 'In this system, women gain power only through access to men' and even more damaging is the likelihood that the 'list system ensures women's quiescence because allegiance is owed to the political party which placed the woman high on its list rather than the voter' (ibid.: 78). A cynical conclusion is that the 'improved presence of women in South Africa's national legislature due to the ANC's quota has done little more than advance the careers of a select group of already well-educated, politically highly well-connected women' (ibid.: 92). The elected women themselves are left without much autonomy to act against the 'tight control' of the party leadership. In the Indian parliamentary scene, based on a sample survey of 15 women MPs, of the 39 in the 1991-1996 Indian Parliament, Rai (2002) finds that 'all the MPs questioned made clear, they are "party women first"; the party whip is rarely flouted'.[8] Thus while most women MPs supported the WRB, party discipline did not allow them to vote for it.

The prevalence of a culture of tight party control leads to a startling criticism of the politics of presence that 'simply having members of marginalised groups present when unjust decisions are taken serves to legitimise these decisions because legitimacy is thought to rest not on what is decided, but on who was present when it was decided' (Vincent 2004: 84). One can imagine the scary scenario of a legislature with 30 per cent women voting to increase defence spending at the cost of spending on education—reluctant women legislators' voting hands being tied by a party whip—thus legitimising the decision from 'women's point of view' simply because they were present. Now if women were present in even larger numbers, one could argue that justification of questionable decisions from 'women's point of view' would lose its appeal. Writing on the South African experience, Sheila Meintzes identifies as the 'major challenge' 'the disjuncture between progressive planning and policy development and the necessary capacity to implement them' (Meintzes 2005: 235). She also confirms the evidence, like Vincent, of persistence of an 'androcentric culture' where women parliamentarians face sexism and sexual harassment.[9] On the whole it seems that the presence of women, whilst instrumental in passing progressive legislation, has had an uneven impact on setting a gender sensitive transformative political agenda in South Africa.

Focusing on the experience of women brought to power in local government in India, Duflo (2005) concludes that although reservation 'brings to power a group of relatively inexperienced and less-educated politicians, there is no evidence that this comes at the expense of the quality of decision making ... and at least one group (women) is less likely to take bribes'. Duflo recommends reservation as a 'powerful redistributive tool'.

The messages are mixed. What is clear, as Petra Meier (2002) argues following Lovenduski and Norris (1993) is that 'studying aspects which influence the women's position in politics in a vacuum, can lead to single-cause, simplistic and deterministic explanations. Therefore it is important to approach the various aspects of an electoral system in a holistic perspective'.

In the interest of providing such a holistic perspective, I have brought together readings from historical, theoretical, practical and political perspectives.

Historical background

The first section looks at the historical antecedents of the current demands for reservations for women in elected bodies. A refusal of 'preferential treatment' is the highlight of the letter from Naidu and Nawaz to the British Prime Minister in 1931. The accompanying Declaration states unequivocally that 'we look upon nominations, reservation of seats, and the co-option in any sphere of activity as a pernicious and humiliating system which must run counter to all real progress'. There is a touching belief in the 'open door of competition' and an unsullied aspiration to find 'our rightful place in the Councils and Federal Legislatures of our country' by 'merit and merit alone'. More than 40 years later in 1974, when the Committee on the Status of Women in India (CSWI) fields its report, two of its writers, Vina Mazumdar and Lotika Sarkar, find themselves dissenting with the decision of the majority. They 'regret' that the decision to recommend the constitution of women's panchayats and reservation of seats for women in municipalities did not extend to legislative bodies too. Commenting on the chequered history of the efforts of women's organisations to bring CSWI recommendations to fruition, Mazumdar courageously accepts the 'volte-face' in her understanding of nation-building. She reassesses her earlier criticism of special representation, noting the resistance amongst the 'daughters of independence' to 'being equated with Scheduled Castes and Tribes'.

The tension between reservations based on caste and those based on gender is acutely observed by Mary E. John, in a historical picture 'spanning the last century' in her essay, 'Reservations and the Women's Movement in Twentieth Century India'. She points out the internal differences between Sarojini Naidu and Muthulakshmi Reddi, both signatories of the Declaration on behalf of women's organisations to the Premier calling for 'no privileges', due to their different starting points. Reddi had been a supporter of reservations, but later came to drop the demand. Worthy of note is John's observation that 'Gandhi's intense personal relationships with women were a conduit for turning demands for reservations or special electorates into signs of anti-nationalist betrayal'. Upper-caste women, following Gandhi, opposed reservations, and in the process 'communal' or 'minority' rights were counterposed to 'women's' rights. At the present juncture, John sees 'the chance to conceive of alternate modernities. This is nothing less than an opportunity to link—rather than oppose—women's rights to rights based on caste, class or minority status in the broader context of a common democratic struggle'. Two essays in the next section (Rai, and Dhanda) attempt to forge such links.

Theoretical issues

One of the earliest detailed discussions on the policy of reservations for women by Nandita Gandhi and Nandita Shah raised theoretical issues of setting strategic priorities for the women's movement in this excerpt from their work, *The Quota Question*. Anne Phillips' chapter on 'Quotas for Women' from her book *The Politics of Presence* is one of the most cited works on the subject of gender quotas. A pertinent reference to the Panchayati Act in India and to the measures taken by the African National Congress in its first democratic election in South Africa sets the global tone of the discussion. She challenges the taken-for-granted attitude in most discussions for or against gender quotas that women *are* under-represented in elected assemblies. If the elected represent ideas of people they represent, then there is no reason why women's ideas should not be represented by men as women are not any more under-represented than any other group whose ideas do not get a fair hearing. Even if women have distinct interests and/or needs, it could be argued that men should in principle be able to voice them. Phillips reminds us with a 'strong dose of political realism' that women cannot really expect 'the degree of vigorous advocacy that people bring to their own concerns', for which the *presence* of women in elected assemblies is the key. Thus she concludes 'changing the gender composition of elected assemblies is a major, and necessary, challenge to the social arrangements which have systematically placed women in a subordinate position'. Whilst the presence of women is also important as symbolic representation and relates to the self-image of the represented, it should not be seen as an end in itself. Representation is a 'process', in need of constant reinvigoration by electors' participation in holding the elected accountable.

In her paper, 'Democratic Institutions, Political Representation and Women's Empowerment', Shirin Rai recommends an enhanced use of the language of empowerment to assess whether a selective inclusion of women in the Parliament can challenge 'established hierarchies'. In her assessment the quota step is 'important—but inadequate'. The key question for her is 'which type of quota?' Rai points out the alleged 'inherently undemocratic' nature of any quota policy, but does not, however, challenge the conception of democracy underpinning this criticism of quotas. Her empirically grounded observations that non-party women do not seem to be approaching women MPs and that greater representation is being demanded at a time of deteriorating privileges for the worst off women both point towards a more cautious approach. She is mildly sceptical of the use of gender quotas because she urges that increase in women's numbers within Parliament and local bodies must result in 'real benefits' for women. By implication, the increase in numbers is not itself a 'real' benefit.[10] The opposition here between apparent versus real benefits parallels one between affirmative versus transformative remedies.[11]

A philosophical justification for quotas, not taken up by Rai, would need to address this binary opposition. There is an underlying tension between affirming the difference of women by recognising their separateness in a 'reservation policy' and transforming their status through social and economic measures, seemingly eliminating the need for reservations. On Rai's argument, drawing on Nancy Fraser's perspective, affirmation on its own would not be a 'real' benefit if not accompanied by transformation. But is there an opposition between affirmation and transformation? Is not the one always accompanied by the other? The two sides of the opposition are not fixed as it is assumed in arguments for bypassing affirmative strategies. The symbolic processes of culture are not separate from the material processes of political economy. As Iris Young emphasises, 'recognition' (the overt aim of affirmative strategies) is often demanded for the 'sake of redistribution' (the overt aim of transformative strategies). Fraser's view that 'transformative remedies' must be contrasted with 'affirmative remedies for injustice, which alter end-state patterns of distribution and recognition without disturbing the underlying framework'[12] presupposes that there is some recalcitrant 'underlying framework'. A theorist of such a framework might simply want to flash her 'socialist' badge but if one aims to save the 'idea of socialism' understood as 'transformative redistribution' then the metaphoric divisions between apparent/real, surface/depth, superficial/underlying and, of course, affirmative/transformative must be reconsidered.

However, I agree with Rai, that it is important to emphasise 'questions about strategising'. The 'long-standing caste-based quotas' deserve added scrutiny in devising effective strategies for transformation.

In my article, 'Representation for Women: Should Feminists Support Quotas?'[13] I aimed to change the focus of the discussion from a preoccupation with the consequences of instituting a policy of gender quotas to a deeper understanding of what it means to 'engender' democratic political participation and to act in solidarity with women. It was an attempt to clear the theoretical ground, as it were, to foster a genuine dialogue amongst different viewpoints claiming to speak on behalf of women. It was not my claim that consequences are irrelevant,[14] but simply that they are inconclusive. We are operating in a framework of 'probabilities rather than certainties'.[15] I suggested as a principle that '*we must judge public policies in terms of their sensitivity to the identities of people for whom they are designed*' (emphasis in original). Policies that are insensitive to the identity concerns of people undermine conditions of genuine reciprocity and thereby destroy the possibility of a politics of solidarity. By suggesting that we consider gender quotas in terms of 'identity concerns' I wanted to initiate discussion on 'the complex question of how to negotiate the identities of women from lower/backward castes and minorities with a view to empower *them*' (emphasis in original). I also speculated that the praxis of elected women in local bodies would make them likely to 'support gender quotas in the parliament' (ibid.: note 16). Research on the experience of women as policy makers is included in this volume.

Nivedita Menon, sets out avowedly to 'problematise' the terms of discourse used in the debate over reservations for women. Unlike Rai who recommends the use of the language of empowerment, Menon warns that terms 'like empowerment, civil society and democratisation, which form part of the new liberalisation discourse [...] have been given a restricted meaning'. The legitimacy built by women activists has been misappropriated by the state that seems to be speaking on behalf of 'women'. Thus, whilst backward caste identities are unacceptable, 'as far as the ruling elites are concerned, "women" are something they can deal with'. She argues that identities do not 'exist independent of ideology' therefore 'women' too is not a neutral category that exists 'independently of all political considerations'. She supports 'a radical politics of subversion', which compels thinking beyond the quotas question. In practical terms she suggests 'a revisioned PR (proportional representation) system' open to 'newer kinds of political configurations—the anti-big dam movements, anti-nuclear energy movements, alternative sexualities/gay and lesbian rights movements'. I agree with Menon that a PR system, given the current restricted choice of political parties, would be deficient. However, I am tempted to add that the additional political configurations she mentions could well be a part of a new 'Green Party'.

A quandary which women's groups find themselves in with respect to caste quotas 'within quotas', is well exemplified by Manasa. The group found itself unable to decide whether or not to support the Women's Reservation Bill. Raising the demand for reservations for Other Backward Classes (OBC) within reservation might put the Bill 'into the freezer for another 20 years'; endorsing it as it is without sub-quotas leaves the problem 'how do we plan to lobby for later amendments so that OBC women get adequate representation in politics?' (Manasa 2000: 3453)

Lama-Rewal (2001) makes the important point that legally 'the introduction of a sub-quota for OBCs and Muslim women would require beforehand the implementation of quotas for OBCs and for Muslims as a whole in political assemblies'.[16] It might be simple to grant that OBCs also need to be adequately represented, but it is not so simple to suggest a legally and politically defensible strategy to turn the idea into a workable model of representation.

Women as policy makers

Gail Omvedt's reflections on the experience of women in panchayats in Maharashtra, were written *before* the constitutional institution of reserved seats in village panchayats and local bodies. In 'Women, Zilla Parishads and Panchayat Raj', she counters the presumption that women would only be puppets in the hands of rich male peasants of upper-caste families. She cites the experience of women fielded from the Shetkari Sangathana to conclude that 'where women come into local political power as a part of a collective fight, they do so with a bias towards the low caste and poor peasants among them, and with a consciousness of the need to combat communalism and casteism'. They also take up 'need-oriented' development programmes. All this is achieved in the face of hostility and resistance to their leadership.

Stéphanie Tawa Lama-Rewal's, 'Women in Calcutta Municipal Corporation' reports the findings of a survey in 2000 to assess the first phase of the implementation of 33 per cent women's quota in the city's municipal corporation. To test the contentious issues that have divided opinion on the worth of the Women's Reservation Bill it used as data, the results of questionnaires, interviews, direct observation and archival analysis from the survey. It asks whether quotas are conducive to gender justice, to efficiency of assemblies and to representing women's interests. It also studies the impact of rotating reserved constituencies. Its findings are instructive. First, since personal financial resources matter, poor people have 'a definite handicap in municipal politics' and in this case elite women have benefited. Second, being a woman is seen as both a disadvantage in some ways as well as an advantage. However, when asked if, given the opportunity they would consider contesting at the state Assembly level, '89 per cent of the women interviewed expressed their readiness to go further into their political career'. The advantage of being a woman is the 'special relationship with the women of their constituency' giving them access to the CMC, which Lama-Rewal argues is a 'major argument in favour of the ability of reservations to promote political participation'. Third, the findings show a considerable distance between women's organisations (except women's sections of political parties) and women councillors. Interestingly both men and women appreciate the honesty, sincerity, hard work and patience of women councillors. This, in my view, could be a basis for bridging the distance between women activists of non-party organisations and women councillors. Clearly, reservations have produced an 'opportunity effect' as women have contested as independents. The reserved wards have also facilitated greater visibility of women candidates and women party workers. Lama-Rewal concludes that 'contrary to what M. Kishwar had anticipated, more and more women actually contest—and win—against male opponents'. She has, however, partially verified the 'nurturing' argument put forward by Kishwar against rotation of reserved constituencies as it 'generates a game of musical chairs detrimental to the career of women and men councillors and to the interests of voters'. Finally, increased participation, according to her research, does not automatically lead to changing the agenda of the house which she speculates is due perhaps to a credibility issue, to the reluctance of women councillors to be seen as promoting only women's interests.

This finding is at odds with the research reported in the next paper by Raghabendra Chattopadhyay and Esther Duflo, 'The Impact of Reservation in the Panchayati Raj'. They summarise the findings of their village level research in two districts, Birbhum, in West Bengal and Udaipur, in Rajasthan. They show that 'women invest more in goods that are relevant to the needs of local women: water and roads in West Bengal; water in Rajasthan. They invest less in goods that are less relevant to the needs of women: non-formal education centres in West Bengal; roads in Rajasthan.' Their findings challenge the scepticism that women or Scheduled Castes (SCs) are not capable of being independent leaders. According to their results, 'despite the handicaps they may face in terms of education and prior experience, and the preconception of weak leadership, women have a real impact on policy decisions', and the gender of the pradhan affects the provision of public goods. They conclude that 'reservation may be a tool to ensure not only adequate representation but also adequate delivery of public goods to disadvantaged groups'. Finally, they warn that tagging a two-child norm for members of the panchayat, as is being mandated in some states, would adversely affect the candidacy of women and SCs for leadership and that this would be 'an unfortunate outcome' given their findings that the presence of women and SCs in leadership positions makes a 'difference on the ground'.

R. Geetha specifically focuses on anecdotal experiences of women across the country in 'Panchayat Raj Institution (PRI) and Women's Reservation'. In general, according to her, women councillors complain of lack of respect, and of the dual burden of household plus political duties. More significantly, she notes that some women have lost their wages because employers are reluctant to employ a sarpanch or even an ex-sarpanch.[17] Their assertion of independent ways of working and protracted resistance to misuse of power by upper-caste men has been met with horrific violence in some cases, especially those involving dubious land deals. Nevertheless, there are success stories as well. Jalaja Chandran in Kerala managed to use part of the state's outlay of funds for panchayat activities to institute a counselling centre and a legal aid cell. Geetha takes care to point out that this financial backing was due to the LDF government at that time; the new UDF government has reversed some of the decentralising processes started before. Amongst the success stories, the role of Muslim women in Kerala's panchayats, totalling 300 across the district,[18] is noteworthy as they 'were becoming bold, assertive and ready to take on the injustice of their male controlled world'. The stories of Muslim women panches in other states—Fatima Bi in Andhra Pradesh and Nazra Khatoon in Bihar—are exemplary. However, dalit women panches have had a very hard time: in one case, that of Premawati of Uttar Pradesh, the dalit woman elected as panch was not even able to take charge due to upper-caste networking against her.

Alternatives to Women's Reservation Bill

One of the most cited articles on this subject by Madhu Kishwar 'Women and Politics: Beyond Quotas' is followed by Vasanthi Raman's short commentary suggesting that gender oppression must be addressed in 'more subtle and nuanced ways' than is likely to happen by the WRB in its present form. She does support affirmative action for women, but suspects that the WRB 'will willy-nilly strengthen and shore up the interests of the dominant groups'. Nonetheless, she also expects that women's representation from all sections will strengthen the 'democratisation process within communities.'[19]

'Enhancing Women's Representation in Legislatures' by Jayaprakash Narayan, Dhirubhai Sheth, Yogendra Yadav and Madhu Kishwar under the auspices of the Forum for Democratic Reforms is one of the most detailed proposals put forward by anyone in opposition to the WRB.[20] It notes the continuous decline in the participation of women in politics since the freedom struggle, partly due to the increasing violence against women. It acknowledges the need for improving the participation of women in government and politics. Amongst the problems with the present Bill, it lists the adverse affect of rotation of constituencies. On this issue the experience of rotation in wards in municipal corporation elections could be a pointer. According to the research included in the section on Women as Policy Makers, rotation does seem to be a cumbersome process. My earlier theoretical argument in support of rotation (see my article in this volume) was based perhaps on an unrealistic expectation of the readiness of electors to engage in principled rather that personality-oriented politics. I did not give importance to the need for longer-term personal nurturing relations between elected and electors. Was I wrong? In some countries representatives are not allowed to hold two terms consecutively, but that does not hinder their accountability. Therefore it seems that there is no necessary link between accountability and the number of terms an incumbent can hope to serve. When the same people are re-elected, they might make the same promises again and break them again; peoples' criticism of their failures could get further muted for fear of facing the wrath of the politician in power yet again. For new entrants to politics, it might be argued, more stability in office is necessary, which rotation upsets. An alternative that eschews rotation is worth devising and I offer a suggestion to that end in my conclusion.

The Alternative Bill, as it has come to be known, rehearses most of the arguments put forward by Kishwar in her earlier piece.[21] Particularly questionable is the assertion that women 'will lack the legitimacy and opportunity needed to prove their ability and acceptability. Leadership acquired in such a manner will be seen as unnatural, artificial and foisted'. Once again we can learn from the experience of women elected by reservation in local government. Clearly, a number of women have proved their ability *through their work* and thereby earned the confidence of the electors to contest and win in the second round even from non-reserved seats. The proposals of the Alternative Bill could, perhaps, have had a better hearing amongst a wider section of politicians and feminist activists, without the burden of such unjustified proclamations. Further, in the proposed Alternative Bill, the punitive measure suggested in case a party does not field the mandated percentage of women candidates is not at all realistic. Besides the impossibility of determining justly which two male candidates should lose their party symbol when the party errs, the enforcement of such a penalty would vest far too much power in the Election Commission. It is intriguing that the urge for democracy has not tempered the suggestion of the Forum to rely so much on the enhanced role of an unelected body. Nonetheless, some proposals for embedding the Bill in wider electoral reforms, such as the requirement to field election expenses, are entirely welcome, although given the creative accounting powers of chartered accountants, we should be wary about how earnestly the policing of political parties' accounting practices can be done. The focus on party nomination practices is also very sensible.[22]

Enforcement of legislation for party quotas is a tricky business.

Methods of enforcement can range from rejection of party lists failing to meet the mandatory quota (as in Mexico) to fines for non-compliance (as in France). The implementation of French Parity legislation has been uneven, as financial penalties for non-compliance are calculatedly brooked by political parties and individuals. (Stokes 2005: 87). What the French experience shows is that fines may not work to enforce legislation for enhancing greater presence of women in political decision-making bodies. Men are clearly extremely reluctant to give up their seats, so either we need the backing of stricter laws or work out solutions that do not require men to give up their seats.[23]

Krook (2005) provides a very detailed political history of the WRB in India in comparison with the passage of the parity law in France. The most important aspect of this (underdeveloped) comparison is the purported difference in the underlying norm appealed to. Krook aims to show that while the quota provision in India relies on group interest, parity law uses the idea of difference between the two sexes as a universal difference cutting across race, class and background. But Krook has overplayed the contrast between the notion of 'group interest' in the Indian case, and of a (redefined) universalism of the French case. The quota legislation applied on caste basis may be read as one of protecting 'group interest' but when the different quota legislation for women's enhanced participation is being considered, there does not have to be any appeal to 'group interests'.[24]

Gail Omvedt writing on 'Women and PR' agrees with Madhu Kishwar that an alternative is needed to the WRB, which is 'after all, a very badly written Bill.' Unlike other commentators, she rates the 'Alternative Bill' as 'a major advance on the original proposal.' However, her own preference is for a move to a system of proportional representation (PR). Whilst she supports the retention of a quota for Scheduled Castes and Scheduled Tribes within a PR system, she does not think that Muslims, OBCs or women would need a quota to enhance their representation in legislatures. In a more recent paper Omvedt (2005) continues to prefer a move towards proportional representation, but is also supportive of either party candidate lists or even multi-seat constituencies as 'more democratic' than reservations for women in legislative bodies.

Medha Nanivadekar discusses another alternative in 'Dual-member Constituencies: Resolving Deadlock on Women's Reservation'. She argues in favour of accepting dual-member constituencies, with one man and one woman for seats held by men, and both women for seats held by women MPs. She also proposes the extension of this process to the Rajya Sabha.

Conclusion and a suggestion

On 15 July 2003, Manohar Joshi of the Bharatiya Janata Party, the Lok Sabha Speaker at the time, convened an all-party meeting in New Delhi to discuss the WRB in which several 'different proposals' including the Election Commission proposal, double-member constituencies and reportedly, one of increasing the strength of the House, were put forward. As to the consensus, none was achieved. (*The Hindu*, 16 July 2003).

The 'new' BJP proposal put forward for consideration was of double-member constituencies:

> Our Party believes that the basic purpose of the Women's Reservation Bill, which seeks to significantly increase the level of women's representation in Parliament and State Legislatures, should be realised without any further delay. In order to secure this objective, the BJP is now of the considered view that 33 per cent of the seats in the Lok Sabha be made Double-Member Constituencies. One of the two seats be mandatorily reserved for women in these constituencies, which would change on a rotational basis. This would increase the total number of members in the Lok Sabha by 181. The same approach can also be adopted in the State Legislatures.
>
> BJP Press Release (2003)

This proposal was dismissed forthwith by Ms Ambika Soni of the Congress party rejecting the dual-member constituencies mooted by the BJP, insisting that the Bill should be passed in its original form; 15 lakh signatures in support of the Bill were to be presented to the President, A.P.J. Abdul Kalam by a delegation of the Mahila Congress. The National Federation of Indian Women (NFIW) and All India Progressive Women's Association (AIPWA) were also opposed to the double-member constituencies' formula, describing it as an 'eyewash'. AIPWA president, Ms Srilata Swaminathan saw in this move a treatment of women 'as appendages of males'. The 'Election Commission' proposal of mandatory candidate quotas for women at party level, in its turn was strongly rejected by the Mahila Morcha, BJP's women's wing. Kanta Nalawade, the president of Mahila Morcha reportedly said: 'Women do not want the right to simply contest elections, they want the right to win elections'.[25] Badly put, no doubt; awkwardly this appeal to 'right to win' expresses the desire of ambitious women to be at the helm of political decision-making. Interestingly, in a previous all-party meeting[26] convened by the Prime Minister on 7 March 2003, the Shiv Sena openly opposed the WRB but favoured the EC's proposal (*The Hindu*, 8 March 2003). The fissure in the ranks of the Hindutva Right has been pointed out by Tanika Sarkar (1999); women (and men) within the parties of the Right are divided on the issue of women's reservation in Parliament.[27]

It would be a mistake to either uncritically accept or reject a proposal merely because of the ostensible Left/Right leanings of the party it originates from. It may be added that if the BJP wants to institute quotas in their candidate party lists it should not be opposed; any step towards institutionalising mechanisms for increased presence of women is better than none. Such a step should not be seen as essentially an obstacle to the passing of (some version of) the WRB; rather, ways of incorporating such a voluntary policy within a legally enforced one should be sought.

Writing on Mexico, Baldez shows that a voluntarily adopted policy of gender quotas may not be actually enforced. The percentage of women elected to the Mexican Congress decreased in the 2000 election notwithstanding the presence of women in prominent leadership positions, and despite a decade of efforts to increase women's representation. 'This reversal challenged assumptions that the election of women would continue to increase over time, a realisation that prompted feminist legislators to intensify their efforts to pass an enforceable gender quotas law at the national level' (Baldez 2004: 241).

The current government under the leadership of the United Progressive Alliance came to office with the promise in its Common Minimum Programme to 'take the lead to introduce legislation for one-third reservation for women in Vidhan Sabhas and in the Lok Sabha' amongst other measures.[28] These words have yet (as of 2007) to translate into action.

An interesting lesson from the Mexican experience is that one state, within the federal structure, could take the lead in passing an electoral law instituting enforceable gender quotas. The rest of the country may follow, as indeed it did in Mexico. A further lesson is the lobbying strategy used by Mexican women to circumvent the notorious 'machismo' of Mexican men: women politicians lobbied men from other political parties than their own; it worked, because men found it harder to snub women without listening to them. Women got heard.

Clever lobbying may be handy, but legislation is a must.[29] Even those opposed to the WRB have clearly acknowledged the need for it. Indeed one prominent critic Yogendra Yadav (2001) has lamented the 'lack of attention to the challenge of institutional design in radical circles'[30] and more recently reiterated his support for the Alternative WRB, by now known as the Election Commission Proposal as it only requires an ordinary amendment in the Representation of the People Act. Anticipating objections from his opponents he wrote that the 'party quota option is not a "dilution" of the existing Bill but a better way of realising the objectives' (Yadav 2003). Objections to the Election Commission Proposal came from the Right (as noted above) as well as the Left (Karat 2003).

My own suggestion is for *doubling the number of seats in the Lok Sabha, by making all constituencies into dual-member constituencies with the restriction that both the members cannot be of the same sex.* So we should have two differently sexed people representing every constituency: this leaves open the possibility that a person of a non-specific sex can jointly represent a constituency along with a man or a woman. Before this is laughed off as a philosopher's pipe dream, note that the number of people's representatives in China which has a comparable population, is 2980 and in a country with a considerably smaller population, the UK, the number of representatives is considerably *more* than in India.[31]

All lovers of representative democracy argue for greater accountability of elected representatives. This could be partly achieved by decreasing the 'accessibility gap'—if I may call it that—between an ordinary citizen and an MP. Sixty years after independence the 'MP-population' ratio in India has increased, of course increasing the accessibility gap. Is it not time that we considered increasing the number of representatives? The advantage of my proposal is that it will take care of the pro-incumbency factor—blighting the selection of women to winnable seats in the Election Commission Proposal; it will stem the ire of OBC men as it does not undo the gains made by them in the Lok Sabha; it does away with the objection of 'dilution' made by women's groups against the dual-member constituencies proposal for a third of the seats. My proposal ups the ante, with the hope that the players will be encouraged to reach a settlement that might satisfy all, even if, for conflicting reasons—to cut losses, hit the jackpot or simply to break even! This proposal is obviously not a panacea. Neither 'culture' by itself nor 'top-down' initiatives on their own can be relied on to deliver the goods. It seems that 'sustainable human development' combined with legal and structural reforms, in an environment of a gradual shift in the public opinion in a 'more egalitarian and liberal direction' is most likely to entrench substantial gains for women.[32]

Notes

[1] For Dr Ambedkar's writings see Ahir (1997) and Rodrigues (2002); for his differences with Gandhi on issues of representation see Tejani (2007).

[2] Anne Phillips' widely cited *The Politics of Presence* (1995) unsurprisingly pays no homage to Ambedkar, but it behoves Indian feminists to recall the arguments of the astute constitutionalist who emphasised the importance

INTRODUCTION

of the 'presence' of members of the collective whose interests are otherwise inadequately represented.

3. I agree with Baldez (2004: 236) that 'international influence, including changing norms and transnational activist networks' is an important factor promoting the use of gender quotas.

4. The 73rd and 74th Indian Constitutional Amendments on Panchayati Raj Institutions have been widely cited in cross-national comparative literature on gender quotas.

5. Pertinent for this task is a comprehensive document (Squires 2001) published by the Equal Opportunities Commission UK setting forth a detailed analysis of the level of women's parliamentary participation in the UK and factors affecting patterns of representation in other European and industrialised countries including Australia, Finland, France, Germany, Spain and Sweden.

6. Pakistan has the highest percentage in South Asia of women representatives; due to an act passed in 2002 under General Pervez Musharraf. But women are nominated from lists presented by political parties and picked according to the share of each party in the elected seats to a total of 17 per cent in the national assembly. In 2002, of 342 elected, 72 (21.2 per cent) were women. Women's organisations demand direct elections rather than nominations. (Omvedt 2005).

7. In Germany in the 1980s, the Greens had led the way by pledging 50 per cent quota in party posts followed by the Social Democratic Party; both parties 'enforced a more even gender distribution on their lists' compared to other parties who cluster the women at the bottom of their lists. (Kolinsky 1993) The Green Party UK has two principal speakers, at least one of whom has to be a woman.

8. Rai (2002) also notes the strategies that women MPs have employed to access the public sphere are coloured by their largely 'elite' class composition. The most worrying finding is that 'there has been limited interaction between women representatives and the women's movement'.

9. Pegu (1999) reports on the conference sponsored in Rajasmund, Rajasthan by the UN Population Fund to reflect on grass-roots politics where most women said that 'the worst demoralising factor was the male habit of mouthing abuses and denigrating womanhood'. Even in this environment of hostility, women have grown in confidence. The poignancy of an illiterate women's 'autonomous' use of newly acquired power is expressed in the words of Nandu Devi, pradhan of Ral Mangra panchayat in rural Rajasthan: 'The male panches try to take advantage of my illiteracy... Before signing any document I make a neutral person read it out to me'. (ibid.)

10. Rai (2005: 181) concedes that women representatives 'do attempt to address women's basic needs, and are approached by women's groups to address their problems, and there is even some evidence that on the whole women representatives are less corrupt and bring to local governance some

degree of credibility in the eyes of the people'. Clearly these are 'real' benefits by anyone's definition of real. Rai also writes that 'low-caste women find it difficult to represent their own communities satisfactorily, while at the same time they are unable to represent any generalised interests of women' (ibid.). I am not sure what these 'generalised interests of women' are supposed to be, but I do agree that there is evidence of difficulties that dalit women representatives experience *because* they are dalit (Pegu 1999; Sainath 2003). In my view, low-caste poor women representatives can be strengthened in their ability to be autonomous in their function as representatives by effective training and basic remuneration.

[11] See Fraser (1995) and Young's criticism of her, mentioned but not addressed by Rai, in Young (1997). See also Young (2000).

[12] See Fraser (1997).

[13] The EPW article reproduced here is a revised and expanded version of Dhanda (1998-9).

[14] In a rather impassioned and personalised published response to me, Madhu Kishwar (2000) was especially chagrined at my omission of the 'Alternate Women's Reservation Bill' co-authored by her and a group of three other luminaries.

[15] See Phillips (1995: 82).

[16] Lama-Rewal (2001) provides a good historical background of the use of 'women' as a political category and rightly observes that 'if gender has become legitimate as a political category, it remains less legitimate than caste, class and tribe' (1439). I also agree with her suggestion that field studies are called for and have included her findings in this volume (see her article).

[17] See the story of Basanti Bai in Madhya Pradesh.

[18] Paradoxically, a majority of these women belong to the Indian Union Muslim League, a party opposed to the introduction of women's reservation at the parliamentary and state legislative level.

[19] Raman (2002) again stresses that the 'levers of change have to be sought in an overall democratisation of society'. She confirms that overall the experience of women in PRIs has been 'positive'. Especially noteworthy is that women 'have responded overwhelmingly and participated with full enthusiasm'.

[20] A very innovative proposal, not included in this selection, has been suggested by Mukesh Dalal (2000) that a variable number out of 'women's quota' seats with an upper ceiling of say 50, should be *added* to the total 543 in the Lok Sabha, when there is a shortfall from one-third seats of winning women, so that the number of women elected with the addition of quota seats comes as close to one-third (i.e. 181) seats as possible. Some women runners-up, he suggests, should be co-opted as winning candidates by using the quota. But this proposal does not consider the very likely scenario when in election after election the shortfall of ordinarily winning women persists. It is based on an optimism that within the space of a few

INTRODUCTION

elections there would not be any need for the additional quota seats.

[21] See Madhu Kishwar's article in this volume.

[22] As Dahlerup (2002) writes: 'One conclusion is especially relevant for the introduction of quotas: that in almost all political systems, no matter what electoral regime, it is political parties, not the voters, that constitute the real gatekeepers into elected offices. Consequently, the party nomination practices should be kept in focus.'

[23] I suggest such a solution.

[24] For elaboration of non-group-interests arguments in support of quota legislation see my paper.

[25] The outcome was exactly as the Rajya Sabha MP Shabana Azmi had predicted. 'I don't think the Bill will be passed in its current form. It is high time that all women accept this and try and chalk out appropriate suggestions and changes which could be incorporated in the Bill to enable its passage in Parliament', Ms Azmi reportedly said in an interview on BBC Hindi. She was sceptical of party candidate quotas too for fear of women being allotted losing constituencies *The Hindu* (20 May 2003).

[26] The Pattali Makkal Katchi, the Janata Dal (U), the Muslim League, the Samata Party and the Telegu Desam Party did not participate in this meeting.

[27] Sarkar (1999) writes: 'The need to field women candidates is obvious [...] The interesting thing is the careful insulation of such candidates from women's issues and organisations even within the Sangh parivar [...] I found it interesting that Samiti office-bearers and pracharikas were quite contemptuous about the issue of women's reservation in Parliament, arguing that it denoted a tragic dilution of the principles of merit'.

[28] 'The UPA Government will take the lead to introduce legislation for one-third reservation for women in Vidhan Sabhas and in the Lok Sabha. Legislation on domestic violence and against gender discrimination will be enacted. The UPA Government will ensure that at least one-third of all funds flowing into panchayats will be earmarked for programmes for the development of women and children. Village women and their associations will be encouraged to assume responsibilities for all development schemes relating to drinking water, sanitation, primary education, health and nutrition. Complete legal equality for women in all spheres will be made a practical reality'.

[29] In Argentina, the difference between having and not having a quota became clearly evident when the quota legislation was suspended for a 40-year period. The percentage of women in the national chamber of deputies with a quota was 22 per cent in 1955 and dropped to four per cent during this 40-year period (Stokes 2005: 90). Following legislation in 1991 that required a minimum of 30 per cent women to be placed in electable positions on closed party lists, the federal state of 23 provinces out of which 21 have adopted gender quotas, Argentina now ranks ninth in the world with 35 per cent women in the lower house (See appendix 2, Inter Parliamentary

Union, 31 January 2007, http://www.ipu.org/wmn-e/world.htm) and 43.1 per cent in the Senate.

[30] 'If there is any need to tinker with the electoral system, it is with a view to address two specific problems: under-representation of women and Muslims. In both cases the under-representation is gross and structural, and therefore, unlikely to be overcome in the normal course of things. Both these are fit cases for redesigning institutions. But it needs to be ensured that the proposed change would achieve the objective and its side effects will not outweigh the benefits. The Women's Reservation Bill that proposes to reserve one-third seats in the legislatures does not meet these elementary criteria' (Yadav 2001: 12).

[31] Besides China and the UK (646), Cuba, Germany, Democratic People's Republic of Korea, Italy, France, Indonesia and Turkey all have larger lower or single houses than India (with 545 seats in the Lok Sabha).

[32] See Inglehart and Norris (2003).

References

Ahir, D.C. 1997. *Dr Ambedkar and Indian Constitution* New Delhi: Low Price Publications.

Baldez, Lisa. 2004. 'Elected Bodies: The Gender Quota Law for Legislative Candidates in Mexico'. *Legislative Studies Quarterly*, XXIX. 2 May. pp. 231-58.

Ballington, J. and Karam, A. eds. 2005. *Women in Parliament: Beyond Numbers, A Revised Edition*. Stockholm: International Institute for Democracy and Electoral Assistance (IDEA). http://www.int-idea.se/women

Bidwai, Praful. 2004. 'Creating Equal Opportunities: Say Yes to Affirmative Action'. *The Times of India*. 9 August.

BJP Press Release. 2003. 'Resolution on Reservation for Women in Parliament and State Legislatures' at National Executive Meeting. Raipur. 18-20 July 2003. http://www.bjp.org/NEM/July_1803a.htm

Dahlerup, Drude. 2002. 'Quotas—A Jump to Equality? The Need for International Comparisons of the Use of Electoral Quotas to Obtain Equal Political Citizenship for Women'. Paper prepared for IDEA Workshop. Jakarta, Indonesia. 25 September.

Dalal, Mukesh. 2000. 'Women's Reservation: Another Approach'. *Manushi*. Issue 120. September-October.

Dhanda, Meena. 1998-99. 'Justification for Gender Quotas in Legislative Bodies: a Consideration of Identity and Representation'. *Women's Philosophy Review* 20. Winter. pp. 44-62.

Duflo, Esther. 2005. 'Why Political Reservations?' *Journal of the European Economic Association* 3 (2-3). pp. 668-78.

Fleschenberg, Andrea. 2005. 'Engendering Electoral Politics—Quota Regulations as a Means of Increasing Female Political Representation?' Discussion Paper No. 10 of the project *Dynasties and Female Political Leaders in Asia* series. eds. Claudia Derichs and Mark Thompson.

Fraser, Nancy. 1995. 'From Redistribution to Recognition? Dilemmas of Justice in a "Post-Socialist" Age'. *New Left Review* 212. pp. 68-93.
———. 1997. 'A Rejoinder to Iris Young'. *New Left Review*. 223.
Inglehart, R. and Norris, P. 2003. *Gender Equality and Cultural Change Around the World*. Cambridge: Cambridge University Press.
Karat, Brinda. 2003. 'Alternative as dilution'. *The Hindu*. 15 May 2003.
Kishwar, Madhu. 2000. 'Equality of Opportunity vs Equality of Results: Improving the Women's Reservation Bill'. *Economic and Political Weekly*. 18 November. pp. 4151-56.
Kolinsky, E. 1993. 'Party Change and Women's Representation in Germany' in *Gender and Party Politics*. eds. J. Lovenduski and P. Norris. London: Sage Publications. pp. 113-46.
Krook, Mona Lena. 2005. 'Competing Claims: Quotas for Women and Minorities in India and France'. Paper presented at the General Conference of the European Consortium for Political Research. Budapest, Hungary. 8-10 September.
Lama-Rewal, Stéphanie Tawa. 2001. 'Fluctuating, Ambivalent Legitimacy of Gender as a Political Category'. *Economic and Political Weekly*. 28 April. pp. 1435-40.
Lovenduski, J. and P. Norris. eds. 1993. *Gender and Party Politics*. London: Sage Publications.
Manasa. 2000. 'Karnataka and the Women's Reservation Bill'. *Economic and Political Weekly*. 28 October. pp. 3849-53
Meier, Petra. 2002. 'A Step Forward? A Gender Perspective on the Reform of the Belgian Electoral System'. Working paper in the context of 'les rencontres du CEDEM'. Liège. 14 November.
Meintzes, Sheila. 2005. 'Case Studies: South Africa' in *Women in Parliament: Beyond Numbers, A Revised Edition*. eds. Julie Ballington and Azza Karam. pp. 230-37.
Omvedt, Gail. 2005. 'Women in Governance'. Paper for UNIFEM-IDRC Regional Conference on Development Effectiveness through Gender Mainstreaming: Lessons Learnt from South Asia. New Delhi. 10-12 May.
Pegu, Rinku. 1999. 'Packing a Panch: Rajasthan: Women Panchayat Members Stand up to Male Chauvinism'. *The Week*. 21 November.
Rai, Shirin. 2002. 'Class, Caste and Gender—Women in Parliament in India'. Stockholm: IDEA (http://www.idea.int)
———. 2005. 'Reserved Seats in South Asia: A Regional Perspective' in *Women in Parliament: Beyond Numbers, A Revised Edition*. eds. Julie Ballington and Azza Karam. pp. 174-84.
Raman, Vasanthi. 2002. 'The Implementation of Quotas for Women: The Indian Experience'. Paper for IDEA Workshop. Jakarta, Indonesia. 25 September. http://www.quotaproject.org/cs/cs_India.pdf
Rao, Anupama. ed. 2003. *Gender and Caste*. New Delhi: Kali for Women.
Rodrigues, Valerian. ed. 2002. *The Essential Writings of B.R. Ambedkar*. New Delhi: Oxford University Press.

Sainath, P. 2003. 'Unmusical Chairs' in *Gender and Caste*. ed. Rao. New Delhi: Kali for Women. pp. 336-40.
Sarkar, Tanika. 1999. 'The Pragmatics of the Hindu Right'. *Economic and Political Weekly*. 31 July-6 August. pp. 2159-67.
Squires, J. and M. Wickham-Jones. 2001. *Women in Parliament: a comparative analysis*. Equal Opportunities Commission UK.
Stokes, Wendy. 2005. *Women in Contemporary Politics*. Cambridge: Polity Press.
Tejani, Shabnam. 2007. 'Reflections on the Category of Secularism in India: Gandhi, Ambedkar, and the Ethics of Communal Representation, c. 1931' in *The Crisis of Secularism in India*. eds. Anuradha Dingwaney Needham and Rajeswari Sunder Rajan. Duke University Press. pp. 45-65.
The Hindu. 8 March 2003. 'We will go ahead with the women's bill: PM'.
———. 20 May 2003. 'No party is serious on Women's Bill: Shabana'.
———. 16 July 2003. 'Unanimity claimed and contested on women's Bill'.
Vincent, Louise. 2004. 'Quotas: Changing the Way Things Look Without Changing the Way Things Are'. *The Journal of Legislative Studies*. vol. 10. no. 1. Spring. pp. 71-96.
Yadav, Yogendra. 2001. 'A Radical Agenda for Political Reforms'. *Seminar* 506. pp. 3-17.
———. 2003. 'Quota Options'. *The Hindu*. 9 May 2003.
Young, Iris Marion. 1997. 'Unruly Categories: A Critique of Nancy Fraser's Dual Systems Theory. *New Left Review* 222. pp. 147-160.
———. 2000. *Inclusion and Democracy*. Oxford: Oxford University Press.

Section 1
Historical Background

Section I

Women's Challenges to Reservations in Pre-Independence India

*Letter to the Premier
From Mrs Sarojini Naidu and Begum Shah Nawaz*

St. James' Palace
SWI
16th November 1931

The Prime Minister
Chairman of the Minorities Committee
Downing Street, S.W.

Dear Prime Minister,
We herewith beg to submit the official Memorandum jointly issued on the status of Indian women in the proposed new Constitution by the All India Women's Conference on Education and Social Reform, the Women's Indian Association and the Central Committee of the National Council of Women in India. These three premier Organisations include the great majority of progressive and influential women of all communities, creeds and ranks who are interested in social, educational, civic or political activities, and the accredited leaders of organised public opinion amongst women.

The manifesto signed by the principal office-bearers of these important bodies may be regarded as an authoritative statement of representative opinion, duly considered and widely endorsed, on the case and claim of Indian women.

We have been entrusted with the task of presenting to the Round Table Conference their demand for a complete and immediate recognition of their equal political status, in theory and practice, by the grant of full adult franchise or an effective and acceptable alternative, based on the conception of adult suffrage.

We are further enjoined to resist any plea that may be advanced by small individual groups of people, either in India or in this country, for any kind of temporary concessions or adventitious methods of securing the adequate representation of women in the Legislatures in the shape of reservation of seats, nomination or co-option, whether by Status, Convention or at the discretion of the Provincial and Central Governments. To seek any form of preferential treatment would be to violate the integrity of the universal demand of Indian women for absolute equality of political status.

We are confident that no untoward difficulties will intervene in the way of women of the right quality, capacity, political equipment and record of public service in seeking the suffrages of the nation to be returned as its representatives in the various Legislatures of the country.

We ask that there should be no sex discrimination either against or in favour of women under the new Constitution.

Will you be so good as to treat our covering letter as part of the official document submitted to you on behalf of our Organisations.

Yours sincerely,

(sd.) *Sarojini Naidu*
(sd.) *J.A. Shah Nawaz*

Declaration by AIWC and WIA, 1933

The Joint Memorandum on the Status of Indian Women in the proposed New Constitution of India issued last year by the All India Women's Conference, the Women's Indian Association and the Central Executive Committee of the National Council of Women in India has already received publicity through circulation to all the Members of the Round

Table Conference, the British as well as the Indian Governments, the Members of the British Parliament, the Members of the Indian Legislatures and other men and women interested in the question both in England and in India. The Indian Press, when publishing the Memorandum, commented very favourably on the principles embodied therein.

The signatories to this Declaration, however, feel that, in spite of the unanimous opinion of the main Women's Organisations in India, their views have not received the consideration that was and is their due and lest the weighty demands of the thinking womanhood of India be lightly set aside, we wish once more on behalf of the Organisations which we have the honour to represent, to inform the Governments of Britain and India, as well as the general public, that we firmly adhere to our opinions as already expressed in our Joint Memorandum. Any Constitution for India which does not provide for adult suffrage and no special expedients and does not recognise the fundamental rights of citizenship in India, as interpreted by us in the aforesaid Memorandum, will meet with our unqualified disapproval.

We are aware that certain expedients have been suggested, e.g.,

A. Property qualification for franchise on the basis of wifehood or widowhood, if the woman does not hold property in her own right;
B. Literacy qualification for franchise;
C. Nomination for Legislatures;
D. Reservation of seats or co-option in Legislatures.

All such expedients are, in our opinion, wholly undesirable for the following reasons:

1. We look upon any qualifications for the vote based on property as undemocratic and, as such, wholly against the spirit of the age. At the same time an expedient of this nature is quite contrary to the interests of the humble poor who constitute India's main population;
2. Owing to the almost incredible illiteracy prevalent amongst

the women of India any such qualification stands clearly self-condemned;
3. We look upon nominations, reservation of seats, and co-option in any sphere of activity as a pernicious and humiliating system which must run counter to all real progress. However impartially carried out it must, by its very nature, engender an inferiority complex amongst those for whom it caters, a contingency to be avoided at all costs. It may even tend to create a spirit of communication amongst women which we, at any rate, are determined shall not be the case. We realise to the full and with immeasurable sorrow to what an extent this canker amongst men has retarded and is retarding the progress of our beloved land.

We submit, therefore, that adult franchise immediately applied, without special expedients, constitutes the only way by which the men and women of India can possibly come in to their own. We do not think that there will be insurmountable difficulties in achieving these objects forthwith if sufficient efforts are made.

Even if men are in favour of expedients meanwhile, we wish to make it quite clear that women do not stand by them in this demand. For ourselves, we have made up our minds that even if a few or no women are returned for the present to the Legislatures by the open door of competition, we shall not attach any importance thereto—for we are certain that our cause is righteous and that in the end it will prevail.

We urge the Governments of Britain and India not to ignore the principle that we are setting before them and we call upon all our brothers and any individual sisters who may differ from us to follow our lead. There can be no live consciousness of nationhood or true patriotism until we are willing to sacrifice to the uttermost for a principle.

As representatives of important women's organisations we know that we have a strong body of opinion which lends full support to these views besides that which is voiceless today behind prison bars and we hope our Declaration will be the means of securing for Indians, men and women, a real voice in the governance of their country.

Finally, we wish to broadcast an earnest appeal to Women's Organisations throughout the world—remote in distance but kindred, no doubt, in spirit—to stand by the women of India in their fight for real emancipation at this important stage in the history of India.

(sd.) Muthulakshmi Reddi   Dr Muthulakshmi Reddi
                                Ex-President, AIWC
                                Secretary, WIA

(sd.) Amrit Kaur   Rajkumari Amrit Kaur
                                Chairwoman, AIWC

(sd.) Jahanara Shah Nawaz   Begum Shah Nawaz
                                Vice-President, AIWC

(sd.) Dorothy Jinarajadas   Mrs Jinarajadas, WIA

(sd.) Ammu Swaminadhan   Mrs Swaminadhan, WIA

(sd.) Hilla Rustomji Faridoonji Mrs Rustomji Faridoonji
                                Vice-President, AIWC

(sd.) Sharifa Hamid Ali   Mrs Hamid Ali, AIWC

(sd.) Lakshmibai Rajwade   Rani Rajwade
                                Organising Secretary, AIWC

Statement by AIWC, WIA and NCWI to the Joint Select Committee 1935

Relevant extracts from the Statement made by the three elected women representatives of the All India Women's Conference, the Women's Indian Association and the National Council of Women in India.

We, the elected representatives of the three main Women's Organisations in India are glad that we have been given an opportunity of placing the Indian Women's point of view before the Joint Select Committee.

Fundamental rights

The question of franchise for women and their status in the new constitution of India has exercised our minds greatly during the past three years, for it is a matter that concerns in a vital manner the entire womanhood of our country.

Our Organisations have throughout stood for Adult Franchise or failing that, any system based thereon which would, after a short transitional period, lead to the goal which has been universally recognised as the ultimate desideratum.

We still adhere to our opinion that Adult Suffrage is the only logical and desirable method of fairly enfranchising a whole people and if it had been accepted, as we suggested, as means of the group system for the first few elections all the differential qualifications and resort to expedients divorced from basic principles and the welter of communalism into which our country is to be further embroiled, by means of not only a cumbersome but an exceedingly expensive machinery, would have been avoided.

We have repeatedly urged that we do not desire the communal virus to enter into our united ranks. We totally refuse to be made party pawns for the purposes of weightage for the convenience of any community. We desire direct election on an entirely un-communal basis. By merit and merit alone do we wish to find—and we are confident we shall find—our rightful place in the Councils and Federal Legislatures of our country.

It naturally follows that we are opposed to reservation of seats for ourselves and are whole-heartedly in favour of joint electorates by which means alone, we are convinced, can India rise to her full stature.

We strongly urge the necessity of the specific recognition of woman's inherent right to full citizenship and equal opportunities with men for public service to the country. Therefore, in the Declaration of Fundamental Rights, we wish it to be clearly stated that 'sex' shall be no bar to any public employment, office, power or honour and in the exercise of any trade or calling.

The above memorandum was read out before the members

of the Joint Select Committee by Rajkumari Amrit Kaur, one of the members of the delegation in an eloquent and impressive voice which created a profound impression upon the committee.

We acknowledge our immense gratitude to those Men and Women who have helped our cause.

The right to franchise

The present franchise for women as provided in the Government of India Act of 1935 is unsatisfactory. The three all-India women's organisations in India had demanded adult franchise based on a system of joint electorates of all men and women. This was turned down as impracticable. The main reasons given were administrative difficulties, inability on the part of Indian men to come to an agreement over the communal problem, and the fact that in the opinion of the government existing social conditions made too rapid an advance dangerous. It was also against the express wish of these organisations that special seats were reserved for women. They felt that women could not contest on equal terms with men.

In the Central Assembly as at present constituted under the Government of India Act 1919, there is one women member who has come in from a general constituency.

Woman has been deprived of her inherent right of citizenship and the vote of the conservative section, generally opposed to progressive reform, has been doubled by giving the woman a vote not in her own right as an individual, but as a wife. The additional voting qualifications granted have themselves proved a handicap and will reduce the number of women enrolled.

It was feared that the Indian woman would not go to the polls in exercise of her civic right. This fear was not, however, well-founded.

Recommendations

We fully endorse the declaration of the Fundamental Rights of Citizenship in India made by the Karachi Session of the Indian National Congress in 1931 to which we have already referred in our Introduction.

1. 'All citizens are equal before the law, irrespective of religion, caste, creed or sex'.
2. 'No disability attaches to any citizen, by reason of his or her religion, caste, creed, or sex in regard to public employment, office of power or honour, and in the exercise of any trade or calling'.
3. 'The Franchise shall be on the basis of universal adult suffrage'.
4. 'Woman shall have the right to vote, to represent and the right to hold public offices'.

Reprinted in *Indian Journal of Gender Studies*, Vol. 6, Number 1, January-June 1999, (pp. 129-33).

Dissenting Voices

LOTIKA SARKAR & VINA MAZUMDAR

**Note of Dissent to *Towards Equality*
(Report of the Committee on the Status of Women in India, Government of India, 1974)**

As members of the pre-Independence generation, we have always been firm believers in equal rights for women. For us the recognition of this principle in the Constitution heralded the beginning of a new era for the women of this country. As we have never been supporters of special representation or class representation in any form, in academic discussions we had often criticised the system of reservations for Scheduled Castes and Scheduled Tribes, as a legacy of the colonial period which institutionalised the backwardness of certain sections of our population.

When we started out on this investigation, it had not even occurred to us to seek the opinion of the people about the system of representation provided in the Constitution. For us, it was a settled fact, embodying a principle of democracy in which no change could be considered. This is why we never thought of including a question on the point in our questionnaire, nor did we think of asking this question of the people whom we interviewed during our early tours. Only when the problem kept being posed repeatedly before us by various groups of women in the course of our discussions did we become aware that a problem like this was real and very much in existence. The Committee has accepted the reality of the problem and our Report has presented both sides of the basic argument.

We regret our inability to agree with the Committee on the decision that was taken. While we, too, feel that our investigation and examination of this question was not adequate to recommend a major change in our system of representation, we consider that it would not be proper for us to turn our back on the pressing reality of the problem. A political system cannot be based on ideology alone but must keep in touch with the actualities of the social situation and so adjust its operation as to achieve the desired goals of the society. The mechanics of a system, if they do not grapple with the needs of a society, can defeat the ultimate objective in the long run. It is for this reason that we are compelled to dissent from the Committee's decision on this point.

Our reasons for dissenting on this matter are consistent with the findings that run throughout the Report, that despite progressive legal changes, the actual condition of life of the mass of Indian women has not changed much. The continuing under-representation of women prevents their proper participation in the decision-making process in the country. The success of a few in reaching positions of power and dignity may, to the uninformed eye, suggest the existence of full opportunities for such participation, but we have shown that this is far from so in the political process or in economic activity, in education and in general social status. The number of women elected to Parliament constitute less than five per cent of the members. The proportion of women in the pre-Independence Central Legislature (elected under the Government of India Act 1935) was 3.4 per cent. The infinitesimal gain of 1.6 per cent in proportion over a quarter century (and the pattern has been a zig-zag one), when taken with the decline in the absolute number of representatives during the last 10 years, is a sufficient indicator of the reluctance of our society to accept the principle of equal representation for women.

The second problem in a way stems from the inadequate representation of women in these bodies. The basic principle underlying universal franchise is the need to involve all classes and sections of the population in the process of decision-making so that the policy reflects the problems, needs and aspirations of the whole of society, and not of a limited group. Every democracy has to pass through this phase, when a limited group of persons, small in number as well as narrow in their class composition, acts as the voice of the people. The institution of universal franchise, in the course of its functioning, should gradually expand the representative base of this group and alter its class composition. As Professor Sirsikar points out, this is already happening in the case of the male legislators in this country within the short period since Independence. In the case of women, however, the story is quite different. More than one-third of the women in Parliament belong to professional groups which means the urban middle class. Most of these members are college-educated, and a fair number have overseas education as well. Quite a few of the women legislators in the states, as well as the centre, belong to royal or zamindari families or have 'agricultural interests' arising out of landed property. As compared to their male counterparts, the background of the women legislators is considerably narrower and represents mainly the dominant upper strata of our society.

This restricted origin apart, Indian women legislators suffer from other inadequacies. A considerable number of them, as we were informed again and again, have not worked their way up in the political system from actual work among the people, but have been drafted into the system at different levels because of their contacts with persons in positions of power and influence. Our discussions with some individual members of this group revealed that they lacked enough awareness and understanding of the basic problems affecting the majority of women in our society. We were also told repeatedly that women members in the legislative bodies have not displayed adequate alertness and initiative in posing these problems before the Government, the legislatures of the people of this country. To cite a few examples, it is a regrettable fact that in spite of the Law Commission's recommendations (15th Report of the Commission, 1960) regarding the reforms needed in the Christian Law of Marriage and Divorce to ameliorate the disabilities of Christian women, the Bill was shelved without any dissenting voice from among the women Members of

Parliament. In the case of another recommendation of the Law Commission (41st Report, 1969), regarding reforms in the Criminal Procedure Code, to end the claim for maintenance to divorced wives, the law was passed after specifically excluding Muslim women from this category. In this case too, the women Members of Parliament failed to register any protest against this injustice to a large section of women in our society.

In voicing our criticism we would not like it to be thought that we are merely condemning without understanding the difficulties under which our women legislators have to function. As we have pointed out, their small numbers and their dependence on the support of their political parties, which are all dominated by men, have aggravated their inhibitions and weaknesses in asserting righteous but unpopular causes. Most of us have had to experience the tremendous force of these inhibitions bred by cultural values over generations. It is far easier for a woman to be outspoken when she is backed by a large group, than when she has to stand alone. We have also seen the courage with which some women have taken up the cudgels in defence of some unpopular causes, and the degree of social pressure, character assassination and social ostracism that they have had to face for such action. They deserve the admiration of the womenfolk of this country, but unless we can enlarge their ranks, it is our firm belief that the social revolution that Gandhiji had expected to be the end result of women's participation in the 'political deliberations of the nation' will not be achieved.

The reasons given by our colleagues for rejecting the demand for reservation in the legislatures evade, in our opinion, the real issues and are based on an ideological principle which does not take into consideration the needs of women in present-day India. No one who has studied the history of the last 200 years would deny the signal contribution made by distinguished men to the women's cause. The greatest of them, however, always observed that the real cause of women's low status in this country lay 'in men's interested teaching' and in women's acceptance of them. To believe that these champions of women's cause reflected the thinking of the majority of men in this country would be a travesty of history. If that had been the case, they would not have had to face the kind of social opposition that was unleashed on them at every step. It is certainly not expected that women alone will represent women; or progressive measures in their favour, just as men also do no[t] do so. The fact that some men have managed to stand out in defence of women's rights shows that, with more women actively participating in the political process there will be more spokesmen with actual knowledge of women's problems. Larger numbers will also help to break the somewhat exclusive class composition of this group.

About the argument that the system of special representation might precipitate fissiparous tendencies, we cannot do better than quote Professor Sirsikar's answer. Anticipating this criticism, he observed: 'Women are not marginal to society as the minority group might be. They are not a dispensable part of the society—they are as essential as men for the very sustenance of the society'. A system of reservation for women 'would not create what is feared by the critics, isolated pockets ... this may make exacting demands on women ... but would motivate women to come forth to shoulder these responsibilities'.

When one applies the principle of democracy to a society characterised by tremendous inequalities, such special protections are only spearheads to pierce through the barriers of inequality. An unattainable goal is as meaningless as a right that cannot be exercised. Equality of opportunities cannot be achieved in the face of the tremendous disabilities and obstacles which the social system imposes on all those sections whom traditional India treated as second class or even third class citizens. Our investigations have proved that the application of the theoretical principle of equality in the context of unequal situations only intensifies inequalities, because equality in such situations merely means privileges for those who have them already and not for those who need them.

Our colleagues did appreciate the reality of the problem of under-representation and the failure of the large majority of women to overcome social resistance to asserting their political and legal rights. This is implicit in the recommendations for the constitution of women's panchayats and for the reservation of seats for women in municipalities. We regret that they could not agree to the logical extension of the same principle to legislative bodies. We have been compelled to explain our decision at considerable length because we feel that the problem that we have posed requires careful consideration by all who strive for an equalitarian and a just society.

Lotika Sarkar
Vina Mazumdar
31 December 1974

Reprinted in *Indian Journal of Gender Studies*, Vol. 6, Number 1, January-June 1999, (pp. 134-17).

Historical Soundings

VINA MAZUMDAR

The freedom movement developed many dimensions—on issues of foundations of national identity, the nature of the state, and the rights of citizens. There were wide differences among leaders and sections on each of these. The need to promote a sense of patriotism stimulated various forms of cultural nationalism, some of which sought to romanticise and glamourise India's past. The more honest and long-term visionaries, on the other hand, admitted the necessity of rejecting some basic elements of the Indian social system and cultural institutions 'to bring about the moral and political regeneration of the Indian people'.

Despite nationalist historiography seeking to provide historical rationale for an Indian nation, Gopal Krishna Gokhale [leader of the moderate faction of the Indian National Congress], was honest enough to admit that the creation of such a new political entity necessitated giving to all the historically oppressed sections of Indian people a stake in that future. A philosophical and moral justification for this same thesis came from many different regions through the 19th and the earlier part of the 20th century. Democracy, equality before the law, and universal adult franchise were therefore not just abstract principles borrowed from the West but political and cultural necessities to defy our 'inherited social institutions and values'. Unfortunately the clarity of these ideas were dimmed by the politics of conservatism and communalism, aided and abetted by the policies of the Raj—ending in the partition of India.

The removal of institutionalised inequalities required

institutionalised counter measures. The Constitution makers acknowledged this in the case of the Scheduled Castes and the Scheduled Tribes. The issue of reservation for women did come up but was rejected by the leaders of the women's movement despite a demand from the rank and file. A quarter of a century later, faced with the repeated demand from junior political cadres of various parties and the unanimous advice of a group of social scientists who had undertaken studies for the Committee on the Status of Women in India (CSWI), the majority of members adopted a somewhat equivocal position. While agreeing that rural women's life experiences, aspirations, problems and perspectives had remained undervalued as well as invisible to the new state, and that rural society had remained unaware of some of the basic principles and ideology of the Constitution, *the committee unanimously recommended the establishment of statutory women's panchayats* with an integral connection to other Panchayati Raj Institutions.

The Panchayat Acts of most states reserved one or two seats for women—to be filled by nomination, if no one was returned by election. This provision in effect became a token gesture and remained unknown to most people. Instead, the committee recommended that the reserved seats be occupied by elected office-bearers of the women's panchayats, who would be both genuine representatives and accountable to women. For municipalities, a majority recommended reservation of seats for women, not as tokenism but as an effective intervention.

In the case of state assemblies and Parliament, however, a majority decided to uphold the position of the earlier women leaders. Neera Dogra, Lotika Sarkar and I, dissented from this position, pointing out that the committee had failed to address the problem of under-representation caused by institutionalised inequalities which 25 years of democracy had failed to dislodge. We also felt that the committee should have paid greater heed to the pleas of some social scientists that reservation for women was necessary 'for the health of Indian democracy'.

It is significant that this was the one issue on which members of the committee could not reach a consensus. *Towards Equality* contained many unexpected, unknown and somewhat shocking revelations which disturbed many of the members, but the chapters were processed through the drafting committee. The recommendations also received the approval and endorsement of all members, with few modifications. There were debates on some of the recommendations but agreement was finally reached on all of them. Occasional reservations on the style of presentation, or the title of the report were also resolved. I would like to take this opportunity to record my personal tribute to the late Maniben Kara, the oldest member of the committee, for backing the decisions of the drafting committee and persuading other members to withdraw their objections. But the stand taken by Neera Dogra, Lotika Sarkar and myself on the reservation issue upset even Maniben and our Chair, Phulrenu Guha.

Paragraphs 7.102 to 7.117—the last section of the chapter on political status—show that most of the arguments which have been raised during the recent debates on the Reservation Bill were anticipated in the debate within the committee. The three notes of dissent (pp. 354–7) provide some explanation for these differing views. I do not propose to repeat them here except to state that for Lotika Sarkar and myself, our position represented an ideological and conceptual shift which was to develop into a search for a new identity for ourselves in the maelstrom of the politics of nation building.

As 'daughters of Independence' we had been critics of special representation or class representation, regarding these 'as a legacy of the colonial period which institutionalised the backwardness of certain sections'. Twenty-five years later, we discovered considerable resistance among women of our and an older generation to being equated with Scheduled Castes and Tribes. Over the last 22 years, however, the Indian women's movement, as we see it, has done a complete volte-face on this position. We have found our understanding of nation building changing radically as we sought to come closer to the life experiences, the unacknowledged wisdom and knowledge, the priorities and perspectives of poor peasant and working women in the informal sector across the country (and the subcontinent), forcing us to raise questions about the meaning of development, of freedom, traditions, modernisation, social progress and the dynamics of economic, cultural and demographic changes that we had never asked before.

The committee's recommendations on panchayats and municipalities went into cold storage during the decade that followed as far as the government was concerned. With an increase in grassroots organisations, however, the new groups of poor women demonstrated far greater dynamism and challenge. The issue of reservation was periodically raised by political activists as well as serving women legislators in various government sponsored conferences.

In 1985, the government of Rajiv Gandhi indicated its desire to give greater priority to women's issues (the President's Address to the Parliament, January 1985). Interpreting the hint in the President's Address as an opportunity to initiate new policy initiatives, Secretary, Social Welfare, R.P. Khosla called and asked for my suggestions. He agreed to (a) re-open the CSWI's recommendation on panchayats; (b) seek a mandate in the promised New Education Policy to engage educational institutions actively in women's empowerment; and (c) get the Planning Commission to reconsider the special component approach for women in all sectoral development—as recommended by the Working Group on Employment of Women (1977–78), but rejected by two successive Planning Commissions.

C.P. Sujaya, the new Joint Secretary in charge of the women's division promptly went to work digging up old files. Within a few months the women's division within Social Welfare became a Department for Women and Child Development within the Ministry of Human Resource Development, with an all women cast—from minister in charge, Margaret Alva, to the juniormost officers. The Department of Rural Development introduced a minimum 30 per cent quota for women within all anti-poverty programmes. The Government of India also announced the constitution of a core group to prepare a National Perspective Plan for Women.

Outside government, we concentrated on exerting pressure to work gender equality into the education policy and in assisting the Ela Bhatt Commission (National Commission on Self-Employed Women and Women in the Informal Sector) to gather evidence for a new report on women in the poverty sector.

The first half of 1986 witnessed a major failure of the women's movement—to prevent the enactment of the Muslim Women's (Protection of Rights in Divorce) Act; and a victory—with the incorporation of a section on Education for Equality within the education policy. I must take this opportunity to record a part of unrecorded history. In 1985, the Additional Secretary, Education, in charge of exercises leading to the formulation of a new policy, assured me that the draft policy could contain something on 'women's issues', but told me to forget the word 'equality' as it was no longer an objective of the government. But his colleagues who had accompanied him agreed with me that a national seminar to be convened by the Ministry must be titled Education for Women's Equality.

The seminar did take place and its outcome was the incorporation of the section on Education for Equality—starting with women, and going on to Scheduled Castes, Tribes, minorities and others. The seminar emphasised that the issue could no longer be confined to improving women's access to education. It had to be viewed in the context of a need to develop the national education system to incorporate gender dimensions, perspectives and the value of human equality itself, assigning an active participatory role to educational institutions in the 'empowerment of women'.

The euphoria of 1985 had given way to disillusionment by 1988 when the first draft of the National Perspective Plan for Women to the Year 2000 was released. The chapter on Political Participation acknowledged the problem of under-representation and recommended 30 per cent reservation for women in all elective bodies—from panchayats to Parliament—but put in a proviso that in the initial years this quota may be filled by nomination/co-option. National women's organisations called a debate to discuss the NPP. This particular recommendation was rejected outright as 'subversion of the Constitution'. Instead, the debate asked for 30 per cent reservation for women in panchayats and municipalities only 'with due representation for women belonging to dalit and tribal communities'—but to be filled only by election. The participants justified their position by acknowledging the need for a new kind of 'leadership from below'. The final version of the NPP recommended 30 per cent reservation only in panchyats and municipalities, to be filled by election. This version was then incorporated into the 64th Constitutional (Amendment) Bill, 1989, which after a chequered history finally emerged as the 73rd and 74th Constitutional Amendments, 1992 enacted by Parliament unanimously, just two weeks after the demolition of the Babri Masjid [6 December 1992].

As a result of the situation created by the Babri Masjid affair these two historic amendments, conferring constitutional status on local self-government as an integral part of the Indian governance structure, and mandating one-third reservation for women in all these bodies, with in-built quotas for SC and ST women, attracted no media or public attention for some months, and were quietly ratified by April 1993. The response of women to these two measures in the elections that followed in several states and the political dynamism demonstrated by women voters in some of the assembly elections between 1993 and 1996, persuaded women's organisations into putting forward a joint demand for reservations in state assemblies and Parliament before all parties prior to the general elections of 1996. The demand was accepted and features in the manifestos of the major parties. The Common Minimum Programme, drafted to establish the United Front government included the same promise.

There has been a clear ideological divide among the Indian intelligentsia on the issue as well as the consequences of reservation on the Indian political system. While no one could openly question the need to discard practices like untouchability, regarding universal adult franchise alone as capable of transforming an age-old hierarchical, patriarchal and divided social system into a representative democracy was like asking for the moon. The philosophers of the Raj (Henry Maine,

H.H. Risley et al.) had always been at pains to point to the vertical and horizontal divisions among the peoples of India to prove that democracy would be totally unsuitable in India's context.

There was, however, another set of thinkers within the Raj who pointed to India's past history of an effectively functioning local self-government and pleaded that the 'interests of governance' required 'representatives of people', as otherwise 'the task of governing this country in detail is too much for us'—a small alien bureaucracy. Apart from any considerations of political ideology, the practical issue of resource mobilisation needed for governance itself required the support of such representatives, as otherwise the Raj would end with bloodshed on a far higher scale than the events of 1857. A gradual extension of the principles of local self-government by elected bodies and an increasing association of elected representatives at higher levels was therefore suggested as an administrative necessity. It was uncanny to discover in a document prepared in 1872 (Sir George Clarke, Member, Governor General's Council, 1872) not only the same arguments, but virtually the same language as in the Balwantrai Mehta Committee Report of 1956 on democratic decentralisation.

The tricky question, however, had always been about the *basis* of representation. The defenders of British supremacy— even at the cost of efficiency of governance—inevitably moved in the direction of sectional rather than territorial representation, based on a religious divide and only a single class divide—between the propertied and the non-propertied. By the early 1890s, H.H. Risely's theory of the different 'nation-building' capacities of Hinduism and Islam provided a basis for the two-nation theory, finally introduced as a principle in the Morley-Minto Reforms (1909) along with separate representation of landed propertied interests.

An attempt by some enthusiasts of the same school to introduce the principle of caste representation had, however, to be abandoned in the face of tremendous opposition, not only from nationalist leaders but also a large section of the British bureaucracy and the Secretary of State, John Morley, himself. Similar opposition from the same two groups had also come against representation by religion and 'estates', but Risley—in charge of processing all these papers for the Council Committee on Reforms—managed to suppress the entire evidence, leaving the Council Committee as well as the Secretary of State unaware of the strength of opposition.

On the other hand, the Census policy of not only enumerating the population by castes and religion but 'grading them in a hierarchical order' introduced by Risley in 1901, promoted organised rivalry between the different castes through formation of various caste associations and discouraged what many bureaucrats and scholars of Indian society had noted as fluidity and mobility between different caste groups in the social hierarchy—assisted by an increasing migration from the place of origin to other parts of the country and changes in occupation (drawn from the author's DPhil thesis).

Since British women had to wait till 1920 to win the right of suffrage, the question of women's representation never entered these discussions until a women's delegation placed their demands before the Montagu-Chelmsford Committee in 1917. Even at that time, the women leaders demanded universal adult franchise rather than a franchise restricted by property, education, and gender. It surfaced again in the debates leading up to the Government of India Act of 1935, but the political atmosphere had by that time become so vitiated by a growing rift between the two major communities and the organised demand for special provisions for the 'depressed' classes, that the division within the ranks of women's organisations and leaders on the issue of special reservations for women was ignored by the national leadership and many later accounts of the constitutional history of India.

The defenders of reservation used the logic of special provisions 'to bring about women's uplift', a logic very similar to that being offered in defence of representation of the depressed classes. Some of them were at one stage even prepared to restrict such special provisions only to urban women, among whom they believed some 'awakening' had already taken place.

Requested by the All India Women's Conference to argue on their behalf, Sarojini Naidu made her personal objections very clear, but carried out her responsibility of communicating the AIWC's plea to the government and the national leaders.

The net outcome of these discussions were (a) a highly limited franchise for women—qualified either by their status as wives of voters or by education; and (b) a token reservation of 3.3 per cent of women among members of the central legislature. This was only a slight extension of the principles introduced within provincial legislatures after the Reforms of 1919.

Social scientists who advised the CSWI in 1974, compared the 1935 provision with the average four per cent presence of women in Parliament between 1952 and 1971 with universal franchise but without reservation. 'The existing limitations on the role being played by the minority of women legislators may increase if their number declines further with the continuation of the already recognised trend in this direction' (Upendra Baxi: Provisions relating to women in the Indian Constitution—an analytical examination undertaken for the CSWI). Baxi also argued that a transitional provision of reservation to 'break through' the existing structures of inequality would not be retrogression 'from the doctrine of equality of sexes and the principles of demographic representation', but would serve the long-term objectives of equality and democracy better than 'the present system where inequalities get intensified'.

Pleading for a qualitative change in the very character of the Indian legislature and the process of representation, V.M. Sirsikar argued that reservation for women would not introduce further divisive tendencies because 'women are not marginal to society as a minority group might be' (V.M. Sirsikar: Politicisation of women in India). On the other hand, it could increase women's participation and motivate them to shoulder their political responsibilities. Iqbal Narain regarded such a measure as an integral aspect of the necessity of broadening the political elite structure. 'At a later stage of development, changes in the socio-economic order may buttress changes in the political status of women but it has to be the other way round in present day India' (Iqbal Narain: Political status of women in India).

It is significant that the first argument offered by the CSWI for rejecting these suggestions was 'to preserve male support in improving the status of women!' Another quarter of a century later, in my dual capacity as a political analyst as well as an activist in the women's movement, I can only record my view that the warning signal given to us by this body of male social scientists should have received greater consideration and weightage from my colleagues on the committee. Baxi had also warned that without increased participation of a larger group of women in these bodies, the 'rate and type of changes' in the position of women could take an adverse and distorted direction.

Critics of the existing provisions of reservation in the Constitution as the cause of increased hostilities, rivalries, and political instability ignore the fact that without the triple provision for reservation in education, public employment and political representation, the kind of breaches that have been made in the thousands of years old institutions of 'social exclusion' in the case of Scheduled Castes and Tribes would not have taken place and India's claim to be regarded as the world's largest democracy would have remained a misnomer. The prediction of many foreign pundits about the impossibility of India continuing as a democratic state have been repeatedly defeated by the behaviour of the Indian electorate through successive elections.

It should also be remembered that the hostilities supposed to have been enhanced by 'Mandalisation' were not through a demand for political reservation but reservations in employment. The women's movement, however, has never espoused a demand for reservation in employment unanimously. Within the organisations, this has remained an unresolved debate. In the early decades after Independence, the special provision clause under Article 15(3) was used by many state and national agencies to respond to demands from the National Council for Women's Education to provide some weightage to women seeking enrolment in higher education. The University

Grants Commission relaxed eligibility conditions for grants to colleges catering exclusively to women. These special provisions were withdrawn after the CSWI report, because the committee argued that such additional investment should be concentrated on women still outside the educational process, rather than in higher education where women were able to hold their own.

The Working Group on Employment of Women (1977–78) which included a cross-section of activists from women's studies and policy analysts, rejected the suggestion of the Ministry of Labour and Employment for job reservation, though this was already being introduced by several state governments. The argument the Group offered was that job reservation would benefit very few, but damage the women's cause by losing the support of trade unions and other needed allies. What the Group recommended, instead, was reservations and special investment in training institutions, and preparation of a negative list of occupations which were truly hazardous for women's health and reproductive capacity, instead of leaving it to the sweet will of employers to decide what was 'unsuitable for women'. Many of us have continued to support this approach and oppose job reservations as a risky strategy.

[A leading Janata Dal politician], Sharad Yadav's argument that the women's movement and organisations cannot represent OBC (Other Backward Classes) women can be challenged by volumes of research undertaken by women's studies scholars which have particularly highlighted the oppression of OBC women as a case of 'oppression from prosperity'. I leave it to women's organisations to prove that their membership does include a large number from these strata. The question to Sharad Yadav, however, remains: since OBC men have increased their numbers in Parliament so substantially, who is really responsible for the fact that there are only three OBC women in Parliament? Is it the women's movement which has been fighting for better land rights for women in the agricultural communities, greater participation by them in panchayati raj institutions, and increased opportunities from them to participate in organisational activities? Or does the responsibility lie with the political parties whose promises of 'social justice' demonstrate the same patriarchal face as Brahminism or 'Manuvad'?

The women's movement has, till date, opposed all attempts to use its demand for one-third reservation as a bargaining counter, because any dilution now will ultimately be targeted at the panchayati raj provision, to which the movement had given first priority. Women's empowerment, like national integration—a phrase which has done more to damage the Indian polity than any provisions for reservation—is historically linked with (a) the end of 'the sanskritisation process' which 50 years of 'modernisation' operating 'democratically' has not been able to weaken (and globalisation has only enhanced and accelerated); and (b) development of new social institutions and values which can challenge social hierarchy, patriarchy and the politics of the accident of birth buttressing the theory of purity-pollution, which has always haunted our history.

Europe, which gave birth to the principles of territorial representation, is now finding it difficult to maintain it with increasingly multiculturalist societies. It is time for India to try out some new experiments in achieving real democracy in a multicultural context and provide a new basis for formation of political identities. The women's movement could offer some lessons, but where are the *statesmen* thinking in term of the 21st century?

Published in *Seminar*, Number 457, September 1997, (pp. 14-19).

Reservations and the Women's Movement in Twentieth Century India

MARY E. JOHN

Strange as it may seem—since feminists are above all else agreed on the political nature and consequences of gender relations—women's relation to politics has actually seen a waning of interest from a historical point of view. Furthermore, while our understanding of the 19th century has been successfully 'recast' from feminist perspectives, the early 20th century, the very decades that witnessed the establishment of women's organisations and saw women engaging for the first time with the public sphere of politics, has been comparatively sparsely studied. The effects of this overall neglect are particularly visible today in the wake of the rather sudden revival of concern over women's lack of presence in the political sphere, brought upon by the convergence of a global concern over 'governance' and the question of reservations for women in the different tiers of government.

On its part, the subject of reservations—that is, the creation of statutory quotas for specific groups in the legislatures, public services and institutions of higher education—has repeatedly emerged as a critical issue in the political history of 20th century India. No other policy measure has raised so many fundamental questions about the nature and composition of Indian society, and how the structures of modern governance may promote citizenship and equality within it. And yet—even though they have often provoked major conflicts and controversies both before and after Independence—reservations policies have not produced the kind of informed public debate or serious scholarship associated with other policies. Women's relation to reservations has to be seen within this larger context as well.

In the last few years, major sections of the women's movement in India have been campaigning actively, with considerable public support, to institute reservations for women in Parliament. This marks a radical change of perspective because ever since the 1930s, and even as recently as the 1970s, most women's organisations and their supporters resisted and openly rejected proposals for reserved seats. The pro-reservation stance seems to have begun in the late 1980s in response to the 73rd and 74th Constitutional Amendments which introduced 33 per cent reservations for women in local self-government institutions—the village panchayats and urban municipal bodies respectively. (These Amendments were brought into force when Rajiv Gandhi was Prime Minister at the Centre as a 'top-down' measure, hardly as a response from 'the grass-roots'. Even more interesting is that these legislations in favour of local self-government and quotas for women were passed without any debate, much less controversy.) This was followed by the subsequent demand for a similar provision in Parliament and state assemblies (first tabled as the 81st Amendment Bill in 1996), to the point where increasing women's representative presence seems to have become something of a contemporary battle-cry. However, instead of simply urging for the rapid passing of the 81st Amendment Bill and viewing its repeated stalling as a defeat at the hands of patriarchal forces, this essay attempts to open up the issues involved to further debate. Indeed, we may even have to concede that, given the complexities of our recent history, the Bill itself may only be the proverbial tip of the iceberg.

India today is hardly alone in having focused on the low presence of women in legislative and parliamentary bodies. Securing the participation of women in the institutions of democracy and governance is now an important item on the global agenda—so much so that it is acquiring the ubiquity and scope that was associated not so long ago with 'women and development'. While I am hardly opposed to the globalisation of women's issues, I cannot help but noticing certain dangers here. First of all, there is the danger that 'global' becomes a stand-in for the older term 'western'. This not only means that the particularities of non-western contexts can be obscured, but, less obviously, that profitable comparisons among non-western countries are rarely considered. This is especially important for the region of South Asia, whose political history must be examined for its intra-regional developments and conflicts. Secondly, and equally damaging, is the effective historical shortsightedness that invariably governs 'new' global agendas, agendas which consequently begin their narratives in the 1980s or even as recently as the 1990s, the decades of economic liberalisation and globalisation in India.

What is thus almost always left unaddressed in discussions of women's representation in political institutions in India is its long history. The present essay argues, therefore, that we must begin by untangling the multi-stranded history of reservations, and acknowledge the deep imprint it has left on the political common sense and the conceptual vocabularies that we have inherited. This is not an easy task, for most of this history has been and continues to be invisible to us. It is particularly marked and marred by the legacy of colonial modernity. Even when shifts and breakthroughs have occurred, as they no doubt have during the course of the women's movement in the subcontinent, they did not precipitate wholesale or one-sided changes, nor did they ensure that prior assumptions and ways of thinking were discarded, or even that the presuppositions accompanying such shifts were explicitly stated. This makes our contemporary feminist common sense a rich but also a contradictory combination of past and present beliefs and ideologies, where blocked critiques have gone hand-in-hand with the deepest questioning. Finally, the fact that a subject like reservations carries such a powerful emotive charge, especially among the middle classes, is yet another reason why a special effort is needed to uncover the many latent fears and tensions that may be implicated.

In this context, two significant moments in the history of the 20th century are urgently in need of further investigation: first, the 1920s and 1930s, including especially Ramsay Macdonald's 'Communal Award' of separate electorates in 1932,

Mahatma Gandhi's famous Poona fast, and the conflicts over reserved seats among women's organisations; and second, the years surrounding independence and its ratification, when the new nation-state and its Constitution were being shaped. It seems to me that these two periods are critical components of the pre-history of the 1990s and the revival of the demand for reservations for women during this decade. In other words, we cannot afford to contextualise the current debate solely in terms of India's prior experience with the 73rd and 74th Amendments for reservations in panchayats and municipalities—a broader canvas spanning the last century is indispensable.

Caste and communalism have been vital in the history of reservations. Though both these issues came to a crisis and were sought to be resolved at moments which were also critical for the 'women's question', we have yet to understand the consequences of these conjunctures for feminist politics. As we shall see, during the late colonial period, *'women's rights' were invariably posed in opposition to the political claims made by 'untouchables' and 'minorities'*. This has had a direct impact on how these issues were 'resolved' after independence, and on contemporary predicaments concerning gender. I would like to argue that, today, the revival of the demand for women's reservations offers us the opportunity to interrogate these colonial and post-colonial frames of reference within which we have been organising—and often misrecognising—our world. At stake is nothing less than the (as yet largely unexamined) conception of an *alternate modernity*.

The early 20th century context and the women's movement

Let me begin, then, with the opening decades of the 20th century, when the question of reservations for women was first articulated in the context of new initiatives by British colonial policy-makers towards their subject population. As we are only beginning to discover, these decades, especially the 1920s and 30s, were a 'turning point', representing a 'new conjuncture' on many interrelated fronts: for a nationalist movement whose popular base expanded on an unpredecented scale, for tribals, peasants and workers, for the anti-Brahmin movements in southern India, for the history of the Dalit movement, as well as for the often violent production of communalism.[1] The British, on their part, were actively involved in negotiating these diverse struggles and growing demands for freedom, through a strategy of devolution of power by stages, with the declared intent of enabling 'the gradual development of self-governing institutions' under a new Indian Constitution. This colonial response was replete with contradictions and manipulations, perhaps even more so than their prior efforts to justify their civilising mission through the regulation of social reform. The implications of this for the development of movements such as the women's movement were nothing less than severe.

In terms of the history of the women's movement, the early decades of the 20th century mark the acknowledged beginning of a fresh phase in women's organising. 'The educational experiments of the late 19th and early 20th centuries', it is said, 'produced a "new woman" with interests that went beyond the household.' (Forbes 1996: 64). The new demands of becoming modern, however, set off major uncertainties about the relationship between so-called 'social' issues—hitherto defined as promoting female education, raising the age of marriage, encouraging 'scientific' methods of child-care, handicraft production and so on, and an as yet undefined domain of the 'political', especially political activity vis-à-vis the state. I believe that this complex and often conflicted relationship between the social and political, including the changing contours of both these realms, has been definitive for the self-understanding of the women's movement right up to the present. Moreover, this relationship directly shaped different women's responses when the question of reservations for women in the legislatures and councils was posed.

Historians of the women's movement have invariably underscored the critical, over-determining role of colonialism and the growing force of nationalism for approaching women's politicisation in the 20th century. The 'paradox', according to Tanika Sarkar, was that the grounding of public political action (even revolutionary terrorist protest on the part of some women) was formulated in a 'language, imagery and idiom ... steeped in tradition and religion as self-conscious alternatives to alien Western norms'. This in turn froze women's revolutionary potential where domestic or family relations were concerned. (Sarkar 1989: 241) Partha Chatterjee's formulation of the nationalist resolution of the women's question addresses the same problematic, but the vantage point is different. Nationalism was able to successfully resolve the major conflicts produced in the wake of social reform during the 19th century by producing a 'modern women' who was to be the embodiment of the spiritual superiority of the nation. From the turn of the 20th century, nationalists 'refused to make the women's question an issue of political negotiation with the colonial state'; moreover, they granted women the vote without the need for a suffrage movement. In other words, by containing the real history of the women's question within the middle-class home, the colonial (and post-colonial) public sphere was effectively degendered. Indeed, Chatterjee goes on to remark on the 'seeming absence of any autonomous struggle by women themselves for equality and freedom'. Instead of being in public competition with men, distinctions '*between* women in the world outside the home' were far more significant. It was against conceptions of excessively 'westernised', 'traditional', and 'low-class' women that the new norm was fashioned—the modern woman whose education and emancipation were tied to the spiritual qualities of self-sacrifice, benevolence, devotion, and religiosity, thus setting in place a revised patriarchy whose legitimacy rested precisely on being disavowed. (Chatterjee 1994: 131–33; emphasis original). Unfortunately, Chatterjee's account stops with the turn of the 20th century, and does not comment at all on the complex evolution of a women's movement in the subsequent decades. In effect, then, his arguments have the following twin corollaries: on the one hand, women ceased to be relevant in the next phase of nationalist struggle; on the other hand, women's political rights were resolved in cultural terms, as spiritual bearers of Indian nationhood. The question I wish to pursue here is whether such assumptions can be sustained, or whether in fact 'women' continued to be critical precisely when the ground of cultural nationalism moved in the direction of the political claims of citizenship.

Now it is indeed possible to find prominent women who drew from (while also transforming) the potent ingredients of cultural nationalism to become quite extraordinary embodiments of public politics, and who enacted this new woman on many stages—colonial, national and international. Sarojini Naidu was arguably one of the most famous of them. Already in 1918 she persuaded her Congress audience that giving women the vote would by no means interfere with the 'destinies' of men and women, which were 'separate' ones, but united by nationalism. Nor, in the decade that followed, can it be denied that it was the British who refused to grant women the right to vote and stand for elections on the same terms as men, even though this demand enjoyed the support of most of the women's organisations of the time, the Home Rule League, the Muslim League, and the Indian National Congress, including an initially opposed Gandhi. By 1930, major women's organisations were also deliberating the question of reservations of seats in political bodies apart from women's voting rights. In her much-publicised Presidential Address to the All India Women's Conference in Bombay of the same year, Sarojini Naidu made it unequivocally clear that women did not want preferential treatment [i.e. any form of nomination or reservation], for this would amount to an admission of women's 'inferiority'. This was why she was no feminist. Women's task was nothing less than the 'spiritual reform of the world' (AIWC 1930: 21). Thus, even nationalism in her view limited the scope of women's transformative potential. On another occasion she evoked 'the indivisibility of womanhood—frontiers, wars, races, many things make for division—but womanhood combines. The queen and the peasant are one, and the time has come when every woman should know her own divinity' (Reddi 1964: 124). Cultural distinction and political rights appear to flow seamlessly into one another, and with this crucial consequence: whereas cultural nationalism rested on claims of difference, women's politics drew upon the universal language of unity and indivisibility.

But if a figure like Sarojini Naidu could turn the experience of colonial subjection into a romantic project of feminine spiritualism and humanism, in one and the same breath dismissing feminism in the name of women's global unity, this cannot be said for many others who became active in setting up women's organisations and promoting women's issues. For some of these women who were drawn towards agendas of social reform under the changing and politically turbulent decade of the 20th century, the question of political rights, engagement with the colonial state, the demand for the franchise and the contentious issue of reserved seats were not so easily 'resolved'. It may be worth recalling that the first demand for women's right to vote (presented to Montagu in 1917) appears to have been something of an accidental by-product: The initial deputation by Margaret Cousins, (an Irish feminist and secretary of the Women's Indian Association in Madras), with the backing of D.K. Karve and the Senate of Poona's Indian Women's University, was for compulsory free primary education for both girls and boys. It was only when she was informed that the terms of the Montagu-Chelmsford enquiry were strictly 'political', meant to initiate a constitutional process of self-government, that she claims to have linked the demand for education to the need for Indian women's franchise (Reddi ed. 1956; Pearson 1989: 201–2). Sarojini Naidu led a separate delegation demanding that women be included on the same terms as men in any political settlement for India.

Unlike Sarojini Naidu, Muthulakshmi Reddi's relationship to the question of reserved seats was quite different. Born into a devadasi family in the southern Tamil country, she was educated and became trained as a medical doctor. In 1926 her name was submitted by the Women's Indian Association (WIA) for nomination to the Madras Legislative Council (which, along with Bombay in 1921, was the first to extend the franchise to women on the same terms as men, i.e. subject to property and income criteria). With some reluctance she agreed, only, she said, to use politics to advance her sisters' cause. Muthulakshmi

Reddi's own descriptions and explanations of her work as a legislator were multi-voiced: accounts of women's inferiority, their lack of economic independence and inheritance rights, the need for marriage law reform, abolition of the devadasi system, and so on, required reservations 'to represent the women's point of view'. As mistresses of the home, moreover, women were ideal administrators of the municipality. At the same time she voiced her feelings against separate electoral rolls for women—'we do not want to form a separate caste' she said, for 'men and women rise and fall together'. Moreover, in a situation where a majority of educated women were not qualified to vote, separate electorates would enfranchise conservative women 'not conversant with the moving world' (Reddi 1930: 155–61). She also questioned men of the depressed and backward classes and minorities, her 'Adi-Dravida brothers and Mohammedans', who stressed more upon other grievances than the education of their girls (p. 123). Indeed, the 'backwardness of Hindu women' was much worse, she asserted, than the condition of backward class or minority men (p. 155). Unlike Sarojini Naidu, therefore, Reddi's visible feminist struggle to carry forward an agenda of social reform sharpened her misgivings about the differences between women—'modern' and 'conservative', and eventually appears to have led to her own rethinking about the very purpose of reservations, when it brought in, in her view, 'undeserving' women.

In one of the first extensive studies of the Indian women's movement, Jana Everett tried to account for such differences amongst women in their relation to politics and reservations by referring to the 'uplift' and 'equal rights' factions among women's organisations (Everett 1979). Since then, a number of studies have analysed this enormously complex period in the history of the women's movement, especially from the point of view of the mixed fortunes of different women's delegations before the British government, and the responses of British colonialists and feminists.[2] In a recent intervention, occasioned precisely by the present revival of interest in the subject of reservations, Geraldine Forbes has referred to different phases on this issue between 1918 and 1935 in terms of women's relationships to politics and voting rights. It was only after 1930 (after the Lahore Declaration and the Nehru Report promising women 'equal rights') that the idea of universal franchise formed the relevant backdrop for varying stances towards the issue of reservations (Forbes 2002). Clearly there were deep differences and conflicts even within women's organisations such as the All India Women's Conference (AIWC), established in 1926, which became the most influential national women's organisation in the next decade. In an earlier study, Forbes has pointed out how 'one by one, women who had previously supported nomination and reserved seats [such as Muthulakshmi Reddi] added their voices to the demand for "equality and no privileges" and "a fair field and no favour".' The official stance of the three major women's organisations in 1932 against any 'privileges' notwithstanding, 'there was a great deal of support for special electorates and nominated seats,' especially from provincial assemblies and local bodies (Forbes 1996: 107–8).

Any account of the growing pressure on women to drop their demands for reserved seats must make space for the extraordinary relationship of Gandhi with women and the women's movement that developed during the 1920s. Much has been written about Gandhi's surprised discovery of women's remarkable potential as public political actors, especially during the civil disobedience campaigns, and his subsequent conversion to the cause of women. It was men, he said, who needed to learn from the Indian woman's supreme powers of self-sacrifice. This aspect of Gandhi has been the subject of both celebration and critique. It is, I think, less well-known that Gandhi's intense personal relationships with women were the conduit for turning demands for reservations or special electorates into signs of anti-nationalist betrayal. His influence was also paramount for how women's organisations approached communalism and untouchability, as we shall see. Partha Chatterjee's claim, then, that for nationalism the colonial public sphere must be degendered, undergoes a subtle, but highly significant transformation with Gandhi. At the height of political nationalism, the public glorification of femininity became the very ground for persuading women of the illegitimacy of their demands for special political representation.

When the next Franchise Committee was set up at the close of the Second Round Table Conference to tour India and collect opinions in 1932, a memorandum from the all-India women's organisations (the WIA, AIWC and NCIW [National Council of Indian Women]) reiterated their demand 'for the Universal Adult Franchise—irrespective of any property or literacy qualification, and with no expedients such as nomination and reservation of seats'. When their demands were not met, (once again British opinion claimed that the majority of Indian women were 'not ready', that implementing the franchise across the country would be 'impractical', even though their own recommendations sought to engineer an improvement in the male/female vote ratio from 20:1 to 5:1), women's organisations agreed to work out some sort of transitional compromise. It is surely significant that while they opposed many of the colonial recommendations such as the wifehood qualification, their compromise included the restriction of women's franchise to urban areas. This was because, as their written statement put it, they attached 'equal importance to the quality as well as the quantity of the woman's vote'; an urban vote would ensure 'a more independent and well-organised vote—factors of vital importance ... at the present juncture'; thus enabling 'the educated womanhood of India to coordinate the woman's vote on the right lines' (AIWC 1933–34: 18). At the same time, opposition to any kind of reservation was reiterated—'merit and merit alone' was to be the criterion, even if it meant fewer seats. Those voices that believed special electorates and nominated seats would enable a truer representation and amelioration of the social problems facing women were sought to be won over, or accused of being disloyal.

On one level, therefore, we can see how these women's strategic choice in favour of formal political equality was not unrelated to their own social, educational and individual advancement. The most significant issue here is, of course, that they thereby naturalised their own representative claims to speak for all of Indian womanhood, while professing a language of no privileges or favours. Moreover, their official opposition to nominations and reserved seats did not stop them from demanding the presence of women in the central and provincial legislatures, district, municipal and other local bodies, indeed, on any commissions or committees affecting women and children, from the League of Nations to the Censor Board (AIWC 1934-35: 70, 187). Finally, as Gail Pearson has pointed out, 'the very method—reserved seats—by which women were accepted as part of the Indian parliamentary culture [under the terms of the Government of India Act of 1935] was first vehemently opposed by those nationalist women whom it was later to benefit' (Pearson 1989: 199).

In other words, the significance of this formative period in the history of the women's movement lies in how, precisely at the height of political nationalism, a new contradictory identity was cemented. A very specific 'woman' and a corresponding construction of femininity—in terms of class and caste, refinement and subjectivity—became the bearer, not just of Indian culture, but of a new *universal citizen*. From the 1930s onwards, it was women's organisations more than any other group, even including the Congress Party, that clung tenaciously to universal formal rights, of which they were the truest embodiment.

It would be a major mistake, however, to isolate women's protests against the idea of reservations and special electorates, from their resolution against the British 'Communal Award' of 1932, as it was known, which sought to provide separate electorates and reserved seats to Muslims, Christians, Sikhs and Anglo-Indians, and made 'special' provisions for the depressed classes, as they were called. Though pledged not to get involved in party politics and stay focused on matters relating to women's status, prominent figures, within the AIWC were able to condemn the award by interweaving their conception of the 'best' system of representation with the theme of the unity of all women. As Rajkumari Amrit Kaur put it 'there is no question as to the reality of unity amongst us women. We want to send our *best* women and our *best* men to the councils—therefore we do not want the canker of communalism amongst us. Once we are divided into sects and communities all will be lost ...'

(AIWC 1932–33: 51). Seconding the resolution, Aruna Asaf Ali referred to the 'evil of separatism'. 'We women must do our uttermost to see that our country is not left to the mercies of job hunters. The legislatures must be filled with those who really feel that the country's interests stand above personal or communal considerations' (p. 53). Other members, however, raised questions and objections. Begum Sakina Mayuzada opposed the resolution, saying that desiring the good of one's community did not imply she wished harm on others, and K.B. Firozuddin raised the problem that Muslim women representatives might be prevented from competing under a system of joint electorates due to their comparative educational backwardness. But these views were brushed aside as creating barriers and 'artificial communal hedges', which would only lead to being told yet again that 'we are unfit for Self-government'. A separate resolution was passed condemning the practice of untouchability, calling on women to work wholeheartedly for this abolition and for the equal admittance of the so-called untouchables in public spaces and institutions. Gandhi's fast was referred to in the subsequent discussion as having brought 'this disgrace to Hinduism and the Hindu community' finally into prominence all across the country (p. 60).

Women's organisations thus insisted that they were untouched by communalism, in spite of clear expressions of disagreement. As far as possible, declarations of dissent were not recorded by the AIWC Franchise Committee, even when it came from such important figures as Begum Shah Nawaz. 'Minority' opinions were regarded as numerically unimportant, since 'it had been decided that only the majority vote counted' (Forbes 1979: 15). But, as Forbes goes on to add, members of these organisations had always known that Muslim women were in a minority. Maitrayee Chaudhuri has also perceptively commented on the opposed perceptions of communal representation for different women. While the unity of women and the nation were endangered by communal electorates in the dominant discourses, it was the very settlement of the communal question that would ensure the safety of the nation in the notes of most Muslim women members (Chaudhuri 1993: 157).

Communalism, minorities and majorities

The host of issues thrown up in the name of the Communal Award need much more examination than either women's organisations appear to have been capable of at the time or that feminist historians have provided since. In the space of this paper, it is only possible to mention some of the more important aspects, beginning with the very construction of the notion of 'communalism' itself. Right into the 20th century, liberal nationalists envisioned the future India as being made up of discrete religious communities, Hindu, Muslim, Sikh, Christian and so on (whatever the problems attached to such a vision, and parallel efforts to demarcate boundaries between 'social' and 'political' domains). They even publicly espoused the role of separate electorates. However, from the 1920s, and not only because of the series of Hindu-Muslim riots in many parts of the country during that decade, the meaning of 'communalism' changed dramatically and came to be conceptualised in zero-sum terms, in a relation of opposition to a much narrower definition of nationalism. Nationalism now claimed to stand *above* and *outside* the primordial pulls of religious community or caste (Pandey 1990: 235), loyalty to country had to exceed that of any sectarian attachments (whose public political place therefore had to be diminished), until, finally, any reference to communities, was not just synonymous with religious community, but with all that was pernicious in the British policy of 'divide and rule'. Understandings such as these were clearly dominant in organisations like the AIWC.

Much of this must be familiar and commonplace. But there is another dimension to communalism whose contours and strategies are far less clear, in spite of its apparent obviousness and democratic structure—this is the language of minoritism and majoritarianism, which evolved side-by-side with the demands of a new 'purified' nationalism. Its lasting effects cannot be underestimated, especially if we are to make meaningful links between the establishment of organisations such as the Hindu Mahasabha and the Rashtriya Swayamsevak Sangh (RSS) in the 1920s, the aggressive construction of the 'Hindu community' as a beleaguered, fragile majority in their own homeland, growing fears among Muslims that they were now condemned to being a minority in need of protection, having lost out in modern opportunities and advancement, and the complex politics attached to caste. Prominent national women's organisations' own naturalisations of the 'Hindu', in the context of claiming the space of a united women's movement, in fact contributed to the creation of a 'secular-Hindu' movement, and the minoritisation of other groups.

Leaders like Jawaharlal Nehru juggled between the 'untenability', in his view, of a communal system of political representation, and claims that the Congress must make it 'the business of the state to give favoured treatment to minority and backward communities'. This was in 1930. Even though the Constituent Assembly as late as 28 August 1947 (after Indian independence and the creation of Pakistan) sought to ratify the special rights of minorities, which explicitly included reservations of seats in the central and provincial legislatures, a principle of representation in the Cabinet, and a due share in the services, by the time the question was re-opened in 1949 after the horrors of the Partition violence had subsided, it did not take much to dismantle and drop them altogether. The distress and ambiguity of the moment was such that it was even possible to radically undermine the political relevance of notions such as minorities and majorities in a secular independent state making a break with the colonial past. However, it was not as though these terms were abandoned. Nehru, for example, continued to use them, along with the asymmetry of political power that the majority/minority dyad implied, when he declared that any demand for safeguards by minorities betrayed a lack of trust in the majority, while also advising the majority not to ride roughshod over the minorities. Already in 1947, when the Objectives Resolution of the Constituent Assembly had resolved to provide adequate safeguards for 'minorities, backward and tribal areas, depressed and other backward classes', the term 'minority' was dropped, and 'class' was said to be sufficiently inclusive. As a result of the efforts of B.R. Ambedkar, the phrase which finally found its way into Article 16(4) of the Constitution of India was 'any backward class of citizens'. Ambedkar himself appears to have used 'community', 'caste' and 'class' in the course of his deliberations more or less interchangeably. But overall, the tenor of these debates was such that the rights of minorities had to be encapsulated as primarily cultural and religious, not political.[3]

The question of caste

If this is how relations between reservations and minorities were played out from the time of the Communal Award to the framing of the new Indian Constitution, what about caste? How, in particular, did questions of reservations and caste impinge on the women's movement? These may well be the hardest questions of any that this paper hopes to open up for further discussion. It appears fairly certain that Gandhi's campaigns against untouchability during the 1920s played the most direct and immediate role in shaping women's organisations' views on caste. These were the very years that saw the emergence of non-Brahmin and Dalit movements in the southern and western regions of the subcontinent. These movements were making their presence felt in existing working-class and peasant organisations; through 'reformist' struggles of improvement as much as more 'radical' claims to cultural autonomy from upper caste society; and significantly as a political force, by demanding representation in education, administration as well as on legislative bodies. In the case of the Princely State of Mysore, for instance, historical developments brought together Muslims, Christians and castes such as the Vokkaligas and Lingayats under a common 'non-Brahmin' banner as far back as 1874 in a bid to break the monopoly of Brahmins in the Mysore government services. The first Backward Classes Committee of its kind was appointed in 1918 as a result of this political awakening amongst groups who were able to give voice to their lack of presence and representative power in the administrative system (Thimmaiah: 1993). The Self-Respect Movement in Madras included critiques of caste and gender in their attacks on

Brahmin and upper caste dominance (V. Geetha and Rajadurai: 1997; Anandhi S. 1998)

In this context, the effects of Gandhi's campaigns against untouchability on women's organisations are disturbing. Having also been instrumental in nominating Muthulakshmi Reddi to the Madras Legislative Council, a women's organisation like the WIA was, for many years, positively disposed towards reserved seats for women. Gandhi's fast against granting special electorates to the depressed classes on 20 September 1932 following the announcement of the Ramsay Macdonald Award a month before, which was described as his fast 'against untouchability', was not just widely reported in the journal of the WIA (significantly named *Stree Dharma*) but dramatically broke their own demand for reserved seats and nominations. Right up to Gandhi's fast, the WIA maintained that although adult franchise was the real answer,

> for a transition period it suggests the reservation of 20 per cent of the seats in the new and enlarged legislatures and proposes that they be voted for by proportional representation by the newly elected members of Council from a panel of names sent forward by the officially recognised associations of women. (cited in Forbes 1979: 14)

But once Gandhi's fast began, 'this was the last time such a possibility [by the WIA] was entertained.' This meant that women's self-sacrifice of *their* interests, as proof of their devotion to Gandhi, was achieved by a less visible denial—the political rights to representation of the 'untouchables' or 'depressed classes'. Indeed, it is not even clear to what extent women's groups were even aware just how such political rights were in fact being articulated, and especially of Ambedkar's own demands and representations to the British. By 1930, Ambedkar stated that the depressed people whom he represented needed political power, which could only be gained within the framework of an independent India. His demand at the First Round Table Conference was for a unitary state, adult suffrage, and reserved seats and special safeguards for untouchables. Historians of the Dalit movement like Gail Omvedt have asked themselves why, of all things, the Second

Conference and the Ramsay MacDonald Award of separate electorates should have developed specifically into Gandhi's opposition to Ambedkar, and not to the other minorities, the federal power accorded to the princely states, or, for that matter, to any of the other interest groups—landlords, commerce and industry, universities and labour—who were all granted special representative rights under the terms of the Award. 'Of all the participants in the first conference, Ambedkar's position (adult suffrage and reserved seats) was actually closest to the nationalist one' (Omvedt 1994: 169).

Though detailed information on women's participation in Ambedkar's movement is only just being unearthed, historians such as Meenakshi Moon and Urmilla Pawar drew attention well over a decade ago to the range of issues taken up by Dalit women's organisations in the early 20th century. According to them, during the late 1920s and '30s 'women conducted meetings to support separate electorates for the untouchables and passed resolutions accordingly' (Moon and Pawar 1989: 69).

But the dominant voice in the mainstream women's organisations was definitely that of Gandhi's. 'Those who speak of political rights of untouchables do not know how Indian society is constructed,' he declared to the Minorities Committee. 'So far as Hinduism is concerned, separate electorates would simply vivisect and disrupt it' (in Sitaramayya 1969: 909). Indeed, Gandhi went on, it would be preferable if the Untouchables converted to Islam or Christianity. An adequate answer for Gandhi's exclusive confrontation with Ambedkar must therefore account for the unique constructions of the 'Hindu', not just for explicitly Hindu organisations, but within the Congress itself. A complex mix of the politics of numbers which required proof of the numerical supremacy of Hindus at any cost; an inability to look upon untouchability as anything more than a social problem, a 'blight' that upper castes must purify; and Gandhi's own reconception of Hinduism and reformed caste relations as an 'indivisible family', one for which he was ready to lay down his life—all of these might go some way towards recognising why the politics of caste was so especially threatening.

In any event, after a four-day fast, a compromise had to be reached and the Poona Pact was signed, involving a two-tier system of voting between untouchables and a general electorate. By 1935, when the Government of India Act was finalised, the distinct careers of the notion of the depressed classes (which continued to be the preferred term of the British), political concepts of 'backwardness' which were evolving in Mysore and Madras; and the pivotal question of 'untouchability' as a unique disability and form of social exclusion, came together when the need to draw up a 'Schedule' or list of castes was required for 'special' electoral representation. As a number of commentators have pointed out, the selection of the 'Scheduled Castes' as they came to be called, proceeded without the benefit of a connotative definition, since no single criterion could be found that worked for the whole country. Even though leaders like Ambedkar kept the focus of untouchability on those who suffer from the contempt and aversion of higher caste Hindus, questions of economic backwardness and lack of education were also drawn upon, especially for regions of the north and east (Galanter 1984). By the time the Constitution was ratified in 1950, the principle that was applied came to rest on groups which had *historically* suffered both hostile discrimination and disadvantage, and for whom, three kinds of preference were envisaged: special electoral representation in the legislatures, preferential employment, and preferential treatment. (Interestingly enough, the listing from 1935 was to remain more or less stable in the post-independence period, with only minor additions after that.)

After the ratification of the Schedules for specific castes and tribes in the Constitution, the numerous pre-independence struggles and coalitions in the names of the 'Backward classes or communities', 'Non-Brahmins', 'depressed classes' and so on, underwent a major change, to re-emerge as the so-called 'Other Backward Classes' in the language of the state. As the name suggests, this was a residual category, meant to designate those groups (apart from the Scheduled Castes and Scheduled Tribes) who were nevertheless deemed to be in need of special treatment.

The constitutional resolution of the women's question

In comparison to the trajectories of the political rights of minorities, backward classes and the 'untouchables', the direction taken by women's rights from the 1930s to 1950, was significantly different. We have already seen how the Communal Award not only fundamentally affected women' organisations' understanding of caste and communalism, but stiffened the resolve of many to hold onto 'equal rights' at any cost. In the years leading up to and following the Government of India Act of 1935, women's organisations were successively betrayed. The first to do so were the British, who refused to provide any declaration of fundamental rights or non-discrimination on the basis of sex for holding public office in the 1935 Act. Some modifications were made regarding qualifications for voting in different provinces, (wifehood remaining primary), which expanded male and female electorates to 43 per cent and nine per cent respectively. Forty-one reserved seats for women were allocated among different communities. In the next elections of 1937, a total of 56 women candidates entered the legislatures, out of which only 10 came from general seats and five were nominations. Women's organisations therefore felt specifically betrayed by the Congress. If it was Gandhi who had been the most vociferous advocate against reserved seats for women, the Congress now had little room for any women candidates other than those who were staunch party workers in any case. Finally, for all their efforts to enlarge the number of women voters, 'there was no necessary corollary between the politicisation of women and the actual advancement of their cause' (Nair 1996: 140).

Eleven women were nominated to the Constituent Assembly to participate in its deliberations on the ultimate finalisation of the Constitution. According to Vina Mazumdar 'there is little doubt that it was the willing and spontaneous participation of women in the civil disobedience movements rather than the radical ideas of sexual equality that finally tilted the balance in favour of political equality between the sexes in the Congress Party and later in the Constituent Assembly' (Mazumdar 1979: xvi). As she notes, the 'Constitution fathers' never debated the issue, nor did they realise the social and political implications of what they were granting. Partha Chatterjee, as we have seen, has argued that the question was settled much earlier, on the grounds of 'cultural' not 'political' nationalism, which enabled middle class 'modern' women's entry into the public sphere by domesticating the nationalist project within the home.

I have been suggesting that the issue of women's rights was both more complex and more significant than either of these two views indicate. Conflicts over the relationship between 'social' issues and the abstract universal language of political rights 'irrespective of caste, creed, race or sex' took concrete form in the protracted problem of reserved seats. Women's organisations were caught in contradictory proclamations of the 'unity of all women', the sameness of their condition, and so on, even as they effectively 'reserved' for themselves—urban, educated, modern and progressive—the right to represent Indian womanhood. These claims to unity had to be maintained, moreover, in the face of the loss of Muslim women's membership, and the effective negation of distinct political right to the 'untouchables'. The period of political nationalism thus saw multifaceted processes of avowal and disavowal—the celebration of a convoluted feminity by Gandhi, the claim to representativeness by dominant women's organisations, and the emergence of women as model bearers of political unity and universal citizenship, all of which were consolidated through definitive, if not always explicitly understood processes of exclusion.

The Constituent Assembly was not the place, however, where women members discussed any of these contradictions. On the contrary, they appeared eager to declare their opposition to any special privileges in the form of reservations. Thus Renuka Ray, for instance, referred to the Government of India Act of 1935, where 'the social backwardness of women had been sought to be exploited in the same manner as the backwardness of so many sections in this country by those who wanted to deny its freedom' (CAD 1947: 668). Reservations prevented women from standing from general constituencies, and constituted 'an impediment to our growth and an insult to our very intelligence and capacity' (p. 669). It is worth noting that this intervention took place 'spontaneously', so to say, in the context of a discussion over requests for the modification of territorial representation for the remote and sparsely populated hill tribes of Assam. Vallabhbhai Patel took full advantage of the situation, regretting, as he put it, that men had not yet come up to the standard of women: 'Let us hope that nothing will be provided in the Constitution which would make exception in favour of men [in a situation] where women object [to similar exceptions being made in their favour]' (p. 674).

The pattern whereby 'communal' or 'minority' rights were thus counterposed to women's rights—always to the detriment of the former and invariably by underscoring the superiority of women's demands for universal rights and claims to unity—took many forms during these years. It emerged in the Constituent Assembly Minorities Sub-committee in 1949 when 'freedom of religious propaganda and practice' was seen to conflict with 'social reform' for women. It took an interestingly different form in what became the very first Constitutional Amendment. Champaka Dorairajan, a young Brahmin woman, petitioned the High Court of Madras in 1951 claiming that her fundamental right (to pursue a medical education) was being denied by the Madras system of proportional 'communal' reservations in higher education.

Now it might seem that these two examples disprove my arguments. After all, though the Madras Court struck down the system of reservations of the Madras government as unconstitutional, the Supreme Court subsequently ordered the incorporation of Clause 15(4) concerning special provisions 'for the advancement of any socially or educationally backward class of citizens' into the Constitution. In the Minorities Sub-Committee, though the other members initially agreed to Rajkumari Amrit Kaur's suggestion that religious freedom be limited to religious worship, in the end both the terms 'practice' and 'propagation' were retained, with the proviso that this did not preclude social reform (*Roshni* 1941: 150–61). In my view, however, cases like these helped to cement concepts undergirding the very nature of caste (i.e. backwardness) and minorities (i.e. religion), and to pit these concepts as *problematic and even regressive* in opposition to the more genuinely universal claims of modern womanhood.

More than two decades later in 1974, the Committee on the Status of Women rejected by majority vote the recommendation to reintroduce into independent India reservations for women in legislative bodies. (Of all the issues taken up by the committee—in the fields of work, law, education and so on, this was the only question which required a vote to settle different opinions among the members.) Amongst the many shocking discoveries of their report *Towards Equality* were the declining trends in the number of women legislators and the reluctance of political parties to sponsor women—in the very wake of freedom and the universal franchise. Amongst the reasons advanced by the Committee for not wishing to reintroduce reservations for women was that 'women are a category, not a community'. The tendency to make a case in favour of women's rights in opposition to notions of backwardness and minority groups is visible even here. Thus the 'note of dissent' (written in support of women's reservations) by Vina Mazumdar and Lotika Sarkar begins by recalling their own misplaced prior criticisms of 'the system of reservations for Scheduled Castes and Scheduled Tribes, as a legacy of the colonial period, which institutionalised backwardness of certain sections of our population' (in Mazumdar 1979: 363). Against the argument that a system of special representation might 'precipitate fissiparous tendencies', they cited the views of one of the experts, Professor Sirsikar: 'Women are not marginal to society as the minority group might be. They are not a dispensable part of the society ...' and 'would not create what is feared by the critics, isolated pockets' (p. 365–66).

Questions for the present

The 1990s, have been watershed years in India's history, a time of transition, when the nation-state we took for granted was subjected to unprecedented pressures from without and within. This has been the decade of the liberalisation of the economy, the anti-Mandal agitation against the extension of reservations to the Other Backward Classes, and the emergence of lower caste parties such as the Bahujan Samaj Party and the Samajwadi Party. This was also the decade of the demolition of the Babri Masjid and the ensuing riots, and the rise to dominance of a Bharatiya Janata Party-led coalition that is currently in power at the centre. It is in this context that the 81st Women's Reservation Bill for one-third reservation for women was first tabled in Parliament in 1996, and was soon mired in the conflict over the demand for special quotas for women of the Other Backward Classes and minorities.

The resurgence of caste and minority issues within a 'women's issue' seems to take us right back to the pre-independence years, but with at least one significant difference: five decades after independence, we are forced to recognise the divergent post-independence trajectories of 'gender,' 'caste,' and 'community'. The post-independence women's movement, reborn in the 1970s, has come a long way from early 20th century struggles, and from successive efforts to 'resolve' the women's question. Even if old debates on tradition and the westernness of feminism have not disappeared, it is now clear that gender oppression must take on board the entire question of modernity, since patriarchal power is manifested in multiple contemporary forms, both public and private. Women are not just considered to be victims of tradition, centuries of oppression, or the ruses of colonial subjection. Feminism is visible and enduring; it is a viable, if problematic, part of our present.

However, the political careers of caste and community have been far more confused. They are 'still' with us, it is so often said, implying thereby that they are the products of a pre-colonial or colonial past. Their very legitimacy as active sites of contemporary struggle is frequently in question. In the case of caste for instance, the heavy emphasis on the historical past and backwardness of caste discrimination, which was to be rectified by compensatory policies, might help us understand the peculiar place of caste, (often better described as a non-place), in the imagination of the nation-state in the decades following independence. The preferential programmes and policies aimed at the Scheduled Castes and Scheduled Tribes were never premised on the recognition of *injustice in the modern present*.[4] Backward class commissions were regionalised, unable to carry out their assigned tasks meaningfully, stymied by the negative attitudes of the State, the indifference if not hostility of academia and the national press. Preferential policies have therefore existed in a climate which soon turned them into exceptions to the rule of equality, inimical to the national interest. Most difficult of all, upper caste domination became largely invisible in a 'casteless' ethos. There was little support for constitutionally sanctioned reservations even from Left and democratic organisations, an attitude that has undergone a change only after the Mandal agitations. Prior to the 1990s, this has been part of the common sense of most sections of the women's movement as well. Similar problems have held back our understanding of the post-colonial marginalisation of minorities and the consolidation of secular-Hindu dominance.

That is why it seems to me that the revival of reservations for women in the 1990s—after Mandal, Ayodhya and globalisation—offers us the chance to conceive of alternate modernities by rethinking the predicaments that surround women's rights. First of all, we need to revisit the late colonial period when women's political rights were effectively set in place. This paper has done no more than provide a sketch which must be filled out if not revised by further exploration. Feminist historians such as Geraldine Forbes have emphasised the obsession of pre-independence women's organisations with the 'right kind of woman' (whether they were pro- or anti-reservationist). Mrinalini Sinha has gone so far as to claim that 'liberal Indian feminists played a pivotal role in the fashioning of a "bourgeois" liberal Indian modernity' (Sinha 2000: 626).

It is obviously tempting to think that, with the benefit of hindsight, feminists today are better placed to realise the insufficiencies of the modernising impulses of their pre-independence sisters. I am not so sure, if only because of the shortsightedness with which sections of the women's movement have suddenly become so positively inclined towards reservations for women. Where has this change come from? Have we taken on board the fact that the introduction of reservations for women in local bodies—first brought in by the state of Karnataka in 1983 and promulgated by Parliament at the national level a decade later—was very much a state-initiated and politically motivated venture (even allowing that the authors of *Towards Equality* in 1974 had made an explicit recommendation in favour of reservations for women in the panchayats)? There are definite indications that the move of 25 per cent reserved seats for women in Karnataka was not unrelated to the rise of backward caste politics in that state. Nivedita Menon has also argued that the timing of the Women's Reservation Bill in the 1990s cannot simply be understood in terms of the rebirth of the women's movement and the resulting emergence of women's issues in the public domain from the late 1970s onwards—the other factor is 'the transformation of the caste composition of Parliament and the growing presence of backward castes through successive elections' (Menon 2000: 3836).

This is not the place for a detailed account of the career of the Women's Reservations Bill and the kinds of debates that have surrounded it. However, one issue is worth highlighting. The biggest change from the colonial period has to do with the ease with which feminists today question abstract constructions of citizenship—at least in relation to the passing of the Bill. On any number of occasions the partriarchal biases of parties and politicians, indeed of the family itself, have been indicted for having ensured the effective exclusion of women from parliamentary politics. But feminists have been rather reluctant to think through the *diverse* patriarchal forces which constrain women's life chances, their ambitions, and their ability to represent women's and men's experiences politically. The growing economic and social disparities that are a hallmark of liberalisation should also alert us to the reality that partriarchy in contemporary society is neither a single monolith nor a set of discrete unconnected enclaves, but rather, a complex articulation of *unequal partriarchies*.

Therefore, even if the demand for 'quotas within quotas'

had never been raised, a feminist perspective on the question of reservations for women today would have to take account of subjugated patriarchies. This requires *linking*—rather than opposing—women's rights to rights based on caste, class or minority status in the broader context of a common democratic struggle. To recognise caste and communalism as modern forms of inequality (rather than as symbols of our 'backwardness'), they need to be integrated with questions of class and gender, thereby transforming our understanding of all of them. This also means re-examining the last 50 years of independence, and focusing much more carefully on the social composition of the dominant elites, especially among the so-called middle classes and within the women's movement. As Gail Omvedt put it recently, these classes have been reproducing themselves in an 'informational vacuum' (*The Hindu* 25 March 2000). To concentrate solely on poverty and disadvantage, as we have been doing so far, is no longer enough. Of course, these constitute little more than starting points—however necessary—for engaging with the issue of reservations for women within the context of the vexed but critical question of women's relation to politics and to power as such. There is little room for naivete or for any simple beliefs that women as women—whether from dominant or subaltern groups—make better political subjects. The point is rather that diverse women have been struggling within the domain of the political under very disparate circumstances and for quite some time. Any progressive-democratic debate on the Women's Reservation Bill that wishes to learn from the legacy of the 20th century must engage with these multiple realities as fully as possible.[5]

Acknowledgements

I am grateful to audiences in Hyderabad, Delhi, Colombo and Lahore for their comments on different presentations of the main arguments of this essay. An earlier version of this paper has been published under the title 'Alternate Modernities? Reservations and the Women's Movement in Twentieth Century India', Economic and Political Weekly, Review of Women's Studies, *vol. 35, nos. 43–44, 28 October 2000.*

Notes

1. For further details on this period, see Sarkar 1983, Pandey 1990, and Omvedt 1994.
2. There are a number of studies that dwell on different phases in the development of women's organisations and their battle for the franchise. These include Everett 1979; Forbes 1979, 1996; Chaudhuri 1993; Kumar 1993; Nair 1996; Pearson 1989; Sinha 1999.
3. See various volumes of the Constituent Assembly Debates. For different interpretations on the loss of political rights to the minorities see Ansari 1999, and Bajpai 2000. Though Bajpai's extended discussion of the competing conceptions of backwardness and minority rights is instructive, I am not convinced of the overall frame of her argument that the historical creation of Pakistan had little to do with the weakening of minority rights. Also the idea that notions of backwardness were upheld by 'dominant' sections of the Assembly overstates the case, especially when we consider the overall aversion to caste by precisely these dominant sections.
4. Discussions with Satish Deshpande have helped clarify the importance of this issue for me.
5. The 'Alternate Women's Reservation Bill' prepared by the Forum for Democratic Reforms and widely publicised by Madhu Kishwar was circulated as an explicit response to the shortcomings of the WRB. For all its claims to have improved on the 81st Amendment Bill, it displays a not very well-hidden resentment that women even need reservations. While the freedom movement is lauded for having brought 'outstanding women' into politics, the emergence of OBC parties are squarely blamed for having 'blocked the participation of women at key entry points'. Even more disturbing is the cavalier mode in which 'resentment' towards reservations for SCs and STs is discussed. Whatever the limitations of the 81st Amendment Bill, one is hard put to figuring out how this constitutes an advance.

References

All India Women's Conference Annual Reports (AIWC). 1931–37.
Ambedkar, Dr Babasaheb. *Writings and Speeches* vol. 1–12. Government of Maharashtra: Education Department.
Ansari, Iqbal A. 1999. 'Minorities and the Politics of Constitution Making in India' in *Minority Identities and the Nation*, eds. Gurpreet Mahajan and D.L. Sheth. Delhi: Oxford University Press.
Bajpai, Rochana. 2000. 'Constituent Assembly Debates and Minority Rights'. *Economic and Political Weekly.* 27 May 2000.
Chaudhuri, Maitrayee. 1993. *Indian Women's Movement: Reform and Revival.* New Delhi: Radiant.
Chatterjee, Partha. 1994. *The Nation and its Fragments: Colonial and Postcolonial Histories.* Delhi: Oxford University Press.

Constituent Assembly Debates: Official Report (CAD). 1946–50. various volumes. Delhi.

Everett, Jana M. 1979. *Women and Social Change in India.* New York: St Martins Press.

Forbes, Geraldine. 1979. 'Votes for Women' in *Symbols of Power: Women in a Changing Society I.* New Delhi: Allied Publishers.

———. 1996. *Women in Modern India.* Cambridge: Cambridge University Press.

———. 2002. 'Women of Character, Grit and Courage: The Reservation Debate in Historical Perspective' in *Between Tradition, Counter Tradition and Heresy: Contributions in Honour of Vina Mazumdar.* eds. Lotika Sarkar, Kumud Sharma and Leela Kasturi. New Delhi: Rainbow Publications.

Galanter, Marc. 1984. *Competing Equalities: Law and the Backward Classes in India.* Delhi: Oxford University Press.

Kumar, Radha. 1993. *A History of Doing: An Illustrated History of Movements for Women's Rights and Feminism in India, 1800–1990.* New Delhi: Kali for Women.

Mazumdar, Vina. 1979. 'Editor's Note' in *Symbols of Power: Women in a Changing Society I.* New Delhi: Allied Publishers.

Menon, Nivedita. 2000. 'Elusive "Women": Feminism and the women's reservation bill'. *Economic and Political Weekly.* vol. 35. nos. 43–44. 21 October 2000.

Moon, Meenakshi and Urmilla Pawar. 1989. 'Women in the early untouchable liberation movement'. *South Asia Bulletin.* vol. 9. no. 2. pp. 68–71.

Nair, Janaki. 1996. *Women and Law in Colonial India: A Social History.* New Delhi: Kali for Women.

Omvedt, Gail. 1994. *Dalits and the Democratic Revolution: Dr. Ambedkar and the Dalit Movement in Colonial India.* New Delhi: Sage.

Pandey, Gyanendra. 1990. *The Constitution of Communalism in Colonial North India.* Delhi: Oxford University Press.

Pearson, Gail. 1989. 'Reserved Seats—women and the vote in Bombay' in *Women in Colonial India: Essays on Survival, Work and the State.* ed. J. Krishnamurthy, Delhi: Oxford University Press.

Reddi, Muthulakshmi. 1930. *My Experiences as a Legislator.* Triplicane, Madras: Current Thought Press.

———. 1964. *Autobiography: A Pioneer Woman Legislator.* Madras.

———. 1956. ed. *Mrs. Margaret Cousins and her Work in India.* Adyar: Women's Indian Association.

Roshni. 1941. Journal of the AIWC.

S. Anandhi. 1998. 'Reproductive Bodes and Regulated Sexuality: Birth control debates in early twentieth century Tamil Nadu' in *A Question of Silence? The Sexual Economies of Modern India.* eds. Mary E. John and Janaki Nair. New Delhi: Kali for Women.

Sarkar, Sumit. 1983. *Modern India, 1885–1947.* Delhi: Macmillan.

Sarkar, Tanika. 1989. 'Politics and women in Bengal—the conditions and meaning of participation' in *Women in Colonial India: Essays on Survival, Work and the State*. ed. J. Krishnamurthy. Delhi: Oxford University Press.

Sinha, Mrinalini. 1999. 'Suffragism and Internationalism: The Enfranchisement of British and Indian women under an imperial state'. *The Indian Economic and Social History Review*. 36, 4.

———. 2000. 'Refashioning Mother India: Feminism and Nationalism in Late-colonial India'. *Feminist Studies*. vol. 26. no. 3. Fall.

Sitaramayya, Pattabhai B. 1969. *The History of the Indian National Congress 1835–1935*.

Thimmaiah, G. 1993. *Power Politics and Social Justice: Backward Castes in Karnataka*. New Delhi: Sage Publications.

V. Geetha and S.V. Rajadurai. 1997. *Towards a Non-Brahmin Millenium: From Iyothee Thass to Periyar*. Calcutta: Samya.

Section II
Theoretical Issues

The Quota Question: Women and Electoral Seats

NANDITA SHAH & NANDITA GANDHI

The necessity for reservations

How effective will women be in elected bodies? Will women in politics be able to assist the women's movement or be a hindrance to it? Should we support such a move? This is an attempt to put forward some of the arguments and trends of thinking on 30 per cent reservations of seats for women in Maharashtra. We believe this is a first step and will be followed by a much wider debate, sharing of experiences from different parts of the country and theorising to enable us to evolve a more holistic stand on this issue.

> With the decline of women elected candidates and the party's apathy to field more women, we actually do not have any choice but to accept reservation for women.
>
> Mrinal Gore

The Left party women have expressed a concern for the declining number of women candidates. Only a handful of women from the generation of freedom fighters like Mrinal Gore, Ahiliya Rangnekar, Manju Gandhi, Pramila Dandavate are still active in politics. All of them acutely feel the lack of younger women to take their place, lead their organisations and keep alive their struggles. This trend in declining numbers is confirmed by statistics. The last Maharashtra State Legislature election of 1989-90 had a total number of 288 seats which were contested by 6268 male candidates and 148 female candidates i.e. 2.3 per cent. Only five female candidates were elected to the Legislature. This wide gap between the number of male and female contestants and elected members can also be noticed for the Lok Sabha election from Maharashtra in 1989. For a total number of 48 seats there were 573 male candidates and 20 women candidates. Only two women made it to the Lok Sabha.

Nationally the situation is not very different as we can see in the table below:

Women Contestants in the Lok Sabha Elections

Year	Total Seats	Seats Contested by Women	Seats Won by Women
1952	489	51	23
1957	494	70	27
1962	494	65	33
1967	520	66	28
1971	518	86	21
1977	542	70	19
1980	542	142	28
1984	542	173	43
1989	543	189	28

[Reference Handbook: General Election 1989, Press Information Bureau, Ministry of Information and Broadcasting, Government of India]

The numerical decline of women candidates has to be seen against the backdrop of an increase in the female voters and the reduction in the gap between men and women voters. In a small constituency like Chimur in Maharashtra, there were more women voters than men for the recent general elections—84.36 per cent women as against 73.8 per cent men (Thakkar 1990). For the State Legislative Assembly election, more women voted in 43 out of the 288 constituencies (*The Independent*, 13 February 1990). Whilst many factors determine voting patterns, what is clear is that women form a sizable vote bloc and can not be ignored.

Women politicians put the blame for this sad decline on the laps of their parties. Was it not the support of the nationalist movement and political parties which encouraged women to struggle for franchise and participate in the electoral process?

And how are the parties now facilitating women's entry into the political process today? Ironically these same parties for the first time since their inception have made the most lavish promises to women. All of them speak about removing gender discrimination and providing economic opportunities. The Janata Dal manifesto promises to reserve 30 per cent government jobs for women. The Bharatiya Janata Party would like to make a wife a co-sharer in her husband's wealth and income. The Congress-I, besides 30 per cent reservation for women in local self government, promises to include women's names in land and house ownership and to spread consciousness amongst women about their rights.

In the electoral field, each party had promised to field 30 per cent women as their candidates. But as most electoral promises, this one remained unfulfilled.

Regional parties have fared as badly if not worse. 'The idea that a woman candidate would necessarily get women's votes seemed to have initially caught the fancy of political parties but even this was not a sufficient factor to push for more women candidates' (Thakkar 1990).

It is this apathy of the political parties to field women that one finds many women standing in elections as Independent candidates with very little success. There is an increasing trend in the general elections of Independent members contesting on their own but both men and women find it very difficult and lose out in the end. The following table gives an idea:

Lok Sabha Elections in Maharashtra

Year	Total Seats	Total Candidates	Independent Candidates	Elected Independents
1980	48	415	234 (56%)	0
1984	48	498	377 (75%)	1
1989	48	593	347 (58%)	1

The all-India statistics of the General Elections also confirms that while more than 50 per cent candidates were Independent, only five were elected in 1984 and 12 in 1989 elections. None of them were women.

> The main reason for lesser number of elected women candidates is not that they are not good or that they don't have support from the electorate but that they have to face the hurdles of a patriarchal society at every [step].
>
> Neelum Gohre

Most parties are reluctant to field women candidates. Women are considered liabilities, inexperienced and resourceless. They are usually not considered for electoral politics unless they are supported by some godfather or party bigwig and have the patronage of political families. Many times they are given difficult constituencies with little chances of winning or asked to step down during electoral adjustments. In short women except for the important leaders have felt like unwanted relatives or reserves waiting in the wings for an opportunity.

On their parts, the parties say that much as they would like to encourage women there are very few who have the time and capacity to be seriously interested in politics. But parties hardly ever question the existing societal and partriarchal notion about women's primary role and duty as a wife and mother which restricts their participation in the public sphere. Most often woman are bearing a double burden of work within the household and in the work place. Political activity would become a triple burden. Popular notions also perceive politics as something unsuitable for women's temperament and abilities. How often have we heard the comment, 'Kya leaderni banne jati hai?'

Some women may with courageous determination overcome the physical constraint of domestic and other work and the restrictive partriarchal notions which generally deter them from politics. But all of them are vulnerable to references and charges of a sexual nature. Character assassination is a sure way to destroy a woman politician's progress. They have to keep disproving rumours of affairs, secret marriages or relationships. Instances of molestation or rape, which may have happened against their will, can make them public controversies and disqualify them from electoral politics. However, political parties are not so squeamish in fielding wife beaters, rapists or molesters as their candidates. These rigid and moralistic double standards hamper women in yet another way. Unlike men, they have to be more careful in taking very confrontationist struggles as a way to get political prominence. The potential of sexual assault as political revenge is a stumbling block. Whereas for men, courting arrest, stints in jail and fights with authorities are 'sacrifices' which lead to greater political prominence.

A striking difference between male and female politicians is their class and regional background. Men from a lower class and caste background, with little education have been able to move upwards from local bodies and organisations to occupy national level high positions of leadership. It is nearly impossible for a woman with a similar background to do so. Most of the women politicians in Assemblies and the Parliament come from economically well off families or from royal backgrounds and are high-caste Hindus. Women who have aspired for Prime Ministership are the daughters or wives of leaders. In fact the family plays the role of the political patron in women's political careers. Those without such families have to seek out male patrons and bear the brunt of sexual rumours as in the case of Jayalalitha and M.G. Ramachandran in Tamil Nadu.

Women wanting to enter the political field find the dice loaded against them. Poor, rural and semi-literate women lose out even before they can begin. Those from wealthier families with political connections survive the first round. If they are careful and stay away from all sexual insinuations and find patrons or powerful lobbies to support them, their parties are willing to risk their candidature. It is therefore not surprising that in Indian politics most women politicians have not worked their way up but '... have been grafted on the political system at different levels because of their contacts with persons in positions of power and influence' (Status of Women Report 1974). About 30 to 40 women politicians have stayed in politics for a long time. Many of them have contested thrice and some all elections. 'This shows that the circulation of women elites in the electoral processes and thus in the Parliament and state legislatures have been slow and restricted' (Mazumdar 1979).

> What is generally noticeable not only in South Asia but all over the world [is] that women are often in the front ranks when a political

struggle is in its ideological phase but they become invisible when the struggle enters the phase of distributing the fruits of power.

Rounaq Jahan

It is to the credit of the women's movement that the focus of study has shifted from women's formal i.e. voting and leadership patterns to their informal or mass level political participation. There are adequate data to show that women have played an important role in political struggle and have fought along with men in all major agitations and movements against colonialism, for wages, against rising prices, for control over land, etc. They have sat in dharnas, gheraoed officials, gone to jail, borne police beating and shouldered the burdens of struggle. Women have often played a supportive role sheltering activists, nursing or as messengers in underground movements. And in emergencies and crisis situations women have taken over leadership and sustained the movement.

Now that women's activism and militancy has become visible the question being asked is why should it be that women should hold the protests and men hold the positions of power? Women are now ready to contest for leadership positions. Rural women attending a series of seminars organised at the Dandekar School for Political Economy (1982–84) in Lonavala spoke of bossism and corruption in the local level governments and asked why they could not contest for those positions? (Omvedt 1990) Forty women activists sat for four days discussing various aspects related to electoral politics like functioning of the panchayati raj system, the criteria for selecting candidates, need for a women's front, etc. at a training shibir in Ambethan (June 1987). Women in many villages of Maharashtra have organised women's panels in the gram panchayat elections. The Shetkari Sangathana had put up nine all-women panels for gram swaraj elections in July 1989 out of which seven were successful (*Afternoon Despatch & Courier*, 9 July 1990)

It is argued that if women enter the corridors of power they will be able to take up women's issues within state structures and also effect changes in the party and local bodies. They will have access to state resources which can support women's groups and provide services to them. Their positions and actions can legitimise the women's cause in the eyes of the people and parties. Women have in a short while learnt the skills of managing, debating and policy making. They have generated a lot of confidence in not only themselves but amongst neighbouring women and villages. Women are more likely and less afraid of approaching women corporators directly rather than male ones. Wherever women have contested, regardless of whether they have won or lost, they created waves of confidence and determination.

On the other hand some ask: will not reserved seats isolate women from mainstream politics? Women have replied that SC and ST reservation have not isolated them from mainstream politics but in fact acted as a pressure on the political system without which the dalits and their issues might have remained outside the field of public debate (Mazumdar 1979). Most women view reservations as a stepping stone to join general politics.

Saroj Kashikar, a Janata Dal MLA said, 'Reservation should not be like a *lakshman rekha* wherein women will be kept away from general constituencies. What the party is likely to do is field a woman in a reserved ward, when it is de-reserved the standing woman corporator will most probably be shifted to another reserved constituency. This would mean that she will have no one constituency and continuity in an area. They should not be stopped from contesting from general constituencies' (*The Independent*, 21 March 1990).

Neelum Gohre had contested through the Republican Party of India (Prakash Ambedkar group) for the Lok Sabha elections from Bombay in 1989. She said, 'Reservation at the lower level will definitely help women enter the political field and to prove themselves. It will then be up to them to win elections at the higher levels on merit.' However, academicians like Vina Mazumdar and Lotika Sarkar are against the idea of reservation for women only at the local level. They think that a political system cannot be based on ideology alone but must keep in touch with the actualities of the social situations. Considering the many hurdles that women have to face, reservation for women should be extended to all the levels of legislature both at the State as well as at the Centre (Status of Women Report 1974).

The Committee on the Status of Women recommends reservations to reverse the declining trend in the number of women legislators, to help women gain confidence and to provide greater space to articulate their views. Women elected through the system of reservation will have a greater sense of responsibility and concern for the problems affecting women, thus ensuring the presence of a body of spokespersons for women's cause in the representative bodies of the states. This would also lead to greater mobilisation in the electorate and within the parties. Women's participation at the local level will help bridge the gap between the state and parliamentary levels. It will also alter the very character of decision making and will compel the political parties to change their strategies and tactics. They argued that such a transitory measure will not be retrogressive to the doctrine of equality of sexes or to the principle of democratic representation but in fact would serve the objective of democracy and equality better by democratising the representational base.

They further demanded that reservation should be accompanied by measures which will aid the process of women's participation. There should be a permanent committee in each municipality to initiate and supervise programmes related to women's welfare and development. They recommended establishment of statutory women's panchayats at the village level as a integral part of the Panchayati Raj structure, with their own autonomy and resources to manage the affairs related to welfare and development programmes for women and children (Status of Women Report, 1974).

Just a political gimmick

It is not only the opposition parties but also many women's groups which have opposed the introduction of reservation of seats for women. The former have mainly attacked it on the grounds of political manoeuvring as they, unlike the Congress party, do not have many women members to field for elections. They have raised specific doubts that the actual functioning like the rotation system will be so manipulated that wards which are under the influence of the opposition parties will be reserved to put them at a disadvantage. Secondly, the male corporators of the reserved wards are likely to lose interest in their constituency. Or they will put up their female relatives for one term only to regain it back later. The very purpose of reservation will thus be defeated. In Maharashtra, the Bharatiya Janata Party and the Shiv Sena, through their supporters filed a petition against reservations which was dismissed by the High Court.

However, none of the political parties including the two behind the scenes petitioners have directly opposed reservations of seats for women. Individuals, intellectuals, progressive comrades within smaller parties and other organisations have generally supported reservations as a step towards encouraging women's greater political participation. But unlike men, women not under a moral compulsion to prove their 'support' or 'feminism' have been more critical and raised fundamental questions regarding its effect on women and the movement.

Many of the newer women's groups including some Marxist Leninist affiliated groups are wary of the electoral processes, the state as well as the motivations of the political parties in their sudden interest in women's electoral participation. Neither of the three have been particularly concerned with women's oppression which is the reason for the emergence of these groups as autonomous bodies. The state continues to play an important role in the perpetuation of the unequal relations between men and women through its development policies, half hearted legislations, etc. The state also attempts to co-opt any movements or any section of society that it sees as either challenging its authority or disturbing the status quo. Whenever a movement like the dalit, tribal or women's has put forward radical issues or demands for change, the state has responded by creating an illusion of acceptance. In 1975 as a token gesture to the International Women's Year it gave women the unimplementable Equal Remuneration Act and in 1983 it conceded to amending the rape laws but bypassed the anti-rape campaign's major suggestions.

The political parties have never seen women as a viable

'bloc' of votes (till recently) and fused their specific interests with their class, caste, religion or regional identities. And both the State and the parties have abused the 'democratic' process, degraded it with their manipulation, rigging and corruption which has not only discouraged women from entering the race but robbed them of their democratic rights of representation.

Thirty per cent reservations will force the parties to recruit women or lose the particular reserved constituency. The question is what sort of women will the parties recruit? Newspaper articles have reported the disgust of opposition leaders at the introduction of reservations for women and have applied for permission to field their wives and relatives (*Indian Express*, 12 September 1990).

These women will have no political experience, ideology or enthusiasm. Numbers will definitely make women visible in the party structure but how will they contribute to alter some of the root causes which have prevented women from entering these parties? How will they challenge the parties for incorporating societal patriarchal norms which do not take women's double burden at home and at work into account, which have a rigid hierarchical structure that provides no space for the development of their skills and by its silence accepts the double standards of sexual morality for men and women? Will these women be able to point out that parties have always mobilised women in times of crisis and protest, channelised their militancy, opened new horizons for them but without taking up their own issues or giving them any leadership positions?

The other part of the same argument claims that more women in the representative bodies will not only show the social and political advancement that women have made but also facilitate the raising of women's issues. There is a strange paradox at work here. In 1980 in the Lok Sabha election some 142 women contested from a total of 544 seats but only 28 won. Far from this dismal situation, outside the parliament, a new phase of the women's movement had emerged and initiated a national anti-rape campaign. These new 'spokespersons' continued their agitations against all forms of violence against women like bride murders, wife battery, sexual harassment etc.

which had hitherto been considered as non-political, social issues.

The two dissenting voices (Phulrenu Guha and Maniben Kara) in the Committee for Status of Women Report had other reasons to reject the reservation demand. They considered it retrogressive to accept such favoured treatment as women have always been competing with men as equals. Such an acceptance reinforces the common belief that women are weaker. 'It should be our aim to see that the masses of women of all classes become equal partners with men in all senses in society. Separate seats will weaken the position of women. They must come up on the strength of their own abilities and not through special provisions' (Status of Women Report 1974).

Secondly, such reservations even as a transitory measure will only help a few women from the upper class and caste who are already in a privileged position. Thirdly, they argued that reservations once granted are very difficult to withdraw and this would only perpetuate the already unequal status of women instead of eliminating it. They condemned reservations as a measure which becomes a sort of vested interest in women's backwardness. Rather than reservations, women should be made conscious of their rights, they should be educated to take responsibilities and public opinion should be created for their increased political participation.

Many of Guha's and Kara's arguments are still echoed today. The Constitution recommends reservations for weaker sections of society and so far the Scheduled Castes and Tribes have been granted such measures. But women do not form a caste, do not occupy a particular region, are not a community but are across class, caste, regional etc. groups related only to each other by virtue of their sex.

Women are not sole inhabitants of a constituency nor do they represent a specific grouping so the sex of a candidate cannot be the basis for selection. Women's interest though different in some ways from men cannot be isolated from the economic, social and political interests of the rest of society. Besides, there is a danger of projecting women as only women's leaders and ghettoising women's issues. Reservations will only reinforce the concept of separate identities and hamper the integration of women in society.

The women's cause, as is shown by our history especially the nationalist movement, has been taken up by progressive women and men. The concept of reservations implies that only women will be interested in raising women's issues. In the context of rising fundamentalism and right-wing conservatism, there is a greater likelihood of the women of the Bharatiya Janata Party and the Shiv Sena winning elections. Will right-wing women raise women's issues and if so will they not raise them in their own particular manner? In Bombay we have had two militant demonstrations by Shiv Sena women. One for scrapping late night foreign classic films on TV because children stayed up late to watch 'obscene' scenes. The second one was to protest against the preference given by a Christian managed school to children of their own community and not Maharashtrians. Women from the Bharatiya Janata party in Pune had taken out a demonstration a few years ago to refute that women were unhappy or in any way oppressed as claimed by other women's organisations. Perhaps, argue some women, it might be better to have sympathetic socialist-minded men than right-wing women in power.

The question which has bothered women's organisations is—can we gauge the material and ideological efficacy and strengths which the movement might derive from women seizing positions of power? Should women's organisations actively encourage women to enter the formal political process? One stream of argument points to the notional power which women hold because they are always in a minority in elected bodies and even after being elected women rarely get to be in positions where they can be part of the decision-making process. The situation is worse in villages where men expect women members to keep silent. An activist in Uttar Pradesh reported that when one of them made bold to speak her mind in a village panchayat she was physically threatened and ordered out. It is argued that this continuing struggle within formal structures is more time consuming, emotionally draining and less effective than the struggle from outside.

By entering the electoral process women are accepting the already set hierarchical pattern between the electors and the elected without any hopes of being able to change it. They will have to dilute their programmes and cater to a wider mass of the electorate; bear the burden of council matters at the expense of their other programmes; and be extremely careful of their public image which might prevent them from raising any controversial issues. Most women politicians will get trapped between party requirements and its marginalisation of women' issues and women's groups and objectives of the movement.

In order to see that their own programmes and policies are considered and executed they have to devote all their time and energy to persuasion of their colleagues and officials, play the numbers game and trade obligations with other council members. This in effect removes them from other non-official or movement work and from their day-to-day contact with their local organisations and communities. Once elected the nature of their accountability to the local women will be reduced as they will be forced to make decisions on their behalf and the feedback of information and necessity of debate will be bypassed due to lack of time and excessive work.

Then as Gangaben, a dalit and active social worker in her community, asks: should not women and organisations reject being wooed by the carrot of elections as it is a definite way to remove and alienate them from their community? Rather should they not put their energies in taking up basic issues and programmes for women?

Interview with an Activist

Gangaben Solanki is a 34-year old dalit Gujarati woman who has been working in her basti for the last 10 years helping women informally, solving their marital problems, accompanying them to the police and other authorities as well as organising cultural programmes. She is employed in a municipal school and works at home looking after her two children and husband. She has often locked horns with the local dalit party's leaders and caste leaders in putting forward the women's question. Her natural dynamism and deep concern for women makes her an instinctual feminist and activist. When 30 per cent reservations of seats for women was announced, she formulated her viewpoint based on her own experiences and thoughts.

When I first heard of 30 per cent I felt quite happy about it. Women, social workers like me who work in a community and all of us in the women's groups, need official support for everyday living. It's not only taking out morchas and having campaigns. Some women have problems when they are out hawking with the municipality or with the police. They can be also given stall space through the corporation. In my case I was allocated a house but the files just lay there for three years. So many women who become widows have to go to corporators, pay bribes or do sexual favours to get their room in their name.

If women are elected then women can go to them, without feeling afraid, and ask for help. For example, they may need certificates or other official papers. Men have been corporators for years, they have contacts with builders and have perfected the art of fooling people. It is common for them to give slum dwellers taps or latrines by asking them to waive their rights over the land. Or they take a commission from builders. Wherever there are old buildings they tell the tenants that they will repair them but in actuality they take money from the corporation. Women candidates can expose such goings-on. See, no one is concerned about women, why look the gift horse in the mouth? So I thought if this government for whatever reason is giving something to women we should just take it.

Around that time my caste panchayat had its elections. Do you know that still women have no right to vote. We have the right to vote for the corporation, for the Assembly and Lok Sabha but not for the panchayat! I went there with a huge board and sat there explaining to people why women should also be allowed to stand for the panel. They did not like it at all. They made me move my board saying that according to rules I could not sit near the election booth. Their enemies (those who were against them) brought me tea and gave me space. They thought that it was a good thing I was doing. I went around the basti and spoke to men and women. It is such a problem for women coming before the panchayat. Suppose there is a dispute, divorce or battering, these are all the problems to be solved by the panchayat. But what happens, the woman feels hesitant coming before a group of men, her own in-laws are there so she cannot speak freely and her family is not aware of what she really wants. Again women have to go to the panchayat for all sorts of certificates like domicile or asking them to pressurise a husband who is refusing to pay maintenance.

People were quite impressed and the leaders offered me a seat. They said you should stand and very soon party leaders also heard of this and came to offer me a ticket. They said, you will not have to do anything, just stand and we will take care of everything for you. One of them even offered me money for all the election work. I thought, look at this, usually they select all sorts of women for giving a ticket. Some of them have a bad character or are in the illicit liquor trade. One of them used to break municipal water pipes and sell water to the people for Rs 10 a bucket. This 30 per cent is going to encourage the parties to select any type of woman especially their mothers or wives who will listen to them. If I stand, not only will I have to resign from my job but do what they say. As a woman I will never have the same status as men corporators. And then who will take care of the women of my caste here?

So I thought nothing doing, I am not going to be sucked into this sort of thing! Being elected to the corporation will be more of a symbolic thing. Male leaders will continue to rule over the community. If I stay where I am I could do much more for women and see that they get a better deal from the panchayat. By pushing me out of the community the male leaders will continue doing exactly what they have been doing so far, solve problems according to their beliefs or money power. Alright suppose I was elected, what would be my position in the corporation? I will not be allowed to do anything I want. I will have to get involved mainly in party politics. Do you know that there has been no woman mayor or sheriff in Bombay in the last 40 years?

All sorts of other thoughts also came up. Elections will make women oppose each other. If there is another woman like me in my basti then another party will promote her, so both of us who might have co-operated earlier in helping women will now stand against each other. Then who knows women can also become corrupted like the male corporators. Practically I don't know how I would be able to manage. The party is hardly going to manage my home for me. But then I think that god

> knows how many schemes exist gathering dust that we don't even know of. As elected members women could do so much good. If you ask me straight off to say yes or no should there be reservations, then I think that reservations for women should be there but I am doubtful about it.

Raising some questions

Within the movement, women have either accepted 30 per cent reservations of electoral seats as an unfortunate necessity or rejected it as a clever political ploy. Undoubtedly it is a political gimmick coming from Sharad Pawar, a chief minister, who has never shown much concern for women in his long political career. But the use of 30 per cent reservations at this juncture reflects simultaneously the frenzied state of realpolitik in Maharashtra as well as the recognition of women as a political grouping and force. We, as members of social organisations and women's groups, need to debate this issue and share with each other our thoughts and experiences. What is the ideological base from where we draw our arguments and what do we perceive as our strategy for the women's movement?

The 'unfortunate necessity' argument

This argument of women politicians is only part of the reasons for our extending support to 30 per cent reservations. No doubt, more women in the party and state bodies will highlight the entry of women in a primarily male dominated field; it will begin processes of change in the language used and decorum in the body; and will bring confidence to the candidates and women in general.

A larger number of women could also join hands across party lines in case of extreme atrocities and basic services for women. As women experiencing oppression they are likely to have more empathy with other women and their problems. In fact they have the potential to be more sympathetic not only to women but other oppressed sections like dalits and tribals.

We disagree with the argument that inexperience and political naivete will hamper women and show them as incompetent and ineffective leaders. It does not take long in that environment to learn the ways of political functioning and trading. On the contrary, women's unfamiliarity might be advantageous to the public because their presence might serve as obstacles to the ways of corruption.

Women once elected have been able to use power quite effectively. Newspaper reports and personal interviews with activists show that at the gram panchayat level, with an all-women's panel and with the backing of their party, women have made a significant impact. In July 1989, the Shetkari Mahila Aghadi put up nine all-women panels for the panchayat elections out of which seven were elected. The first thing they did was to shut down all liquor shops and appoint new teachers in the school. In Metikheda village, they installed 90 taps and many gobar gas plants. The other interesting fact was that '... the nature and even physical place of electoral activity changed, drinking was forbidden during the last three days and slanderous propaganda was laughed off' (Omvedt 1990). This is just one example.

However, the main reason for encouraging those women who feel like stepping into the political world is not such reasons or the fact that they can bring services for women or that they will 'humanise' or 'clean up' politics. But that their presence will herald the erosion of one area of the sexual division of labour between men and women in society—men in the outside, public world and women in the private world of the home. It will challenge the cliché that politics is no place for women. And the acceptance of women as leaders will in the long run change to some degree the prevalent humiliating and condescending attitude towards women in general.

Hopefully such processes will first begin within the party structures. Veteran women politicians can take courage to begin a much needed internal debate with their male colleagues on the relationship of the party to women and their role in the revolutionary process. Such debates will point out some basic conceptual and structural problems and the necessity for recognising the deeply embedded patriarchal notions which control women and which cannot be overcome by patronage and tokenism.

Thirty per cent reservations provides an opportunity to widen the base of individuals participating in the electoral process. It can begin a process of democratisation which can introduce different women from various socio-economic backgrounds instead of the few middle, upper-caste women who now hold positions in elected bodies. Further these women together with the women's movement can create new relationships of feedback, accountability and responsibility with the electorate which can be put forward as an alternative to the existing distanced and once-a-term contact.

Reform versus revolution?

Reservation has been criticised and rejected also because activists think that at the most it will bring in some services but does not have the potential for any fundamental changes. Perhaps here we need to reflect on what we mean by reforms and revolution.

Every movement and every historical period has posed the reform versus revolution contradiction before its activists. In the context of 30 per cent reservation of electoral seats there is a curious and ironic reversal of roles. Those who have traditionally opposed the strategy of reforms or changes and redress within the existing political framework are the Left parties. They consider themselves the vanguard party destined to lead the working class and the struggle against the entire social and political system of capitalism. This revolution will establish a new order and ultimately a new socialist society. All other issues except those that lead to revolution are considered reformist. Their struggle is against the capitalists and the State, the primary instrument of the capitalist class, which will oppose, co-opt and repress such radical movements. The Communist Party abandoned its strategy of armed revolution for the electoral path to power after the end of the Telangana Struggle in 1951. The two communist parties, the socialist and now several Marxist Leninist ones are part of the parliamentary system, actively mobilising, organising and seeking electoral approval. Their shift justifies all actions which enhance their chances of coming to power. Mobilising women, raising their political consciousness, involving them in the electoral process, with the aid of 30 per cent reservation, is part of their strategy and struggle.

Strangely some of the newer groups which have been attacked as 'apolitical' 'bourgeois' and 'reformist' (Randive 1986) by the established Left parties reject 30 per cent reservations as a reformist measure, co-option by the parties and the State of its activists and uncomplimentary to its objectives of empowering women in their basic struggles, changing the unequal relations between men and women, between the classes and castes in society.

This raises the question—what issue can be termed as reformist or revolutionary? The Left party women with their numerous years of experience and political activism and the 'new' groups with 15 years behind them have undoubtedly learnt a few political lessons. The understanding of what is a women's issue itself has changed since the beginning of the 1980s when rape, domestic violence and bride murders were elevated from being social and humanitarian issues to political ones. The new phase of the women's movement removed these 'personal' issues from the confines of the home and showed that they were not individual or private incidents but institutionalised relationships of power over women. Today we denounce the division of women's issues or women oriented issues and general issues as a false one. Each issue concerns women as it does men and has a women's perspective to it.

We should be aware that it is also impossible to label any one issue as reformist or revolutionary. What we have to concern ourselves with is how it can help in furthering the objectives of the movement. We will have to evaluate each issue in relation to the changing societal forces, the strength of the movement, opposition to it, state intervention and linkages with other movements. Each issue has the potential to be part of the broad strategy of the women's movement. Thirty per cent reservations cannot be called a reformist issue because no one considers it an end in itself or a panacea for women's oppression. Neither is it a revolutionary issue because working from within state bodies adversely affects its potentiality. Nor can we be indifferent to it. Because to ignore it or reject it would be lapsing into welfarism, agreeing to an armed version of Marxism Leninism or reverting to anarchism.

The demand of 30 per cent reservation will have to be seen in the context of our understanding of the goals and strategies of the women's movement. We in the women's movement are struggling to transform unequal and oppressive relations between women and men, between caste, class and races. We want to work towards a world in which resources are not used for power and destruction but for growth and nurturance; where women and men share in the decision-making in a decentralised democracy; and where poverty, violence, intolerance of religious and cultural differences are eliminated.

Though there is not one common strategy adopted by the diverse women's groups within the movement, most believe in a systematic and organised struggle in all spheres of life—within the home, at the workplace, against the State and in society in general to ensure equality, freedom and dignity to all women and men. All structures and institutions have to be challenged from both outside and inside, creating a collective consciousness and strong pressure groups. Our immediate priority is to ensure survival needs through access to and control over the means of production, basic amenities, prevention of violence and atrocities on women and challenging the deep-rooted patriarchal notions and beliefs.

In the wide canvas of inter-related long and short term strategies, reservation of electoral seats for women is but a part. It is of importance because it combines possibilities of struggling from within and the provision of services which will strengthen women's struggle for survival. The women's movement can support elected candidates to raise issues, expose manipulation and create a new relationship of accountability to the women electorate. The creation of such vigilance and genuine answerability are not easy tasks but it could be the beginning of a democratisation of the electoral process. We feel that the women's movement should accept 30 per cent reservation and work towards its effectivity. We should limit reservations to only local levels and review its efficacy after 15 years. Such a review should take place in the form of public debate where women's organisations, academicians and other social organisations take a leading role. It is only after such a review that we should decide the need to continue reservations at local level and/or to extend them to Assembly and Parliament.

References

All statistics related to elections, unless specified, are from the Election Department, Mantralaya, Maharashtra Government.

Jahan, Rounaq. 1987. 'Women in South Asian Politics'. *Mainstream*. 15 August.

Mazumdar Vina. 1979. '*Symbols of Power—Studies on the Political Status of Women in India*'. Allied Publishers Private Ltd.

Omvedt Gail. 1990a. 'Women, Zilla Parishads and Panchayat Raj—Chandwad to Vitner'. *Economic and Political Weekly*. 4 August.

———. 1990b. 'The Farmers Struggle in Maharashtra' in *A Space Within the Struggle*. ed. Ilina Sen. New Delhi: Kali for Women.

Randive, Vimala, 1986. 'Feminist and the Women's Movement'. New Delhi: All India Democratic Women's Association.

Status of Women Report. 1974. *Towards Equality*. Government of India.

Thakkar, Usha. 1990. 'Women and the Recent Elections in India'. Paper presented at the Seminar on 'Indian Politics after Elections—1989. UK: University of Hull. May.

Women and Media. 1990. 'Reservation of Seats for Women—A brief backgrounder'. Paper presented at Seminar on 'Women and Politics with reference to Reservations'. 21 July.

Excerpt from *The Quota Question: Women and Electoral Seats* by Nandita Shah & Nandita Gandhi, Akshara Publications, Bombay, 1999.

Quotas for Women

ANNE PHILLIPS

Though the overall statistics on women in politics continue to tell their dreary tale of under-representation, this under-representation is now widely regarded as a problem, and a significant number of political parties have adopted measures to raise the proportion of women elected. That the issue is even discussed marks a significant change. Even more remarkable is that growing support for a variety of *enabling* devices (day-schools, for example, to encourage potential women candidates) now combines with some minority backing for measures that guarantee parity between women and men. Parties in the Nordic countries took the lead in this, introducing gender quotas for the selection of parliamentary candidates from the mid-1970s onwards, but a quick survey across the globe throws up a number of parallel developments.

When the African National Congress contested its first democratic election in South Africa, it operated a quota for women in selecting the candidates for seats. Recent developments in Indian local government have applied a quota system of people from Scheduled Castes (this is already practiced in employment and education) to elected positions at the village, block, and district level; the Panchayati Acts additionally require that one-third of the seats be reserved for women. Five years ago, the British Labour Party adopted a 50 per cent target for the number of women elected, to be achieved within three general elections. At its annual conference in 1993, it decided to establish all-women short lists for candidate selection in half the 'target' marginals and half the seats where sitting members will retire; since local parties have overall control of their selection process, it hoped to achieve this through amicable agreement.[1]

The bitter hostility such developments can arouse warns against easy optimism, but even the bitterness testifies to a sea change in political attitudes. Positive action to increase the proportion of women elected is now on the political agenda. It has become one of the issues on which politicians disagree.

In some ways, indeed, this is an area in which those engaged in the practice of politics have edged ahead of those engaged in its theory. Gatherings of party politicians are significantly more likely to admit the problem of women's under-representation than gatherings of political scientists; for, while the former remain deeply divided over the particular measures they will support, most can manage at least a lukewarm expression of 'regret' that so few women are elected. The pressures of party competition weigh heavily on their shoulders. In an era of increased voter volatility, they cannot afford to disparage issues that competitors might turn to electoral advantage. Hence the cumulative effect noted in Norwegian politics, where the Socialist Left Party first adopted gender quotas in the 1970s, to be followed in the 1980s by similar initiatives from the Labour and Centre Parties, and by substantial increases in the number of women selected by the Conservative Party as well.[2] Hence the impact of the German Green Party, which decided to alternate women and men on its list for the 1986 election; the threat of this small—but at the time rapidly growing—party contributed to the Christian Democrats' adoption of a voluntary quota, and to the Social Democrats' conversion to a formal one.[3] Hence the otherwise surprising consensus that has emerged among Britian's major political parties—at central office level if not yet in local constituencies—in favour of selecting a higher proportion of women candidates.[4] None of this would have happened without vigorous campaigning inside the political parties, but the campaigns have proved particularly effective where parties were already worried about their electoral appeal.

The results are not as yet striking, and outside the Nordic

countries political elites continue to be resolutely male: a solid phalanx of dull-suited men, with only the occasional splash of female colour. A comparative survey from 1990 showed the proportion of women in legislative assemblies reaching 38 per cent in Sweden, 34.4 per cent in Norway, 33.5 per cent in Finland, 30.7 per cent in Denmark; then dropping to 21.3 per cent in the Netherlands, 15.4 per cent in Germany, 8.5 per cent in Belgium, 6.3 per cent in the UK, and a mere 5.8 per cent in France.[5] Subsequent elections have brought further modification (the Netherlands has now reached Nordic proportions, while the UK figure jumped to over nine per cent at the following general election), but the prospects for continuing improvement almost certainly depend on the willingness of political parties to make sex an additional criterion in choosing their candidates. Background changes in society have their effect, and the marked increase in women's labour market participation, combined with the equalisation of educational qualifications between the sexes, is likely to feed through gradually into a greater number of women elected. But any more rapid improvement depends on deliberate choice. It is frequently noted that those countries that have adopted multi-member rather than single-member electoral constituencies offer more favourable conditions for women politicians, for when parties are choosing a slate of candidates it looks more obviously indefensible if all of these turn out to be men.[6] The most dramatic changes, however, have occurred where parties are pressured into positive action, setting a minimum target for the number of women elected, or, as in the common Nordic alternative, requiring a 40 per cent minimum for either sex.

Critics of gender parity[7] have tended to home in on what is really a second-order question. Taking it almost as given that the current under-representation of women in elected assemblies is a problem, they focus on what they perceive as the unacceptable solution of positive action. There is a surprising degree of consensus that women *are* under-represented, and few critics have bothered to contest this point. More remarkable still, critics rarely dwell on the essentialist presumptions of 'a' women's perspective, or the dangerous potential for women politicians pressing only narrowly sectional concerns. It is as if there are just too many women for them to be considered as a unified or sectional group, and too obviously spread across every social dimension and every conceivable political persuasion. So, while concerns about social divisiveness and sectional narrowing are part of the standard fare in arguments against other forms of group-based representation, opponents of gender quotas are most likely to take their stand on a general critique of affirmative action, on the paucity of 'experienced' women, and the risk that the overall calibre of politicians will fall.

The argument then becomes a subset of more general debates, focusing on supposed tensions between selection by gender and selection by merit. Those opposed to gender quotas or other such affirmative actions typically insist on the dangers of abandoning meritocratic principles; and they warn the aspiring politicians of the derision that will pursue them if they reach their positions through their gender alone.

> Quotas are patronising and self-defeating. Appointing or selecting women on grounds other than ability will rebound, not just on those individuals but on women generally. To say it is merely wiping out a disadvantage is disingenuous. Women will be making progress by denying men an equal chance to compete. How can any woman politician claim to be taken seriously in such circumstances? An unfairness will have been replaced by a deliberate rigging of the rules.[8]

> The really reactionary mentality belongs to those who argue that women must be cosseted and promoted by virtue of their sex in a way that men are not.[9]

Such arguments lend themselves to a series of empirical contestations, some of which have explored the availability of qualified women, while others query the startling presumption that existing incumbents were chosen on merit. (This last point is nicely summed up in a widely repeated comment that we'll know we have genuine equality when the country is run by incompetent women.) One of the points raised in the wider literature is that, even in the most seemingly meritocratic of systems—the selection of students for academic courses or the appointment of academics to university jobs—there is normally a cluster of vaguer characteristics which can override the stricter numerical hierarchy of grades or publications or degrees.[10] The implication is that selection by 'merit' and selection by ethnicity or gender are not such poles apart, for there is no process of admission or appointment that operates by a single quantifiable scale, and the numbers are always moderated by additional criteria. These more qualitative criteria ('personality', 'character', whether the candidates will 'fit in') often favour those who are most like the people conducting the interview: more starkly, they often favour the men. The point applies a fortiori to the process of selecting candidates for political office, where no one really knows what the qualifications should be.

A related point frequently raised in the general literature is that justifiable measures for remedying social disadvantage can come into conflict with what seem equally justifiable claims by individuals who would have got on the course or into the position if they had been around just 10 years earlier. Such individuals then seem to be paying unfairly for something that was hardly their personal fault, and even those most committed to affirmative action will sometimes argue a moral case for compensating those who seem singled out to pay what should really be regarded as a social debt.[11] Whatever conclusion we may reach on this, it is a problem that has less obvious application in the political realm. When Abigail Thernstrom wrote her indictment of what she saw as racial gerrymandering in the USA, she noted how extraordinary it was that, in an era marked by sharp challenges to affirmative action in the fields of education and employment, no one seemed particularly bothered by its equally extensive application in the field of political representation.[12] The explanation for this lies in our very different relationship to electoral office, which we rarely conceive as a matter of individual rights. The most ardent defender of an individual's 'right' to a particular course or a particular position rarely talks of the individual's 'right' to be elected to parliament: outside the great political dynasties, few people think of political office in these terms.

These have been the issues most likely to arise in popular or media discussion, but from my perspective they remain mere skirmishing around the edges. The emphasis is entirely on the legitimacy of particular measures: how is one to justify quotas, guarantees, positive action, what its critics regard as 'reverse discrimination'? The arguments then parallel and reproduce those applied to the use of gender quotas in education or employment, with little sense of what makes political representation different from either of these. This elision obscures more fundamental issues of representation, and this is the first point I want to stress. The argument for gender parity in politics can proceed perfectly happily on the basis of correcting a previous injustice, but where this treats being an elected representative as much the same sort of thing as being a doctor or lawyer or engineer, it does not grapple adequately with what we mean by representation. It may be that this limitation is part of the appeal: that arguing for more women in politics as if this were simply an extension of more women in medicine or more women in law is what makes the case so effective. But what concerns me here is not so much the pragmatic choices over which kind of argument to employ. I want to address the theoretical basis of the arguments, and what they imply about representation.

I

Arguments for raising the proportion of women elected have fallen broadly into four groups. There are those that dwell on the role model successful women politicians offer; those that appeal to principles of justice between the sexes; those that identify particular interests of women that would be otherwise overlooked; and those that stress women's different relationship to politics and the way their presence will enhance the quality of political life. The least interesting of these, from my point of view, is the role model. When more women candidates are elected, their example is said to raise women's self-esteem, encourage others to follow in their footsteps, and dislodge deep-rooted assumptions about what is appropriate to women and men. I leave this to one side, for I see it as an argument that has no particular purchase on politics per se. Positive role models are certainly beneficial, but I want to address those arguments that engage more directly with democracy.

The most immediately compelling of the remaining arguments is that which presents gender parity as a straightforward matter of justice: that it is patently and grotesquely unfair for men to monopolise representation. If there were no obstacles operating to keep certain groups of people out of political life, we would expect positions of political influence to be randomly distributed between the sexes. There might be some minor and innocent deviations, but any more distorted distribution is evidence of intentional or structural discrimination. In such contexts (that is, most contexts) women are being denied rights and opportunities that are currently available to men. There is a prima facie case for action.

There are two things to be said about this. One is that it relies on a strong position on the current sexual division of labour as inequitable and 'unnatural'. Consider the parallel under-representation of the very young and very old in politics. Most people will accept this as part of a normal and natural life-cycle, in which the young have no time for conventional politics, and the old have already contributed their share; and since each in principle has a chance in the middle years of life, this under-representation does not strike us as particularly unfair. The consequent 'exclusion' of certain views or experiences may be said to pose a problem; but, however much people worry about this, they rarely argue for proportionate representation for the over-70s and the under-25s.[13] The situation of women looks more obviously unfair, in that women will be under-represented throughout their entire lives, but anyone wedded to the current division of labour can treat it as a parallel case. A woman's life-cycle typically includes a lengthy period of caring for children, and another lengthy period of caring for parents as they grow old. It is hardly surprising, then, that fewer women come forward as candidates, or that so few women are elected. Here, too, there may be an under-representation of particular experiences and concerns, but, since this arises quite 'naturally' from particular life-cycles, it is not at odds with equality or justice.

I do not find the parallel convincing, but my reasons lie in a feminist analysis of the sexual division of labor as 'unnatural' and unjust. The general argument from equal rights or opportunities translates into a specific case for gender parity in politics only when it is combined with some such analysis; failing this, it engages merely with the more overt forms of discrimination that exclude particular aspirants from political office. Justice requires us to eliminate discrimination (this is already implied in the notion of justice), but the argument for women's equal representation in politics depends on that further ingredient which establishes structural discrimination. Feminists will have no difficulty adding this, and the first point then reinforces the general argument already developed. The case for the proportionate representation of women and men is not something we can deduce from an impossibly abstract equation of fair representation with proportional representation, as if each and every characteristic can be mapped out in the legislative assemblies. Nor is it automatically mandated by the discovery that there are fewer women in politics than men. Something else has to be added before we can move from a description of women's under-representation to an analysis of its injustice.

The second point is more intrinsically problematic, and relates to the status of representation as a political act. If we treat the under-representation of women in politics as akin to their under-representation in management or the professions, we seem to treat being a politician as on a continuum with all those other careers that should be opened up equally to women. In each case, there is disturbing evidence of sexual inequality; in each case, there should be positive action for change. The argument appeals to our sense of justice, but it does so at the expense of an equally strong feeling that being a politician is not just another kind of job. 'Career politician' is still (and surely rightly) a term of abuse; however accurately it may describe people's activities in politics, it does not capture our political ideals. If political office *has* been reduced to yet another favourable and privileged position, then there is a clear argument from justice for making such office equally available to women. Most democrats, however, will want to resist pressures to regard political office in this way. So, while men have no 'right' to monopolise political office, there is something rather unsatisfying in basing women's claim to political equality on an equal right to an interesting job.

Reformulating the equal right to political office as an equal right to participate in politics makes it sound much better, but does not otherwise help. A rough equality in political participation has entered firmly enough into the understanding (if not yet the practice) of political equality for us to see an imbalance between the sexes as a legitimate cause for concern. Extending this, however, to the sphere of representation simply asserts what has to be established: that representation is just another aspect of participation, to be judged by identical criteria. The under-representation of women in elected assemblies is not simply analogous to their under-representation in the membership of political parties or the attendance at political meetings; for, while we can quite legitimately talk of an equal 'right' to political participation, we cannot so readily talk of an equal 'right' to be elected to political office. As has already been noted, the deduction from the one to the other lays itself open to irritated complaints of missing what is new about representation.

What we can more usefully do is turn the argument around, and ask by what 'natural' superiority of talent or experience men could claim a right to dominate assemblies? The burden of proof then shifts to the men, who would have to establish either some genetic distinction which makes them better at understanding problems and taking decisions, or some more socially derived advantage which enhances their political skills. Neither of these looks particularly persuasive; the first has never been successfully established, and the second is no justification if it depends on structures of discrimination. There is no argument from justice that can defend the current state of affairs; and in this more negative sense, there *is* an argument from justice for parity between women and men. The case then approximates that more general argument about symbolic representation, stressing the social significance that attaches to the composition of political elites, and the way that exclusion from these reinforces wider assumptions about the inferiority of particular groups. But there is a troubling sense in which this still overlooks what is peculiar to representation as a political act. When democracy has been widely understood as a matter of representing particular policies or programmes or ideas, this leaves a question mark over why the sex of the representatives should matter.

II

An alternative way of arguing for gender parity is in terms of the interests that would be otherwise discounted. This is an argument from political realism. In the heterogeneous societies contained by the modern nation-state, there is no transparently obvious 'public interest', but rather a multiplicity of different and potentially conflicting interests which must be acknowledged and held in check. Our political representatives are only human, and as such they cannot pretend to any greater generosity of spirit than those who elected them to office. There may be altruists among them, but it would be unwise to rely on this in framing our constitutional arrangements. Failing Plato's solution to the intrusion of private interest (a class of Guardians with no property or family of their own), we must look to other ways of limiting tyrannical tendencies, and most of these will involve giving all interests their legitimate voice.

This, in essence, was James Mill's case for representative government and an extended franchise, though he notoriously combined this with the argument that women could 'be struck off without inconvenience' from the list of potential claimants, because they had no interests not already included in those of their fathers or husbands. (He also thought we could strike off 'young' men under 40 years of age.) Part of the argument for increasing women's political representation is a feminist rewrite and extension of this. Women occupy a distinct position within society: they are typically concentrated, for example, in lower paid jobs; and they carry the primary responsibility for the unpaid work of caring for others. There are particular needs, interests, and concerns that arise from women's experience, and this will be inadequately addressed in a politics that is dominated by men. Equal rights to a vote have not proved strong enough to deal with this problem; there must also be equality among those elected to office.

One point made by Will Kymlicka is that this argument may not be enough to justify parity of presence. In a recent discussion of demands for group representation in Canada, he makes a useful distinction between arguments for equal or proportionate presence (where the number of women or Aboriginal peoples or francophone Canadians in any legislative assembly would correspond to their proportion in the citizenry as a whole), and the case for a threshold presence (where the numbers would reach the requisite level that ensured each group's concerns were adequately addressed).[14] When the group in question is a numerically small minority, the threshold might prove larger than their proportion in the population as a whole; when the group composes half the population, the threshold might be considerably lower. On this basis, there could be an argument for greater than proportionate representation of Aboriginal peoples, for example, but less than proportionate representation of women—not that women would be formally restricted to 25 per cent or 30 per cent of the seats, but that they might not require any more than this in order to change the political agenda. It is the argument from justice that most readily translates into strict notions of equality; the argument from women's interests need not deliver such strong results.

The above is a qualification rather than a counter-argument, and in principle it still confirms the legitimacy of political presence. A potentially more damaging argument comes from those who query whether women do have a distinct and separate interest, and whether 'women' is a sufficiently unified category to generate an interest of its own. If women's interests differed systematically from men's (or if women always thought differently on political issues), then the disproportionate number of men in politics would seem self-evidently wrong. The concerns of one group would get minimal consideration; the concerns of another would have excessive weight. But where is the evidence for this claim? Does not the notion of a distinct 'women's interest' just dissolve upon closer attention?

The idea that women have at least some interests distinct from and even in conflict with men's is, I think, relatively straightforward. Women have distinct interests in relation to child-bearing (for any foreseeable future, an exclusively female affair); and as society is currently constituted they also have particular interests arising from their exposure to sexual harassment and violence, their unequal position in the division of paid and unpaid labour, and their exclusion from most arenas of economic or political power.[15] But all this may still be said to fall short of establishing a set of interests shared by all women. If interests are understood in terms of what women express as their priorities and goals, there is considerable disagreement among women; and, while attitude surveys frequently expose a 'gender gap' between women and men, the more striking development over recent decades has been the convergence in the voting behaviour of women and men. There may be more mileage in notions of a distinct woman's interest if this is understood in terms of some underlying but as yet unnoticed 'reality', but this edges uncomfortably close to notions of 'false consciousness', which most feminists would prefer to avoid. Indeed, the presumption of a clearly demarcated woman's interest which holds true for all women in all classes and all countries has been one of the casualties of recent feminist critique, and the exposure of multiple differences between women has undermined more global understandings of women's interests and concerns.[16] If there is no clearly agreed woman's interest, can this really figure as a basis for more women in politics?

There are two things to be said about this. The first is that the variety of women's interests does not refute the claim that interests are gendered. That some women do not bear children does not make pregnancy a gender-neutral event; that women disagree so profoundly on abortion does not make its legal availability a matter of equal concern to both women and men;

that women occupy such different positions in the occupational hierarchy does not mean they have the same interests as men in their class. The argument from interest does not depend on establishing a unified interest of all women: it depends, rather, on establishing a difference between the interests of women and men.

Some of the interests of women will, of course, overlap with the interests of certain groups of men. The fact that women are more likely to depend on public transport, for example, forges a potential alliance with those men who have campaigned for better public transport on social or environmental grounds; and the fact that women are more likely to press the interests of children does not mean that no man would share their concerns. In these instances, it may be said that the election of more female representatives will introduce a new range of issues—but that many of these will be ones that some men will be happy to endorse. In other instances, the differences are more inherently conflictual. Women's claim to equal pay must, logically, imply a relative worsening of male earnings; and outside extraordinary growth conditions, women's claim to equal employment opportunities must reduce some of the openings currently available to men. Women have no monopoly on generosity of spirit, and even in these more conflictual situations they can expect to find a few powerful allies among the men. What they cannot really expect is the degree of vigorous advocacy that people bring to their own concerns.

The second point is more complex, and arises with particular pertinence when a history of political exclusion has made it hard even to articulate group concerns. When Hanna Pitkin explored Edmund Burke's rather odd understanding of representation, she noted that he conceived of interests as a matter of 'objective, impersonal, unattached reality';[17] this then became the basis on which he argued for 'virtual' representation, by people not even chosen by the interested group. Burke certainly thought that all major interests should be duly represented, but the very objectivity of the interests allowed for their representation by people who did not immediately share them. The more fixed the interests, the more definite and easily defined, the less significance seemed to attach to who does the work of representation. So if women's interests had a more objective quality (and where transparently obvious to any intelligent observer) there might be no particular case—beyond what I have already argued about vigorous advocacy—for insisting on representatives who also happen to be women. We might feel that men would be less diligent in pressing women's interests and concerns, that their declared 'sympathy' would always be suspect. But if we all knew what these interests were, it would be correspondingly easy to tell whether or not they were being adequately pursued.

Interest would then more obviously parallel political ideas or beliefs. It would become something we could detach from particular experience, as we already detach the 'interest' of pensioners, or children, or the long-term unemployed. Each of these (perhaps particularly the example of children) is problematic, but in each of them we can more legitimately claim to know what is in a group's interest. Attention then shifts to more traditional ways of strengthening the weight attached to the interests, perhaps through writing them into party programmes or party commitments. The alternative emphasis on changing the composition of decision-making assemblies is particularly compelling where interests are not so precisely delineated, where the political agenda has been constructed without reference to certain areas of concern, and where much fresh thinking is necessary to work out what best to do. In such contexts there is little to turn to other than the people who carry the interests, and who does the representation then comes to be of equal significance with what political parties they represent.

This argument echoes what was a widely shared experience in the early years of contemporary feminism. The now derided emphasis on consciousness-raising groups offered more than a luxury occasion for some women to get together and moan: the sharing of experience was part of a process in which women freed themselves from a cycle of passivity and self-denial, stretched their sense of what was possible and desirable, and reached different conclusions about what they might want.

Those involved in this experience frequently talked of their difficulties in finding a voice, the way that dominant definitions of politics blocked out alternatives, or hegemonic culture controlled what could or could not be said. The emphasis then shifted from an objectively defined set of interests (which just needed more vigorous pursuit) to a more exploratory notion of possibilities so far silenced and ideas one had to struggle to express. And in this later understanding of the processes that generate needs and concerns and ideas, it was far harder to sustain the primacy of ideas over political presence. If the field of politics has already been clearly demarcated, containing within it a comprehensive range of ideas and interests and concerns, it might not so much matter who does the work of representation. But if the range of ideas has been curtailed by orthodoxies that rendered alternatives invisible, there will be no satisfactory solution short of changing the people who represent and develop the ideas.

The more decisive problem with the argument from interests lies in the conditions for accountability to the interested group. Does the election of more women ensure their representation? At an intuitive level, an increase in the number of women elected seems likely to change both the practices and priorities of politics, increasing the attention given to matters of child care, for example, or ensuring that women's poor position in the labour market is more vigorously addressed. This intuition is already partially confirmed by the experience of those countries that have changed the gender composition of their elected assemblies. But what does this mean in terms of political representation? Elections are typically organised by geographical constituencies, which sometimes coincide with concentrations of particular ethnic or religious groups, or concentrations of certain social classes, but which never coincide with concentrations of women or men. Elections typically take place through the medium of political parties, each of which produces candidates who are said to represent that party's policies and programmes and goals. In what sense can we say that the women elected through this process carry an additional responsibility to represent women? In the absence of mechanisms to establish accountability, the equation of more women with more adequate representation of women's interests looks suspiciously undemocratic. If the interests of women are varied, or not yet fully formed, how do the women elected know what the women who elected them want? By what right do they claim their responsibility to represent women's concerns? The asymmetry between noting a problem of exclusion and identifying the difference that inclusion brings about is particularly pointed here. However plausible it is to say that male-dominated assemblies will not adequately address the needs and interests of women, it cannot be claimed with equal confidence that a more balanced legislature will fill this gap.

III

The third way of formulating the case for gender parity approaches it from almost the opposite direction. It sees the inclusion of women as challenging the dominance of interest group politics, and expects women politicians to introduce a different set of values and concerns. This is something that has had a long history in feminist thinking; for, while women have repeatedly complained that their interests were being ignored by the men, the very same women have often presented their sex as the one that disdains interest and transcends the limits of faction. In the campaign for women's suffrage, for example, it was often suggested that women would bring a more generous morality to the political field; in the recent development of eco-feminism, it is often argued that women have a deeper, because trans-generational, relationship to the needs of the environment.

In some formulations of this, feminists have made a strong distinction between interest and need, arguing that the emphasis on interests treats politics as a matter of brokerage between different groups, and that the equation of politics with the rational calculation of interests is at odds with women's own understanding of their needs and goals.[18] As Irene Diamond and Nancy Hartsock put it, '[t]he reduction of all human emotions to interests, and interests to the rational search for gain reduces the human community to an instrumental, arbitrary, and deeply unstable alliance, one which rests on the private desires of isolated individuals.'[19] Need, by contrast, is thought to appeal to a more basic and common humanity; instead of asserting a stake in political battle, it formulates claims in more obviously moral terms.

This distinction engages directly with that common objection to a politics of presence which views it as increasing the role of interest in politics. When the demand for more women in politics is formulated in terms of interest, this seems to accept a version of politics as a matter of competition between interest groups; it talks the language of defence or protection, and treats politics as a zero-sum game. But when the demand is formulated in terms of need, this potentially raises things to a higher plain. The substitution of needs talk for interests talk may then offer a more radical challenge to the practices of contemporary democracy, querying the very nature of the game as well as the composition of the players.

My own position on this is somewhat agnostic. Interest can sound rather grasping and competitive, but it does at least serve to remind us that there may be conflicts between different groups. Need has more obvious moral resonance, but it originates from a paternalist discourse which lends itself more readily to decisions by experts on behalf of the needy group.[20] My own rather commonsensical solution is to use both terms together. Note, however, that the opposition between need and interest does not substantially alter what is at issue in demands for more women in politics, for need is as contested as interest, and either requires a greater female presence. As Nancy Fraser has argued, the interpretation of needs is itself a matter of political struggle, spanning three crucial moments: the struggle to establish (or deny) the political status of a given need; the struggle for the power to define and interpret the need; and the struggle to secure its satisfaction.[21] At each moment it matters immensely who can claim the authoritative interpretation; and, while much of the battle for this rages across the full terrain of civil society, groups excluded from state agencies or legislative assemblies will have significantly less chance of establishing their own preferred version. Neither needs nor interests can be conceived as transparently obvious, and any fair interpretation of either then implies the presence of the relevant group.

The broader claim made by those who disdain the politics of interest is that increasing the proportion of women elected introduces new kinds of behaviour and values. It is often suggested, for example, that women will be less competitive, more co-operative, more prepared to listen to others; that women bring with them a different, and more generous, scale of values; that women raise the moral tenor of politics. These arguments are always associated with women's role as caring for others, and often more specifically with their role as mothers. Jean Bethke Elshtain, for example, presents a stark picture of contemporary politics as dominated by the most crass individualism and expressed in the most impersonal of languages: a world that begins and ends 'with mobilisation of resources, achieving maximum impacts, calculating prudentially, articulating interest group claims, engaging in reward distribution functions'.[22] The relationship between mother and child then appears as a paradigm for a less interest-regarding set of values. Mothers cannot put their own interests first, for they can never forget the vulnerability of the human child. The politics that develops out of this cannot accept the conventional separation of politics from morality, and it offers the most profound and hopeful challenge to the sordid instrumentalism of the modern world.[23]

Elshtain is only moderately (if at all) concerned with measures that might increase the proportion of women elected, for much of her critique of the current relationship between public and private revolves around an analysis of that world of 'formal' male power which has absorbed more and more spheres of social life into its orbit. She sees little to gain in the absorption of women into the same circuit. But her broadly 'maternal feminism'[24] finds many echoes in current explorations of women's role in politics, perhaps most notably in the Nordic tradition which sees women as bearers of a new 'politics of care'. Feminists have challenged the 'misplaced analogy to the marketplace'[25] which is said to weaken both the theory and practice of politics; they have elaborated alternative theories of power which stress power as energy or capacity rather than dominance; and they have suggested that we try out what society would look like if we conceive it from the perspective of mothering rather than that of 'economic man'.[26] Running through all such arguments is a consistent contrast between women and the politics of self-interest. The kind of changes we can anticipate from women's increased political presence are seen as relating to this.

My problem with such arguments is not that they presume a difference between men and women. As Catherine MacKinnon puts it in a nicely pointed question, 'I mean, can you imagine elevating one half of a population and denigrating the other half and producing a population in which everyone is the same?'[27] We do not have to resort to either mysticism or sociobiology to explain social differences between women and men, and it would be most peculiar if the different responsibilities the sexes carry for caring for others did not translate into different approaches to politics and power. These initial differences may be far outweighed by the common experiences men and women will later share in making their way through political life. I incline to the view that politics is more formative than sex, and that the contrast between those who get involved in politics and those who do not is deeper than any gender difference between those who are elected. But this remains at a more speculative level. The real problem with basing the case for more women in politics on their supposed superiority over men is that this loads too much on women's role as mothers.

As Mary Dietz, in particular, has argued,[28] the characteristics that make a good mother are not necessarily those that make a good citizen, and the generous care women may give to their dependent children is hardly a paradigm for a democratic politics that should be based on equality and mutual respect. Nor is it particularly useful to present women as better or more moral than men. 'Such a premise would posit as a starting point precisely what a democratic attitude must deny—that one group of citizens' voices is generally better, more deserving of attention, more worthy of emulation, more moral, than another's. A feminist democrat cannot give way to this sort of temptation, lest democracy itself lose its meaning, and citizenship its special name.'[29]

Which is not to say that women will not, or should not, make a difference. In a recent study of Norwegian MPs, Hege Skjeie uncovered a remarkable consensus across the parties and between the sexes that gender does and should make a difference, with a clear majority thinking that gender affects priorities and interests, and that women represent a new 'politics of care'. Translated into areas of policy initiative, this generated a rather predictable list: politicians of both sexes saw women as particularly concerned with policies on welfare, the environment, equality, education, and disarmament, and men as more interested in the economy, industry, energy, national security, and foreign affairs. (Transport was the only area regarded as equally 'male' and 'female'—not because transport is intrinsically more gender-neutral, but because it has become important, for different reasons, to both women and men.) Against the background of a strong Norwegian tradition of social representation, which has long assumed that political representatives should 'mirror' differences between town and country and balance territorial concerns,[30] it has been seen as perfectly legitimate and desirable that women politicians should represent different concerns. Indeed, '[a] mandate of "difference" is now attached to women politicians ... Women have entered politics on a collective mandate, and their performance is judged collectively.'[31]

The precise implications of this remain, however, ambiguous. The widely presumed association between women and a politics of care leaves it open whether women will concentrate on policies to enhance child care provision, thereby to increase women's participation in the labour market, or on policies that will raise the value and prestige of the care work that women do in the home. What resolves this in the Norwegian context is not so much gender as party. Women associated with parties on the left of the political spectrum are more likely to interpret a politics of care in terms of the first set of priorities, while women associated with parties on the right will tend to the second interpretation. In this as in other policy areas, party loyalties are usually decisive, and, though Skjeie notes a number of cases of women forming cross-party alliances on particular issues, she finds little evidence of women refusing the ultimate priorities of their parties. 'The belief in women's difference could still turn into a mere litany on the importance of difference. Repeated often enough, the statement that "gender matters" may in turn convince the participants that change can in fact be achieved by no other contribution than the mere presence of women.'[32]

IV

This leads directly into the key area of contention, already signalled in my discussion of interest. Either gender does make a difference, in which case it is in tension with accountability through political parties, or it does not make a difference, in which case it can look a rather opportunistic way of enhancing the career prospects of women politicians. Aside from the symbolic importance of political inclusion, and women's equal right to have their chance at a political career (a fair enough argument, but not intrinsically about democracy), we can only believe that the sex of the representatives matters if we think it will change what the representatives do. Yet in saying this, we seem to be undermining accountability through party programmes. We are saying we expect our representatives to do more—or other—than they promised in the election campaign. If we are either surprised or disappointed, for example, by the limited capacity to act on a cross-party basis, this must be because we see an increase in the number of women politicians as challenging the dominance of the party system, or the tradition of voting along party lines. Those who have felt that tight controls of party discipline have worked to discourage serious discussion and debate may be happy enough with this conclusion. But in the absence of alternative mechanisms of consultation or accountability, it does read like a recipe for letting representatives do what *they* choose to do.

Though it is rarely stated in the literature, the argument from women's interests or needs or difference implies that representatives will have considerable autonomy; that they do have currently; and, by implication, that this ought to continue. Women's exclusion from politics is said to matter precisely because politicians do not abide by pre-agreed policies and goals—and feminists have much experience of this, gained through painful years of watching hard-won commitments to sexual equality drop off the final agenda. When there is a significant under-representation of women at the point of final decision, this can and does have serious consequences, and it is partly in reflection on this that many have shifted attention from the details of policy commitments to the composition of the decision-making group. Past experience tells us that all male or mostly male assemblies have limited capacity for articulating either the interests or needs of women, and that trying to tie them down to pre-agreed programmes has had only limited effect. There is a strong dose of political realism here. Representatives *do* have autonomy, which is why it matters who those representatives are.

This is a fair enough comment on politics as currently practised, and shifting the gender balance of legislatures then seems a sensible enough strategy for the enfeebled democracies of the present day. But one might still ask whether representatives *should* have such autonomy, and whether it would change the importance attached to gender composition if the politicians were more carefully bound by their party's commitments and goals. Consider, in this context, the guidelines that were introduced by the US Democrats in the early 1970s, to make their National Convention (which carries the crucial responsibility of deciding on the presidential candidate) more representative of the party rank and file. Dismay at the seemingly undemocratic nature of the 1968 Convention prompted the formation of a Commission on Party Structure and Delegate Selection, which recommended more extensive participation by party members in the selection of delegates, as well as quota guidelines to increase the proportion of delegates who were female, black, and young. As a result of this, the composition of the 1972 Convention was markedly more 'descriptive' of party members than previous ones had been: 40 per cent of the delegates were women, 15 per cent were black, and 21 per cent were aged 18–30.[33] But the reforms pointed in potentially contradictory directions, for they simultaneously sought to increase rank-and-file participation in the selection of delegates, to bind delegates more tightly to the preferences of this rank and file, and to ensure a more descriptive representation according to age, gender, and race. As Austin Ranney (one of the members of the Commission) later noted, the success of the first two initiatives undermined the importance of the third. By 1980 the overwhelming majority of delegates were being chosen in party primaries which bound them to cast their votes for one particular candidate; they became in consequence mere ciphers, who were there to register preferences already expressed. 'If that is the case,' Ranney argues, 'then it really doesn't matter very much who the delegates are.'[34] The more radical the emphasis on accountability, the less significance attaches to who does the work of representation.

Bob Goodin offers one way out of this impasse, which stresses the importance of symbolic representation and the way this relates to people's self-images in politics.[35] Empirical studies of the 1972 National Convention suggest that increasing the proportion of female and black delegates had minimal impact on the kinds of views represented at the convention, and that neither sex nor race made much of a difference. But such investigations may miss the point, which is that 'people's self-images are, at least in part, tied up with politics'.[36] If the pattern of representation gives no recognition to the communal attachments through which people live their lives, then this is felt to be intolerable, even when changing that pattern of representation has no discernible impact on the kinds of policies adopted. Politics is not just about self-interest, but also about self-image: '[b]e they manifestations of silly sentimentality or not, symbolic appeals have a powerful political pull which social scientists cannot ignore.'[37]

Goodin's argument captures much of the popular impetus towards gender parity, for people do recoil from the representation of themselves by such an 'unrepresentative' sample, and do feel that changing this matters even if it subsequently proves to make no further difference. One of the principles associated with legal judgements is that justice must not only be done but be seen to be done. By the same token, we might well say that representatives must not only be representative but also be seen to be so. It would be foolish to underplay this element, but it would also be misleading to consider it the only thing at issue in demands for political presence. Women *do* think that it will—or should—make a difference when more women are elected as representatives ... Where this is so, it conflicts with alternative strategies for keeping representatives accountable.

This points to a significant area of divergence between current feminist preoccupations and what has long been the main thrust in radical democracy. Radical democrats distrust the wayward autonomy of politicians and the way they concentrate power around them, and they typically work to combat these tendencies by measures that will bind politicians more tightly to their promises, and disperse over-centralised power. Feminists have usually joined forces in support of the second objective: feminism is widely associated with bringing politics closer to home; and women are often intensely involved in local and community affairs. But when feminists insist that the sex of the representatives matters, they are expressing a deeper ambivalence towards the first objective. The politics of binding mandates turns the representatives into glorified messengers: it puts all the emphasis on to the content of the messages, and makes it irrelevant who the messengers are. In contesting the sex of the representatives, feminists are querying this version of democratic accountability [...]

The first part of the argument for gender parity in politics derives from principles of justice, and its power is essentially negative: by what possible superiority of talent or experience could men claim a 'right' to monopolise assemblies? There is no convincing answer to this ultimately rhetorical question, and on this more limited ground of equal access to elected office it is easy enough to establish the case. There are all kinds of second-order questions, relating to how legitimate objectives can be best achieved; and all kind of pragmatic judgements to be made on specific proposals, none of which flows directly from conclusions on overall objectives. But the real problem with the argument from justice is that it remains a subset of more general arguments for equal opportunities and affirmative action, and as such it gives too little weight to the difference between being a representative and being a lawyer or professor. It may be said that changing the composition of elected assemblies plays a particularly important symbolic role, that it involves a more powerful and visible assertion of women's equality with men than changing the composition of management or the professions. But this still confines it to the realm of symbolic representation, without any clear implications as to what further difference this representation should make.

The argument from either interests or needs, by contrast, anticipates a difference in the kinds of policy decision that will be made, and this more directly challenges existing conditions of representation and accountability. Representation as currently practised rests on what most of the practitioners will admit is pretence; a pretence that the choices offered to the electorate exhaust the full range of possible alternatives; a pretence that party manifestos and programmes wrap up coherent packages of interests and beliefs; a pretence that government is just a matter of implementing the choices the electorate has made. The pretence cedes tremendous power to those individuals who are eventually elected ... The power of the representatives is not, of course unlimited; if nothing else, they have to tread in wary judgement of how much the electorate will swallow, and in contemporary mass democracies they pay close attention to the messages that arrive daily through opinion polls. But opinion polls register opinion on what is already on the political agenda, and have never proved a particularly effective way of introducing new possibilities and concerns. They cannot give a significant voice to those groups that have been excluded from arenas of power.

Changing the gender composition of elected assemblies is a major, and necessary, challenge to the social arrangements which have systematically placed women in a subordinate position; and whether we conceive of politics as the representation of interest or need (or both), a closer approximation to gender parity is one minimal condition for transforming the political agenda. But changing the gender composition cannot guarantee that women's needs or interests will then be addressed. The only secure guarantees would be those grounded in an essential identity of women, or those arrived at through mechanisms of accountability to women organised as a separate group. The first has neither empirical nor theoretical plausibility; the second is impossible under current electoral arrangements, and perhaps unlikely in any event. So the case for gender parity among our political representatives inevitably operates in a framework of probabilities rather than certainties. It is possible—if highly unlikely—that assemblies composed equally of women and men will behave just like assemblies in which women have a token presence; it is possible—and perhaps very likely—that they will address the interests of certain groups of women while ignoring the claims of others. The proposed change cannot bring with it a certificate of interests addressed or even a guarantee of good intent. In this, as in all areas of politics, there are no definitive guarantees.

Although the importance I have attached to the gender of the representatives conflicts with much of what Hanna Pitkin has argued about the limits of mirror representation, it should be clear from this chapter that I am very much at one with her in seeing representation as a process. Fair representation is not something that can be achieved in one moment, nor is it something that can be guaranteed in advance. Representation depends on the continuing relationship between representatives and the represented, and anyone concerned about the exclusion of women's voices or needs or interests would be ill-advised to shut up shop as soon as half those elected are women. This is already well understood in relation to the politics of ideas; for getting one's preferred party elected to government is usually seen as the beginning rather than the end of the process, and only the most sanguine of voters regards this as settling future policy direction. The warning is even more pointed in relation to the politics of presence, for the shared experience of women as women can only ever figure as a *promise* of shared concerns, and there is no obvious way of establishing strict accountability to women as a group. Changing the gender composition of elected assemblies is largely an enabling condition (a crucially important one, considering what is *disabled* at present) but it cannot present itself as a guarantee. It is, in some sense, a shot in the dark: far more likely to reach its target than when those shooting are predominantly male, but still open to all kinds of accident.

Notes

[1] This device reflects the constraints of the British electoral system, which operates with single-member constituencies and first-past-the-post election, and is not then amenable to the more normal quota procedures.

[2] H. Skjeie, 'The Rhetoric of Difference: On Women's Inclusion into Political Elites', *Politics and Society*, 19/2 (1991).

[3] J. Chapman, *Politics, Feminism, and the Reformation of Gender* (London, 1993), ch. 9.

[4] J. Lovenduski and P. Norris, 'Selecting Women Candidates: Obstacles to the Feminisation of the House of Commons', *European Journal of Political Research*, 17 (1989).

[5] S. McRae, 'Women at the Top: The Case of British National Politics', *Parliamentary Affairs*, 43/3 (1990).

[6] P. Norris, 'Women's Legislative Participation in Western Europe', in S. Bashevkin (ed.), *Women and Politics in Western Europe* (London, 1985).

[7] I use the term 'parity' to indicate a rough equality between the proportion of women and men elected. My use of this term should not be confused with the arguments that have recently surfaced within the Council of Europe for so-called parity democracy. See J. Outshoorn, 'Parity Democracy: A Critical Look at a "New" Strategy', paper prepared for workshop on 'Citizenship and Plurality', European Consortium for Political Research, Leiden, 1993.

[8] M. Phillips, 'Hello to the Gender Gerrymander', *Observer* (3 October 1993).

[9] Editorial, *London Evening Standard* (24 June 1993).

[10] See P. Green, *The Pursuit of Inequality* (New York, 1981), especially ch. 6.

[11] This argument is comprehensively discussed in G. Ezorsky, *Racism and Justice: The Case for Affirmative Action* (Ithaca, NY, 1991), especially ch. 4.

[12] A.M. Thernstrom, *Whose Votes Count? Affirmative Action and Minority Voting Rights* (Cambridge, Mass., 1987), p. 9.

[13] There *are* parties that operate quotas for youth (usually defined as under 30), but no one, to my knowledge, argues that voters aged between 18 and 25 should have a proportionate representation in Parliament.

14. W. Kymlicka, *Multicultural Citizenship: A Liberal Theory of Minority Rights* (Oxford, 1995), ch. 7.
15. Since segregation is the fundamental ordering principle of gendered societies, women can be said to share at least one interest in common: the interest in improved access. See H. Skjeie, *The Feminization of Power: Norway's Political Experiment (1986–)* (Oslo, 1988).
16. See e.g. C.T. Mohanty, 'Feminist Encounters: Locating the Politics of Experience', in M. Barrett and A. Phillips (eds.), *Destabilizing Theory: Contemporary Feminist Debates* (Cambridge, 1993).
17. H. Pitkin, *The Concept of Representation* (Berkeley, 1967), p. 168.
18. J. Jacquette, 'Power as Ideology: A Feminist Analysis', in J.S. Stiehm (ed.), *Women's Views of the Political World of Men* (New York, 1984).
19. I. Diamond and N. Hartsock, 'Beyond Interests in Politics: A Comment on Virginia Sapiro's "When are interests interesting?"' *American Political Science Review*, 75/3 (1981), p. 719.
20. This is one of the arguments made by Anna Jonasdottir, who sees needs talk as potentially paternalist, and not sufficiently insistent on the political involvement of those in need; see her 'On the Concept of Interest, Women's Interests, and the Limitation of Interest Theory', in K.B. Jones and A. Jonasdottir, *The Political Interests of Women* (London, 1988).
21. N. Fraser, 'Struggle Over Needs: Outline of a Socialist–Feminist Critical Theory of Late Capitalist Political Culture', in N. Fraser, *Unruly Practices: Power, Discourse and Gender in Contemporary Social Theory* (Cambridge, 1989).
22. J.B. Elshtain, *Public Man, Private Woman: Women in Social and Political Thought* (Princeton, 1981), p. 246.
23. J.B. Elshtain, 'The Power and Powerlessness of Woman', in G. Bock and S. James (eds.), *Beyond Equality and Difference* (London, 1993).
24. The phrase comes from Sara Ruddick's 'Maternal Thinking', *Feminist Studies* 6 (1980).
25. J. Mansbridge, 'Feminism and Democracy', *American Prospect*, 1 (1990), p. 134.
26. V. Held, 'Mothering versus Contract', in J.J. Mansbridge (ed.), *Beyond Self-Interest* (Chicago and London, 1990). Held is careful to clarify that she is not proposing the mother–child relationship as the paradigm for all social relations; she follows Michael Walzer in considering that different paradigms will be appropriate in different domains.
27. C.A. MacKinnon, *Feminism Unmodified: Discourses on Life and Law* (Cambridge, Mass., 1987), p. 37.
28. M. Dietz, 'Citizenship with a Feminist Face: The Problem with Maternal Thinking', *Political Theory*, 13/1 (1985); M. Dietz, 'Context Is All: Feminism and Theories of Citizenship', *Daedalus*, 116/4 (1987); N. Fraser, 'The Ethic of Solidarity', *Praxis International* (1986).
29. Dietz, 'Context Is All', pp. 17–18.
30. H. Valen, 'Norway: Decentralization and Group Representation', in M.

Gallagher and M. Marsh (eds.), *Candidate Selection in Comparative Perspective* (London, 1988).

[31] Skjeie, 'Rhetoric of Difference', p. 234.

[32] Ibid. p. 258.

[33] This compared with 15 per cent women, five per cent black people, and only four per cent aged 18–30 at the 1968 National Convention; see J.I. Lengle, 'Participation, Representation, and Democratic Party Reform', in B. Grofman, A. Lijphart, R.B. McKay and H.A. Scarrow (eds.), *Representation and Redistricting Issues* (Lexington, Mass., 1982), p. 175.

[34] A. Ranney, 'Comments on Representation within the Political Party System', in B. Grofman, A. Lijphart, R.B. McKay, and H.A. Scarrow (eds.), *Representation and Redistricting Issues*, (Lexington, Mass., 1982), p. 196.

[35] R.E. Goodin, 'Convention Quotas and Communal Representation', *British Journal of Political Science*, 7/2 (1977).

[36] Ibid. p. 259.

[37] Ibid.

Published in A. Phillips, *The Politics of Presence*, Clarendon Press, Oxford, 1995 (pp. 57-83).

Democratic Institutions, Political Representation and Women's Empowerment

SHIRIN M. RAI

This article examines whether the current debates about quotas for women in political institutions in India can form part of a wider debate on women's empowerment. It explores the reasons for this articulation of demands by women's groups in a country where quotas have had a problematic symbolic history of nearly 40 years. Is this the way to reach a feasible politics? Is there a way forward for representing 'women's interests' through political constituencies? Is this close engagement with the state appropriate at a time when the pressures of globalisation through liberalisation are creating immense social inequalities and tensions within the country? Surely any debate on empowerment should start with questions about better life-chances? Such questions form the bases of debate on quotas in India.

The term empowerment has largely been ignored in the mainstream of political science. For example, it does not appear at all in the *Oxford Dictionary of Politics*.[1] On the other hand, empowerment has found great currency within the feminist discourses. From early on debates about participatory politics at the local levels have been important within feminist politics.[2] While issue was taken by some over the costs of participation, the focus was on the concept of participation rather than on empowerment. Empowerment as a concept has emerged out of debates on education, especially in the work of the Brazilian exponent of consciousness-raising Paulo Friere, and increasingly within the literature on social movements. 'The notion of empowerment was intended to help participation perform one main political function—to provide development with a new source of legitimation', writes Majid Rehnama in the *The Development Dictionary*.[3] It is a legitimation of oppositional discourse as well as of oppositional social movements, of programmes, of methodologies, of policies—both macro and micro. Empowerment has been re-emphasised in the feminist literature on politics as well as on development matters. Bystydzienski, for example, defines empowerment as 'a process by which oppressed persons gain some control over their lives by taking part with others in development of activities and structures that allow people increased involvement in matters which affect them directly'.[4]

Feminists have preferred using the term empowerment in preference to power for many reasons—its focus on those who are oppressed, rather than the oppressors, its emphasis on 'power to' rather than a starting assumption of 'power over', and its insistence upon power as enabling, as competence, rather than power as dominance.[5] Starting from a grass-roots, social movements perspective, empowerment as a term has recently come to be expanded to include institutional strategies for empowerment. Thus we have growing concerns being expressed regarding the under-representation of women in political institutions. The Beijing Declaration of the United Nations, in 1996, for example links participation in institutional politics with their empowerment in the social and economic life: 'The empowerment and autonomy of women and the improvement of women's social, economic and political status is essential for the achievement of both transparent and accountable government and administration and sustainable development in all areas of life'.[6]

Empowerment is a seductive term. It encompasses a politics oppositional to the state on the one hand, and the economic forces of neo-liberal markets on the other. The actors in this oppositional politics are 'the people' variously defined, and identified. This categorisation of the people is important for suggesting an alternative model of politics—based on the concept of needs that are articulated by the people rather than the state, and processes of politics that are participatory and democratic at the local level close to home, rather than representative and bureaucratised in far away corridors of state power. Empowerment then is the knowing and the doing; the feasibility of such politics which allows us to feel empowered whatever our contexts. This is the great seduction. What becomes obscured from view in this discourse of empowerment are wider political implications of the concept as well as the strategy of empowerment.

While there is emphasis on participatory politics within the empowerment approaches, there is little reflection upon the machinery of social and state power itself. It has been argued that empowerment

> is not a process organised from the helm of government, but it does require a strong state, that is, a state in which executive power is centralised, and departments (or provinces) are not colonised, and also one in which security agencies are not a law unto themselves ... [T]his might enable people to take greater advantage of the opportunities available to them in the existing market structures, and would in any case be a necessary condition for changes in those structures to achieve their stated aims of income or asset redistribution.[7]

This points clearly to the importance of the state, its politics, ideology, and its institutions—bureaucratic as well as political (political parties, for example)—as part of the debates on empowerment. Without such a multi-layered analysis there are good grounds for arguing that a discourse of empowerment is not really a discourse of power. It addresses itself to its audiences as if they were all potential converts to 'the cause'. Further, there is a tendency towards homogenising the actors engaged in the struggles for empowerment. There is 'the people', or 'women' without a sufficiently differentiated profile of what these categories mean. As the Indian debate on quotas below shows, the need to focus on the politics of difference among women is important for the credibility of strategies of empowerment as well as for their long-term viability. So, the examination here does not seek to delegitimise the concept of empowerment. On the contrary, it seeks to reinstate it so as to take into account the issue of power. Empowerment of whom?

By whom? Or through what? Empowerment for what?

The current debates on institutional strategies of women's empowerment in India are examined below. With reference to recent work the writer has engaged with Indian feminists participating in this debate, as well as earlier work with women parliamentarians, she argues that social class, political ideology, and communal identities are important to our understanding of this current phase of feminist politics in India. As has been stated elsewhere, the issue of class is at the heart of the process of engendering development, and it is at our own peril that we forget it.[8] This is not simply to forestall a backlash, but also to address issues of difference among women and to rethink women's empowerment. The next section sets out the story of two debates that took place in India over the last decade—one resulting very quickly in quota legislation for women, the other resulting in terrible differences among various groups which have delayed the passing of the women's quota bill at the national level. Echoing Nancy Fraser,[9] who argues that while justice requires both recognition of difference and an insistence upon redistribution of socio-economic resources, the two have come to be seen as disassociated from one another. The argument here is that political representation would be a strategy of recognition rather than redistribution, thus limiting its transformative potential. There follows a conclusion assessing what, if anything, do the Indian debates on quotas for women teach us about the possibilities, and limitations of this strategy for the empowerment of women.

The Indian experiments with quotas

The local, the national, the political

On 22 December 1992, the Indian Parliament passed the Constitution (73rd and 74th) Amendment Acts. These amendments 'enshrined in the Constitution certain basic and essential features of Panchayati Raj Institutions [PRI] to impart certainty, continuity and strength to them'.[10] These two amendments responded not only to a growing political demand for greater decentralisation of power, after a crisis of governability at the centre in Indian politics in the 1990s, but also to the emerging demand of women's groups for greater visibility for women in politics. 'A unique feature of the new phase in panchayats and municipalities in India is that it has ensured one-third representation for women in the local bodies and one-third of the offices of chairpersons at all levels in rural and urban bodies for them'.[11] This has created the possibility for about 1,000,000 women to get elected to village panchayats and urban municipalities; so far around 716,234 women are holding elected positions in the country and in some states such as West Bengal, more than the mandatory 33.3 per cent women have been elected. What is more remarkable about this already remarkable success story is that all political parties co-operated to get this legislation passed.

The 1996 elections in India resulted in a Parliament which contained fewer women members than the previous three parliaments—women contested only 11 per cent of the total seats, and the 1996 Parliament has only 36 women Members of Parliament (MPs) out of a total of 545, as compared with 44 in the previous Parliament. At the same time, the coalition which was eventually returned to government committed itself to introducing legislation in the first session of the new Parliament, ensuring a quota for women of 33 per cent in future Indian parliaments. Such a quota would ensure that out of 545 seats in the Lok Sabha, 182 seats will go to women. Constituencies reserved for women would not be fixed, but would be rotated at random. All parties, irrespective of their ideological standpoints, initially agreed to support this legislation. The Bill was introduced in the first term of the new Bharatiya Janata Party (BJP) led government in Parliament, but it has been referred to a Joint Select Committee of the Indian Parliament due to differences among parties about the detail of the proposed Bill. The debate on the Bill in the Indian press reveals that there is a lack of general political will among parties to pass the 81st Constitution Amendment Bill, which would ensure this quota for women. Women's groups have largely supported the measure, though some important voices within the women's movements have spoken out against the Bill.

One could speculate about the reasons why the various political parties, who supported the ratification of the 74th Constitutional Amendment Act on 24 April 1993 which provided for a quota of 33 per cent for women in panchayats (village councils) and their leadership, have been more reluctant regarding similar legislation at the parliamentary level. Could it be that enhanced representation of women in the national Parliament spells a far greater and immediate challenge to the gendered status quo within the party political system? The panchayats while symbolic of grass-roots democracy in India, have never been resourced well enough to be important to the political processes in Indian politics. Or is it that the pattern of quota systems in India has shown that elite-based strategies of empowerment are less helpful to groups seeking greater recognition than those based upon grass-roots institutions? The message from established political parties and state institutions is mixed. While a strengthening women's movement has been able to politicise the issue of gender representation successfully, mainstream political bodies have not embraced the gender justice agenda wholeheartedly.

At this point it is also important to consider the reasons for the near consensus that has emerged among the women's groups on the issue of quotas. While many women's groups have supported the move for quotas (a significant number of these are attached to political parties), some feminists have opposed this move as 'tokenist'. The first group of feminists focuses on the under-representation of women in party politics; the second is concerned about the elitist character of parliamentary politics and the dangers of expropriation that women face in seeking inclusion into this overwhelmingly male space.[12] Feminists who oppose the Bill do so as much on grounds of detail as principles. Kishwar, for example, also opposes the focus on reserving constituencies which will force women to contest only against other women and will 'ghettoise' them. She wishes to see a system of 'multi-seat constituencies where one out of three candidates has to be a women'.[13] Concerns about co-optation, and elitism remain real for many feminist and women's groups in India: 'the link between reservations in Parliament and "empowerment" of women is at best tenuous, and may even be a way of closing off possibilities of further radicalisation of Indian politics ... If we attempt to recover feminist politics as subversion ... we would need to move away from politics as merely seeking space within already defined boundaries of power'.[14]

Women's interests, women representatives

In a recent article Hoskyns and Rai have argued that policies based on a recognition that certain groups are under-represented can also be seen as a means of political gate-keeping, and that in certain circumstances the recognition of gender-based groups may be seen as less disruptive of the hierarchy of power relations than the recognition of groups more clearly based on class. 'Gender' can be accommodated on this reading—but only if it loses its class dimension. The argument then is that 'the privileging of gender over class, together with the grip of the political parties on access to the political system, results in a particular profile of women representatives which in turn raises issues about accountability'. A conclusion drawn from this is that 'this selective inclusion of women in the political process is important—but inadequate in challenging the established hierarchies of power relations'.[15] If development agendas are to be re-articulated, if transformation of the lives of women has to take place in tandem with that of the gender relations within which they are enmeshed, then the issues surrounding economic and social class relations have to be addressed.

For the moment, the main thrust of academic research and institutional initiatives continues to focus on other categories of difference than class. The salience of class in political life remains weak and representation continues to be regarded as a strategy for reordering political hierarchies. This political bias is reflective of what, in a recent article, Nancy Fraser has called the politics of affirmation.[16] Fraser argues that while justice requires both recognition of difference and an insistence upon redistribution of socio-economic resources, currently the two have been disassociated from each other. Representation, on this analysis, would be a strategy of recognition rather than redistribution, thus limiting its transformative potential.

Fraser distinguishes two broad approaches to remedying injustice that occur across the recognition-redistribution divide. The first she calls the affirmation approach, which focuses on 'correcting inequitable outcomes of social arrangements without disturbing the underlying framework that generates them'.[17] The second she calls the transformative remedy, which focuses on 'correcting inequitable outcomes precisely by restructuring the underlying generative framework'.[18] Whereas affirmative remedies reinforce group difference, transformative remedies tend to destabilise them in the long run. Fraser sees the combination of socialism and deconstruction as the remedy best suited to resolving the recognition-redistribution dilemma. In doing so she seems to suggest that the disordering of group difference is the long-term strategy best suited to the process of transformation. Young's argument with Fraser on this issue points to the problematic of setting up such binaries of analysis, and therefore positioning choices in a zero-sum fashion.[19] However, Fraser's discussion of the recognition-redistribution dilemma does pose important questions for a study of gender and representation. How far can representation as a concept and strategy meet the needs of the majority of women? The debate in India about the concrete provisions of the quota legislation is salutary in this regard.

Social backwardness and quota politics

What is evident from the introduction of the 81st Amendment Bill, and indeed from the legislative changes in the form of the 74th Amendment Act, is that political representation of women has become an important issue in Indian politics. The success of the women's movements in placing the issue of political under-representation of women on the agenda of political parties and governments begs the questions, why and how? Why has this issue become important for the women's movement in the last decade, and how have women's movements been able to get recognition for this agenda? In part this is perhaps the result of the 'troubling impasse'[20] that the Indian women's movements are facing in the 1990s. The liberalisation policies have seen women increasingly being pushed into the unorganised sector of work. The decline of the trade union movement—never very sensitive to women's issues in the first place, but changing under pressure of women's movements—has also resulted in the increased vulnerability of working class women. Despite tremendous struggles waged by women's groups against violence against women, convictions have been established only with great difficulty. The late 1980s also saw the hardening of divisions among women's groups—between 'academic' and 'activists', between women on the right wing and left wing of politics, between those working with mass organisations and those working with international non-governmental organisations. In this context the early focus of women's groups—on women's work, violence, and capitalist relations in, and outside the home—became obscured. Together with these developments, the international context of women's organisations changed. While the demand for women's inclusion in policy-making institutions had appeared first in the late 1970s, it found increasing expression in the formulations of 'women's interests' in the late 1980s and gathered momentum with former Prime Minister Rajiv Gandhi's proposals in 1991 for a reservation of seats for women in the village panchayats. Reservations (or quotas) have had a long and chequered history in India.

A history of 'reservation' policies

When the Indian state was taking shape, the question of caste was predominant in the debates about the crafting of a new Constitution as well as a new social order. The arguments were cast in both philosophical and pragmatic terms. Political equality could not be realised without social and economic equality, which were attached to the whole edifice of social power. In India, the caste system is the 'steel frame' that has underpinned Hindu society despite all its polytheism and plurality. The inherent inequality of birth built into this system did not allow the individual the way out of the particular positioning within the social system. Individualisation could not therefore work as a strategy for social mobility.

The Indian Constituent Assembly decided to enshrine in the Constitution a special 9th Schedule that would allow the policies of affirmative action through reservations. At the pragmatic level it was clear to the Congress party leadership that the consequences of not tackling this issue of caste-based inequality could only be political instability which a fledgling democracy could ill afford. The legislation was based on the idea of 'Social Backwardness' which was seen as a social 'placing [of] individuals/groups in particular disadvantageous position by delimiting their life chances'. The determinants of this 'social backwardness' were both the objective position of a group in terms of economic conditions in the social structure as well as the prevailing value system.[21]

A further amendment was made to the original legislation in 1951 which enables the state to make 'special provisions for the advancement of any socially and educationally backward classes' of citizens or for Scheduled Castes and Scheduled Tribes. Similar provision was made in Article 16(4) for reservation of posts in favour of any backward classes of citizens which in the opinion of the state 'is not adequately represented in the services under the state'. Both these clauses refer to 'classes of citizens' and not individuals; group (minority) rights were therefore acknowledged as important by the Indian political elites almost from the start. This recognition is the basis of the quota debates and demands for women. However, the question of caste has posed very divisive questions for the women's groups engaged in these debates.

India has undergone a fracturing of its one-party dominant political system since the death of Mrs Indira Gandhi in 1984. Today, coalition politics, and caste interest groups are extremely visible and active in India. Parties based on regional and caste identities have gained prominence in the political processes and system. At the time of the consideration of the quota legislation for women in Parliament in 1993–94, the party consensus that had allowed a smooth passage of the 73rd Amendment Act broke on the question of caste representation within the quota for women. Political parties like the Janata Party and the Samata Party argued fiercely for the quota for women to be distributed along caste lines; that the caste-based reservation already in place should be reflected in the newly proposed quota for women. On the other hand, other regional parties such as the Tamil party All India Anna Dravida Munnetra Kazhagam (AIADMK) have supported the Bill and given vital support to the initiative at the time when it was most needed. The saga of the non-passage of the Bill shows the fluidity of the Indian political situation—a fluidity that women's groups have been able to take advantage of, and at the same time fallen foul of.

The arguments for quotas

The arguments for quotas for women in representative institutions are fairly well rehearsed. Development policies are highly politically charged trade-offs between diverse interests and value choices. 'The political nature of these policies is frequently made behind the closed door of bureaucracy or among tiny groups of men in a non-transparent political structure'.[22] The question then arises, how are women to access this world of policy making so dominated by men? The answers that have been explored within the Indian women's movements have been diverse—political mobilisation of women, lobbying political parties, moving the courts and legal establishments, constitutional reform, mobilisation and participation in social movements such as the environmental movement, and civil liberties campaigns. It is only now, however, that women's groups have come together to demand increased representation of women in India's political institutions.

Women's groups are now arguing that quotas for women are needed to compensate for the social barriers that have prevented women from participating in politics and thus making their voices heard. That in order for women to be more than 'tokens' in political institutions, a level of presence that cannot be overlooked by political parties is required, hence the demand for a 33 per cent quota. The quota system acknowledges that it is the recruitment process, organised through political parties supported by a framework of patriarchal values, that needs to carry the burden of change, rather than individual women. The alternative then is that there should be an acknowledgement of the historical social exclusion of women from politics, a compensatory regime (quotas) established, and 'institutionalised ... for the explicit recognition and representation of oppressed groups'.[23] That this demand for quotas has been formulated first with respect to grass-roots institutions (panchayats), is reflective of the unease felt by many women's groups with elite politics and elite women.[24] The National Commission for Women, set up in 1991, has consistently supported the demand for a quota for women in Parliament and other representative institutions. In the 1996 elections, it called for all women voters to exercise their franchise in favour of women candidates regardless of the political party they represented. This call was at one level the logical result of the Commission's support for quotas for women. If the purpose of the quotas is to increase the number of women in parliament, then the gender variable is the most important one to consider at the time of voting. However, women's groups in India have had close links with political parties.

This means that the question of representativeness is also tied closely to the question of political platforms:

> In a system which is party-based, whether it is men or women, they will represent the viewpoint of the party ... Women voters while making their choice [of candidates] will have to judge which of these platforms will be closest to viewing their concerns with sympathy. They will also have to judge which of these platforms is intrinsically against women's equality and vote against the candidate regardless of whether it is a man or a woman.[25]

This concern with party politics has been further increased by the growing mobilisation of women by the right-wing political parties in the name of cultural authenticity and the recognition of women as bulwarks against erosion of traditions, calling for a political response from the women's groups on the centre/left of politics.[26] The consensus on the quota policy has also evolved with the successful enactment of the 73rd and 74th Amendment Acts. The feeling now is that these Acts will ensure a grass-roots political involvement of women; that as women become active in panchayat politics, their capabilities to participate in national politics will increase. The question of elitism will thus be answered.

The consensus on having a quota for women has also gained from the support (however ambivalent) of the political parties. I have pointed out the changing character of the Indian political system. With the break up of the old system of one-party domination there has also arisen the need for a mobilisation of new constituencies. Women have been identified by most parties as one of the most important, and possibly the most neglected, constituency, that needs to be brought into the political mainstream. This mobilisation has become an issue only because of the strength of the women's movement in India, but it has taken different forms when different political parties have sought to engage women.[27] The terms of engagement of various political parties have differed, and they have sought to highlight only their own political agendas in the debate. So, while the right wing has supported an undifferentiated quota for women, parties with significant lower caste constituencies have been generally more ambivalent, this even when reflecting upon the need to mobilise women into their parties. The pressure on political parties to support the quota has therefore been matched by their concern about the terms on which the quota is to be constructed.

So, as the consensus around the need for a quota has evolved, it has also raised new and important issues for women's groups and movements. In particular the question of how to deal with difference among women has been critical here. The current emphasis by women's groups on the representation of women in political institutions can thus be read in the light of the tension between on the one side the politics of universalism as symbolised in the Indian context in the debates about citizenship, and on the other side the constant and real fear of co-optation of the feminist projects by the political elites.

The arguments against quotas

At the theoretical level two sets of arguments have been used: first, that any quota policy is against the principle of equal opportunity, and therefore, inherently undemocratic; that it is also against the principle of meritocracy. The second set of arguments are regarding the nature of interest representation—whose interests are being represented? Can women be regarded as a homogenous group? How are differences among women to be acknowledged and then translated into a quota policy? The motives of those opposing the Bill have been varied too. Some are moved by dilemmas that women's movements will have to face: 'It [the legislation] can either be an authentic expression of womanhood in politics, in which case it profoundly alters the way we all are, or it can be a device to co-opt women into structures of power and ways of authoritarian thinking ... and yet express a vision of the universe in which the male [remains] the principal agent ...'[28] Others look clearly to the feasibility of such mechanisms of change: 'How can these poor women panches [panchayat members] oppose the same men whose fields they work for livelihood? First organise them and put economic power in their hands, only then can they oppose men.'[29]

Then there are those who have initially supported the quota Bills and then violently opposed them because of the issue of representation of different minority interests. The two political parties that have managed to scuttle the passage of the Bill—Samajwadi Party, and the Rashtriya Janata Dal—have taken the position that to be fair, the Women's Reservation Bill has to reflect the caste distinctions in the country; that 'gender justice, abstracted from all other forms of social justice, is an urban middle-class concept and, therefore, of little use ...'[30] These parties demand that the 33 per cent quotas be differentiated by a fixed quota for women belonging to OBCs (Other Backward Classes and minorities). The argument is also that the quota Bill is 'the creation of a new constituency which is not defined by social or economic criteria, strictly speaking, and whose characteristics are, in fact totally unknown—even the representatives of this [reserved] constituency would be unable to say what it is that women stand for and men don't...'[31] Finally, there is the issue of priorities—whether the Indian political system faced with many challenges can also deal with another 'divisive' issue: 'The country is facing many serious problems ... it was not the right time to bring the Women's Reservation Bill', said Prabhu Nath Singh of Samata (Equality) Party in the parliamentary debate on the Bill.[32]

The debate on the quota Bill has been bitter. Feminists and women's groups have come in for violent verbal abuse from those opposing the Bill. They have been caricatured—'short-haired memsahibs' and as 'biwi (wife) brigades'; their agendas have been called divisive for the country. However, the debate has also provoked considerable discussion of what is needed to make women's participation in politics meaningful, and how can there be an acknowledgement of differences among women at the same time as meeting the need for quotas for women in parliament. Most of the arguments have been framed by liberal politics: increased emphasis on education for girl children and women, gender-sensitive training of police, and bureaucrats, review of the functioning of family courts and various laws relating to issues like divorce, adoption, and share of property for women have all been aired as development policies to ensure women's empowerment. The question before the feminist groups in India is how this increase in women's numbers within Parliament and at the local level will result in real benefits for women, and women's movements.

Caste, class, gender: dilemmas for feminisms

If we examine the profile of the women representatives in the 1991–96 Indian Parliament, we find that they were mostly middle-class, professional women, with little or no links with the women's movement. A significant number of them accessed politics through their families, some through various student and civil rights movements, and some because of state initiatives in increasing representation from the lower castes in India. This selective inclusion of women into mainstream politics has tended to maintain divisions within the women's movement posing difficult questions for representation of and by women—between feminist/professionals and activists, and between women members of different political parties.[33]

A survey of women MPs also suggests that these women have benefited from the growing strength of the women's movement, which has put the issues of women's empowerment and participation in politics on the national agenda, and to which various party political leaders have responded in different ways. However, none of these women have come into political life through the women's movement. Their access to women's organisations is generally limited to the women's wing of their own parties. As party women with political ambitions, women MPs respond to the institutional incentives and disincentives that are put to them. All these factors limit the potential of these women MPs representing the interests of Indian women across a range of issues. As a result there seems to be little regular contact between women's groups and women MPs. The exception here is of course the women's wing of political parties which do liaise with women MPs. This does allow the possibility of women MPs becoming conduits between the party's leadership and its women members. They are also consulted from time to time by the party leadership on issues regarding the family, and women's rights. But non-party women's groups do not seem to be approaching women MPs.[34]

In the context of the discussion of difference among women, there are several interesting aspects of the debate about quotas in India. First, there is the consensus that has emerged among women's groups and political parties that quotas are a valid and much-needed strategy of enhancing women's participation. We need more information about how this consensus came to be crafted and on what terms.

Second, that this consensus has been far more stable in the context of village and township council, that is lower levels of governance, than at the national level. We could ask whether this has something to do with the extent to which the panchayat level quotas have challenged social hierarchies, or is it more predictably about the reluctance of male elites to keep women out of national level institutions where power is concentrated?

Third, at various points the question of greater representation has been discussed in terms of women 'transforming politics', by representing women's interests in a deeply patriarchal society, and also, especially in the context of high levels of political corruption (the expectation being that women will not behave in as corrupt a way as men do). Here, we could ask why are such burdens being placed on women and not men, but also more pertinently, given the discussion about differences among women, what are the philosophical bases upon which we can argue for greater representation of women in political institutions?

Fourth, the question of difference among women was raised in the debates on quotas for women, in the first instance by men and not by the various women's groups. The result was a rather nasty and divisive debate where those demanding a quota for women were portrayed as manipulative, westernised feminists wishing to keep low-caste women out of the equation, and therefore working against the interests of the 'ordinary Indian woman'. This serious charge was only partially challenged by women's groups which were largely endorsing an undifferentiated quota strategy. This experience of the high political cost that women's groups had to pay for assuming that issues of difference could be put to one side in a deeply divided social context raises questions about strategising. It establishes the importance of dealing with difference among women within socio-economic contexts of great inequality. Here a consideration of the particularity of the political system becomes extremely important. In the Indian context, the long-standing caste-based quotas should have been taken centrally into account by women's groups articulating demands for quotas for women. Also, consideration should have been given to the new alliances and fractures among political parties operating in an unfamiliar context of coalition politics, in a country where until recently one party, Congress, dominated the political system and set the political agendas. Why an alliance of strong, sophisticated and active women's movements was unable to do so, is another issue that merits exploration.

Concluding remarks

In making these points, this article is not arguing against the need for greater representation of women in political institutions, nor denying the positive impact that such representation can and has had. Neither does it in any sense intend to undervalue the campaigns and struggles on the part of women which have been and are still necessary, to make these advances possible. It is also not suggesting any easy correlation between class and social positioning with political behaviour. Instead the concern is to make a contribution to a more self-reflective analysis of what increasing representation on the basis of gender alone may mean in practice, and of what may be being erased in the process. For it remains the case that in India, and more broadly, the greater representation of women in politics is taking place at a time when the conditions of women with the least access to resources and the fewest privileges are steadily deteriorating. This more reflective approach is essential to constructing a politics of alliances that women and women's organisations must engage in now if they are to be effective, in a still largely male political terrain.

The Indian example has many insights to offer to women engaged in similar struggles in other countries and contexts. First, it points to the 'rethink' within the Indian women's movements regarding strategies of empowerment. A shift has occurred among these groups regarding an engagement with the state and its institutions. It is now increasingly seen as an essential part of women's struggles to improve their lives. This shift is so fundamental that it spans across party political lines, creating a new consensus on this issue. In the words of the doyenne of Indian Women's Studies, Vina Mazumdar, it is now accepted that 'politics is not a dirty word' for women. Changes in policy-making machineries are critical to the improvement of women's life chances.[35]

Second, the Indian example points to the importance of levels of governance in crafting strategies of political empowerment if women are to engage with the state. The quota Bill in 1993 which provided for 33 per cent of seats in the village and town councils was passed without a murmur of opposition from any political party, and yet when something similar was demanded at the national level, the consensus fell apart. Disassociating empowerment politics from local politics allows us an explanation as well as a context for this discrepancy.

Third, the Indian example critically points to the importance of the recognition of difference among women and women's groups. Because women's groups arguing for the quota did not think it strategically necessary to proactively raise the issue of difference among women on the basis of caste, they were wrong-footed politically. Empowerment for whom? became the issue when they had sought to ask the question about empowerment for what?

Finally, the Indian example shows that there is no simple correlation between an enhanced visibility of women in political institutions and a sense of empowerment of 'women' in the polity in general. In short, the question of empowerment cannot be disassociated from the question of relations of power within different socio-political systems. In order to challenge structural impediments to greater participation of women in political institutions, we need to have regard to the multi-faceted power relations which contextualise that challenge. In this regard, the debates on empowerment need to be opened up to the questions raised above. Seductive as the language of empowerment is, it needs to and can be much more.

Acknowledgements

The author thanks the anonymous referees of the journal and participants in the 'Rethinking Empowerment' panel of the International Studies Association annual conference March 1999, in Washington, DC, for comments on an earlier draft. The author benefited greatly from the feedback.

Notes

[1] I. McLean, *The Oxford Dictionary of Politics* (Oxford: Oxford University Press, 1996).
[2] A. Phillips, *Engendering Democracy* (Cambridge: Polity Press, 1991).
[3] M. Rahnema, 'Participation', in W. Sachs (ed.), *The Development Dictionary* (London: Zed Press, 1992), p. 122.
[4] J.M. Bystydzienski (ed.), *Women Transforming Politics: Worldwide Strategies for Empowerment* (Bloomington, IN: Indiana University Press, 1992), p. 3.
[5] Bystydzienski, ibid., p. 3.

[6] United Nations, *Platform for Action and the Beijing Declaration* (1996), p. 109.
[7] J. Friedman, *Empowerment* (Oxford: Blackwell, 1997), p. 7.
[8] C. Hoskyns and S. Rai, 'Gender, Class and Representation: India and the European Union', *European Journal of Women's Studies*, Vol. 5 (November 1998), pp. 345–65.
[9] N. Fraser, 'From Redistribution to Recognition? Dilemmas of Justice in "Poststructuralist" Age', *New Left Review*, 212 (July/August 1995), pp. 68–93.
[10] G. Matthews, 'Restructuring the Polity: The Panchayati Raj', *Mainstream*, Vol. XXXV, No. 22 (10 May 1997), p. 22.
[11] Matthews, ibid., p. 25.
[12] R. Kapoor, *The Times of India* (1996), p. 11; M. Kishwar, 'Do we need "biwi brigades" in parliament', *The Times of India* (22 December 1996), Review Section, p. 2.
[13] Ibid.
[14] N. Menon, 'Reservations and Representation', *Seminar*, Special Issue on 'Empowering Women', No. 457 (September 1997), p. 41.
[15] Hoskyns and Rai, op. cit., pp. 345–65.
[16] Fraser, op. cit., pp. 68–93.
[17] Fraser, op. cit., p. 82.
[18] Ibid.
[19] I.M. Young, 'Unruly Categories: A Critique of Nancy Fraser's Dual Systems Theory', *New Left Review*, No. 222 (March–April 1997).
[20] G. Omvedt, *Reinventing Revolution, New Social Movements and the Socialist Tradition in India* (New York: M.E. Sharpe, 1993), p. 96.
[21] G. Shah, 'Social Backwardness and Reservation Politics', *Economic and Political Weekly* (Annual Number, 1991), p. 65.
[22] K. Staudt, *Managing Development* (London: Sage, 1991), p. 65.
[23] I.M. Young, *Justice and the Politics of Difference* (Princeton, NJ: Princeton University Press, 1990), pp. 183–91.
[24] I. Agnihotri and V. Mazumdar, 'Changing Terms of Political Discourse: Women's Movement in India, 1970s–1990s', *Economic and Political Weekly*, Vol. XXX, No. 29 (1995), pp. 1869–78; Centre for Women's Development Studies (CWDS), *Confronting Myriad Oppressions: Voices from the Women's Movement in India* (New Delhi: Centre for Women's Development Studies, 1994).
[25] B. Karat, 'Vote for Policies, not Gender', *Indian Express* (3 February 1996), p. 8.
[26] CWDS, op. cit., pp. 22–4.
[27] For the particularity of right-wing mobilisation of women see U. Butalia and T. Sarkar, *Women and Right-Wing Movements: The Indian Experiences* (New Delhi: Kali for Women, 1995).
[28] Soumitra Das, *The Times of India* (22 July 1998), p. 10.
[29] Ella Bhatt, *The Times of India* (23 December 1996), p. 13.

[30] Editorial, *The Statesman* (13 July 1998), p. 8.
[31] Ibid.
[32] *The Statesman* (15 July 1998), p. 1.
[33] S. Rai, 'Gender and Representation: Women in the Indian Parliament, 1991–1996' in A.M. Goetz (ed.), *Getting Institutions Right for Women in Development* (London: Sage, 1997).
[34] S. Rai, 'Women Negotiating Boundaries: State and Law in India', *Social and Legal Studies*, Vol. 4 (1995).
[35] See ibid.

Published as 'Democratic Institutions, Political Representation and Women's Empowerment: The Quota Debate in India' in *Democratisation*, Vol. 6, No. 3, Autumn 1999, (pp. 84-99), Frank Cass, London.

Representation for Women: Should Feminists Support Quotas?

MEENA DHANDA

A gender quota in legislative bodies is controversial. It raises troubling doubts about what it means for a collectivity to be 'represented'. It challenges our precritical notions of respect for differences between women. It questions our most fundamental allegiances to groups and forces the issue of who we want to be identified with. As a relatively untried political measure, it arouses a mixture of fear and excitement. Thus, the prospect of a gender quota perturbs the open-minded as well as the avowedly partisan citizen. But, on reflection, gender quotas are not as much of a political conundrum as they are made out to be. There is a growing body of political thought that can lead us to greater clarity about the use of gender quotas. There is even considerable evidence from different parts of the world to suggest that gender quotas might be worth betting on.[1]

It will be my concern in this paper to offer a defence of gender quotas in legislative bodies. In order to make a convincing case, I shall, at one level, engage with the substantive issues raised in the debates surrounding the potential political and socio-cultural consequences of the institution of a gender quota in the Indian Parliament by a Constitutional Amendment. At a different level, I shall build an argument for a reframing of the debate in terms of concerns of identity and representation. The surprising effect of my reinterpretation is to provide a strong justification for the use of a gender quota in legislative bodies; incidentally, disproving (in a sense) that philosophy leaves everything as it is. Philosophical reflection can bolster our confidence as we juggle our priorities in undertaking the specific tasks of changing the world to make it a better place for women.

Those who have advocated the cause of affirmative action for the inclusion of Indian women in local as well as central government for almost a decade now, argue that 'institutionalised inequalities' require 'institutionalised counter measures' (Mazumdar 1997: 19). The fruit of their labour was the 73rd and 74th Amendments to the Indian Constitution enacted unanimously by Parliament in 1992. This legislation guaranteed a 33 per cent reservation in the elected representatives to local government when it was 'quietly ratified' in April 1993. According to Vina Mazumdar, this legislation brought about the 'political dynamism' of women voters, leading her to conclude that 'it is time for India to try out some new experiments in achieving real democracy ... (ibid.: 19).

As against the above, it has been argued by some 'that reservations are not a matter of principle; that they are at best a limited intervention in a larger repertoire of affirmative action strategies designed in specific contexts ...' (Singh 1997: 12). Still others seem opposed to reservations in Parliament, on account of a superficially higher order principle. This is expressed as 'It is no good getting seats without any work to show for it ... If eternal vigilance is the price of liberty, eternal striving is the price we must pay for entering politics' (Dhangambar 1997: 22). In a similar vein, Kishwar (1996) draws cynical conclusions about the likely calibre of women parliamentarians who might unfairly benefit from a quota. Further, fears of a 'growing statism' are expressed to turn feminists away from any simple equation between reservations in the Parliament and empowerment of women. It is also contended that, not only will the designed entry of women pervert the course of justice, it may actually create a far more objectionable scenario. 'To try and push reforms without necessary social support is mere adventurism, mere symbolism ... the damaging impact of ill-thought intervention, even if the intention is noble, is no less serious than inaction and paralysis' (Singh 1997: 13). It is argued that what ought to be done, instead of instituting gender quotas, is to address the underlying *causes* of women's exclusion.

There is a common thread that binds both the proponents of quotas and their opponents. It lies in the nature of their political arguments. A bulk of the debate on the question of gender quotas has been conducted in *consequentialist* terms. There are those who point out the benefits that accrue to women when they receive a helping hand, and others who predict gloom and doom if women were to expectantly clutch it.

Without meaning to undermine the significance of the often very astute observations on the Indian political scene, we might want to concentrate on a slightly different set of related concerns. Even though I shall engage in some detail with the consequentialist arguments offered by Madhu Kishwar (1996) in Section I of the paper, I shall set aside predictions of the 'what if' kind in Section II. There, I shall pay closer attention to the concept of the public sphere, and the idea of acting in solidarity with women, presupposed in the debate. In Section III, I shall elaborate my version of an identitarian justification of gender quotas. I shall compare my justification with the support for gender quotas from the argument for 'a politics of presence' developed by Anne Phillips (1995) in Section IV. Hopefully, by the concluding section of the paper, I shall have lent some support to an affirmative answer to the question: Should feminists[2] support the women's Bill[3] for an amendment to the Indian Constitution which seeks to put in place institutional measures to guarantee a 33 per cent reservation for women in the Indian Parliament and state legislatures?

It is my contention that the issue of gender quotas is better grasped if we reconceptualise what it means to act politically in the interests of women. I shall use two concepts that I find particularly illuminating in this regard. The first is the idea of a 'heterogeneous public' (Fraser 1992) and the second that of conceptualising gender as 'seriality' (Young 1994; Kruks 1995). The first helps to accommodate a variety of political action women engage in to fight the constraints on their political life. The second helps to clarify what it means to act in solidarity with women.

In general, gender quotas raise problems that are echoed in feminist debates about the status of women as a group given their multiple/different locations in the polity (Kruks 1995; Young 1994). Likewise, in the theoretical work on the conception of the political itself and the supervening debate on the relative merits of using the Parliament and/or the 'subaltern counterpublics' as arenas of effecting social transformation (Fraser 1992 with due acknowledgement to Spivak), we find some useful conceptual tools. Finally, the increasing use of historiography in feminist political theory (Sparks 1997; Sarvasy 1997) reinforces the necessity of positioning a general problem, such as of gender quotas, in the specific locale in which it arises in particular forms.

My arguments suggest that the question of whether particular women *actually* identify with other women sufficiently to envisage the shared project of greater representation of women in legislative bodies, is a question of their *praxis*. Theory helps us imagine alternative responses to the constraints and confinements we face, but which of those alternatives is, and must be, embraced is an existential matter. My purpose in engaging in theory is to make some accommodations seem easier than they may seem at first. I shall argue that it is possible to defend gender quotas, without becoming an apologist for state protectionism. And it is possible to defend gender quotas without undermining the political potentiality of groups of women being motivated to political action on the distinct bases of caste and/or class solidarity or indeed any other group solidarity.

I. Consequentialist objections

I claimed above that those who oppose gender quotas in the Indian context mainly do so on consequentialist grounds. A consideration of the central arguments that Kishwar (1996) offers would clearly illustrate this tendency. In this section, I shall engage with the substantive issues raised by her arguments with a view to bringing the assumptions she makes to the surface.

Kishwar may be counted as someone who has repeatedly advocated power from the ground up, while taking to task those who wield power. She takes care to note that while the electorate is receptive to the idea of women in power, the leaders may not be. Therefore, she argues, we must not look towards pushing women into the legislature amidst 'gangster' politicians, but 'leaders and parties will have to initiate widespread social reform movements within their respective communities' to 'realistically prepare ground for women to emerge ...' (Kishwar 1996). This, she considers, is particularly important for 'backward castes'.

Strikingly, it is women politicians of the 'backward castes' that have 'emerged' in the current climate of flux in the Indian political scene. One is tempted to offer a straight instance of falsification of Kishwar's theory, that women are not yet ready and need a preparatory social reform movement to make a proper entry into politics. The instance is Mayawati, who is the first among 'low caste' women to become the chief minister of a state. It is begging the question of women's ability to be politicians in their own right to claim, as Kishwar does, that her success is owing to her proximity to the 'backward caste' leader, Kanshi Ram. The diagnosis of nepotism also leads Kishwar to a grim portrayal of what would happen if by some stroke of luck the quota system were to be introduced for the representation of women in politics. She predicts that we would witness the onslaught of the 'biwi' brigade. It is difficult to improve upon the response of Kalpana and Vasanth Kannabiran (1997) to this imagined scenario. There is enough nepotism in Indian politics even without women, they argue, so why should the entry of women be seen as especially harmful? But Kishwar's provocative response is that:

> the presence of such proxy figures in parliament ... is actually harmful. Political socialisation of such women legislators, required for being an effective member of state assemblies and parliament, cannot take place smoothly when women members remain filially attached and politically dependent on the male party leaders (Kishwar 1996: 2873).

It is her unquestioned assertion that 'even the most untalented of men do not allow themselves' to be used as proxies (ibid.). Her unstated conclusion has to be that even an intelligent, albeit, dependent woman, makes a worse parliamentarian than the most untalented supposedly independent man. Kishwar is in the company of the honourable Kant who denied active citizenship to women because they 'do not possess civil independence'. In such conditions, women should be 'subject' to the law, he argued, but not participate in making it (Mendus 1987). Kishwar's argument for denying women the ability to be good legislators is not very different from Kant's argument for refusing suffrage to women. Her unacknowledged assumption that 'independence' is a necessary virtue for an 'active' political career requires further investigation that must wait for another occasion.

However, in a consequentialist spirit one may reply that even if some undeserving women benefit in the immediate future, the overall evaluation surely has to weigh long-term desirable consequences against short-term undesirable ones. Finally, the objection of women lacking requisite skills for being active legislators is a matter of interpreting what skills they do have. Certainly, the hurdle of being a woman is not a small one. Learning to overcome it is evidence of having acquired as yet *unnamed* skills. Whether the skills women have are 'inferior' is relative to the purposes for which collectivities come together, and perfection is relative to the particular *kind* of politics one practices.

Whatever be the evaluation of their political skills, women have undoubtedly participated in several traditional political arenas, such as, national liberation struggles. Kishwar fails to notice that the trajectory of women's inclusion in struggles for transformation and later their exclusion is the same the world over. Gandhi's alternative extra-parliamentary politics and Nehru's inability to shake the upper class, upper caste bias of the educated elite may have been contributory factors in the Indian case, as Kishwar argues. However, the underlying reason why women are unable to translate the treasure of their political experience into power, once the immediate struggle is over, might lie elsewhere. In my view, there is nothing particular about Indian 'culture' that needs transformation in order for women to engage in more public forms of politics. As Pateman (1988) shows, the relegation of most women to the 'private sphere' of life is a ubiquitous feature of patriarchy that is further consolidated in the very birth of civil society. Hence, we can endorse the influx of women in the political mainstream, even if in a seemingly contrived manner, as a challenge to the domination of women by men.

The claim that gender quotas will lead to women being entrapped in divisive politics fails to register the fact that electoral politics is a legitimate area of contest. If women may be pitched against other women with justification anywhere, it is here. Moreover, leadership contests have, arguably, little bearing on the possibility of solidarity between people of the same sex. It is the bargaining power of the electorate that makes leaders forge or break alliances with other leaders.

Kishwar also raises a number of technical questions regarding the suggested procedures for instituting a gender quota in legislative bodies. Since these are an integral part of her polemic against quotas it is worth responding to them briefly. One question that seems to worry her is that of why there must be a quota of 33 per cent. A simple argument for a percentage less than the 49 per cent, which is the share of women in the population, is that it is not 'mirror' representation which is being demanded. The argument for a percentage not lower than 33 per cent is that a threshold number of seats that are sufficient to effectively express the interests of women must be secured. Arguably the threshold may in fact be lower than the proposed number. A distinction made by Kymlicka (1995), between the case for proportionate presence and the case for a threshold presence, is useful in this regard. Given that women form almost half the population, they might not require any more than 25 per cent to 30 per cent of the seats in order to change the political agenda. Opponents of quotas, mistakenly assume that the point of the demand is to seek 'mirror representation'. In fact, it is effective power and not 'mirror representation' that is the goal of gender quotas.

A second technical issue regarding the procedures involved in ensuring representation of women is that of reserving constituencies by lot and rotation. Kishwar (1996) argues that reserving constituencies by lot will lead to less responsible politics because every politician will have the exit option, and hence not care to nurture a long-term relationship with the electorate. Alternatively, the necessity of seeking re-election from the same constituency would force politicians to attend to the grievances of the electorate. She has the support of others on this observation. Abhishek M. Singhvi, a senior advocate at the Supreme Court of India, claims along the same lines that:

> A change of constituency every five years ... would snap that fundamental link between the electorate and the elected and completely eliminate all incentive and interest in the development, nurturing and continued prosperity of the constituency which every representative must have and which is the very essence of representative democracy. It would make the very purpose of women's representation empty and devoid of substance (Singhvi 1997: 28).

A quick response to this argument is that it is never the interests of all that are catered to, but only of those who the elected depend upon to secure re-election. If the interests of women voters are to be catered to at all, reservation by lot cannot but be a good device. The reason it would be a good device is that every constituency will have to be alert to the possibility of it being the next reserved one, so that no one who seeks election from a constituency can afford to neglect women's interests.

Finally, it is suggested that while it may be assumed, for the sake of argument, that the gender composition of elected assemblies must change, what is not clear is *how* this change must be brought about. Gender quotas can operate at the party level, where parties target to field at least 30 per cent (up to 50 per cent) women as candidates, but then this is something that a political party may or may not want to institute. On the positive side, the experience of Norway is exemplary in that a range of political parties abides by gender quotas. The '40 per cent rule' included in the Equal Status Act in 1988 requires a 40 per cent representation of both sexes on all public boards, councils and committees. By 1994, there were 39 per cent women in the Storting (the Norwegian Parliament), and 42 per cent out of the 19 member cabinet, (i.e., eight) were women.[4] Gender quotas have operated at the level of political parties in Germany too. The Greens lead with a 50-50 system and the other half of the ruling combine, the Social Democrats, reserve 40 per cent of party posts for women. Almost a third of the Members of Parliament in the lower house in Bonn are women. The Labour Party in UK recently 'twinned' constituencies to ensure that one in two will field women candidates for the Scottish parliamentary elections. The example of Spain is instructive too. Here is a country that gave equal civic rights to women as late as the 1978 post-Franco constitution. The Socialist Party of Spain implements a mandatory 40 per cent quota of women for all its officials and representatives and this has had a demonstration effect[5] in that the ruling Popular Party too fielded a very high proportion of women in the recent European Union parliamentary elections.[6] On the negative side, despite promises in their manifestos, there is little evidence of any significant increase in the presence of women in the political parties of India.

In conclusion, it is obvious that much of the discussion questioning the justification of gender quotas is carried out in a consequentialist framework. The general strategy adopted by most opponents is to point out the harmful consequences of bringing about greater participation of women in legislative bodies by means of a reservation for women. However, there are three points worth making. First, not all the relevant consequences are necessarily taken into account, as is obvious, for example, in the argument about nepotism. Secondly, as the argument about skills and divisions between women illustrates, it is a matter of interpretation and disputation whether the consequences that are noted are good, bad, or neither. Finally, the constraints placed upon innovative transformative politics by historical 'givens' are also a matter of interpretation and relative evaluation, as the argument between Kishwar and Mazumdar shows. Hence, the broadly consequentialist reasoning of arguments against quotas fails to be conclusive.

However, the most important political challenge to gender quotas comes from that part of the electorate that sees itself as only just beginning to emerge in the political mainstream. The leadership claiming to represent this part of the electorate holds that the bid to introduce the women's Bill on gender quotas is an upper caste ploy to stem the rising tide of lower caste men in legislative bodies (Rajshekhar 1998; *Times of India* 1999a).

In order to respond to this challenge, we shall need to reframe the justification for gender quotas in identitarian terms. For this, an excursion into theory to equip us with the necessary conceptual tools becomes urgent.

II. Conceptual tools

I now turn to my second object of engaging with the question of the justification for gender quotas at a second-order level. Political representation is a chief means of participation in representative democratic governments. However, to some people it might seem that the investment in improving the standing of a group within traditionally defined spheres of governance would be misdirected. They would remind us of the potential of recovering 'feminist politics as subversion' (Menon 1997: 41). I think that this is an unnecessary closing off of legitimate political options. There is enough scope for political intervention of the traditional *and* non-traditional kinds, fortunately, matching the different proclivities of political activists and their different locations in the polity. Thus Bickford points out that 'identity plays different kinds of political roles' and 'is related to power in different ways' (Bickford 1997: 119). Without meaning to undermine the profound influence of 'politicising the personal' for many women, then, there is an argument to be made for greater political participation by women through increasing their representation in legislative bodies.

Similarly, questions have to be asked about the meaning of 'public'. Whilst Pateman (1988) has argued that the restricted entry of women into government is no more surprising than the 'fact' of their general exclusion from the 'public' domain, Fraser (1992) has queried the notion of the 'public' operating in this 'factual' claim. Sparks (1997) suggests in a similar vein that the 'public' must be reconceptualised to include the non-traditional arenas where activities aimed at collective goals are carried out. In the idealised picture, 'bourgeois public spheres' are 'aimed at mediating between society and the state by holding the state accountable to society via publicity' (Fraser 1992: 112). But alternative historiography shows that the 'official public sphere ... was, and indeed is, the prime institutional site for the construction of the consent that defines the new, hegemonic mode of domination' (ibid.: 117). The question, however, whether the 'public sphere' must be criticised for being a utopian ideal or exposed as an instrument of domination is not so important. It is, as Fraser herself acknowledges, 'perhaps both, but actually neither' (ibid.: 117). Women's political activities may not have been granted the same status as men's, but women were a part of the public sphere, as members of *weak publics*. Now, think of the sovereign Parliament as 'a public sphere *within* the state', as a 'strong' public in comparison to 'weak publics' (ibid.: 134, her emphasis). What becomes more important, on this construal of the public sphere, is to get a clearer picture of what kinds of public women were excluded, and which women were excluded more than others. We can do this if, 'rather than rejecting identity', we 'delve into its complicated political meanings' (Bickford 1997: 118). The double advantage of such a move is that it allows us, first, to acknowledge the ways in which some women succeed in *directly* participating in the formation of collective goals, through various extra-parliamentary though institutionalised forums. Secondly, it helps us to identify the obstacles that prevent other women from having the opportunity to do so.

In conclusion, Fraser's idea of the 'heterogeneous public' including both, strong and weak publics, allows a variegated understanding of political action. Thus, calls for gender quotas, which necessarily involve the 'protector' state, can sit alongside 'dissident citizenship' (Sparks 1997) expressed in 'dharnas', demonstrations and other political activities of civil disobedience. In the case of India, we do not have to address the underlying causes of women's exclusion 'instead' of the designed entry of women (Singh 1997: 13; Kishwar 1996). We can do both. A dichotomous understanding of the political sphere, by contrast, fails to recognise the multiple possibilities that a diversified, decentralised feminist activism can take up. It also takes a rather crude additive view of the 'situation' of women and misunderstands the nature of 'collective' action. Above all, it misrepresents the praxis of women actually engaged in political action in the various publics they find themselves in.

III. Identity concerns

A theoretical framework more suitable than consequentialism for the discussion of the policy of gender quotas is that of *identity concerns*. Its main principle would be that *we must judge public policies in terms of their sensitivity to the identities of people for whom they are designed*. Note, by contrast, that consequentialism does not suggest what value should be placed on identity as such compared to the value placed on the preferences for other goods. The value of having a sense of identity (for example, as a woman and/or citizen and/or member of a caste) is merely one of many goods that are aggregated along with other goods such as remunerated work or status in society. Let me hasten to add that my object here is not to evaluate consequentialism as such. Rather, I am suggesting that if, as feminists, we are concerned with whether or not the political change of instituting gender quotas is in the interests of women, then we need to look further than weighing consequences of the policy of gender quotas. We need to get clearer about what it *means* to identify with other women.

Some feminists have doubted the worth of identity politics.[7] In order for the principle I am suggesting to have any credence, I need to at least indicate the direction in which an answer to some of the feminists' objections to identity politics lies. For a start let us note that without conceptualising women as a collectivity, 'it is not possible to conceptualise oppression as a systematic, structured, institutional process' (Young 1994: 718). But one's identity, as I understand it, is not just a simple given, but a complex process of 'identification with'. If we want to live in a world where interpersonal relations are governed by mutual respect and acknowledgement of persons, we must pay due attention to the identity concerns of people from the first person perspective. Public policies that deny these identities, or fail to respect them, are objectionable on the ground that they undermine the conditions of genuine reciprocity and therefore destroy the possibility of building a world of closer human ties.

By the first person perspective I mean 'my sense of who I am' to the extent that such a self-identification determines which others I will subjectively identify with for a common project. The later Sartrean distinction between being a part of a collective which is interconnected by the relation of seriality (as in a queue for a bus) and being a part of a group which is bound together by shared projects is very useful in this regard. Feminist theorising of group identity in these terms, differentiating between 'passively mediated ensembles and intentionally created ones' (Kruks 1995: 15; Young 1994), explains the conundrum of seeking motivational identification with other women without presumptively essentialising them.

Women are globally a part of the serial collectivity 'women' which is amorphously defined by their respective *passive* situation in a world constructed as heterosexual and defined by a sexual division of labour. Each one of us is a part of various collectivities. What is distinctive about these is that there is no self-consciousness of having a shared project, although we may be individually negotiating the same problem in the world that is given to us. Out of those collectivities emerge groups of women who share some project or other aimed at removing the constraints on their activity. Such groups may fall back into seriality when the common project is abandoned or lost. Collectivities form the milieu in which those individual women from disintegrated groups may then seek to form other groups with other shared projects.

The distinction between collectivities and groups allows us to dispel some confusion about what may be expected out of the praxis of women demanding gender quotas. Feminists who demand gender quotas must surely know that even women who have formed into a group as women may be called upon to respond to the allegiances of other possible groups (class-, religious-, caste-based ones). Gender quotas will only enable some possibilities for the formation of women's groups that will hopefully be directed by ever more global and valuable shared projects.

The framework of identity concerns also offers an alternative justification for representation. Representative governments need not just be expedient arrangements for public decision-making in rapidly transforming societies. Representation may no longer allow the face-to-face interactions of the direct democracies of ancient times but it can also provide us with the opportunity to identify with others. The process of trusting my vote to a candidate and/or a party I choose to support, is a process in which I can *form* communal bonds of solidarity. My identity is affirmed or denied or negotiated by my participation in the process of choosing representatives. It is with political representation that the really hard questions arise regarding how a group can be carved out of various people who simultaneously belong to different collectivities. A collectivity born out of the relation of seriality, say the collectivity of women demanding gender quotas, has the potential of becoming a group with common goals and shared projects. The point to note, however, is that group formation is not an entirely self-directed activity. There are a host of unintended consequences of collective action that may turn out to be obstacles in future projects and thus hamper the formation of other valuable groups. To that extent, engaging in an exercise of unravelling possible consequences of pursuing a project is useful, without falling in the trap of *justifying* the shared projects in a consequentialist way.

The identity of being a woman, of belonging to the group women, is especially difficult for some to accept as a basis for representation because women are also at the same time poor or rich, educated or illiterate, upper caste or lower caste and so on. Hence, some theorists prefer to address the concerns of women indirectly, as the concerns, for example, of the poor, the illiterate, or the lower caste. The displacement of one identity for another signals the value a theorist places on a particular identity-preserving/undermining policy. For example, one may argue that reservations in the case of the Scheduled Castes were meant to address the economic want they suffer and to undo the social disadvantage that flows from such economic want (Gupta 1997: 1977). From such a point of view, an approach to reservations that seeks to undercut caste identity is more valuable than one that perpetuates it even as both may be motivated by concerns to reverse disadvantages stemming from caste status (ibid.: 1971). One may similarly argue against the demand for gender quotas on the grounds that focusing on gender hampers the formation of a 'class-based' identity. This I take to be another case of a needlessly dichotomous mode of thought. Our identities are mediated by the world in which we live. If the world in which we live is in fact class-divided as well as patriarchal, how could this material mediation be 'overridden' or 'undercut' by an attempt to form women into a group as women? While identifying with women as women in some arenas of public life, working women can still identify with working men in other (overlapping) arenas of public life.

However, more women in the Parliament in effect means that fewer men get in. Here, *as* men and *as* women, the interests of the two collectivities clash. It is hardly surprising that the women's Bill was so easily scuttled in the predominantly male Indian Parliament,[8] before it was finally introduced on 23 December 1999. Moreover, the strongest opposition to the tabling of the legislation for a gender quota came from the leaders of the other backward castes. Men from these caste groups are well aware of the relative disadvantage that women from lower castes have with respect to upper caste women, who are more articulate, educated and independent. They do not expect a gender quota to help them improve the overall political standing of their caste groups, because they fear that the sole purpose of the Bill is to check the increase in the number of backward caste men in legislative bodies.[9]

An identity-based justification for gender quotas must address this fear. On my analysis, the multiple position of lower caste women is a given in which they have to *existentially* form their shared projects. They form one collective with lower caste men, and another with upper caste women. The possibility of forming group solidarities exists on both fronts. The question for them to decide is which of those solidarities they take as opening further possibilities for them. Their identification with women of the upper castes may in their experience be in danger of lapsing them back into a relation of seriality with women. Or they may fear that when the women's Bill is objected to in their name, it is not their disadvantage which is the prime concern but the narrower electoral prospects of lower caste men.

From a feminist point of view what matters is that more women participate in legislative bodies. It is of secondary importance which caste group they come from.[10] But one may ask—can women of one social collectivity represent those of another collectivity? Much discussion in feminist literature has focused on the *problem* of women speaking about women without substituting the dominant modes of the self-understanding of highly-educated, mobile, middle-class, westernised (white) women for the voices of all the other women—the illiterate, the poor, the lower caste, the non-western. It is important to distinguish this legitimate concern of the feminist from the sceptical question about any representation as such. The main difference in the two approaches is that the feminist one is committed to evolving ways of communicating between women and in most cases between women and men. The feminist is therefore cautious of the unintended, but possible consequence of silencing some women in the effort made to 'speak for' them. The plainly sceptical approach, on the other hand, does not raise these problems with any expectation of finding a solution.

The determination of our identities depends to a great extent upon the contingent circumstances we find ourselves in. Further, others often interpret for us what these circumstances are. Different interpretations of the world we inhabit support different identities. Our choice lies in identifying with a particular interpretation of our world out of the different interpretations available to us. Our current self-interpretation is only one among the several interpretations available to us. It is the one that we have identified with in our present location.

IV. Representation

We accept another as our representative if we identify with the interpretation of our world that s/he offers. There is a special relation we may have to our political representatives if our dependence upon them stretches beyond defending our current interests to articulating a possible future in which we matter.

We trust the promise of representation they make to us only if as a minimum requirement, we accept the plausibility of the programme of transformation they offer. A stronger requirement for representation would be that the person who represents me embodies my own hopes and aspirations for the future by sharing projects with me. It is only in this sense that my representative may 'mirror' me.

'Mirror' and 'elected' representation need to be carefully distinguished. The idea of 'group' representation promotes the protection of the interests of smaller, or less powerful, 'groups' under a system of majority rule. However, 'group representation' is an ambiguous term because it can mean either 'mirror representation' or 'elected representation'. On the first interpretation, only someone who shares the *definitive* characteristic of the 'group' can adequately represent others like her. On this view only women can represent women, only Hindus can represent Hindus and only Punjabis can represent Punjabis. On the second interpretation, the *procedure of election* alone determines the adequacy of representation. The identity of those elected, i.e., 'who' they are, is not important. If the elections are rigged, or in some other way not in line with procedures laid down and collectively agreed, then the chosen representatives are not truly elected representatives. Otherwise, 'free' and 'fair' elections guarantee the legitimacy of representation.[11]

The idea of mirror representation rests on the belief that the 'barriers of experience' are insurmountable; for example, it may be claimed that only a woman can understand what it is to be a woman.

> Just as a nobleman cannot represent a plebeian and the latter cannot represent a nobleman, so man, no matter how honest he may be, cannot represent a woman. Between the representatives and the represented there must be an absolute identity of interests.[12]

The founding idea of mirror representation (that only like should represent like) is born out of the struggle of members of excluded groups for recognition of their needs and interests. The experiences of being excluded are expressed in historically specific claims that ought to be read in specific terms. The demand for mirror representation does not necessarily depend upon or lead to the suggestion of any *essential* difference between the experiences of men and woman—save the difference that is *constructed* by their specific location in the dominant social hierarchies of their times. Inasmuch as our identities are socially constructed and our capacities for identification with others limited by our identities, indeed, there may be barriers of experience that are, at particular junctures, insurmountable. Therefore, there may be specific needs and interests that at those junctures remain absent from the political agenda.

The retort of those who support 'elected' representation is that the claim that men cannot understand the needs of women provides an excuse for *not trying* to understand women (making it a self-fulfilling prophecy). A stronger argument for elected representation, as the only coherent notion of political representation, is that non-understanding 'cuts both ways'. If men are deemed unfit for representing women, then women too are supposedly incapable of representing men. Either way 'what' is placed on the political agenda gets limited by 'who' puts it there. Phillips (1995) claims that 'the separation between "who" and "what" is to be represented, and the subordination of the first to the second is very much up for question. The politics of ideas is being challenged by an alternative politics of presence' (ibid.: 5).

By 'a politics of ideas', Phillips means a politics where the ideas someone stands for determine the loyalties of electors and not the identities of candidates. From the point of view of such a politics, the main reason why we elect particular people to represent us must be that we share ideas—political beliefs, goals, aspirations—with them and not on the basis that they are Hindu or Muslim, or brahmin or dalit, or man or woman. This is a conception of a free market of ideas, which works on the assumption that ideas are separable from presence. *Who* our representatives are, on this view, does not matter to whether they can effectively represent us in decision-making bodies such as the Parliament.

However, Phillips' argument is that if we are interested in the transformation of the political agenda, then we must make an attempt to draw people from different collectivities into the process of decision-making.

> Since all the options are not already in play, we need to ensure a more even-handed balance of society's groups in the arena of public discussion ... If fair representation also implies fair representation of what would emerge under more favourable conditions, we have to address the composition of the decision-making assemblies as well as the equal right to vote (ibid.: 45).

Thus, she argues that in some cases the *presence* of people from particular groups is necessary to transform the political agenda. Collectivities such as of women and dalits have been excluded from political decision-making bodies for so long, that 'what' their interests are, *from their own point of view*, is not clearly articulated. This is not to say that they do not *know* what their interests are. One may know what is in one's interest, without being able to translate that knowledge into the language of political demands. The reason why we talk of 'women' or 'dalits' as a potential group is that there is a basis of shared experience— of vulnerability, of threats to dignity, and much else, even if there may be much less of a basis of shared ideas. However, note that while Phillips' analysis lends support to the case for gender quotas in legislative bodies, her warning that changing the gender composition 'cannot present itself as a guarantee' (Phillips 1995: 83) qualifies that support.

An identity-based justification for a gender quota, such as I have offered, also makes a case for representation beyond merely 'elected' representation. However, the brief discussion[13] above suggests that identity concerns do not have an independent value for Phillips but are merely instrumental in ensuring equal representation of the interests of disadvantaged 'groups'. By contrast with her, I work with a stronger notion of identity from the first-person perspective. What matters when choosing representatives, on my analysis, is that one is at least able to identify with the programme of transformation that is offered. However, the stronger requirement—that the chosen representatives embody some of my own hopes and aspirations—necessitates acknowledging an additional symbolic value of same-sex or same-caste representatives. Moreover, if gender quotas are only designed to change the content of the political agenda, as in Phillips, one also ignores that changing the nature of the 'strong public' makes a difference to the relation it has with the weaker publics in which women traditionally participate. Thus, the potential for political participation of women more generally is affected by changing the gender composition of legislative bodies, not just the agendas of these bodies.[14]

V. Conclusion

In the course of this paper, I have argued that justifications for gender quotas in legislative bodies must move beyond an evaluation of the consequences of following such a policy. Reflection on the Indian debate shows that selective emphases and different interpretations of the probable consequences of following a policy of gender quotas lead to a stalemate. I have suggested that paying attention to identity concerns is a more fruitful way of understanding the opposition and support for the use of gender quotas in ensuring the representation of women in legislative bodies.[15] In this respect, the idea of 'heterogeneous' publics suggests that different women have been excluded from parliamentary politics in different ways. Hence, political measures for their inclusion too must be conceptualised with sensitivity to the differences between them. As we have seen in the case of the debate in India, some may favour interventionist policies like gender quotas, while others may favour gradual reform boosted perhaps by efforts to democratise the polity, through education, electoral reforms or even economic advancement. On my analysis, the quarrel between interventionists and gradualists cannot be settled by an impersonal evaluation of the consequences of following either path. However, the picture becomes clearer if we pay attention to what these measures mean *personally* to those who are affected by them, i.e., how they affect their sense of who they are and which groups they can see themselves as forming.[16] In this regard, it is worth noting that at a recent meeting in Chennai, women from more than 40 voluntary organisations, including both rural and urban based, called for a united support for the women's Bill (*The Hindu*, 1991: 1).

I have argued that gender quotas will hold a significant, though limited, promise of enabling the group formation of women motivated by the shared project of increasing their participation in politics. The limitation arises from the fact that it is not just my passive location within a collectivity, but the possibility of my active 'identification-with' others that determines whether or not a project, such as that of the struggle for gender quotas, is valuable. But it would be a mistake to view the group formation that the project of gender quotas promises as essentialising or trapping women in their identity as women. I have emphasised that a closer look at the manner in which groups form out of collectivities, and the open possibility of regrouping that this process allows, should assuage at least some misgivings about identity politics associated with the political measure of gender quotas. To the extent that I have tried to remove such misgivings, especially those expressed by Kishwar (1996), my support for the specific legislation for gender quotas is an indirect one. If an alternative legislation were put on offer, provided that it does not trade on the myth of 'free' and 'fair' elections and provided that it addresses the complex question of how to negotiate the identities of women from lower/backward castes and minorities with a view to empower *them*, then that alternative legislation should also be discussed alongside the currently proposed one.

Acknowledgements

Some of the ideas here were first presented at the annual conference of the British Association of South Asian Studies held at Bath in 1997. I thank Yogendra Yadav, who was present on this occasion, for supporting the idea of a philosophical reflection on an urgent practical matter. A shorter version of this article, focusing on the general philosophical debates connected with women's identity, political participation and representation is published as Dhanda (1999). I am grateful to Christine Battersby, the general editor of Women's Philosophy Review, for permission to reproduce and use parts of the discussion in that article. Diemut Bubeck's help in clarifying many of my fuzzy ideas is gratefully acknowledged. The suggestions for improvement offered by Alan Apperley and Pritam Singh who read and commented on successive drafts were very useful. Tanya Singh retrieved files that I had given up for lost. I thank them all.

Notes

[1] The French Senate has recently passed a motion by a massive 289 to eight votes calling for a Constitutional Amendment to boost gender parity in public offices. If both the houses of Parliament pass the motion, Article Three of the Constitution will be changed to include the words: 'The law will encourage equal access for women and men to political life and elected posts'. What this encouragement materialises into in the shape of new laws is not clear at this stage. But the move has generated a debate in France about the possible use of gender quotas to achieve parity in the gender composition of elected assemblies dividing feminists along the predictable lines of 'grass-roots pressure' versus 'legislative paths' to reform (Henley 1999).

[2] I shall assume a sufficiently general and inclusive marker for who counts as 'feminist'. Let those who disagree tell us why a narrower definition is preferable to the following one. A feminist is someone who is practically guided by the belief that, women suffer systematic disadvantages in social and political terms because they are women. Clearly, in being 'practically guided', a feminist hopes to succeed in removing or at least lessening some of the identified disadvantages. Such a definition might include even those who have avowedly disowned the 'label'.

[3] The 'Women's Bill' (in the first instance called 'The Constitution (81st Amendment) Bill, 1996) proposes to introduce this reservation with the reserved constituencies to be determined by lottery. The one-third women's quota is also applicable to the Scheduled Caste/Scheduled Tribe reservation, except where the number of seats in the SC/ST reserved constituencies is less than three. I shall indicate below the complex nature of the opposition to this measure for including women and the equally complex response it deserves, since this issue raises the general difficulty of prioritising feminist concerns over allegedly 'other' equally justified concerns of inclusion of 'other' marginalised groups. I think that it is absurd to actually try to separate the oppression resulting from one's being a woman from that resulting from one's being a member of a lower/backward caste. Being oppressed as a 'lower/backward caste woman' is not only a specific way of being oppressed as a woman, but also a specific way of being oppressed as a member of a lower/backward caste. Even though it seems that the means one chooses to fight the oppression at a particular juncture have the effect of prioritising a particular practical identity, say that of being a woman, one must remember that it is not merely the 'identity' of being a woman that is

reinforced, but the *real* woman who is empowered. If that real woman is *also* a member of a lower/backward caste, then a member of a lower/backward caste is empowered when she is empowered.

4 Information obtained from Royal Norwegian Embassy (1997). There is no author or date of publication of this leaflet, but its contents suggest a publication date later than 1994.

5 In the light of this and other examples of such a demonstration effect on centre-right parties, it seems otiose to lament that the 'emancipatory slogans of the women's movement of the 1970s and the early 1980s have been hijacked by the Hindu Right to consolidate their hold over upper caste educated middle classes' (Raman 1999). Likewise to say that the 'BJP has no moral right to talk of women's empowerment' (Pati 1998) because some of its MPs publicly proclaim patriarchal beliefs is to miss the significance of internal differences within hegemonic parties. Another way of looking at the matter is of seeing the Hindu Right itself in a more differentiated way, as consisting of some forces that pull it towards more progressive measures and other forces that drag it in the opposite direction. It is possible that the progressive element within the Hindu Right would gain an upper hand, provided that there were a general consensus on the need for legislation in favour of gender equity. Despite my criticism of the complaint about 'hijacking', I am in agreement with Vasanthi Raman in that 'emphasising the dimension of gender oppression at the expense of other oppressions (of caste, ethnicity, class, religion, etc.) glosses over the complex and intricate ways in which gender oppression is embedded in these categories' (Raman 1999). In line with my argument (see note 3 above) she even concedes that 'affirmative action for women would certainly play a role in undermining male and upper caste dominance' (ibid.) provided that our response to gender oppression is 'more subtle and nuanced'. My point is that if the legislation for gender quotas is found too 'crude', then the opposition to this legislation also needs to rise to the task of providing 'more subtle and nuanced' alternatives. Until such alternatives emerge, we should discuss seriously the legislation that is at present on offer.

6 Writing on women in Spain, Burns (1999), explains that in the labour market where women lag considerably behind men, the government has introduced progressive legislation. On the one hand there is the provision to avail a paternity leave of 10 weeks, should a father wish to substitute the mother for part of her 16 weeks maternity leave. On the other hand the labour ministry funds training courses and 'up to 60 per cent of available places on such courses are reserved for women should the programme deal with skills in job sectors where women are under-represented' (Burns 1999).

7 See Bickford (1997) for a comprehensive account of objections to identity politics, and her pertinent replies.

8 The current number of women MPs is 43, which is eight per cent of the total.

9. Thus, Mulayam Singh Yadav (SP) reportedly said that the Congress and the BJP were colluding against the poor and the downtrodden sections (*TOI* 1999a). Interestingly, however, he is also reported to have said that the Samajwadi Party was not against the Bill but wanted a sub-quota for backward classes and minorities. Indeed, some of the National Democratic Alliance (NDA) partners have also expressed the feeling that the demand for sub-quotas should be taken into consideration (*TOI* 1999b).

10. It should be clear from my arguments in favour of identity concerns that should some women choose to prioritise their caste/religious identity, that is their prerogative. The question of the inclusion/exclusion of backward castes and minorities in the system of quotas, expressed in the demand for sub-quotas must be discussed in terms of what backward caste women and women from religious minorities want and can reasonably hope for.

11. But note that 'free' and 'fair' elections may nonetheless exhibit a systematic gender bias. Using data from Indian elections from 1952–97 compiled by the Centre for the Study of Developing Societies (CSDS) data unit, Chandrika Parmar argues that even with an increase in the number and proportion of women contestants 'the success rate of women contestants has steadily fallen' throughout the period 1952–97. 'The logic of free competition', she rightly concludes, 'is likely to work to the disadvantage of women' (Parmar 1997: 50).

12. This is a citation by S. Vegetti Finzi 'Female Identity between Sexuality and Maternity' in G. Bock and S. James (eds.) (1993), *Beyond Equality and Difference*, London, p. 128, from a claim made by a group of Frenchwomen to a place in the Estates General in 1789 quoted by Phillips (1995: 52)

13. For a further discussion of Phillips (1995) see Dhanda (1997).

14. Amartya Sen (2000) argued in a recent lecture that the empowerment of young women was one of the most important factors in controlling fertility and thus stemming the growth of population. Such a view lends support to interventionist measures such as gender quotas or similar effective legislation to increase women's political participation. What we have in front of us is not only the prospect of radically enhancing women's role in political decision-making but also of creating a socio-political environment of greater credibility of women's power. Increasing women's power has ramifications in some very pressing areas of concern such as the control of population through enhancing women' control of their fertility.

15. According to recent reports it appears that there may be a prospect of reconciliation between the ruling party's stance on the Women's Bill as it stands and that of the opposition, especially the SP's objection to it. For whatever it is worth, this is reflected in the PM's speech to the House after the Bill was introduced. He reportedly said that the Bill was 'not the last word' and a solution to the demand for a sub-quota for minorities and backward classes could be found (*TOI* 1999c: 12).

16. One way of determining what gender quotas mean personally to women is to ask them. In the Indian case, I think we will find that women want

gender quotas. This seems to be the likely outcome following the one-third reservation for women in village level local government. According to Mitra and Ansah (1998: 16), 'over a million women now sit as elected representatives in local bodies'. I expect that their praxis will have clarified for them the value of identifying with other women and that due to their experience they are likely to support gender quotas in the Parliament.

References

Burns, Tom. 1999. 'Politics a Fertile Power Base'. Financial Times Survey on Spain. *Financial Times.* 20 May.

Bickford, Susan. 1997. 'Anti-Anti-Identity Politics: Feminism, Democracy, and the Complexities of Citizenship'. *Hypatia. Special Issue on Citizenship in Feminism: Identity, Action and Locale.* ed. Kathleen B. Jones. vol. 12. no. 4. Fall. pp. 111–31.

Dhagambar, Vasudha. 1997. 'Reservations about Further Reservations'. *Seminar* 457. September. pp. 20–22.

Dhanda, Meena. 1997. 'The Politics of Presence', Review of Phillips (1995). *Seminar* 457. September. pp. 59–61.

———.1999. 'Justifications for Gender Quotas in Legislative Bodies: A Consideration of Identity and Representation' in *Feminist Political Philosophy.* eds. Bubeck and Klaushoser. Special issue of *Womens Philosophy Review.* no. 21.

Fraser, Nancy. 1992. 'Rethinking the Public Sphere' in *Habermas and the Public Sphere.* ed. Craig Calhoun. Cambridge: MIT Press. pp. 109–42.

Gupta, Dipankar. 1997. 'Positive Discrimination and the Question of Fraternity: Contrasting Ambedkar and Mandal on Reservations'. *Economic and Political Weekly.* 2 August. vol. XXXII. no. 31. pp. 1971–78.

Henley, Jon. 1999. 'Boost to Equality in French Politics'. *The Guardian.* 6 March.

Kannabiran, Kalpana and Vasanth Kannabiran. 1997. 'From Social Action to Political Action: Women and the 81st Amendment'. *Economic and Political Weekly,* 1 February. pp. 196–97.

Kymlicka, Will. 1995. *Multicultural Citizenship: A Liberal Theory of Minority Rights.* Oxford: Oxford University Press.

Kishwar, Madhu. 1996. 'Women and Politics: Beyond Quotas'. *Economic and Political Weekly.* 26 October. vol. XXXI. no. 43. pp. 2867–74.

Kruks, Sonia. 1995. 'Identity Politics and Dialectical Reason: Beyond an Epistemology of Provenance'. *Hypatia.* vol. 10. no. 2. Spring. pp. 1–22.

Mazumdar, Vina. 1997. 'Historical Soundings'. *Seminar* 457. September. pp. 14–19.

Mendus, Susan. 1987. 'Kant: An Honest but Narrow-Minded Bourgeois?' in *Women in Western Political Philosophy.* eds. Ellen Kennedy and Susan Mendus. Brighton: Wheatsheaf. pp. 21–43.

Menon, Nivedita. 1997. 'Reservations and Representation'. *Seminar* 457. September. pp. 38–41.

Mitra, Sumit and Javed Ansari (with Saba Naqvi Bhaumik). 1998. 'Scuttling the Bill'. *India Today International*. 27 July. pp. 12–18.
Parmar, Chandrika. 1997. 'Factfile 1952–1997'. *Seminar* 457. p. 50.
Pateman, Carol. 1988. *The Sexual Contract*. Oxford: Polity Press.
Pati, Kumudini. 1998. 'Women's Reservation Bill and the BJP Drama'. *Liberation: Central Organ of CPI (ML)*. July–August. pp. 4–7.
Phillips, Anne. 1995. *The Politics of Presence*. Oxford: Oxford University Press.
Raman, Vasanthi. 1999. 'Women's Reservation and Democratisation: An Alternative Perspective'. *Economic and Political Weekly*. 11–17 December.
Rajshekhar, P.T. ed. 1998. *Dalit Voice* (The Voice of the Persecuted Nationalities Denied Human Rights. vol. 17. no. 18. 1–15 August. pp. 3–5.
Royal Norwegian Embassy. 1997. *Women in Politics: Equality and Empowerment*, London/Norway.
Sarvasy, Wendy. 1997. 'Social Citizenship from a Feminist Perspective'. *Hypatia*. vol. 12. no. 4. Fall. pp. 54–71.
Sen, Amartya. 2000. 'Six Billion and All That'. Public lecture in Oxford. 3 February.
Singh, Tejbir. 1997. 'The Problem' in *Empowering Women: A Symposium on Political Reservations for Women*. ed. Tejbir Singh. *Seminar* 457. September. pp. 12–13.
Singhvi, Abhishek M. 1997. 'The Women's Reservation Bill'. *Seminar* 457. pp. 25–30.
Sparks, Hollway. 1997. 'Dissident Citizenship: Democratic Theory, Political Courage, and Activist Women'. *Hypatia. Special Issue on Citizenship in Feminism: Identity, Action and Locale*. op. cit., vol. 12. no. 4. Fall. pp. 74–110.
The Hindu. 1999. 'Call to Pass Women's Bill in Budget Session'. 7 February. p. 1.
The Times of India (TOI). 1999a. 'Women's Bill Runs in OBC Barrier'. 21 December. pp. 1 and 8.
——.1999b. 'Women's Quota Bill to be tabled today'. 23 December. p. 1.
——.1999c. 'High Drama as Women's Bill is Introduced in LS'. 24 December. pp. 1 and 12.
Young, Iris Marion. 1994. 'Gender as Seriality: Thinking about Women as a Social Collective'. *Signs: Journal of Women in Culture and Society*. vol. 19. no. 3. Spring. pp. 713–38.

Published in *Economic and Political Weekly*, 12 August 2000.

Elusive 'Woman': Feminism and Women's Reservation Bill

NIVEDITA MENON

Feminist issues usually appear as something else altogether in public discourse. So for instance, in the Uniform Civil Code debate, the question of women's rights to property and status within marriage gets posed as a matter of community rights versus national integrity. Sexual harassment in the workplace inevitably gets translated into a debate over 'misuse' of laws and the need to protect men from false charges—in public discourse, the victim of sexual harassment is invariably the 'respectable' man, falsely accused. Women getting lower wages than men is recast as a question of differential pay for different categories of work, it being purely coincidental that women are concentrated in the lowest paid categories. In short, an important political task for the women's movement has usually been to problematise the terms of public discourse precisely in order to make visible the gendered aspects of structures of power.

However, the debate over reservations for women is unusual in this respect. When the Women's Reservation Bill (WRB) first appeared as the 81st Amendment Bill in 1996, proposing to reserve 33 per cent of seats in Parliament for women, it burst into public discourse full-blown as a 'women's' (indeed, a feminist) issue, and continues to be debated largely in terms of women's rights. It is becoming increasingly clear however, that the questions thrown up by the timing of the Bill and the responses to it cannot be understood solely within the framework of women's rights. This paper attempts to relocate these questions in a more complex matrix of political identities in order to realise their full significance. I also argue that the debates around the Bill reveal a more fundamental set of questions about the issues of citizenship, representation, and the subject of feminist politics.

Historical background

The question of reservations for women in representative institutions has long been debated in India. The issue of reservations for women had come up in the Constituent Assembly but had been rejected by women representatives as it was felt to be unnecessary, since the working of democracy in the normal course would ensure the representation of all sections of Indian society. The suggestion was also seen to underestimate the strength of women to compete as equals. Over 25 years later, the Committee on the Status of Women in India (CSWI) considered the same question. It was agreed that rural women's experience and problems had remained undervalued and invisible. The CSWI therefore unanimously recommended the establishment of statutory women's panchayats. Prior to this, the Panchayat Acts of most states had reserved one or two seats for women, to be filled by nomination if no woman was returned by election. But this had remained a token gesture and the CSWI recommended instead that the reserved seats be occupied by elected office-bearers of the proposed women's panchayats.

On the question of reservations for women in Parliament and state legislatures, the debate took a shape familiar to us today. The arguments made in favour of reservation were mainly that (a) political parties because of their generally patriarchal character were reluctant to sponsor women candidates, and therefore reservations were necessary; (b) reservations would increase the number of women in Parliament all at once and they would be able to act as a strong lobby. At present, their being in a small minority inhibits their effective participation in the interests of women; (c) the presence of more women in Parliament would lead to a change in direction of debates and policy.

Arguments made against reservations were mainly that (a)

this would run counter to the principle of equality in the Constitution; (b) women cannot be equated to socially backward communities as women are not a socially homogeneous group; (c) women's interests cannot be isolated from those of other economic, social and political strata; (d) such a system would lead to similar demands from other groups and communities, thus posing a threat to national integration. Finally the CSWI by a majority decided to uphold the position taken in the Constituent Assembly and rejected the reservation of seats for women in Parliament and state assemblies.

The latest phase of the debate began with the National Perspective Plan (NPP) 1988–2000 recommending a 30 per cent reservation of seats for women at panchayat and zilla parishad levels. Subsequently states like Karnataka and Gujarat implemented some form of reservation for women in Panchayati Raj Institutions. In 1993, the 73rd and 74th Constitution Amendments provided for one-third reservation for women nationwide in these bodies. By the time of the general elections of 1996, women's organisations put forward a joint demand to all political parties for reservations for women in state assemblies and Parliament (Mazumdar 1997). The major parties supported the demand although they themselves gave less than 15 per cent of their total number of tickets to women. The Reservation Bill was included in the Common Minimum Programme of the United Front which assumed office, and the 81st Amendment Bill was introduced in 1996, proposing 33 per cent reservation for women in Parliament. It could not be passed and was referred to a Joint Select Committee. In 1998 the Bill (now the 84th Amendment Bill), was introduced again by the BJP government to strong opposition, and was derailed once again. Its most recent incarnation is as the 85th Amendment Bill, introduced in December 1999, and its fate continues to be as uncertain as it ever was.

Gender and caste since 1980s

What were the developments between 1974 when women's movement activists in the CSWI rejected reservations for women in Parliament, and 1996, when almost the same representatives of the women's movement demanded such reservations? What were the shifts in the two intervening decades that would explain this change? In the years that passed, there were two significant developments in Indian politics. One had to do with challenges to the legitimacy of the national integrity argument. By the mid-1970s the legitimacy of the post-independence elites had begun to erode with the economic and political crisis precipitated by the failure of development planning. There was a resurgence of militancy in every section of society. Critical questions were arising as to whose interests were being protected by the 'integrity' of the nation state. By the mid-1980s various regional movements were challenging the inherited idea of Indian nationhood, and backward caste assertion had begun to transform the nature of the political arena and the composition of the Lok Sabha. Yogendra Yadav (1999) points out.

> The influx of lower orders into the field of democratic contestation has ... (made) it respectable to talk of caste in the public-political domain. The emergence of social justice as a rubric to talk about caste equity (and) political representation of castes and communities ... is a distinct achievement of this period.[1]

The other development was that women had emerged as a significant force in politics. Women had been at the forefront of the movements against corruption and price-rise that preceded the imposition of Emergency. The 1980s saw the emergence of the vocal and visible autonomous women's groups which placed feminist issues firmly on the public agenda—dowry, rape, violence against women. At the same time it was clear that women were under-represented on representative bodies. Already by the time of the NPP, therefore, there was both an acknowledgement of women's militant participation in politics as well as of their absence in decision-making bodies. Vina Mazumdar, who was member secretary of the CSWI, points out how as 'daughters of independence' her generation had been critical of special representation, but gradually 'we have found our understanding of nation-building changing radically'

(Mazumdar 1997). By 1996 then, the 'daughters of independence' had come to acknowledge that abstract citizenship was only a cover for privilege, and that difference had to be acknowledged.

However, the point I would emphasise here is that the emergence of women as a significant grouping in Indian politics is only one of two factors shifting the consensus on womens' reservations. The other, the transformation of the caste composition of Parliament and the growing presence of backward castes through successive elections is an equally significant development. I will argue that these two very different (even opposed) sets of concerns—feminist and upper caste—tied in at this particular conjuncture to produce the sudden general acceptability of women's reservations.

Is the WRB only about women?

The career of the Women's Reservations Bill in Parliament is striking for the high drama and rhetoric of women's rights that has accompanied it, the passionate opposition to the Bill being generally characterised by its supporters as anti-women and patriarchal. Some of the comments and phrases decrying the derailing of the Bill are illustrative—'a predominantly male Parliament developed cold feet' (Rai and Sharma 2000); '*Sansad par kabiz purush satta*';[2] 'Parliament was divided into men and women, the former all opposed to the Women's Reservations Bill';[3] 'Parliament is like an all-male club and I feel like an unwanted intruder';[4] 'On caste-based arguments in defence of male domination.'[5] Similarly, speculating about the reasons why political parties who supported the reservation of seats for women in local bodies are reluctant regarding similar legislation at the parliamentary level, Shirin Rai and Kumud Sharma wonder, 'Could it be that enhanced representation of women in the national Parliament spells a far greater and immediate challenge to the gendered status quo within the party political system?' Or conversely, 'Is it that the pattern of quota systems in India have shown that elite-based strategies of empowerment are less helpful to groups seeking greater recognition than those based on grass-roots institutions?' (Rai and Sharma 2000). In other words, is it the case that political parties resist the Bill because they fear it will empower women too much or too little? However, as Rai and Sharma unravel the actual arguments of the protagonists and antagonists of the Bill, it becomes clear that while the protagonists make their arguments in terms of gender justice, the arguments against the Bill come from two opposed positions—they stem either from opposition to reservations in general or from a belief that reservations for women should be extended to other disempowered groups (the quotas within quotas position) (Rai and Sharma 2000). The arguments against, in other words, are not 'anti-feminist'. In spite of their own evidence however, the writers continue to frame their discussion in terms of whether mainstream political bodies have 'embraced the gender justice agenda' or not.

It is now evident that to continue to understand the Bill in terms only of attitudes to women would be a partial exercise at best. Rather, I would argue that when we tease out the strands in the debate, we find two sets of arguments for and against.[6] There are feminist (or at least, pro-women) arguments for and against reservations for women, and (implicitly or explicitly) caste-based arguments for and against.

A feminist case for reservations is made in terms of the need for affirmative action to redress the situation of women. This argument comes from Left parties and women's groups. A characteristic statement of this kind is that made by Vasanth and Kalpana Kannabiran, long-time activists of the women's movement. 'Women's participation in the political process is critical both to the strengthening of democratic traditions and to their struggle against oppression.' But they are obstructed in such participation by 'power relations that ... operate at many levels of society from the most personal to the highly public'. It is necessary therefore to appropriate 'spaces in mainstream political arenas and reshape them' (Kannabiran 1997). A CPI(M) MP expresses another facet of this strand when she argues that while reservations policy per se is not democratic, it is nevertheless necessary to rectify existing imbalances. Thus, it is a partial measure, but one that is unavoidable if women are to participate effectively in politics (Bhattacharya 1997). Similarly, an editorial of *ML Update*, the weekly bulletin of CPI (ML)-Liberation, states that while 'formal equality in law hardly brings equality in society', the WRB is important as 'The moot point at this stage is to recognise women in their entirety as an oppressed category in an otherwise male-dominated society.' More importantly, the Bill 'may prove catalytic to the larger entry of women from backward and dalit castes in the political arena' (*ML Update* 1998). The feminist argument for reservations is thus made in terms of creating equality of opportunity in order to make real the formal equality given by the Constitution.

What could be called a pro-women case against reservations is made by Madhu Kishwar, the editor of *Manushi* (which calls itself 'a journal about women and society'), and by the Shetkari Mahila Aghadi (SMA), a peasant women's organisation founded in 1986. Their broad argument has to do with the concern that reservations will only bring to the fore the 'biwi-beti brigade'. The SMA in an 'Open Letter to MPs', signed by Gail Omvedt among others, said that quotas for women 'is being pushed by women in the creamy layer'. Omvedt too, opposes the WRB, terming one of the most disturbing aspects of the debate around it, 'the way it seemed to set (mainly upper caste) feminists against (mainly male) OBC leaders' (Omvedt 2000). The SMA prefers to put up all-women panels for panchayat elections as the experience of reservations in panchayats in Maharashtra has not been favourable—relatives of established male leaders are fielded, and there has been no impact at all on inefficiency and corruption. It suggests a more fundamental transformation in the election system, the introduction of three-seat constituencies, with each voter having three votes, one of which has to go to a woman. One seat is to be for the woman with the highest votes from among women candidates (SMA 1997).

Kishwar too originally backed the proposal of the SMA although now she has come up with a separate proposal (endorsed by Omvedt in a different form) which we will look at later in this paper. Kishwar believes that reservations are unnecessary because 'our country has a well-entrenched tradition whereby any party, politician or public figure who tries to bad-mouth women in public or opposes moves in favour of women's equality is strongly disapproved of. Hence, compared to many other parts of the world, it is relatively easy to get legislation favouring women passed in India' (Kishwar 1996). This is an amazing statement—a cursory look at newspapers would reveal that extremely patriarchal and sexist, at best protectionist, views of women are routinely publicly expressed in the course of rape trials and election campaigns, in police statements on violence against women, and the like. These are contested only by women's groups and women's wings of political parties, usually of the Left. As for legislation favouring women, Kishwar's is a surprisingly naïve understanding of Indian politics, and of how and why laws get passed. Take for instance, the right to abortion which she cites as an example. The Medical Termination of Pregnancy Bill was introduced as a population control measure in 1971 and the debate in Parliament was entirely within those terms. It is not surprising therefore that only two MPs opposed it. Abortion was not being discussed as a question of women's right over their bodies, but on the contrary, as a measure necessitated in order to achieve lower population growth. In the context of countries of the global South where 'overpopulation' is presented as the reason for poverty, state control of fertility is the problem for feminists, not the illegality of abortion. Therefore, the fact that this right took 'decades of struggle in the West' while it was 'enacted in India without a fight', as Kishwar puts it, has to be understood very differently. In other words, the passing of apparently 'feminist' legislation has to be located also in the context of the compulsions of ruling elites in order to understand the complex dynamics involved.[7] Eventually however, Kishwar concedes that 'our democracy has failed to include women in its purview', partly due to the Gandhian legacy which saw women's role in politics as self-sacrifice rather than as a bid for power, and more recently, because of the increasing corruption and criminalisation associated with politics (Kishwar 1996).

I term SMA and Kishwar's position as a 'pro-women' critique of reservations because their objections arise from focusing on women's interests, which they believe would be better served by other measures. The next set of arguments, which I term 'caste-based', take positions for and against reservations explicitly or implicitly, in terms of caste. The most reviled, explicitly caste-based opposition to women's reservations has been the derogatory reference of Sharad Yadav to the 'short-haired' women who would overrun Parliament. While this has been understood as a misogynist statement, we must see it also as expressing a legitimate fear that reservations for women would radically alter the composition of Parliament in favour of upper classes and upper castes—the term 'parkati mahilaen' in this context drawing upon a common stereotype of westernised and elite women. Of course this stereotype is sexist and misogynist, but that is not really the point here, because surely we are under no illusion that all the support for women's reservations comes from those who actively contest and reject such stereotypes. Rather, this kind of opposition to the Bill in its present form has to be recognised as arising from the politics of caste identity.

The idea of reservation for an undifferentiated category of 'women' has been uniformly denounced by politicians and writers speaking for backward castes and dalits. At its most explicit, such an argument attacks the Bill as an upper caste ploy to stem the rising tide of lower caste men in politics (Dhanda 2000).[8] In this context, we must take into account the experience of women's reservations in Panchayati Raj Institutions. Studies in Gujarat and Karnataka have confirmed that the entrenched power of the dominant castes has been strengthened by women's reservations.[9] It is not surprising then, that OBC and dalit leaders are highly suspicious of the WRB. In an interview, Mayawati, the Bahujan Samaj Party leader, demanded that there should be 50 per cent reservations for women, and within this, separate reservations for backward castes and minorities.[10] Mulayam Singh Yadav of the Samajwadi Party has consistently opposed the Bill, saying that in its present form it is anti-minority and anti-dalit.[11]

Most interestingly, Uma Bharati of the BJP (Bharatiya Janata Party), herself from a backward caste, has taken a position opposed to that of her party's. Unlike Sushma Swaraj, the upper caste BJP leader most vocal in support of the Bill, Uma Bharati makes a clear feminist argument for reservations, while asserting that a backward caste or dalit woman is doubly oppressed, and so should have a place within the quota. Characteristically, Uma Bharati does not grant a quota for Muslim women, even while conceding that they are among the most oppressed, for 'in a secular constitution, there can be no place for reservations based on religion'. This could push the country towards theocracy. She does not however, reject the idea of reservations for Muslims altogether. Her solution is instead, to give reservations to Muslim caste-groups included in the Mandal OBCs (Other Backward Classes), for example, julahe, bunkar, ansari. Thus, in a move which challenges BJP's nationalist Hindutva perspective, she decisively privileges caste identity.[12] It is this split within the party that keeps the BJP from pushing through the Bill, rather than mere 'hypocrisy' about gender justice, as many commentators have suggested, for I am persuaded that hypocrisy is all pervasive in politics, and cannot be treated as an explanatory device.

Within the caste-based opposition to the Bill I would place another strand—a defence of abstract citizenship against any kind of affirmative action. That is, an anti-reservation position in general. It is significant that this position is not taken by any political party, and is expressed only by individual commentators in the media. Thus for example we have an editorial in *The Indian Express* which says that the pandemonium in Parliament over the Bill 'is a sorry vindication of this newspaper's traditional position that affirmative action is a wrong-headed idea. Once unleashed, it perpetuates and propagates itself in the most divisive ways. Is Parliament to be parcelled into lots of the historically oppressed, leaving the rest of mainstream India to its own devices?'[13] Chandan Mitra bemoans the fact that 'Already the vicious spectre of casteism has begun haunting the party system' and feared the degeneration of Parliament to a 'caste panchayats' union'. Reservations for women would lead to demands for reservations for other groups, and 'instead of moving towards the 21st century and age of virtual reality, we have been dragged back into medievalism.'[14]

This last anti-reservation position opposing the Bill is an interesting counterpoint to the final position I present—the (implicitly) caste-based support for women's reservations. These two apparently contradictory positions, one rejecting reservations in toto and the other supporting women's reservations while rejecting caste-based reservations, represent similar interests. It is when we examine the latter that we move more directly towards the suggestion I made earlier, that upper caste concerns and feminist concerns tie in at this historical moment on this question. This position pushes for the passing of the Bill and flatly rejects the demand for further quotas. Within this last position I would place the BJP and the Congress. While within the BJP there is considerable contestation of the official party line rejecting 'quotas within quotas', as we have seen, any debate within the Congress is muted. The party seems reconciled to the loss of its earlier dalit and Muslim base, and is pushing for the Bill in its present form.

Madhu Kishwar takes heart from the fact that the very same people who opposed the Mandal reservations for OBCs have accepted the reservations for women 'with apparent grace and enthusiasm'. For her this is further proof of the great women-friendly traditions of India (Kishwar 1996). As a political analyst one cannot help but note, however, that the fearsome future that Chandan Mitra and *The Indian Express* editorial outline is precisely what a blanket 33 per cent reservation for women hopes to prevent. That is, an immediate filling of 33 per cent of seats with women would certainly change the class and caste composition of Parliament back in the short term, to one more comfortable for our elites, which clearly considers itself to be 'the mainstream', as opposed to the 'historically oppressed', as the editorial quoted above unabashedly declares. As Vasanthi Raman points out, OBCs and Muslims, given their numerical strength as well as their social location, pose a greater threat to upper castes than SC/STs, about whom some complacency was still possible (Raman 1999).

Within the broad feminist camp, the suggestion of 'quotas within quotas' has received mixed responses. As Gail Omvedt points out, by now the stark antagonism between OBC and feminist leaders is easing (Omvedt 2000). Most women's groups accept the principle of quotas within quotas, but while some groups are prepared for a redrafting of the present Bill to include such quotas, others, like the Left groups, continue to insist that the Bill must be passed first, and further quotas can be worked out later.[15]

This survey of positions on the WRB throws into relief a set of interrelated questions about (a) 'women' as the subject of feminist politics, (b) citizenship in post-colonial democracies, and (c) the idea of political representation. That is, about women and the women's movement on the one hand and women and the nation-state on the other, with representation as the category mediating both relationships.

Feminism and citizenship

A good question to begin with here could be this: Why are 'women' acceptable to the ruling elites as a counter-measure to deal with rising backward caste presence in Parliament? Why are women and the women's movement not only not perceived as a threat to social order, but even as a force that can restore the control of upper castes and classes? One possible explanation could have to do with the cooptation and domestication of gender issues by the state and NGOs since the late 1980s. The emergence of autonomous women's groups at the beginning of that decade marked a new and militant, highly visible phase of the women's movement, but by the end of the 1990s, almost all of these groups were running on funding from government and international bodies. That is, these groups which began as an attempt to create spaces outside the orthodoxies of party women's wings, are now far from autonomous of the compulsions of getting and retaining funding.

Further, while the 'empowerment of women' is a slogan much in use by government agencies, it has been argued that this kind of government programme aims at empowering women only to the extent of harnessing women's contribution to 'growth'—a goal to attain which there is considerable external pressure on the government. Thus, drives against child marriage serve the purposes of population control. Or to take another example, the growth of grass-roots women's movements centring on the disastrous impact of development policies, like the Chipko Andolan, have posed a challenge to the state. By providing space to women in the planning and implementation of government programmes, such as forest management programmes, protest movements are sought to be led into non-confrontationist channels.[16]

Writing on the increasing circulation of the term 'empowerment' in the context of World Bank-directed new economic policies in India in the 1990s, Manoranjan Mohanty argues that empowerment, particularly of women, is understood in international documents not as a goal but a prerequisite for productive investment. Terms like empowerment, civil society and democratisation, which form part of the new liberalisation discourse therefore, are not a response to the struggles that have marked Indian politics, but have been given a restricted meaning and oriented in order to 'serve the present global drive of western capitalism'. Since market development is a key feature defining the stage of development of 'civil society' in this understanding, those who are weak or unorganised, or who reject the prevailing system are excluded from 'civil society'. Thus, he concludes, 'the agenda of globalisation promotes democracy for those who can participate in the bargaining process' (Mohanty 1995). The growing statism and NGO-isation of the women's movement are a cause for concern in this sense.

This is a feature that the movement is very aware of. A report by six women's organisations from Delhi and Bombay, investigating the dismissal of some employees of the Rajasthan government's Women's Development Programme (WDP), came to the conclusion that the WDP, designed with the active cooperation of feminist activists, had been successful in reducing people's distrust of the state by appropriating the legitimacy garnered by the women's movement. The report urged a serious consideration of the implications of this.[17] So a harsh conclusion that we seem to be forced to confront is that as far as the ruling elites are concerned, 'women' are something they can deal with.

A more complicated reason for 'women' being acceptable while 'OBCs' are not, has to do with the way in which identities emerge in politics. Indian politics has shown often enough that class, religious, caste (or any other) identity has tended to prevail over gender identification. On issues like the Uniform Civil Code (UCC), the anti-Mandal upper caste agitations, or in Hindu right-wing mobilisation, 'women' have tended to rally as upper/lower caste or Muslim/Hindu (Dietrich 1994). The women's movement has been as much attacked by dalit women for being savarna as the dalit movement has been attacked for being patriarchal, and feminists of minority communities have challenged the women's movement for being Hindu by default, in its claim to being secular (Agnes 1994; Omvedt 1990). Thus, by the late 1980s the women's movement had to accept that 'women' as the subject of feminist politics, and gender justice as an issue, would have to be inflected through the lens of other identities. On the UCC for instance therefore, from a straightforward demand for a state-legislated UCC, other positions have emerged within the women's movement, which seek in different ways to support initiatives for reform within communities, or to provide alternative, differentiated legal spaces for women.

In other words, feminist politics has been coming to the difficult recognition that 'women' do not simply exist as a category that is available for feminist mobilisation—the question then remains, who is the subject of feminist politics? If 'women' must be located within the grid of other identities that circulate, then what a 'feminist' position would be, on questions like the UCC and women's reservations, is not so self-evident. For what we are talking about here is more than simply the truism that 'women have many identities'. So we must go much further than saying that 'women' mobilise as upper caste/dalit and so on. Rather, we need to come to the more complex recognition that under different circumstances, and given different kinds of political mobilisation, 'people' identify and come together as 'dalits', 'Muslims', 'working class', or much less often, as 'women'. This is the difficult political fact to face—that women coming together as upper caste/dalit may not necessarily be coming together as upper caste/dalit women. We are forced to see the creation of 'women-as-subject' as the end or goal of feminist politics, not the starting point.

What this means in the context of the WRB is that when confronted with upper-caste concerns that seem to tie in with feminist concerns at this conjuncture, the women's movement must make the moves necessary to undercut the upper-caste project—and quotas within quotas seems to offer that possibility. But this is only the minimum required of us.

We need to push the question much further. Have we taken seriously the ways in which the core operating principle of bourgeois democracy—universal suffrage—is reshaped by the principle of reservations for groups in representative institutions? As Anne Phillips points out, the institutionalisation of group representation seems to conflict with the historical movement of democracy away from group representation and group privilege and towards the ideal where every individual vote counts equally as one. The question of group identity in western liberal democracies has therefore been at the centre of heated debate, the most well known form of which has been the individualist/communitarian debate (Phillips 1995). Will Kymlicka points out however, that the acceptance of group identity and group rights is usually on the understanding that they are 'a temporary measure on the way to a society where the need for special representation no longer exists'. Society should seek to remove the oppression thereby eliminating the need for these rights (Kymlicka 1996).

In post-colonial societies of Asia and Africa on the other hand, the fact that democracy entered before the notion of the individual took root means that our democracy takes very different shapes than it does in the societies of its origin. As a large body of scholarship in our societies shows, liberal individualism never became the uncontested core of anti-imperialist struggles or of post-independence politics. Whether Gandhi and Ambedkar in India or African socialists like

Nyerere or Nkrumah, most nationalist leaders constructed national identities, not through the idea of individual citizenship but through that of communities—caste, religious, ethnic groups. Their language of politics remained non-individualistic, although ultimately there remained a tension between the community defined in various ways as the bearer of rights, and the individual, a tension we know to be reflected in the Indian Constitution.

Representation: identity or ideology dichotomy

The phenomenon of groups seeking recognition in representative bodies on the basis of ethnic, religious or gender identity has been understood by many scholars as the shift from 'ideology' (in which people are willing for their 'ideas' to be represented rather than their 'self') to 'identity' (where the representative must actually 'mirror'[18] the characteristics of the people represented.) Anne Phillips, for instance, terms this the shift from a politics of ideas to a politics of presence (Phillips 1998). The politics of ideas suggests 'a broadly secular understanding of politics as a matter of judgement and debate, and expects political loyalties to develop around policies rather than people'. A politics of presence on the other hand, privileges the question of 'who' rather than 'what' and demands equal representation of women, ethnic minorities, and other groups that see themselves as excluded (Phillips 1998).

In this section, I will problematise the very framing of the relationship between ideas/presence (or who/what) as a dichotomy. I must emphasise that my concern here with the split between identity and ideology does not have to do with establishing the legitimacy of the demand for recognition of 'identity' over 'ideology'. Arguments that justify the need for group representation over abstract citizenship (or identity over ideology) may have relevance in the liberal democracies of the West, which have traced a different route to democracy, as we saw in the last section. However, the experience of societies that came to democracy and modernity through the encounter with colonialism has been such, that group identity has always been the axis upon which democratic institutions turn. It would be instructive here to turn briefly to a comparison with the movement for parity in France.

The parity movement, which emerged in the 1990s, is a demand for complete equality, that is, numerically equal representation for women and men in decision-making bodies, especially elected assemblies. However, the opposition to the idea takes very different forms in the two societies. While in India, the main opposition to the idea of reservations for women poses competing identities (caste/community) against that of 'women' (the 'quotas within quotas' position), in the case of France, the opposition to parity is largely in terms of protecting the category of abstract citizenship from fragmentation. This argument may be expressed either in the form of asserting the equal capabilities of women, to which it is an insult to propose that they need protection of any sort, or in terms of the fear of a rise in ethnic politics once the principle of abstract citizenship is diluted—that is, once women are recognised as a separate category, other groups could start demanding reservations too.[19] Similar in tone, one may note, to the arguments against reservation expressed in the CSWI here, from which there has been such a marked shift in position.

In other words, while the arguments against parity in France are based on a continued belief in the value of the notion of the abstract citizen,[20] unmarked by other factors like class, race or sex; in India the opposition to women's reservations comes from a position that would push further the critique of the abstract, unmarked citizen. That is, in India the opponents of the WRB mainly demand that other marginalised identities too should have representation within the women's quota. So it is not necessary in our context, to rehearse the arguments justifying recognition of difference.[21]

To return to the main argument of this section then, the distinction made between presence and ideas is unsustainable, in my opinion. The distinction can be maintained only if we assume that 'identity' is natural, pre-political—that is, pre-ideology. That 'presence' is pre-'ideas'. However, as I have argued in an earlier section, identities are created and mobilised in and through politics, they do not pre-exist politics. When we make this argument about caste or religious identity in India it is by now generally accepted, for these are no longer seen as natural or primordial identities, but as identities that have taken their present forms over the course of certain historical developments. The huge body of writing and debate over the Uniform Civil Code bears witness to this assertion. However, when it comes to 'women', there continues to be a tendency to view the category as self-evident, when in fact the painful recognition that the women's movement has had to come to terms with is precisely that 'women' as the subject of feminist politics has to be brought into being by political practice.

It is interesting in this context to note that Anne Phillips makes only a minimalist case for 'quotas' while rejecting the idea of 'representation'. Phillips makes a limited argument for a politics of presence—since half the population is female and there is a substantial non-white presence, bodies of elected representatives should reflect this distribution. 'When the composition of decision-making assemblies is so markedly at odds with the gender and ethnic makeup of the society they represent, this is clear evidence that certain voices are being silenced or suppressed' (Phillips 1995). However, she is very clear that the argument is not strengthened, is even weakened, by claims that this quota would represent a constituency. 'Accountability is always the other side of representation, and, in the absence of procedures for establishing what any group wants, or thinks, we cannot usefully talk of their political representation.' This is why 'we should detach the arguments, for example, for parity between men and women, from the arguments for representing women as a group. The case still stands whether the women "represent" women or not' (Phillips 1995). It is illustrative here to go back to the arguments against *parite* in France—one of them is the fear of the large-scale entry of right-wing women into legislatures (Haas-Dubosc 1999). From Phillips' point of view, what the political views are of the women who enter legislatures would be entirely irrelevant—their presence in legislatures is justified by their presence in the population.

The problem with this argument is that Phillips sees 'women' as a category existing in society independently of their politics, when the dilemma for feminist politics arises precisely from the fact that different political configurations produce different identities. Identity does not exist independently of ideology, or, to put it differently, 'presence' is already constituted by a number of identifications, of which gender is only one. To reiterate a point I have made earlier, there are not 'women' who may be right wing or left wing, white or black—there are people who may respond in different kinds of political mobilisation as 'white', 'left wing' or as 'women'. Phillips can see this point when it comes to race:

> In the case of Britain, for example, the all-embracing concept of 'black' people rapidly dissolved into a distinction between Asian and Afro-Caribbean communities, and then subsequently into finer distinctions. What in this context then counts as 'adequate' ethnic representation? Such questions can hardly be answered in isolation from politics and political mobilisations ...

However, she uses this understanding to cast doubt on the legitimacy of demands for ethnic quotas, as opposed to 'more "permanently" relevant categories' such as women (Phillips 1995: 296). The apparent intractability of the category of 'women' blinds Phillips to the implications of her own argument. If 'women' too is recognised as produced by political mobilisation, then quotas for women cannot be promoted in isolation from quotas for other marginalised groups in society.

Here her position is similar to some feminist Muslim voices in the Indian debate (individuals, not groups), which continue to make a feminist defence of women's reservations while totally rejecting the idea of other quotas within the women's quota.[22] The demand of quotas within quotas is seen (Mustafa 1998) as an attempt to 'divide' women into categories like Muslim and OBC. The argument here is that quotas for Muslim women, for instance, will segregate them from the mainstream—surely something that can be said for reservations for women in general? Or that the demand for quotas for Muslim women is suspect because it comes from the same patriarchal quarters within the

Muslim leadership that pushed for the Muslim Women's Bill (Alavi 1998). But again, this argument does not stand, because one of the strongest supporters of the WRB is the Hindu right-wing BJP, which was opposed to the Muslim Women's Bill for entirely communal reasons while it supports the WRB to preserve upper-caste power. This is precisely the point, that 'women' have proved to be remarkably difficult to demarcate within the matrix of other identities in which they are embedded. On the question of gender-discriminatory personal laws as we know, feminist demands for a UCC seemed indistinguishable from the Hindu Right's programme for the same. 'Speaking for women' has been demonstrated to arise from very different kinds of concerns. It is impossible to sustain an argument defending reservations for 'women' on the basis of an assumed shared experience while at the same time rejecting any notion of a shared experience that is 'Muslim' or 'dalit'.

Phillips of course, does not make 'shared experience' a criterion for quotas—as we saw, she considers 'presence' a sufficient condition to justify them. What she shares with the positions discussed above though, is the assumption that the presence of 'women' can be clearly demarcated from that of 'race', 'caste' or 'religious' identity—the belief that while these are politically produced categories, 'women' pre-exist politics.

A recent alternative proposal to the WRB makes the same assumption. Since the WRB seems unlikely to be revived, the Election Commission has proposed that all political parties should mutually agree on the percentage of seats where they will mandatorily field women candidates in parliamentary and Assembly elections. Failure to do so would result in punitive action to be taken by the Election Commission, even up to derecognition.[23] Left parties have criticised this formula, but the opposition is on the grounds that this is a 'compromise formula' that will only ensure tickets for women, not guarantee their victory.[24] However, this seems to me to be the weakest argument against the proposal. The more serious objection to it should be on the grounds of the anti-democratic nature of this kind of policing by the EC, a body not accountable to the people in any way. The principle of parties ensuring female representation internally has worked elsewhere, in the Nordic countries, and in the African National Congress, for example. But in these cases it has been a self-regulating move. In 1980, parties in Norway and Sweden proposed legislation that would commit all political parties to a minimum of 40 per cent women on their electoral lists, but failing the success of this bid, various parties introduced the practice unilaterally (Phillips 1995). There has been no attempt to police the practice except through the sheer pressure of democratic politics.

It is one thing to say that Parliament as an institution of state should at least formally serve as a forum representing all interests and identities, but quite another to insist that political parties as part of political society, should also be modelled on the same pattern. Parties exist in a democracy precisely in order to represent sectional interests. The absurdity of this proposal, that the EC should have the right to regulate the internal matters of political parties, would be immediately evident if the suggestion had been that all parties would be forced to give a percentage of their seats to dalits or upper castes, to Muslims or Hindus, or to working class people. Why does it not seem absurd when the category here is women? The suggestion can seem reasonable only if 'women' is evacuated of all political content, as if it is a neutral category that exists independently of all political considerations. And the burden of this paper has been to show that this is most definitely not so.

Gail Omvedt also supports the alternative proposal that parties should reserve a proportion of their tickets for women, which she sees as an advance on the original WRB. However, she does not explicitly appear to endorse any role for the EC in ensuring that parties do so. Rather, she concedes that the alternative proposal does not guarantee 33 per cent reservation, but it is nevertheless 'a move towards real empowerment— and in a way that brings about the total welfare of society' (Omvedt 2000). It is clear that the only 'guarantee' she assumes is that of political commitment, which gives the proposal a different shape altogether. Omvedt's rejection of the WRB and support for the alternative proposal then falls into place within the context of her general preference for mass politics over legal reform. In 1990, for example, she saw the government proposals for 30 per cent reservation for women that were then circulating, as a response to the collective challenge offered by different 'drives of women for local political power' all over India. That is, she sees legal reforms as a consequence of the pressure created by mass politics, not as the precondition for social transformation (Omvedt 1990). This puts her support for the proposal in a very different category from the form in which it is cast, both by the Election Commission and the Forum for Democratic Reforms (Phillips 1995).

In lieu of a conclusion

This final section brings us to a set of questions that is by no means amenable to easy resolution. If we accept that it is not the individual but the group, defined in whatever way, that is the basis of representation, then we need to evolve a way of leaving open the potential for any group to choose in the future to define itself as one which requires reservation in Parliament. If identities emerge in and through political mobilisation, then we need to guard against the possibility that some identities may freeze into new formations of power, thus blocking the emergence of new identities and new alignments. Cautioning against the possibility of collective rights 'overtaxing' the theory of rights 'tailored to individual persons', Habermas fears that group rights could represent 'a kind of preservation of species by administrative means':

> For to guarantee survival would necessarily rob the members of the very freedom to say yes or no if they are to appropriate and preserve their cultural heritage (Habermas 1994).

Although Habermas uses this critique to limit the recognition of group rights, a debate we have already seen to be framed very differently in post-colonial societies, nevertheless this point must be taken seriously. We would, however, need to take it in the opposite direction to the one taken by Habermas. That is, rather than reasserting the need as Habermas does, for 'political integration of citizens'[26] we would need to push the possibilities of continuing 'pluralisation' (Habermas 1994). Here I refer to the distinction made by William Connolly:

> pluralism is often presented as an achievement to be protected, while the eruption of new drives to pluralisation are often represented as perils to this achievement (Connolly 1995).

If democracy remains unresponsive to the emergence of new configurations of identity, then once-emancipatory identities can entrench themselves into formations blocking further democratisation.

What kinds of transformations of democratic institutions and practices would ensure an 'ethos of critical responsiveness'? (Connolly 1995). Serious debate on radical alternatives is necessary. One of the suggestions doing the rounds is the advocacy of proportional representation (PR) (Omvedt 2000). But to conceptualise PR in the context only of currently existing parties which would get seats in proportion to their votes, is not sufficient. We would have to think of a revisioned PR system that would have room (and continue to make room) for newer kinds of political configurations—the anti-big dam movements, anti-nuclear energy movements, alternative sexualities/gay and lesbian rights movements, to name but a few. A public debate on the potential and limitations of proportional representation is certainly worthwhile, although that too would only be a beginning.

David Scott, discussing the impasse that constitutional negotiations on ethnic politics in Sri Lanka seems to have reached, suggests a more radical reformulation of democracy. He makes a case for the need to re-examine 'the inscription of liberalism and democracy into the colonial and post-colonial state', arguing that this has created a 'whole new game of politics' of which one crucial aspect is its reliance on 'number'. In his view modern liberal democracy is inseparable from the 'statistical principle'. Therefore,

> (t)he task rather is to find the institutional arrangements in which to embody the forms of life of historical communities and then

determining what kinds of mediating frameworks can be established in which these groups can negotiate their claims. What this means in effect, is the establishment of intersecting public spaces—spaces that practice different forms of belonging, in which different self-governing practices can be cultivated, in the different languages of identity (Scott 1999).

The discussion has only begun. For now I would conclude by suggesting that if reservation politics is not to solidify into different forms of elite control over state institutions, if it is to act, as indeed it must, as merely one of the strategies in a radical politics of subversion, then the debate cannot remain limited to the quotas question.

Acknowledgements

I would like to thank Aditya Nigam and Mary John for discussions, comments and references.

Notes

[1] Yadav concludes that from the 1989 election onwards, the electoral political arena has seen greater participation and more intense politicisation, particularly among marginal social groups. The odds that a dalit will vote are much higher today than of an upper caste. The dominant peasant proprietor OBCs were already politicised, but now the lower OBCs are equally militant.

[2] Translatable as 'the patriarchal forces controlling Parliament'. Yogendra Yadav 'Swarth Aur Moh ke beech Fansa Mahila Arakshan Bill', *Dainik Bhaskar*, 26 August 2000.

[3] Seema Mustafa, 'Forget Footing, Men Can't Even Stomach the Bill', *Asian Age*, 18 July 1998.

[4] Krishna Bose, Trinamul Congress MP, in Parliament, reported in *Times of India*, 9 March 1999.

[5] Title of article by Brinda Karat, in *People's Democracy*, 15 June 1997.

[6] The following section develops on an argument I have made earlier in 'Reservations and Representation', *Seminar*, 457, September 1997.

[7] For a fuller discussion of the right to abortion in the context of the Indian women's movement, see my 'The Impossibility of Justice: Female Foeticide and the Feminist Discourse on Abortion' in Patricia Uberoi (ed.) *Social Reform, Sexuality and the State*, Sage Publications, Delhi 1996.

[8] P.T. Rajshekhar, 'The Voice of the Persecuted Nationalities Denied Human Rights', *Dalit Voice*, vol. 17, no. 18, 1–15 August pp. 3–5. Cited by Meena

Dhanda 'Representation for Women, Should Feminists Support Quotas?' *Economic and Political Weekly*, 12 August, 2000, p. 2971.

[9] Indira Hirway, 'Panchayati Raj at the Crossroads', *Economic and Political Weekly*, vol. XXIV, no. 29, 1989; and Utsahi Mahila Abhyudaya in UMA Prachar April–June 1996. Cited by Janaki Nair, 'An Important Springboard', *Seminar*, 457, September 1997.

[10] Press Conference, *The Hindu*, 28 November 1999.

[11] News report in *Times of India*, 9 March 1999.

[12] Uma Bharati, 'Not a Woman's World, Case for OBC Reservation', *Times of India*, 17 July 1998, p. 12, as told to Vidya Subramaniam.

[13] *The Indian Express*, 15 July 1998.

[14] *The Pioneer*, 31 August 1997.

[15] There is now recognition in the Left, although it is grudging, that caste is a reality of Indian politics, and has to be dealt with. The CPI(M)'s Draft of Updated Party Programme (May 2000) acknowledges that 'The assertion by dalits has a democratic content reflecting the aspirations of the most oppressed sections of society. The backward castes have also asserted their rights in a caste-ridden society.' However, this is qualified by the following: 'At the same time, a purely caste appeal which seeks to perpetuate caste divisions for the narrow aim of consolidating vote banks and detaching these downtrodden sections from the common democratic movement has also been at work' (p. 25). The Left engagement with caste is still very uneasy.

[16] Anonymous, 'Women: Invisible Constituency', *Economic and Political Weekly*, 18 May 1996, p. 1173.

[17] Saheli, Sabla Sangh, Action India, Disha, Women's Centre, Forum Against Oppression of Women and Awaz-e-Nizwan, 'Development for Whom—A Critique of Women's Development Programmes' 1991. For a fuller discussion of this issue, see *Gender and Politics in India*, Nivedita Menon (ed.), Oxford University Press, Delhi, 1999. Introduction, pp. 20–21.

[18] A term used by Hanna Fenichel Pitkin in *The Concept of Representation*, University of California Press, Berkeley and Los Angeles, 1967, cited by Anne Phillips in 'Democracy and Difference' op. cit., p. 297. Pitkin was critical of the idea of mirror representation, but Phillips develops the idea more positively.

[19] Ibid., p. 5.

[20] It is necessary here to make a distinction between 'abstract' and 'universal' citizenship. The two have tended to be conflated in western political theory. However, in post-colonial democracies, it becomes evident that while 'abstract' citizenship has been a cover for protecting privilege (e.g. the discourse of 'merit' in upper-caste opposition to the Mandal reservations), 'universal' citizenship continues to be a value to be defended against the disenfranchising moves of the Hindu Right, for instance.

Universal citizenship can even be group-differentiated (and therefore, not abstract) as it is in Canada—see Will Kymlicka, 'Three Forms of Group-Differentiated Citizenship in Canada', op. cit. For an indication of how abstract citizenship can be a mask for privilege, see Partha Chatterjee, *The Present History of West Bengal*, OUP, Delhi, 1997, pp. 45–46. This point has been developed in discussions with Aditya Nigam. Challenging exchanges with Alok Rai and Rajeev Bhargava were invaluable inputs.

[21] We may note that feminist/pro-women arguments against reservations in India do not reject identity politics as such. That is, Madhu Kishwar and the SMA, for example, or Gail Omvedt, all fully endorse the need to see women as a collectivity with shared experiences which require special strategies to be fairly represented in decision-making bodies. Their opposition to the WRB is on the grounds that it is not an effective strategy. This is why Meena Dhanda's carefully argued defence of identity politics as a counter-position to Kishwar is rather off the mark. However, Dhanda's refutation of Kishwar's consequentialist arguments against the WRB is very useful. See Note 25.

[22] Seema Alavi, 'Muslim Women Don't Need Reservation', *Times of India*, 15 July 1998, p. 12; Seema Mustafa 'Forget Footing, Men Can't Even Stomach the Bill', op. cit.

[23] Nirmala George, 'Debate on Women's Bill Is Two Years Old, It's Going Nowhere', Interview with M.S. Gill, Chief Election Commissioner, *Indian Express*, 26 April 2000, p. 9.

[24] Shahid Faridi 'Left Criticises Gill Formula for Women's Reservation', *Asian Age*, 25 April 2000.

[25] The alternative proposal to reservations in Parliament, that instead, parties should reserve a proportion of their tickets for women has a longer history. Mulayam Singh Yadav first made the suggestion in 1998 (as a self-regulating mechanism, without any role for the EC), but it was not seriously considered. Then in 2000, Madhu Kishwar of *Manushi*, along with Jayaprakash Narayan of *Lok Satta*, Hyderabad, Yogendra Yadav of CSDS Delhi and Dhirubhai Sheth of *Lokayan*, Delhi, came out with an alternative proposal to the WRB, as the Forum for Democratic Reforms. This proposal is titled 'Women's Representation in Legislatures' and is an undated publication, jointly by all four organisations. Here reservations are rejected as an effective measure, and instead, the role of the EC in ensuring that parties not only give one-third of their tickets to women, but that these tickets are spread out over all constituencies, is worked out in great detail. Apart from the objection I have outlined in the text of the paper above, in giving the EC this kind of control over the political agenda of parties, there are other problems with this alternative proposal. Meena Dhanda has dealt exhaustively with the kind of argument in the proposal which envisages certain consequences of following the reservation policy. Kishwar originally

laid out these supposed consequences in her article, 'Women and Politics: Beyond Quotas', cited above, and these are outlined once again in this proposal. Dhanda, addressing the earlier article, points out that not all the relevant consequences are necessarily taken into account, and it is a matter of disputation whether some of the consequences presented as negative are indeed so. She concludes, 'Reflection on the Indian debate shows that selective emphases and different interpretations of the probable consequences of following a policy of gender quotas leads to a stalemate.' See 'Representation for Women: Should Feminists Support Quotas?' op. cit. pp. 2970–75.

I shall briefly lay out the other problems with this proposal: (a) Six of the 14 points that outline the problems with the WRB (pp. 3–4, points 1–5 and 9), have to do with the rotation of constituencies. An alternative which thinks in terms of fixed constituencies could perhaps be considered, rather than giving up on reservations in Parliament altogether. (b) Most of the other arguments against the Bill function on the classic assumption made by the privileged to reject reservations on principle. That is, instead of going on the assumption that it is patriarchal structures that keep women out of decision-making bodies, which is why reservations become necessary, the document makes arguments which suggest that the absence of women is because there are not enough capable candidates among them. With this underlying assumption, it becomes easy to make predictions like 'women elected in reserved constituencies will be contesting against other women only, and will lack the legitimacy to prove their ability' (p. 4). Conversely, if parties can choose their female candidates, 'natural leadership' is promoted, and there will be a large pool of 'credible and serious' women candidates. As they will be elected in competition, they will have legitimacy and not be seen as 'beneficiaries of charitable measures' and will not be 'mere proxy or lightweight' (p. 5). Clearly, the assumption is that this would be the case with reservations. Such assumptions are elitist and even offensive. (c) The concern of the proposal is weighted in favour of the interests of the male candidates, rather than those of the electorate or of the women candidates. Thus, an assumption of 'resentment' against women by 'men who get pushed out of their constituencies' is one of the problems outlined, if reservations are enforced (p. 4).

[26] Ibid., pp. 134–35. The reference to Habermas' argument here is only to point to the value of recognising his caution about 'guarantee of survival'. A more nuanced critique of his response to Charles Taylor and his notion of 'two levels of political integration' will have to be made elsewhere. For now, suffice it to say that I do hold that Taylor has not adequately confronted the contradictions produced by the extension of the language of individual rights to such broadly defined values as 'a fully human existence'. (See my 'State/Gender/Community: Citizenship in Contemporary India', *Economic and Political Weekly*, 31 January 1998, p. PE–4).

References

Agnes, Flavia. 1994. 'Women's Movement within a Secular Framework: Redefining the Agenda'. *Economic and Political Weekly*. vol. XXIX. no. 19. p. 1123.
Bhattacharya, Malini. 1997. 'Democracy and Reservation'. *Seminar*, 457. September. pp. 23–24.
Connolly, William. 1995. *The Ethos of Pluralization*. Minnesota and London: University of Minnesota Press. p. xvi.
Dietrich, Gabriele. 1994. 'Women and Religious Identities in India after Ayodhya' in *Against All Odds*. eds. Kamla Bhasin, Ritu Menon and Nighat Said Khan. New Delhi: Kali for Women. p. 43.
Haas-Dubosc, Danielle. 1999. 'Sexual Difference and Politics in France Today'. *Feminist Studies*. vol. 25. no. 1. Spring.
Habermas, Jurgen. 1994. 'Struggles for Recognition in the Democratic Constitutional State' in *Multiculturalism*. ed. Amy Gutman. tr. Shierry Weber Nicholsen. Princeton: Princeton University Press. p. 130.
Kannabiran, Vasanth and Kalpana Kannabiran. 1997. 'From Social Action to Political Action: Women and the 81st Amendment'. *Economic and Political Weekly*. 1 February. p. 196.
Kishwar, Madhu. 1996. 'Women and Politics: Beyond Quotas'. *Economic and Political Weekly*. 26 October. p. 2867.
Kymlicka, Will. 1996. 'Three Forms of Group-Differentiated Citizenship in Canada' in *Democracy and Difference, Contesting the Boundaries of the Political*. ed. Seyla Benhabib. Princeton: Princeton University Press. p. 158.
Mazumdar, Vina. 1997. 'Historical Soundings'. *Seminar*, 457. September. pp. 15–16.
ML Update. 1998. vol. 1 no. 19. 15 July.
Mohanty, Manoranjan. 1995. 'On the Concept of Empowerment'. *Economic and Political Weekly*. 17 June. pp. 1434–36.
Omvedt, Gail. 1990. *Violence Against Women, New Movement and New Theories in India*. New Delhi: Kali for Women. p. 39.
———. 2000. 'Women and PR'. *The Hindu*. 12 September.
Phillips, Anne. 1995. 'Democracy and Difference: Some Problems for Feminist Theory' in *The Rights of Minority Cultures*. ed. Will Kymlicka. Oxford: Oxford University Press. pp. 290–93.
———. 1998. *The Politics of Presence: The Political Representation of Gender, Ethnicity and Race*. Oxford: Clarendon Press. 1995. Reissued in paperback.
Rai, Shirin and K. Sharma. 2000. 'Democratising the Indian Parliament: The "Reservation for Women Debate"' in *International Perspectives on Gender and Democratisation*, ed. Shirin Rai. London: Macmillan. p. 159.
Raman, Vasanthi. 1999. 'Women's Reservations and Democratisation. An Alternative Perspective'. *Economic and Political Weekly*. 11 December. pp. 3494–95.

Scott, David. 1999. 'Community, Number, Ethos of Democracy' in *Refashioning Futures, Criticism after Post-coloniality*. Princeton: Princeton University Press. pp. 162, 188–89.

Scott, Joan W. 1997. 'La Querelle des Femmes in the Late Twentieth Century'. *New Left Review*. no. 226. November–December.

Shetkari Mahila Aghadi (SMA). 1997. 'Reservation on Reservation'. *Communalism in Combat*. June. p. 6.

Yadav, Yogendra. 1999. 'Electoral Politics in the Time of Change. India's Third Electoral System, 1989–99'. *Economic and Political Weekly*. 21–28 August. pp. 2393–99.

Published in *Economic and Political Weekly*, 28 October 2000, WS 35, (pp. 3835-43).

Section III
Women as Policy Makers

Women, Zilla Parishads and Panchayat Raj

GAIL OMVEDT

Zilla parishad and municipal elections are coming in Maharashtra as the last round of the contesting of political forces in the state which began with the Lok Sabha elections last November. The primary task before the Left and democratic forces at this point seems to be to give the final blow to Shiv Sena's bloated but dangerous aspirations for political power (which means blocking the compromising tendencies within parties like Janata Dal) and at the same time try to stand up to the Congress.

But these local elections have a new aspect, reservations for women. After over a year of promises, Sharad Pawar has announced 30 per cent reservations in local body elections, both in the zilla parishads and the municipalities. Both parties and women's organisations are trying to cope with the fact that thousands of women will enter, one way or another, into local bodies. And some—this time fruitless—reaction is setting in: as the 'reserved' constituencies are announced, the male politicians currently holding power in these constituencies are scrambling to do what they can to prevent the loss of their seats. This has begun with the municipalities. Some corporators have already gone to court, and in Kolhapur, the municipality passed by a vote of 14 to 12 a resolution calling for the withdrawal of reservations. Some well-known women, for instance, the writer Durga Bhagwat, have opposed reservations. Such positions have a broader political context because it is the BJP-Shiv Sena combine which is expected to be the most disadvantaged in women's constituencies.

All through 1987, when zilla parishad elections were expected and the Shetkari Sangathana-backed Samagra Mahila Aghadi was proposing all-women panels, the Janata Dal, Dalit and Left parties reacted—'how can we find the women?' Now that 30 per cent is a reality, they are forced to find at least that many women. After decades of a social-political process which kept politics primarily in the hands of men, even in the Left, the parties are short of women cadres with experience in the arenas of power. Yet there are women, and many who have come up through the women's movement. The Congress will be in a better position, relatively, than the Janata Dal and the Left, in the rural areas. There have been channels open to women through its patronage-linked structures of power—the whole network of Mahila Mandals is mainly tied to Congress linked structures; social welfare department programmes have mobilised women; 'autonomous' but Congress-linked women's organisations exist in many areas, including state-wide efforts such as the Maharashtra Mahila Vyaspith linked to the Yashwantrao Chavan Prathisthan. All of this is aside from any officially Congress-connected women's wing. These will simply serve to mobilise women into Congress party politics unless there is some imaginative intervention.

As for the organisations, feminist or otherwise which have been a part of the women's movement, these are also in somewhat of a dilemma. Not until recently have most of these organisations, individually or collectively, thought about the issue of political power, and most discussions and conferences/workshops organised up to now have concentrated mainly on putting forward principles through which the organisations could try to influence candidates to take up women's issues. At a minimum, the organisations and activists might like to mobilise pressure so that they could support women candidates with experience in and commitment to the women's movement, standing under the banner of parties (Left parties, the Janata Dal, perhaps even the Congress) and not just the wives and daughters of leaders. At a maximum, many would support the idea of women standing not under party banners but on a united platform of all women's organisations (Left and democratic!)

coming together—the 'Samagra Mahila Aghadi' idea, if not the name. Some feminists and many ordinary women are even attracted to the idea of a 'women's party'. The problem in all of this, however, is that the women's organisations have very little mobilisable base, worth counting in terms of voting, to put on pressure for any of this.

As for the Shetkari Sangathana Mahila Aghadi, it was this which pioneered the idea of a mass collective fight for power in the zilla parishads. The resolution for all-women panels, made at the Shetkari Sangathana's Chandwad session in November 1986, received little welcome from Left and democratic parties. There was also opposition within the Shetkari Sangathana itself. But, with a good deal of enthusiasm from women, the organisation went forward with preparations in a large number of districts. Nevertheless, over two years later, the Shetkari Sangathana Mahila Aghadi is also in an ambivalent frame of mind about the zilla parishad elections.

Part of the problem is the intervening Assembly elections. At that time the Shetkari Sangathana broke a 10-year policy against electoral position by allowing its candidates to stand; behind this was a kind of upsurge among activists disgusted with political parties and convinced, on the basis of the power shown by their mass movement, that they could do better by contesting directly. Out of 35 Shetkari Sangathana candidates standing on Janata Dal tickets, 10 were women—probably the highest percentage among all organisations in the country. But Sangathana candidates as a whole got somewhat of a shock from the electoral process—of which they had had no direct experience before—and the results. 'We had a very expensive training' is the way one male activist put it. Women, perhaps more than men, were unexpectedly embittered by some of the nastier aspects of elections, and by finding that movement support and idealism were not enough to withstand the power, money and interests operating in the electoral arena; many also found that some of the movement support they had expected was not forthcoming. The overall result for Shetkari Sangathana was not so bad (five MLAs, not counting Janata Dal MLAs close to the Sangathana) but it was much less than they had expected. One of the MLAs is a woman, Saroj Kashikar, but she was elected with a margin of only a few hundred votes, and is today the only woman MLA of the Progressive Democratic Front. The last elections have seen the percentage of women MLAs and MPs actually *decline* throughout India, and Mahila Aghadi women also clearly suffered from this experience. The result has been not only a heavy case of post-election fatigue, but also a wave of further disillusionment about the electoral process in general. It may be that zilla parishad elections—at least for many—will be fought more as a matter of duty than anything else.

And yet, at other levels, the upsurge in the drive for women's participation in local political power has hardly stopped, but has gone on and even increased. Gram panchayat elections were held in 1989 throughout most of rural Maharashtra. Many Shetkari Sangathana people contested these elections or tried to intervene, but there was no official Sangathana programme of all-women panels. Nevertheless, in many villages scattered throughout the state, local men and women of the Sangathana decided to organise such panels and try to capture the panchayats. This was the 'idea' of Samagra Mahila Aghadi, though the name was rarely used since panchayat candidates have individual election symbols. The results are worth investigating. Indeed, since these were all undertaken at local initiative, the 'higher-level' Sangathana activists still have very little information about the actual situation.

There are at least five villages within Shetkari Sangathana-dominated areas where such all-women panchayats have been elected. One of these is Metikheda in Yeotmal district, where the main local activists are Maya and Chandrakant Wandkhade, formerly Sangarsh Vahini activists who had joined Shetkari Sangathana some four or five years ago. Maya, a former schoolteacher, had been a part of some district agitations and had kept constant touch with the nearly 150 women who had been selected as potential zilla parishad candidates in 1987. Then, hearing of an all-women panel elected in Wardha district in early 1989, she and others in the village were inspired to attempt the same thing in their own village election. The all-women panel formed included two adivasis, one dalit, two nomadic tribe women, two kunbis, one brahman and Maya herself (a brahman married to a backward caste man). The village boss' camp opposed them with all the usual tricks, including attempting to buy off or deceive panel members and trying to stigmatise Maya as an 'outsider' with short hair. None of these worked, and the panel was elected, all by large margins. Further, there was a significant change in the entire electoral process: the nature and even physical place of electoral activity changed, drinking was forbidden during the last three days, and slanderous propaganda was laughed off.

Metikheda is the only village where an urban-born activist stimulated the process. In all other cases it has been local women (and their husbands and male supporters) who have taken the initiative—and very often they have confronted not only 'male' political power, but also the forces of communalism, against which the Shetkari Sangathana as a whole has stood up to combat in recent years. In Salod (Amraoti district) the peasants and agricultural labourers not only elected an all-women panel, but this Hindu-majority village chose a Muslim woman as sarpanch.

Perhaps the most inspiring of these villages, though, is Vitner, in Jalgaon district. Vitner is a small, remote village on the banks of the Tapi. The dominant caste (in conventional anthropological terms) here are gujjars, and it was in fact a gujjar woman, Indirabai Patil, who has taken the initiative. But unlike the gujjars of Shahada and Taloda in Dhule district, who are mostly big landowners and merchants and are the traditional enemy of the adivasi-based Shramik Sangathana (one of the early vital rural poor movements in Maharashtra), the gujjars of Vitner are mainly poor peasants. There are no adivasis here; aside from a few houses of dalits, kolis (a backward caste) equal the gujjars in number and are mainly poor peasants and labourers. But all came together for the women's panel, and it was a koli woman, Shubhabai Raisingh, who was chosen as sarpanch. Kolis and gujjars have equal representation on the panchayat, along with one dalit.

But the Vitner peasants went beyond women's political power

to take up another problem of women tackled in the resolutions of the Shetkari Mahila Aghadi's November 1989 conference at Amraoti: the question of women's economic rights. There was extensive discussion both of women's property rights and of their economic earnings (of agricultural labourers as well as the unpaid work of peasant women in agriculture) at Amraoti. One resolution gave a kind of 'immediate programme' for women's economic rights, called the 'Hingoli programme' after the village shibir where it had been first proposed: this called for peasant men of Shetkari Sangathana to assign the income from a portion of their land to the women of the family. The Vitner women and men took up this idea and carried it an important step further. Men of 127 families actually turned over the legal property rights to women—the *sat-baras*—with approximately half to 6–7 acres going to each women. ('We didn't ask any bigger landowners to do this,' says Indirabai, 'because we didn't want to be accused of evading the ceiling acts.') As we went around the small houses and huts of the panchayat members (who are almost all poor peasants or labourers), it was a memorable experience when one proudly said that the 'sarbat' she gave us to drink was made from the lemons 'of my tree'. At a more serious level, women are also saying that now they will have a strong guarantee against their husbands abandoning them—a growing problem in rural Maharashtra.

And an even more memorable experience was the spontaneous 'cultural programme' arranged on the night of 9 May, while the Mahila Aghadi was holding its meeting in Vitner: women danced the *garbha* and *nac*, and one did a hilarious individual dance rendition of a male drunkard. Songs, both in Marathi and Ahirani, have marked the women's movement as seen in Vitner. The fact of a collectivity of peasant men giving legal property rights to the women of their families is a striking initiative in a society whose women are murdered for demanding such rights—and Vitner has been awarded the honorary title of 'Jotiba Village' (after Jotiba Phule) for it and for the election of an all-women panchayat. Besides these 'Shetkari Sangathana villages', the trend towards local-level women's participation can be seen elsewhere: there are at least two other all-women gram panchayats, one in Ralegaon Shinde in Ahmednagar district (famous as the village of the ecologically minded peasant reformer, Anna Hazari) and one in Bitargaon Haveli in Solapur district, a panchayat of all 'thumb-wallas' or illiterate women. Some observers have reported that women here are more under the domination of local male leaders (Hazari and the gram sevak of Bitargaon) but this may itself prove to be a phase, as the women get experience, move out, interact with other women panchayat members and the women's movement elsewhere. And there is an increasing number of women sarpanches in villages throughout Maharashtra.

These cases illustrate a number of points. It will be remembered that at the time the proposal for reservations for women in panchayats first came up, there was a strong critical reaction (coming also from many Left intellectuals) that this was only a gambit of male rich peasants, that the women involved would be only puppets of the men in their families, and that they would be primarily rich peasant and 'dominant caste' women used to the exclusion of the poor peasant/low caste sections. What the Shetkari Sangathana examples show is that where women come into local political power as a part of a collective fight, they do so with a bias towards the low castes and poor peasants among them, and with a consciousness of the need to combat communalism and casteism. They show that while it helps to have at least one educated woman in the 'team', illiterate women can take a leading role and that they provide the main collective strength of the campaign. (The initiator of a women's panel, though one that failed, in Palshi of Satara district was a nomadic caste woman). They show that women, once elected, take up need-oriented development programmes: the villages have reported providing water taps, biogas plants, toilets especially in the dalit areas, playgrounds for the village school.

And they also show the obstacles that women face: as Anjanabai Toras, sarpanch of Erangaon village in Amravati district (herself illiterate) says, 'The former sarpanch refused to hand over charge to us and for four months came and sat in his chair after we were elected. He also gave us a pot of dung and asked us to use it, saying that is what we were meant for'. Such insults will be no surprise to women who have experienced resistance at the village level or at any other level (perhaps even more among the educated classes) to the idea of women taking charge of public affairs. Women have been slandered, the husbands of candidates have been told to 'put on bangles' since their wives' coming forward is an attack on their potency, all types of methods have been used. Today as the reality of reserved seats looms in the municipalities, male leaders are trying to spread the theme that this will hamper development since 'women have no experience, understand nothing'. But neither in the villages nor in the cities are women ready to remain 'dung' any longer.

Published as 'Women, Zilla Parishads and Panchayat Raj: Chandwad to Vitner' in *Economic and Political Weekly*, 4 August 1990, (pp. 1687-89).

Women in the Calcutta Municipal Corporation

STÉPHANIE TAWA LAMA-REWAL

This article presents the findings of a survey conducted in 2000 in the Calcutta Municipal Corporation (CMC), where quotas—33 per cent of seats—for women have been implemented since 1995. Quotas, or reservations, for women (as well as for the Scheduled Castes and the Scheduled Tribes) are one of the boldest provisions of the decentralisation policy defined by the 73rd and the 74th Constitutional Amendments passed in 1992, which gave a constitutional status to local self-government for the first time in the history of independent India. While the 73rd Constitutional Amendment (73rd CA) defines the decentralisation policy at the rural level (a policy commonly referred to as 'Panchayati Raj', or government of the panchayats), the 74th CA deals with urban local bodies, i.e. municipal corporations, municipal councils and nagar panchayats, depending on the size of the city.

Women's quotas in the Indian cities have evoked comparatively little interest so far.[1] This relative indifference contrasts, on the one hand, with the abundant literature generated by women's new role in the Panchayati Raj institutions. And on the other hand, with the heated debate provoked since 1996 by another constitutional Bill, now commonly referred to as the Women's Reservation Bill (WRB), proposing to implement similar quotas for women in state legislative assemblies and in the Lok Sabha.

The case study described here was conceived as an answer both to the debate over the WRB, involving a series of arguments, for and against women's quotas, in need of a confrontation with existing experiments, and to the present research gap concerning the implementation of quotas in Indian metropolitan cities. The size of cities such as Calcutta, Delhi, Mumbai or Chennai in terms of their population, and the type of problems their urban governments have to deal with, means that many of the arguments over the WRB are relevant to the level of the municipal corporations. This study therefore, is an assessment of the first phase of the implementation of women's quotas in the Calcutta Municipal Corporation, which proceeds by testing the major arguments expressed during the debate over the WRB [...]

The debate over the Women's Reservation Bill: on the objectives and means of a greater political representation of women

The main points of the Women's Reservation Bill, drafted by the National Commission for Women, are the following:

- One third of all seats will be reserved for women in the Lok Sabha as well as in the state legislative assemblies;
- Out of the seats already reserved for the Scheduled Castes and the Scheduled Tribes,[2] one third will be reserved for women belonging to either category;
- The constituencies reserved for women will be selected by rotation, for five years.

The debate over the WRB, involving mostly politicians and women's rights activists, has been taking place both in Parliament—where the Bill has been introduced four times in four years, always to face a strong, at times even violent, opposition—and in other fora such as the media, seminars and conferences all over the country. To sum up a long series of discussions, seven major arguments have been developed during this debate.

The arguments supporting women's quotas, on the one hand, can actually be found, as the Norwegian sociologist Hernes has shown, in about any debate on women's political representation. Hernes classified these arguments, all dealing with the *objectives* of a massive presence of women in political assemblies, into three main categories.

Firstly, arguments focusing on *gender justice*: women's presence in elected political assemblies has to be in proportion to their place in society if 'people's representation', central to the democratic principle, is to be meaningful.

Secondly, arguments focusing on *women's interests*: in this line of reasoning women are considered as an interest group, and a large presence of women in political assemblies is deemed necessary for their interests to be adequately represented.

Thirdly, arguments focusing on *women as a resource* for political life: women are here considered as possessing specific qualities or talents, which could fruitfully be tapped by society through their more effective political participation (Hernes 1982).

The opponents to the WRB, on the other hand, did not contest the above mentioned reasons why women should be numerous in political assemblies. Rather, their arguments focused on the perverse effects of women's quotas as they were outlined in the WRB; they criticised quotas as the *means* to reach these objectives.

Firstly, critics focused on the question as to *which women* would benefit from women's quotas, since the Bill does not specify any criteria of eligibility other than sex (except for Scheduled Castes and Scheduled Tribes). The opponents of the WRB have been arguing that (i) nepotism is likely to annihilate the democratising potential of the Bill; and that (ii) such reservations are likely to benefit mostly those women who belong to the privileged sections of society. Gender justice would thus be a mere façade, and social justice might actually suffer from women's quotas.

Secondly, the difficulty of finding enough suitable candidates has been underlined, along with the *risk of incompetent people being elected*.

Thirdly, a backlash by men, threatened by quotas, has been anticipated: men resenting the forced eviction of their male colleagues would be likely (i) not to allow women to contest out of reserved constituencies, and (ii) to confine the beneficiaries of quotas to some kind of *women's ghetto*, allowing them to deal only with areas traditionally considered as 'soft', such as health or education.

Lastly, the proposed system of *rotation of reserved constituencies* every five years has been denounced on two counts: (i) as a major obstacle to the establishment of a nurturing relationship between elected women and their respective constituencies; and (ii) implying that women candidates would always have to oppose other women candidates, thus both undermining the possibility of female solidarity, and depriving women of a chance to prove that they can do at least as well as men candidates.[3]

The following analysis is centred around these seven arguments, i.e. the issues at stake in the Indian debate on women's quotas. The paper follows a broad chronological order, examining, firstly, who are the women councillors elected in 1995; secondly, how they performed as councillors, and how newcomers learned their job; thirdly, to what extent did they represent women's interests; fourthly, what was their impact on the working of the CMC; and lastly, how they dealt with the rotation of constituencies at the time of the next electoral campaign, in June 2000.

Calcutta as a testing ground

Calcutta was selected as the object of this case study because West Bengal was one of the first states to adopt most of the provisions of the 74th CA. Constituencies were reserved for the first time for the 1995 municipal elections, therefore the survey conducted in 2000 could cover the full first term 'with quotas'.[4] [...]

The Calcutta Municipal Corporation Act, 1980, was amended to include the provisions of the 74th CA, whose broad objective is to give urban local bodies 'the institutional capability to deal with problems of urbanisation' (Pinto 2000: 22). Calcutta actually embodies the urban crisis which most cities are struggling with in India today: acute urban poverty, overpopulation, gross inadequacy of civic infrastructures and basic urban services such as water supply, drainage and sewerage, housing, and public health. The 74th CA provides for 'functional decentralisation, financial decentralisation and popular participation in civic affairs' (Mohanty 1999: 221). Its main features are the following:

- It defines the composition of municipal authorities, including that of ward committees in cities with a population of over 300,000 inhabitants;[5]
- It grants municipal authorities a five-year term, with an obligation for state governments to organise elections every five years, conducted by the state election commissions; it also provides, in case a municipality were dissolved before the end of its full term, that the state government shall organise fresh elections within six months from the date of dissolution;
- It provides for the mandatory constitution of a finance commission by the state government, every five years, 'to recommend to their legislatures measures to improve the financial health of municipal bodies' (Mathur 1999: 4);
- It provides for the constitution of district and metropolitan planning committees;
- The Twelfth Schedule of the 74th CA lists the functions devolved to municipal authorities (in the West Bengal Municipal Act, 1993, the obligatory functions of the municipality are grouped under four categories, i.e. public works, public health and sanitation, town planning and development, and administration);
- Lastly, the 74th CA provides that in order to empower the weaker sections of society, seats will be reserved for women (33 per cent in all municipalities), for the Scheduled Castes and for the Scheduled Tribes (in proportion to their population) for five years, on a rotation basis.

This last provision will now be the focus of this study. As far as Calcutta is concerned, since 1985 the CMC has been structured into 141 wards, (each ward comprising 20,000 to 50,000 inhabitants). In 1995, out of 141 wards, 47 were reserved for women, including three wards for women belonging to the

Scheduled Castes, and six more wards were reserved for Scheduled Castes irrespective of gender. Reservations for women (and for SCs/STs) are central to one of the main stakes of the 74th CA—local democracy. The latter is actually a multilayered notion. Local assemblies, because of the daily, concrete character of the problems they are concerned with, and because of the proximity of local representatives to voters, are supposed to be more accessible, more accountable, more responsive to citizens. From the point of view of representatives, local politics is supposed to be more open to otherwise politically marginalised sections, such as women, because of the part-time character of the councillor's job. Lastly, local democracy has long been conceived, under the influence of the liberal tradition, as a school of democracy, a political training ground.

This study then, aims at testing the contribution of women's reservations to local democracy by confronting the different voices, and the practical experiences, of the beneficiaries of reservations with the somewhat general and abstract arguments exchanged during the debate over the WRB.

Methodology of the survey

The fieldwork for this study was conducted in three stages (February, June and November 2000). While the June fieldwork was mostly devoted to participant observation of the campaigning for the municipal elections, the two other field trips in Calcutta were spent conducting a series of semi-directive interviews with councillors, both women and men.[6] The sample of councillors interviewed was designed so as to provide me with informants from all major political parties—i.e. the Communist Party of India (Marxist) (CPI-M), the Congress (I) (Congress), and the Trinamul Congress (TC), Hindus and Muslims, tested politicians and newcomers, old and young people, Scheduled Castes and others. Altogether I interviewed 50 councillors, i.e. 35 per cent of the 141 councillors elected in 1995. Out of these interviewees, 31 were women (60 per cent of the total number of women councillors) and 19 were men (21 per cent of the total number of men councillors). I also interviewed a section of what I assumed to be privileged 'witness-actors' of the reservation policy: CMC officials, representatives of women's organisations of the city, and party cadres. Lastly, I analysed archives of the CMC, more particularly, the minutes of the House meetings from 1995 to 2000.

I. Who are the beneficiaries of women's quotas?

> [Reservations for women] ... will definitely right the wrong and change the imbalance in legislative representation overnight [...] We must have more women if we want democracy to flourish (Najma Heptullah).[7]

> ...chances are that we will be saddled with more 'biwi-beti' brigades because [backward castes] leaders are likely to resort to fielding their mothers or sisters or wives to ensure that the women's quota stays within their caste control ... (Kishwar 1996: 2872).

Even though they do not legislate, councillors are the representatives of the people of their ward: they convey their particular demands to the relevant departments of the Corporation, and in their capacity of members of either the majority or the opposition in the House, they can support or reject more general proposals concerning the city. The municipal corporation is therefore a site both for political participation, articulation of citizens' interests and political debate.

The issue at stake here is that of gender and social justice, insofar as women's quotas might provide the former at the expense of the latter. The implicit assumption behind the 'democratic argument' in favour of quotas is that they will provide access to political representation to a group of people hitherto largely excluded from politics. Women, of course, are a very heterogenous group, and not all women are excluded from the political sphere to the same extent. The problem, then, can be summed up in two main questions:

- Will women quotas (in the absence of caste/class based subquotas other than those for the SCs and STs) actually benefit mostly elite women?

- Will women quotas encourage nepotism, through an increasing number of candidates/representatives 'by procuration', or 'proxies' i.e. women relatives of the sitting councillor, whose only function is to keep the seat within the family?

Social status and political resources of women councillors

In order to answer the first question, I used, as indicators of the social status of the women councillors elected in 1995, their caste/community identity, education level and occupation.

As far as caste/community is concerned, out of the Hindu[8] women interviewed, 37.5 per cent were Brahmin, 46 per cent were Kayastha/Vaidya, 4 per cent were Marwari and 12.5 per cent were Scheduled Castes. Thus 87.5 per cent of the interviewees belong to the higher castes.

Regarding education, here again the proportion of women with a comparatively high level of education is striking: 73 per cent of the interviewed women had a university degree (37 per cent had a BA, 7 per cent had an LLB, 30 per cent had an MA); 13 per cent had reached the Senior Secondary level; 7 per cent were Matriculate; and 7 per cent had quit school after the Middle level.

Lastly, the occupational profile of the women councillors interviewed is the following: 38 per cent of them are teachers, 24 per cent are housewives, 14 per cent lawyers, 10 per cent employees and 7 per cent in business.

The caste, educational and occupational profile of the women councillors interviewed suggest, beyond the elite character of the majority of them, a series of political resources to which these women have access: while caste and education (which is, of course, a resource in itself) provide social prestige, the occupational profile points to resources such as time (available to housewives, but also to teachers who can take temporary leave since they benefit from job security); social popularity (the main resource of teachers); and oratorical skills (such as those of lawyers).

It was unfortunately not possible, in the course of this survey, to assess with precision the income level of the beneficiaries of quotas, but interviews confirmed that the financial resource is also very important. To start with, all candidates have to give a deposit of Rs 150 when they file their nomination (SC candidates, however, are to give only Rs 75). Only those candidates getting at least one-sixth of the votes polled, will then recover their deposit. But more importantly, a candidate must be able to support expenses incurred in wall painting, posters, banners, transport for herself and her supporters, mike hiring charges, dais for the street corner meetings, refreshments to be provided on the voting day to the polling agents and other incidental expenditure. The ceiling imposed by the State Election Commission on contesting candidates was, in 1995, of Rs 25,000. Real expenses are actually much higher: a CPI(M) cadre estimated that campaigning for one candidate costs between Rs 50,000 and Rs 70,000.

Some parties do partially fund their candidates (mostly through a system of coupons sold to sympathisers), but the majority of candidates have to raise funds, i.e. find sponsors, and/or rely on their personal fortune.

Once elected, councillors also have to be able to mobilise financial resources. Their monthly allowance, which was recently raised from Rs 700 to Rs 1300, is supposed to cover the expenses incurred in the course of their work for the CMC. Since it is grossly inadequate, councillors must have some money to spare simply for their transportation or ward office maintenance.

But beyond these basic expenses, Anita,[9] for instance, was proud to recall that when a tree fell over a slum in her ward, she provided the most affected families with shelter at her personal expense, thus spending Rs 38,000, whereas the mayor had given these people only Rs 600 each; in another case of natural disaster, she had to provide food door to door, again at her personal expense.[10] Salima, too, was especially proud of having provided her ward with a free ambulance service, in which she put her own money, as well as 'well-wishers' donations'.[11]

We will see later that councillors can get funds for work in their ward, either from the CMC or from the Member of

Parliament in whose constituency their ward is located. But personal financial resources, as well as the support of 'well wishers' is obviously considered as a major—and legitimate—asset. Poor people, then, have a definite handicap in municipal politics.

The councillors 'by procuration'

The second question relative to the profile of the beneficiaries of quotas was that of 'proxy' representatives, i.e. women whose presence in municipal politics is only a façade, the real councillors still being their male relative whose seat in the latest election has been reserved for women.

How many 'proxies' then, are there among the 1995 batch of women councillors? If one considers as proxy any woman who is elected in a ward previously held by her husband/father/father-in-law, then six councillors, i.e. 11 per cent of the total, fit this description. One must, however, immediately qualify this figure.

Firstly, one must distinguish between 'proxies' and 'inheritors'. The succession of several members of the same family in the position of councillor of a particular ward might just be the local version of an old tradition in Indian politics, in which it is not infrequent for political positions to be inherited from one generation of a family to the other.[12] Inheritors (female and male) get access to their first political position by inheriting it from a male relative, but they then build their own political career on that basis, whereas real 'proxies' pretend to be the councillor only for formality's sake, knowing that once their ward is de-reserved they will leave politics altogether, while their male relative will once again be the candidate.

Shalini is a typical councillor by procuration. Her husband, who was the sitting councillor of her ward until it was reserved for women in 1995, is obviously the real person in charge. He answered all questions on her behalf when I tried to interview her, while she smiled shyly. How then, had she managed to convince voters to vote for her? 'She approached the voters and told them: "our family is looking after the public interest",' he candidly says.[13]

Being the wife of the sitting councillor is indeed, according to all inheritors, a real, and legitimate asset when one seeks election for the first time.

Lata, who was a candidate for the first time in 1995 in the (newly reserved) ward where her husband had been the councillor for 30 years, explains:

> People kept coming to my house to meet my husband when he was the councillor, so I knew them all ... I was guided by my husband whenever I met with problems, and after a few months I took control, and I became the borough chairman [a position her husband held from 1990 to 1995], now my husband does not attend the borough meetings.[14]

She thus presents her status of inheritor as an advantage, since it conferred her both familiarity with the voters and their problems, and a ready-made guide to help her learn her new job; but she takes care to specify that in the course of time she developed enough political skills of her own to be able to be elected and to work as a borough chairperson without any assistance.

Mina goes even further in justifying her being the candidate in the ward held so far by her husband:

> People are happy with [my husband's] work, so they're glad to support me now. They also know that as a teacher, I'm concerned about people's welfare. We're going to work together: first I was helping him, now he's going to help me; and by helping him I've gained some experience of the job.[15]

She emphasises here the solidarity between her husband and herself, presenting their couple as a team, in which both her husband's popularity and her own occupation combine to attract people's support.

Secondly, inheritors are not necessarily a consequence of the reservation system: one of the six women listed above, Chitra, the wife of the sitting councillor elected in 1990, was elected both in 1995 and 2000 *in a non-reserved ward*.

Thirdly, if one means by 'proxy' a councillor who is actually the puppet of another person, then proxies are not necessarily the female relatives of former sitting councillors. Rasheeda recalls with some bitterness how she became a councillor for the first time in her life.

> I was chosen because I was a divorced, Muslim housewife; I knew nothing about politics ... But then I learnt the job, and when I realised that the party didn't want me to do anything, I fought them, and I started working from my house, not from the ward office; the former councillor tried to influence me, naturally; and when the ward was de-reserved in 2000, I wasn't given the ticket again ...[16]

Unlike Rasheeda, therefore, those women councillors who succeeded their husbands in that position could rely—provided, of course, that their husbands were willing to let them fully exercise their political functions—on a major political resource: that of a patron whom they could legitimately acknowledge.

The second election after the implementation of women's quotas is the time when one can actually differentiate proxies from inheritors. Out of the six women elected in 1995 to succeed their husband/father/father-in-law, five were given the ticket again by their respective political parties in 2000: Chitra was re-elected (in a ward still unreserved); Sunita was proud to mention that after having been elected with a 12-vote majority when her ward was reserved, in 1995, she was re-elected with a victory margin of 2500 votes, even though her ward became 'general' five years later;[17] Lata, whose ward was also de-reserved, lost to a male competitor, and so did Mina; Shalini, whose ward was reserved for a second time in a row, was re-elected. Lastly Janaki was not a candidate when her ward was de-reserved; the party ticket was given again to her husband (who was not elected). Thus two-thirds of the female inheritors proved themselves enough to be entrusted with their party's support even though their ward was de-reserved in 2000.

The following table shows two parallel trends: on the one hand, after the dramatic quantitative leap effected by the implementation of quotas in 1995, the number of women elected during the following election kept increasing: thus quotas do not, at this stage, seem to act as a ceiling on the

Table 1: The progression of women councillors and of inheritors in the CMC

Year	Total number of councillors	Women councillors (%)	Inheritors among women councillors (%)
1990	141	6 (4%)	NA
1995	141	53 (38%)	6 (11%)
2000	141	60 (42.5%)	12 (20%)

Source: Calcutta Municipal Corporation

number of eligible women. On the other hand, the number of women being elected to a position previously held by a close male relative is also increasing.

Quotas appear, indeed, to encourage gender justice in terms of the presence of women in the CMC. But the simultaneous increase in the number of inheritors points to the growing importance of the family factor in local politics.

What finally emerges from the questioning of a few social characteristics of the women councillors elected in 1995, is that quotas did not produce social justice: among their beneficiaries there is an over-representation of elite women in terms of caste, education, and most probably in terms of income. Moreover, nepotism is indeed increasing in Calcutta's municipal politics, although one would need to know the number of inheritors among men councillors to be sure that this phenomenon is entirely due to the implementation of quotas.

However, an analysis of the same social characteristics in terms of resources shows that women councillors have access to major political resources such as education, time, popularity, money, verbal skills and, for inheritors, a male patron. These resources will prove to be crucial to the quality of the performance of the beneficiaries of quotas as councillors.

II. The performance of the beneficiaries of quotas

We should try to bring a qualitative change with women's participation in [elected assemblies], rather than bring it down further with women simply joining as puppets in this unholy enterprise (Kishwar 1996: 2873).

In the initial stage, the quality of women representatives is not up to the mark'; it's difficult to get good candidates, especially in 'SC women' wards; but in the long term it will be good (Calcutta's Mayor).[18]

Given the very small number of women who were active in local politics prior to the implementation of the 74th CA, the first foreseeable consequence of women's quotas is that it will translate into a massive eruption of newcomers in urban local bodies. The issue raised by critics of quotas is then that of the choice of democracy *vs* efficiency, common to all debates on affirmative action. On this issue, opponents to the WRB argued that the (partial) success of the Panchayati Raj was no ground for advocating similar quotas in the Lok Sabha and the state legislative assemblies, since the functions performed by legislators were much more complex than those required from local representatives. But what, really, is the role of municipal councillors in a metropolitan city such as Calcutta?

Firstly, councillors have obligations towards the voters of their ward: they must assess the needs of the ward, listen to the grievances of voters, and represent them in the CMC: they convey the voters' demands and needs to the relevant departments of the CMC, to the Mayor-in-Council or to the House, depending on the nature and dimension of the problem. Each councillor can sanction development expenditures of upto Rs 120,000 per year (Mukhopadhyay 2000: 30). If their ward is located within the constituency of a Member of Parliament (MP) from the same party, they also can appeal to the 'MP fund' to effect particular tasks.[19] Moreover, they convey all relevant information from the CMC to the voters, to whom they also provide official documents such as death certificates, student cards etc. They also have to carry a honorific function, and attend events such as inaugurations, school shows etc. taking place in their ward.

Secondly, councillors have obligations towards the CMC: they have to attend borough and House meetings once a month.

Lastly, they have obligations towards the political party they belong to, which means, most often, that they have to be available for a number of party meetings.

In short, councillors represent voters in the CMC, and they represent the CMC and their party in front of voters. Given the number and variety of the tasks which councillors have to fulfil, what are the specific problems—or advantages—of the beneficiaries of quotas, as women and as newcomers?

The difficulty of being a woman and a councillor

Devaki, a lawyer, describes thus her typical working day:

> From 7 to 11 a.m., people come to see me in my house; then I go to the Court; then, in the evening again people come to me; and I often go out to inspect various areas, I have to personally see the problems.[20]

Alpana, a Scheduled Caste woman who belongs to a poorer milieu, starts her day with the household chores; she then goes to school, where she teaches from 6.30 to 10.30 a.m.; after that she comes home, where she receives people's grievances, signs documents, writes letters; from 11.30 a.m. to 2 p.m. she stays at the ward office; then, if necessary, she goes to the CMC main office. She has to be permanently available for the people, she says.[21]

Being a municipal councillor, obviously, is very demanding in terms of time. The beneficiaries of quotas thus have to face the difficult task, familiar to all working women, of juggling their domestic responsibilities with their public obligations. For women politicians, however, this difficulty is even greater since one feature common to domestic and to political work is that both involve a total commitment (Laufer 1995: 378).

The obligations of the councillor necessarily intrude upon her family life, both in terms of time and in terms of space. Councillors are used to receiving people at home, in addition to the time which they spend in the ward office.[22] Here again, the family support appears as a crucial resource—a resource highlighted by inheritors such as Saloni:

> There are only small problems in being a woman councillor; for

instance, who will look after the children? But I'm supported by my family; and, when there is a big problem, my husband is there to help me.[23]

I asked women councillors what, in their experience, was the main inconvenience of being a *woman* councillor. Their answers point to three main types of problems. Firstly, all of them had to deal with the permanent scarcity of time, due to the competing pressure of domestic duties and political obligations (plus, for those women who were employed and did not take leave after being elected, the additional time required by their job):

> I'm very busy from morning till night, but I have to manage my home also, for my family; but my male colleagues seem to ignore it, they don't see that I sometimes need to rest (Aruti).[24]

> I will not continue as a councillor, even though I like politics very much; my child suffers a lot from my absence (Tulsi).[25]

Secondly, they mentioned the incompatibility between some of their political obligations and women's traditional behaviour:

> The problem is not being a woman, but being a housewife; when I have to go somewhere, the problem is that I cannot ride a bicycle ... (Alpana).[26]

> When people come with a problem at night, then I cannot go out, unless the situation really compels me to do so (Devaki).[27]

> There is a problem if I have to go out after midnight, because then I have to get some male comrades to escort me; I also have to defend myself against drug addicts ... (Tulsi).[28]

The conflict between women councillors' role as respectable women and their role as politicians is indeed specially conspicuous when women councillors have to come out of their house after nightfall. To do so involves two kinds of dangers in the Indian context: a physical danger, since violence is more likely to happen in the dark; and a more abstract, but nevertheless very real danger; that of putting one's reputation at risk, since respectable women are, by convention, not supposed to be out at right.

Thirdly, women councillors have to deal with their male colleagues' prejudices.

> There is a discrimination: men councillors do not take us seriously, even though they don't show it openly; but there is no such problem with voters (Tulsi).[29]

> A man can create many problems for a woman; official executives take advantage of our ignorance ... as newcomers, we feel too shy to shout (Sujata).[30]

As newcomers, precisely, what kind of training was available for the newly elected women to learn the councillor's job? All women councillors interviewed declared that they had to learn their new functions hands on, since no training whatsoever was organised for the newly elected councillors in 1995 [...]

Three types of informal training actually emerge from the interviews, most women mentioning more that one type: 44 per cent of the women councillors relied on explanations and instructions from senior party workers; 44 per cent could benefit from advice and suggestions from CMC officials, engineers, and from fellow councillors; and 12.5 per cent were trained by their husband or father-in-law (these women did not mention any other form of training). Lastly, only one woman (a lawyer) mentioned that she had taken a few paying lessons from an engineer in order to better grasp the complexities involved in solving problems such as water supply or drainage.

As far as the more political side of a councillor's job is concerned, however, most newly elected women could actually rely on some previous experience of collective action, mainly through party or front organisation membership. Altogether 77 per cent of the women interviewed had previously been members of a political party and/or of one of the party's front organisations. Among them, 83 per cent mentioned a membership of the party's women's organisation, 48 per cent a membership of the student's organisation and 30 per cent membership of a trade union (some women had been a member of more than one type of front organisation).

Lastly, when asked why, in their opinion, they had been selected by the party to be a candidate in the municipal elections, the women interviewed gave four main types of explanations (again, not mutually exclusive), which also point to various resources available for learning their new functions. Belonging to a 'political family' was a reason mentioned by 37.5 per cent of women; having done 'social work' was also mentioned by 37.5 per cent of women; while 31 per cent of them cited their own 'political background' as an asset, and 31 per cent, again, presumed that their 'profession'—teacher, or lawyer—had made suitable candidates out of them. Therefore the family and the party appear once again as major training resources, while occupations such as social worker, teacher and lawyer, not surprisingly, show a special affinity for politics.

The advantages of being a woman councillor

Being a woman can also be an advantage when it comes to performing the functions of a municipal councillor. The women interviewed all agreed on two main reasons why women can perform particularly well in this role.

Firstly, they underlined the many aspects common (if on a different scale) between the responsibilities of a housewife and that of a councillor.

> Women are born home ministers ... At home, a woman takes care of all problems, so why not on a larger scale? (Alpana)[31]

> Being a councillor is ideal for a woman; it's work that looks a lot like that of housewives: you have to take care of water, of drainage (like in a bathroom) etc. ... (Sunita).[32]

The assimilation of the constituency to a larger household has been a recurring figure of speech in the discourse on women's aptitudes to political functions, ever since the Indian debate on women's right to vote started in 1917.[33] This argument relies on the traditional sexual division of labour, of which it only displaces the contours. As such, its contribution to women's empowerment is dubious. Moreover, this metaphor can backfire:

when taken too literally, it can be used to support the idea that women are fit only for the local, i.e. the more particular, concrete level of politics.[34]

Yet when asked whether, provided they were offered the opportunity, they would consider being candidates in a future election, at the state assembly level, for instance, 89 per cent of the women interviewed expressed their readiness to go further into their political career; among them, 27 per cent asserted their intention to do so unconditionally, while 54 per cent said that their decision would depend primarily on the party.

The second major argument women councillors cited as supporting a larger number of women in municipal politics is that they are much more approachable by women voters.

> Muslims are very conservative, so their ladies can't go to the party office when they have a problem; it was easier for them to have access to a woman councillor (Rasheeda).[35]

Even though she was not given the ticket in the 2000 municipal elections, Rasheeda said that she still acts as a representative of the Muslim women of her ward: she collaborates with the new councillor by conveying these ladies' demands to him. But Hindu women councillors also emphasised how, as women, they could reach, and be reached by, the many women who would either feel too shy to go and meet a male councillor, or who would simply not trust him to understand and deal with problems such as marital disputes, for instance.

> Earlier, the male members of the family would come most often; now women come more than men, to bring me their problems; women of the slums come to me in a group, about problems of water, drainage ... and there are family problems also; husbands drink and beat their wives ... I had the police close the liquor shop (Ketaki).[36]

By underlining their special relationship with the women of their constituency, women councillors indeed present themselves as the representatives of women, insofar as representation involves knowing about people's problems as a first step into putting these problems on the political agenda.

As a conclusion, it appears, on the one hand, that the

performance of the beneficiaries of quotas may have suffered both from their being women, and from their being newcomers in municipal politics. As women, they were constrained by the weight of domestic responsibilities, and by that of gendered normative behaviours; as newcomers, they were necessarily handicapped by the absence of any comprehensive, formal training to prepare them to their new functions.

On the other hand, the women councillors elected in 1995 could rely on a number of resources to palliate this double handicap, such as their family (a relay for domestic work as well as a training resource), their own political experience and sometimes the skills specific to their occupation. Lastly, and perhaps most importantly, the fact that women councillors gave access to the CMC to women, i.e. to 50 per cent of voters, is certainly a major argument in favour of the ability of reservations to promote political participation, in the largest sense of the word. But the question whether elected women do represent women voters is a complex one, and must now be addressed separately.

III. The representation of women's interests

It is not as if women have not occupied seats in the legislatures; it is simply that they have not addressed the questions which pertain to the problems of women adequately, seriously or with sensitivity. Had they done so, we would not have had all these missing women or illiteracy or hunger or homelessness or violence both at home and at the work place. The demand behind the Women's Reservation Bill is that women representatives should address the specific problems of their constituency (N. Chandhoke).[37]

Women's participation in politics is necessary for holistic development ... [Women] are bound to have a better perspective on vital issues such as environment, health care and education, particularly of the girl-child, as these affect them directly (A. Celly).[38]

The figure of 33 per cent, frequently criticised by those who support women's quotas for the sake of gender justice, is often justified as emanating from a study conducted by a

Scandinavian social scientist, showing that one third is the threshold from which a minority can constitute a 'critical mass', i.e. is in a position to have an impact on the decisions taken by the group as a whole (Dahlerup: 1988). By forcing the election of 33 per cent women among municipal councillors, then, the 74th CA seems to aim at a better representation of women's interests through the presence of a critical mass of women in urban local bodies. But the question whether elected women do actually represent—i.e. advocate—women's interests is a complex one, as it involves a series of subquestions: what are the problems perceived, by women councillors, as women's interests, or women's issues? Do women councillors want to represent women's interests? Are they in a position to do so?

In order to answer this set of questions, I relied on three main sources: what women councillors said; the minutes of the proceedings of the House meetings, showing both which issues are raised, and by whom; and what a few representatives of women's organisations of Calcutta—assumed to be the closest thing to a women's lobby—said of their relationship with women councillors.

What are women's interests?

I asked women councillors what were the main problems they had to deal with in their respective wards, and then, what were, in their view, the main problems faced by women in their ward.

The most frequently mentioned women's issue was 'family problems', i.e. mostly marital disputes (42 per cent); then came 'economic problems, unemployment' (25 per cent), 'water scarcity' (21 per cent), 'violence' (21 per cent), the lack of 'latrines' (12.5 per cent), and 'illiteracy' (8 per cent). Interestingly, 12.5 per cent of the women interviewed said that there was no such thing as 'women's problems', but only 'general problems'.

A comparison of this list with that of the most 'important issues in the ward' identified by women councillors, shows that women's issues come among the least frequently mentioned problems, with the notable exception of 'water scarcity', mentioned by 94 per cent of the women interviewed. Lack of latrines (12 per cent), illiteracy of women (12 per cent) and the need for maternity homes (6 per cent) occupy the last three positions on this list, way behind drainage, street lights, road repairs, slum development and solid waste disposal.

But do women councillors consider women voters as their constituency? In other words, do they want to represent women first? If a majority of the women councillors interviewed expressed their concern for the problems of women, most of them, however, strongly opposed the suggestion that they represent women exclusively, or even more particularly. The interviews suggest that they actually draw a strong distinction between what they can do for women in their capacity of individual councillor, within the ward, and what they can do as the group of women councillors within the CMC.

As *individuals*, we have already seen that most women councillors emphasise that being a woman makes them much more approachable for the women of their ward. They underline the commonality of experience which enables them to better understand women's problems:

> Being a woman, it's easier for me to discuss with women, for instance about their need for latrines; men hear but do not work on those problems; we, as women, feel the importance of the problem (Monalika).[39]

> Women talk very freely to me; these are destitute women, victims of atrocities; I give them counselling, and I convey their complaints to the police station (Raina).[40]

However, they underline the fact that dealing with women's problems is not their main function, but rather an addition to their general load of work as councillors.

> Women come to me with their family problems, they're very oppressed; this is an additional work for me; but I'm a member of the State Committee of the Ganatantrik Mahila Samiti [the women's section of the CPI-M], so they also come to me for that reason (Aruti).[41]

> Women's issues don't matter to me, but women of the lower sections are very ignorant, they have very little awareness, although there are

good laws for women; whenever they come to me I help them, because I am also a lady (Anita).[42]

Several women councillors were proud to mention achievements such as the mobilisation of bustee women to make them benefit from a particular self-employment scheme, the construction of a maternity home, how they helped widows to get the pensions to which they are entitled, the mediation role which they occasionally played in family disputes etc.

The comparatively greater involvement of women councillors in projects concerning mostly women is confirmed by one of the senior officials of the CMC. The Bustee Cell of the CMC, created in 1986, is mainly concerned with implementing schemes of self-employment for slum-dwellers; since 1998, one of the most important of these schemes, the Swarna Jayanti Shahari Rozgar Yojana, has been focusing on women slum-dwellers. According to the Deputy Director of the Bustee Cell, women councillors are more interested than their male counterparts in this scheme;[43] it is also easier for them to reach women, to tell them how to form 'neighbourhood groups' to disseminate information about the existing facilities to which they are entitled to apply, she says.

What are the issues raised by women councillors?

But what about women councillors *as a group*? Does the new, massive presence of women councillors have an impact on the agenda of the House meetings? Is there a solidarity between women councillors on women's issues? There seemed to be a consensus on the actual impossibility for them to unite across party lines on any issue.

> For women, I work in bustees, non-formal education, health, widow stipend, maternity relief ... My first aim is to develop the consciousness of women, to make them aware that they can stop depending on others ... [But] as representatives, in the House we don't want to raise issues considered as sectarian, but only general issues ... (Kiran).[44]

> There is no scope for women's issues in the CMC, except for pensions and family benefits (Anita).[45]

Three main arguments are put forth to explain this state of things, invoking (i) party discipline as the dominant factor in alliances within the CMC; (ii) the nature of issues discussed during the House meetings; and (iii), ideological reasons—the latter being mentioned only by councillors belonging to the communist parties.

> Women's issues are not debated. The problems discussed in the House meetings are general problems: roads, lighting, water ... and there is solidarity within the party only (Monika).[46]

> I'm not a feminist: women cannot solve their problems alone; we're oppressed, we have various demands on our hands; but other oppressed sections are there also (workers etc.). We share the same problems; the oppressed class has to move together (Aruti).[47]

In order to assess the impact of women councillors on the agenda of the CMC, I analysed the proceedings of the House meetings for which the board of councillors gathers once a month.

The following table sums up the types of issues raised in front of the House, as well as who—men or women—raised these issues most often. This table does not take into account the yearly budget sessions of the House, in which only the budget as a whole is discussed.

The table is an indicator *among others* of the issues dealt with by councillors; councillors can, and do work on many problems affecting their ward without necessarily attracting the House's attention to it. Many issues take other routes, such as submitting proposals to the Mayor-in-Council (MIC), which might then become a resolution of the MIC placed before the House for approbation; or submitting a problem directly to the concerned CMC department. What this table shows is (a) the nature and the relative importance of the issues discussed in the House; and (b) the respective participation of men and women councillors relative to the various issues at stake.

It emerges from the analysis that water supply is indeed the most pressing issue in Calcutta, an issue raised by male as well as by female councillors; then come all kinds of questions relating to the working of the CMC itself, and not far behind questions relating more specifically to the use of the CMC funds;

Table 2: The issues raised and discussed in the House meetings between 1995 and 2000

Issues	Number of times it was raised by a male councillor	Number of times it was raised by a female councillor	Total number of times it was raised
1. Water supply	25	15	40
2. Functioning of the CMC (rules implementation, personnel management)	23	5	28
3. Illegal constructions	22	3	25
4. Management of the CMC funds	20	5	25
5. Road repair/construction	15	2	17
6. Public health (control of malaria and other epidemics, vaccination campaigns, health centres, food and water quality control) and safety (manholes, fire prevention)	13	2	15
7. Solid waste disposal	12	0	12
8. Drainage/sewerage	10	2	12
9. Illegal activities	11	0	11
10. CMC building plan	8	3	11
11. CMC land use	6	3	9
12. CMC buildings	6	3	9
13. Parks	6	1	7
14. Property taxes	6	1	7
15. Roads renaming	2	4	6
16. Maintenance of historical places	2	4	6
17. Schools	3	2	5
18. Street lights	5	0	5
19. Issuing of licences	4	0	4
20. Pensions	2	2	4
21. Payment of compensations	4	0	4
22. Community halls	3	0	3
23. Public toilets	3	0	3
24. Family benefit schemes	1	1	2
25. Electrification	1	0	1
26. Issuing of certificates	0	1	1
Total	213	59	272

Source: Minutes of the Meetings of the Calcutta Municipal Corporation, 1995–2000.[48]

apart from the functioning and financing of the CMC work, illegal constructions, roads and health are the issues most often raised by councillors.

What is the participation of women to the House debates? Women councillors clearly participate much less in the debates than their male colleagues, who intervene into the debate 3.6 times more often that their female counterparts do, even though they were, from 1995 to 2000, only 1.6 times more numerous.

Moreover, on those issues which the women councillors interviewed defined as women's issues—such as health, (widows) pensions, public toilets and family benefit schemes, they appear to actually intervene much less than men (on public health), just as much as men (on pensions and family benefit schemes), or not at all (on public toilets). Even more baffling are those issues on which women's contribution outnumbers that of men: the renaming of roads, and the maintenance of historical places, i.e. issues relating to culture, and to cultural symbols—so much for the idea that women are necessarily more interested in concrete issues ...

Finally, then, this table shows that the massive presence of women councillors does not seem to influence the agenda of the House: women's interventions are almost never numerous enough to influence the relative importance of the various issues discussed; and they do not intervene on what has been constructed as 'women's issues'.[49] But the table also shows that there *is* scope for issues affecting women within the House debates: schools, maternity homes, public latrines or family benefit schemes are actually discussed. Two hypotheses come to mind in order to explain the weak participation of women to discussions around those issues: (i) women councillors do not consider these issues as major issues, and/or they do not consider themselves as representatives of women; (ii) they do not want to be discredited by appearing to be concerned only, or mostly, with women's, i.e. sectarian issues.

Women councillors and women's organisations

In order to test the first hypothesis, that is, to probe to what extent women councillors want and/or can act as the representatives of women, I tried to ascertain the nature of the relationship, if any, between women councillors (and more generally the CMC) and women's organisations. I thus interviewed representatives of eight women's organisations operating in Calcutta, including the women's sections of two political parties, the CPI(M) and the TC.

The non-party organisations have all been set up by women, and are run by women, to help women as a group, through literacy classes, skill trainings, self-employment schemes, hostels, legal counselling, crèches, health services etc.

The objectives of the women's sections of political parties are more ambivalent. On the one hand, the parties' women's sections provide a parallel, 'women only' site of political mobilisation, thus being within the reach of those women who find it difficult to be party workers; as such, the women's sections devote part of their work to activities meant to improve women's condition, such as income-generating schemes, literacy classes etc. On the other hand the women's sections of political parties constitute a ready-made pool of volunteers to help the party carry activities such as a demonstration or an electoral campaign. The women's sections of political parties are thus organisations by women, but not exclusively for women: their agenda is always subordinated to that of the party.

Both women councillors and women's organisations represent women: while the former can be said, at the very least, to represent women through their mere *presence* in the CMC, women's organisations, which have no electoral legitimacy, represent women through their *advocacy* work. Thus membership of, or even a relationship with, a women's organisation, seemed to be a good indicator of the level of 'gender-consciousness' of women councillors.

Very few women councillors mentioned any membership of a women's organisation other than the women's section of their political party (of which, as we said earlier 83 per cent had been a member at some point). The few women who did so were actually members of the women's cell of organisations such as the Lion's Club, i.e. charitable organisations targeting women, rather than feminist organisations.

From the side of women's organisations, the question whether they had, as such, observed the impact of the new presence of 53 women in the CMC, evoked a series of negative answers.

At first, all interviewees agreed that their relationship with the CMC is hardly there at all; they would get in touch with the CMC only regarding property tax exemptions, when a function organised by them had to be graced by the local councillor, or when problems such as water logging happen on their land.

On second thoughts, however, several of them reflected that the problem is not so much the irrelevance of the CMC's work to their own activies and needs, as the well-known inefficiency of the CMC.

> We don't work with the CMC, because we never get things done (Nari Seva Sangha).[50]

> The Calcutta Metropolitan Development Authority once got a grant for a population programme; they had no idea how to use this money, so they came to us because they knew about the crèches we are running. We were willing to work, but everything had to be done though the CMC doctor, who refused to budge; so we stopped the whole thing ... (Mahila Seva Samiti).[51]

Most of these women activists disapproved of reservations for women, considering it a humiliating provision, and one which does not guarantee any progress for women as a whole.

> 33 per cent won't help much; women councillors are dominated by their parties. But it gives them access; women are given a seat, but are they really enlightened? ... There is scope for women's issues in the CMC (the CMC can check the standards in schools, provide health services, help NGOs ...) but these issues are not addressed; councillors are concerned with power politics (Women's Sahayog).[52]

> We had a project for street children, for which we needed the cooperation of the local councillor; so we approached her, but she was a young woman who did what her husband told her to do, and he was not sympathetic to our idea, plus he did not like people coming to meet her all the time ... (All India Women's Conference).[53]

Women's organisations thus view women councillors as dominated either by their respective parties, or by male relatives. All of them said they hadn't noticed any change in their contacts with the CMC in the past five years.

The representation of Scheduled Castes within the CMC

In order to put to test the second hypothesis, i.e. the alleged impossibility for councillors to represent sectarian interests in the House, I interviewed five councillors (two men and three women), who had been elected in wards reserved for SCs. To what extent did these councillors want to represent more particularly the interests of SC people, and what were their resources (were they willing to do so)?

Four of them were (nominated) members of State/CMC bodies devoted to the welfare of SCs. But they held very opposed views on their role as SC councillors:

> I was nominated by the Mayor as a member of the SC/ST Municipal Committee which monitors several schemes (funded by the Central Government) to improve the condition of SCs/STs. We inform people of the locality about the different schemes ... We are the coordinators between the CMC and the local people. But 99 per cent of voters in my ward are non SC; caste is not a problem in our city life ... I'm not a member of any SC association. Discrimination is there only regarding the scavengers, the Methor; we help them by offering them self-employment opportunities (Talal).[54]

> A good number of voters in my ward are SCs, and they feel better represented by me; thanks to me they have benefited from specific schemes. I faced some contempt from the higher castes during the [electoral] campaign, but I've won their heart through my hard work ... Reservations are necessary to bring up backward classes, since SC councillors bring up SC people's problems in the House, but reservations for women do not seem to me to be necessary (Pankaj).[55]

What is, then, the view of these women elected in 'women SC' wards? Saroj was elected in such a ward, and she too was nominated by the Mayor as a member of the SC/ST/Backward Classes Committee of the CMC. She described what she had been doing for women and SC people, but insisted that '[she] represents everybody similarly'.[56] She suffered discrimination as a SC from senior colleagues, both in and out of her party; but neither women's issues nor SC issues are ever discussed in the House, she says.

Lastly Padma, who was elected the first time when her ward was reserved for women, and re-elected, five years later, when it was reserved for Scheduled Castes, listed a series of problems faced by women, but she could not think of any problem specific to Scheduled Caste people. 'I don't discriminate', she says; 'whoever comes to me will get my help'.[57]

Thus while the notion of interests specific to the SCs is officially endorsed through the existence of a Municipal Committee exclusively devoted to them—a Committee which has no equivalent concerning women—SC councillors held very diverse views as to what their constituency is. What emerges from their answers is that there is a complete lack of consensus on both the need and the ways to better represent SCs' interests [...]

As a tentative conclusion, one might say that the 'critical mass' theory is not validated by the first term of the CMC including women's quotas: a massive presence of women within the CMC is obviously not enough for women's issues to find a better position on the urban government's agenda. Most women councillors are conscious of, and concern themselves with, the problems faced by women in their ward. But they do not want to advocate women's interests within the House, because they do not consider them, or they do not want to appear as if they considered them, as major issues. A similar phenomenon was observed by B. Ghosh in a study of women elected at the rural level in West Bengal:

> Women [panchayat] members know what the special problems of women are. Yet in their perception of development they could not get out of the pervading influence of the ideology of public works and include gender-specific issues on the agenda of the development plan ... They have not perceived their role as the mouthpiece of women. [...] (Ghosh 1996: 152).

The distinction women councillors draw between what they

can do as individuals and what they can do as councillors in the CMC suggest that they work for women almost in a private capacity; clearly, for them the personal is not political. Their non-relationship with non-party women's organisations confirms that they are not women's rights activists; the political party is their main reference, and they adopt the party's priorities. Lastly, the fact that SC councillors have no such reluctance to assert their more particular commitment to SCs interests shows that, contrary to what women councillors said, 'sectarian interests' can be, and are expressed within the CMC. Gender, clearly, does not have the same legitimacy as caste as a basis for solidarity and concern, in short for mobilisation.

IV. The impact of women on the general functioning of the CMC

> Any polity in which violence and crime dominate, women as a group become automatically marginalised—partly out of choice but largely due to the fact that barring exceptions, women cannot effectively compete with men in gangsterism (Kishwar 1996: 2873).

> Everybody knows that women are less easily carried away and are more objective [than men]. They will make politics more sober (T.N. Seshan).[58]

The issue at stake here is whether women constitute a resource for political life. Do women bring to politics (what is assumed to be) feminine qualities? This question is problematic, since it relies on the postulate of the existence of 'feminine qualities', a notion belonging to an essentialist definition of woman which has been the object of much debate within the women's movement, both in India and elsewhere. It is, however, an important question to ask, if only because of the prominence of the 'resource' argument in all debates on women's political representation.

In order to answer this question then, one will need to (i) identify women's qualities; and to (ii) define criteria so as to measure how, and how much, these qualities appear to have an impact on political life.

Women's motherly qualities

As far as the first part of the problem is concerned, interviews revealed a broad consensus on what constitute women's specific qualities. Most people—men and women—seemed to agree with the idea that women, being women, can improve some aspects of municipal life.

To the question 'Do women make a difference in the CMC, and if yes, how?', only six per cent of the women councillors interviewed answered 'no'. Among the others, 69 per cent cited 'women's honesty, their sincerity'; 31 per cent evoked 'women's hard-working qualities'; and 12.5 per cent mentioned 'women's patience'.

> Women are sincere and honest because woman means mother; a mother manages her family, so she can manage a ward also (Lata).[59]

> A woman can serve people better than a man because she's a mother (Salima).[60]

> Many women councillors are more active, more honest, more society/family oriented than men. Women are mothers ... In wards where a woman is councillor, the polio pulse is more satisfactory (Calcutta's Mayor).[61]

Feminine qualities are thus the qualities assumed to pertain to mothers: nurturing capacity, honesty, devotion to others, patience. The 'resource' argument, as it is asserted by councillors, is actually a 'maternalist' argument, which assimilates womanhood to motherhood. The maternalist argument has a strong, emotional appeal—all the more so, one might think, in Bengal, where the 'matrifocal' character of the Hindu cosmology is particularly developed (Nandy 1990: 8). But his is a dangerous argument, as it relies on stereotypes which have been often used in the past to actually exclude women from politics: women, being mothers, are too soft, too emotional, too partial to be able to deal with public affairs, it was argued (Pateman 1989). Moreover, even beyond the mere question of women's political participation, and notwithstanding the highly idealised character of this conception of motherhood, the assimilation of women to mothers validates their social legitimisation through motherhood only, thus strongly restricting women's freedom in orienting their lives.

Standing out of the apparent consensus on women councillors' motherly qualities, however, the Municipal Secretary's assessment provides a much needed nuance:

> Women councillors are usually quiet, but they can become violent sometimes; once, the women councillors gheraoed the Chairman of the House on a party issue; it's easy for them to do that, because there is no female marshall in the House; otherwise the Chairman would have been quickly rescued! ... Young women councillors are very active; also many women councillors are constructive in their suggestions; they are more assiduous than men, they're more disciplined ...[62]

The incident described here suggests not only that women are not necessarily non-violent, but also that they are able to manipulate the conventions of behaviour between genders to pursue very unwomanly ends. Moreover, the qualities he refers to—activity, discipline—are different from the usual motherly attributes, and evoke, rather, attitudes typical of newcomers eager to prove themselves.

The impossibility of testing the 'resource' argument

In order to proceed towards a testing of the maternalist argument, one would now need (i) to measure men and women councillors' respective attitude towards corruption, their sincerity and their patience; (ii) to assess their respective nurturing capacity; and (iii) to compare the amount of work put in by them—*all other factors being equal*. Such an endeavour is obviously fraught with methodological as well as practical difficulties. The problem of the 'resource' argument is indeed that it relies on a series of clichés which are hardly testable.

It is not possible, then, to say whether or not the new, massive presence of women within the CMC has made the latter a more transparent, more dedicated, more efficient institution. The resource argument, finally, appears to be an assortment of stereotypical representations whose bearing on the political reality is largely unverifiable.

V. The rotation of constituencies reserved for women

> ... accepting 33 per cent permanent reservation for women is ... the equivalent of a 'zenana dabba' (ladies compartment) in every train. Men then come to expect women to remain confined to the ladies section ... (Kishwar 1996: 2872).

> Women legislators, when elected under a rotating quota will not be able to nurse their constituencies on a long-term basis, because after de-reservation of that constituency, they are not likely to get a ticket for the same seat (Kishwar 2000: 4152).

The system of rotating, reserved constituencies has attracted the greatest number of criticisms during the debate over the WRB. The issue at stake here is again, a complex one. Firstly, reserving constituencies for women means restricting the openness of the electoral competition—which is then closed to men—and therefore formally goes against the democratic principle according to which every citizen has an equal right not only to vote, but also to contest in any election. The counter-argument, of course, is that the fact that women have been unable to constitute more than four per cent of councillors in Calcutta since 1952 shows that while electoral contests were formally open, they were really largely closed to women.

But even more than the fact of reserving constituencies, it is the rotation of those which has attracted the strongest criticisms. Rotation is obviously the necessary counterpart of the reservation of constituencies: it balances, over a series of three successive elections, the unequal status of reserved *vs.* general constituencies. But critics of the WRB assumed that reservations would arouse such a resentment among men that those women who were elected for the first time in a reserved constituency would not be given the ticket for a second time once the constituency is de-reserved and becomes general again. Therefore, the rotation of reserved constituencies has been expected to be detrimental to the political career of the beneficiaries of quotas as well as to politics in general since it deprives elections of their 'sanction' aspect, thus diminishing the accountability of elected representatives towards voters.

The June 2000 municipal election in Calcutta, being the

second election subsequent to the implementation of women's quotas, offered a wealth of details and nuances about the actual impact of the rotation of reserved wards on municipal politics.

Being a candidate

Getting the party's ticket, or registering oneself as an independent candidate, is the first step of the municipal election. What happened in the newly reserved wards[63] in 1995? And what happened in the de-reserved wards in 2000?

The pattern of reservations is actually not quite unpredictable. It is available with the State Election Commission, which defined this pattern for three elections to come. Parties and potential candidates in a given ward are therefore in a position to anticipate a strategy, taking reservations into account: most wards become general after having been reserved, but some of them are reserved for two elections in a row, and yet others become reserved for a different category.

In 1995, the sitting councillors whose wards were newly reserved were usually not given the party ticket, except for a few party leaders (such as the mayor) who were given the ticket in a different ward.

Who then, were the women candidates in the newly reserved wards? According to a woman cadre of the CPI(M), the eligibility of a potential woman candidate is assessed according to her 'popularity'; moreover, she must have done some social work, have a clean image and some political principles; but being a party member is not necessary. She added that it was actually not difficult to find enough suitable candidates at the municipal level.[64] Indeed in 1995, women constituted 33 per cent of candidates but 38 per cent of the elected councillors, which points to a high rate of winnability. However, both in 1995 and in 2000, the average number of candidates was slightly higher in general wards than in reserved wards.

In the 2000 elections, out of the 47 wards that had been reserved for women five years earlier, 39 became general again (since five of these wards were reserved for women once again, and three were reserved for the Scheduled Castes).

Table 3: The number of candidates in reserved and in unreserved wards

Year	Average number of candidates in reserved wards	Average number of candidates in general wards
1995	5.5 (2 to 11)	6.5 (3 to 15)
2000	6.6 (2 to 12)	8.5 (3 to 21)

Source: State Election Commission, Calcutta

What happened, in these de-reserved wards to the former beneficiaries of quotas? Out of the 39 female sitting councillors, 51 per cent were given the ticket by their respective political parties to contest elections in the same ward; 18 per cent were given the ticket to contest in a different, reserved ward; and 31 per cent did not contest the elections. Altogether then, more than two-thirds of the beneficiaries of quotas retained the support of their party after de-reservation of their ward, even though one-fourth of these women had to campaign in a new ward, which is necessarily more challenging than campaigning in the ward where and for which one has been working for five years.

What about the anticipated backlash by men? Out of those six women councillors who had been elected in 1995 in general wards, in 2000 one was given the ticket in a different, reserved ward; the five others were given the ticket in the same ward—but for three of them, their ward was newly reserved for women.

Lastly, even though getting a party ticket is a definite advantage in the electoral competition, a number of women contested as independents, emboldened by the fact that their ward was reserved for women. Reservations then appear as generating an opportunity effect. However, we have seen earlier that campaigning is an expensive endeavour; thus potential candidates must have some network to rely on for their campaign; this was the case, for instance, of an independent woman candidate, who mobilised the children to which she had been providing free school, to paste and paint her electoral posters all over her ward.

Campaigning

The campaign for municipal elections, like any electoral campaign, is a time suffused with political symbolism, as politics then becomes literally a show. Any electoral campaign, of course, is firstly about visibility—of the party, its symbol, more rarely its agenda. Reservations for women combined, in June 2000, with the high visibility of Mamata Banerjee—whose portrait was all over the city—and to a lesser extent with that of yet another woman, Indira Gandhi (interestingly preferred by the Congress(I) to the present president of the party, Sonia Gandhi), to give the impression of a highly feminised municipal election.

The campaign is organised along a series of pre-defined steps, each involving, beyond the candidate, different types of actors. The first half of the three-week long campaign usually consists in going from door-to-door, starting with areas where the candidate has more supporters. At this stage, the candidate personally introduces herself to as many voters as possible: her name, her face must become familiar, and they must be associated with the right party (and with the right party symbol). Sitting councillors then seize this opportunity to remind voters of their past achievements, and promise to do more; sometimes they face the wrath of voters, at other times they are thanked for what they have done. New candidates generally meet voters more briefly, only occasionally criticising the sitting councillor and announcing what they plan to do for the ward.

The first round is usually prepared for by party workers, who go all over the ward in the preceding days to make a detailed list of those people who will actually vote on the polling day (thus removing from the list of targeted people those residents who are not on the voters list, those who vote in another ward, and those who will be absent on the D-day). This 'scrutinising' phase is meant both as a way to organise the door-to-door, and as a way to check electoral rigging.

The second phase is devoted to processions and (street corner) meetings, where not only the candidate, but also party workers address groups of voters. A municipal campaign is thus a highly collective endeavour, mobilising different kinds of party workers: men and women, leaders and simple members.

In June 2000, the campaign going on in the 47 wards reserved for women seemed to open up a new, important political space for women. Even without reservations, women and men campaign together, but there is a sexual division of the campaign work: while men take exclusive care of wall painting and slogan-shouting, more women accompany the candidate in the door-to-door. Their presence at that stage is crucial, since only women are allowed to enter the house (and meet the women of the household) in conservative families.

Reserved wards provided a greater visibility not only to women candidates, but also to women party workers, who were more numerous and more prominent in the entourage of women candidates than in that of male candidates;[65] and most importantly, perhaps, for women voters, who obviously found it easier to speak freely with a female rather than with a male candidate. The door-to-door phase of the campaigning is an opportunity many voters seize, to voice their needs, their grievances. One positive impact of reservations might well be that the sheer presence of so many women in the campaign will help women at large take themselves more seriously as citizens concerned with (local) politics.

Yet at the same time the reservation of a ward seems to eliminate all references to the gender of candidates. In such a context, nobody refers to the advantage or the inconvenience of having a woman as councillor. Candidates are introduced by party workers without any reference ever to their gender:

> I cannot request anything as a woman, but only as a party member; I campaigned for the party, not for myself ... (Devaki).[66]

> The party took charge of the campaign; they talked on my life, my work, my social activities, my family, and I visited every house, I explained what I had done (Ketaki).[67]

Inheritors are an exception in this regard, since they always highlight the family dimension of their candidature. During the door-to-door, Mina, wife of the sitting councillor, was introduced as 'Mina S., the wife of Talal S.', while her husband remained discretely at the back of the group of people who surrounded her. Inheritors, however, are not necessarily less assertive than other women candidates. Thus Mina seemed to enjoy more authority over the party workers accompanying her than Preeti, who got the ticket as an acknowledgement of her long involvement with her party, but who nevertheless, seemed to follow her fellow party workers.

But if the gender dimension seemed to be largely excluded from the campaign in reserved wards, other 'sectarian interests', however, were being highlighted. One independent Gujarati candidate, for instance, built her whole campaign on the need for the Gujarati community to be represented within the CMC; she was eventually not elected.

Lastly, a municipal electoral campaign usually focuses on local issues only (that is, mostly the condition of civic amenities), but that particular campaign was more political in tone. The political stakes of the June 2000 campaign were indeed high, since these municipal elections were considered, both by the ruling Left Front and by the opposition, as a test of the Trinamul Congress' capacity to challenge the former's 23-year old domination of the state, and assert itself as a credible alternative. Since the 1985 elections, which put an end to the supercession of the CMC, the Left Front had always won Calcutta; but when general elections were held in 1998 and then in 1999, all three Members of Parliament elected from Calcutta belonged to the opposition (TC and BJP); the 2000 municipal elections were then construed by the opposition, as the definite proof that Calcuttans wanted a change. Winning over the CMC was presented as the first step in the great change to come, that is, overtaking the Left Front in the Assembly elections scheduled six months later. This exceptional, highly symbolical dimension of the local election was attested by the active support provided by the party leaders to local candidates. It might also, incidentally, have helped giving credibility to women candidates as politicians in their own right.

Getting elected

The table below shows, firstly, that in 1995 the voting rate was actually higher in reserved wards than in non-reserved wards, which goes against the idea that voters would disinterest themselves from an electoral competition in which all contestants are women. Unfortunately, data disaggregated by sex are not available; we are thus not in a position to ascertain whether women voters voted more in those wards that were reserved for women.

Table 4: The electoral participation in reserved and unreserved wards

Year	Average electoral participation in reserved wards (WSCW)	Average electoral participation in general wards
1995	74.2% (52% to 85.6%)	72.4% (49.3% to 95.8%)
2000	62.5% (33.1% to 89.9%)	64.6% (42.2% to 89.9%)

Source: State Election Commission, Calcutta.

Table 4 also reveals that the 2000 municipal election was marked by a clear fall in the voting rate, which is probably due to the high degree of violence that characterised this election. One can notice, moreover, that the relative position of reserved and unreserved wards is then reversed, the voting rate being now higher in the latter.

Tabel 5: The proportion of women councillors, including in non-reserved wards

Year	Total number of councillors	Women councillors (% of the total number of councillors)	Women councillors elected in general wards (% of the total number of women councillors)
1990	141	6 (4.2%)	6 (100%)
1995	141	53 (38%)	6 (11%)
2000	141	60 (42.5%)	13 (22%)

Source: State Election Commission, Calcutta.

Table 5 contradicts the 'zenana dabba' theory. The increasing number of women elected, on the one hand, belies the most frequently denounced perverse effect of quotas, i.e. that instead of being a minimum figure, quotas actually automatically become a maximum figure, a ceiling. On the other hand even though, as we saw earlier, the number of inheritors among elected women increases with the second election, the number of women elected in non-reserved wards also increases. The fact that the number of women elected in non-reserved wards has been consistently, so far, superior to what it was prior to the implementation of reservations, points to the stimulating effect of reservations on women's participation in municipal politics. Thus, contrary to what Kishwar had anticipated, more and more women actually contest—and win—against male opponents.

But the 'nurturing' argument stands partially verified. Even though more than half the sitting female councillors whose ward had been de-reserved were given the party ticket for a second time, the rotation of reserved wards does generate a game of musical chairs for a number of men and women councillors, which is problematic both for their political careers, and for their accountability to voters.

Conclusion

The confrontation of the various arguments on the virtues and dangers of quotas for women in elected assemblies, with the voices and experiences of the first batch of women elected in the Calcutta Municipal Corporation subsequent to the implementation of such reservations, now allow us to take stock of the first phase of this implementation.

One of the major arguments supporting women's quotas—that women's specific qualities and talents constitute a 'resource' for political life—actually appears to be unverifiable, at least in the short term, even though the notion of women's qualities, which are really mothers' qualities, is largely accepted by the women as well as by the men interviewed.

The 'male backlash' argument, put forth by opponents to

women's quotas, stands contradicted in every possible way: on the one hand, more and more women are being given the party ticket in non-reserved wards while on the other, more and more women get access to relatively powerful positions within the CMC, such as borough chairperson or member of the Mayor-in-Council. Moreover, the fact that the number of women elected in general wards increases from one election to the other also goes against the argument that quotas would result in a 'women's (electoral) ghetto': More and more women actually contest—and win—against male candidates.

All other arguments stand partially verified. On the important 'gender justice *vs* social justice' debate, it appears that quotas do favour gender justice insofar as they seem to boost women's participation in municipal politics. Far from putting a ceiling on the number of elected women, they actually result in an increasing number of women councillors. Yet the survey showed that, on the one hand, elite women are over represented among the beneficiaries of quotas and on the other, that nepotism is indeed on the rise, with the number of inheritors increasing from one election to the other—a phenomenon which is doubtless encouraged by the rotation of reserved constituencies. Reservations, therefore, do not distribute political opportunities among women equally.

As one turns to the 'democracy *vs* efficiency' debate, however, both the elite character of women councillors and the increasing importance of the family factor in municipal elections, translate into a series of resources which are crucial to the performance of the beneficiaries of quotas. As women and as newcomers, most of them are doubly handicapped when confronting the multiplicity of the tasks they have to perform as councillors. Their social status in terms of caste, education and occupation suggests their comparatively greater access to such major political resources as prestige, education, time, verbal skills and money. Family support is another essential resource, as it provides a relay for domestic work, an escort if need be, and, for inheritors, a legitimate political patron.

The rotation of reserved constituencies actually constitutes another aspect of the 'democracy *vs* efficiency' debate, insofar as it balances the status of reserved and general constituencies over a series of three successive elections, and in doing so, generates a game of musical chairs detrimental both to the career of women and men councillors and to the interests of voters.

Lastly, on the all important question of the representation of women's interests, women's quotas appear to be far less effective than their supporters would have us believe. While the new presence of so many women councillors seems to give access to the CMC to all those women who would never have dared to address a male councillor, both interviews and the minutes of the House meetings showed that women councillors do not openly represent women's interests in the CMC. Women councillors, clearly, are no feminists: they do not consider women's issues as major issues and they have no relationship whatsoever, with (non-party) women's organisations. The 'critical mass' effect, obviously does not operate automatically, or, at least, not immediately.

But the time factor is precisely one of the main limitations of this study, confined as it is to the very first phase of the reservation policy, that is, to the first batch of women councillors benefitting from quotas. A follow-up study over the second and third election is very much needed to assess whether the impact of reservations as I observed it in 2000 is a durable one, or if the representation of women's interests, for instance, will be more and more effective with every election.

Such a longer-term focus would also consider the larger dimension of reservations for women, including (i) the ability of the beneficiaries of quotas at the local level to progress towards higher levels of politics, with or without quotas in state assemblies and in Parliament; (ii) the capacity of quotas to transform the norms of gendered behaviour by providing new role models for women; and (iii) the possibility that a massive presence of women in political assemblies may challenge the sexual division of domestic work.

Lastly, Calcutta, or Kolkata (as it is known since January 2001) is obviously not representative of Indian cities, nor even of Indian metropolises. West Bengal in general, and the state capital in particular, are characterised by a comparatively high level of literacy, a high level of political consciousness, and a special reverence for women as mothers.

Moreover, the political equations in West Bengal since 1998 might have influenced the situation of women candidates in the 2000 municipal elections. To what extent did Mamata Banerjee make a difference? As the leader of the opposition in the state from 1998 onwards, and as a Union minister[68] who has, in the past two years, strongly expressed her support to the Women's Reservation Bill, one might wonder what her impact was on the women of her party. She certainly seems to be a powerful role model for the women party members of the Trinamul Congress, who often mentioned their admiration of her physical courage.

Prior to the 2000 elections; Mamata Banerjee had underlined that she would extend particular support to the women councillors of her party, as part of her growing self-representation as a champion of women's rights. On the whole indeed, the Trinamul Congress proved to be the most supportive party for women sitting councillors. The TC, being a young party, certainly needed to consolidate the influence of its representatives; giving the ticket to sitting women councillors was a way to thank them for shifting their loyalties from the Congress to the TC.

Is Calcutta, then, an exception in the Indian urban landscape? Comparisons are now called for, to differentiate the role of factors pertaining to the regional political culture from that of more structural factors, in the impact of reservations for women in local elected assemblies.

Notes

[1] The few existing studies on this subject include Barry, Honour & Palnitkar (1996), Arora & Prabhakar (1997), Nanivadekar (1997a, 1997b), Gill (1999a, 1997b), and MARG (2000).

[2] Since 1950 SCs and STs have had reserved seats in the Lok Sabha and the Vidhan Sabhas in proportion to their importance in the total population.

[3] Madhu Kishwar, the co-editor of the journal *Manushi*, has consistently been at the forefront of this criticism of the WRB; she is one of the

members of the Forum for Democratic Reforms, who drafted an Alternative Women's Bill, proposing to shift women's quotas at the party level (Kishwar: 2000).

[4] Calcutta is not, however, the first metropolitan city where women's quotas have been implemented in India; similar quotas were implemented in the Bombay Municipal Corporation as early as 1992, subsequent to the policy of reservations for women in Local Self Government Institutions adopted by the government of Maharashtra in 1990 (Nanivadekar: 1997a, 1997b).

[5] In the CMC, however, only nine ward committees were formed between 1995 and 2000, due to the reluctance of political parties to comply with this provision.

[6] Three interviews with female councillors were conducted in 1996 and 1997, in the context of my PhD thesis (*La représentation des femmes sur la scène politique. Etude comparée du Bengale occidental, du Maharashtra et du Népal*, Institut d'Etudes Politiques d'Aix-en-Provence, 1999).

[7] *The Economic Times*, 16 March 1997.

[8] 13 per cent of councillors in Calcutta are Muslims; but Muslim women constitute only 7.5 per cent of the total number of women councillors.

[9] The names of people quoted have been changed.

[10] Interview, February 2000.

[11] Interview, February 2000.

[12] This 'dynastic factor' is neither new, nor restricted to Indian politics alone—it has long been a traditional feature of French local politics as well.

[13] Interview, June 1996.

[14] Interview, February 2000.

[15] Interview, June 2000.

[16] Interview, November 2000.

[17] Interview, November 2000.

[18] Interview, February 2000.

[19] Under the 'Local Area Development Scheme', each MP can spend two crore rupees per year for the development of his/her constituency; these funds actually seem to be a major resource for getting work done in wards whose councillors belong to the opposition parties.

[20] Interview, June 1996.

[21] Interview, January 2000.

[22] Some councillors do not even have a ward office. Saloni, for instance, is used to sitting in a particular place in various markets of the ward, where people know they can find her.

[23] Interview, November 2000.

[24] Interview, October 1997.

[25] Interview, January 2000.

[26] Interview, January 2000.

[27] Interview, June 1996.

[28] Interview, January 2000.

29. Interview, January 2000.
30. Interview, February 2000.
31. Interview, January 2000.
32. Interview, November 2000.
33. See Forbes 1979.
34. Thus Bengali women were given, in 1923, the right to vote and to be elected at the municipal level only. Again, *Towards Equality*, (Report of the Committee on the Status of Women in India, Government of India, 1974) recommended, in its conclusion, the creation of women's panchayats at the local level exclusively.
35. Interview, November 2000.
36. Interview, February 2000.
37. *The Hindu*, 6 December 2000.
38. *The Pioneer*, 22 April 1996
39. Interview, January 2000.
40. Interview, February 2000.
41. Interview, October 1997.
42. Interview, February 2000.
43. Interview, November 2000.
44. Interview, November 2000.
45. Interview, February 2000.
46. Interview, January 2000.
47. Interview, October 1997.
48. We are giving here an account of the proceedings concerning the period between September 1995 and November 2000, covering altogether 54 monthly meetings of the House (the proceedings of the meetings held between February and September 1996 were not available).
49. Out of the 54 meetings analysed through their proceedings, only once was a question relating exclusively to women raised: this was a request that the ladies' room in the councillors' club be enlarged, and it was expressed by a male councillor. Two other examples of specific requests occurred: the claim for barracks to be built for Harijan workers (expressed by a Brahmin, male councillor), and the request that Urdu reporters be appointed by the CMC (expressed by a Muslim, male councillor).
50. Interview, November 2000.
51. Interview, November 2000.
52. Interview, November 2000.
53. Interview, November 2000.
54. Interview, February 2000.
55. Interview, February 2000.
56. Interview, February 2000.
57. Interview, November 2000.
58. *India Today*, 15 October 1996.
59. Interview, February 2000.
60. Interview, February 2000.

[61] Interview, February 2000.
[62] Interview, November 2000.
[63] I deal here with all the wards reserved either for women or for SC women.
[64] Interview, November 2000.
[65] Salima, for instance, estimates that about a quarter of the 250 party workers who are engaged in her campaign are women.
[66] Interview, June 1996.
[67] Interview, February 2000.
[68] She resigned from that position in March 2001.

References

Arora, S.C. & R.K. Prabhakar. 1997. 'A Study of Municipal Council Elections in India. Socio-Economic Background of Women Candidates in Rohtak, Haryana'. *Asian Survey*, 37(10). pp. 918–26.

Barry, J., T. Honour, & S. Palnitkar. 1996. 'Women and Local Politics in Mumbai and London: The Quota Innovation'. Paper presented to the Regional Symposium on Women in Local Government (Asia). Mumbai: March 4–8.

Dahlerup, D. 1988. 'From a Small to a Large Minority: Women in Scandinavian Politics'. *Scandinavian Political Studies*. vol. 11(4).

Forbes, G. 1979. 'Votes for Women. The Demand for Women's Franchise in India, 1917–1937' in *Symbols of Power*. ed. V. Mazumdar. Bombay: Allied Publishers.

Ghosh, B. 1996. 'West Bengal' in *Present Status and Future Prospects of Panchayati Raj in India*. New Delhi: Institute of Social Sciences.

Gill, R. 1999. 'Seventy Fourth Constitution Amendment and Political Empowerment of Women in Punjab: A Study in Urban Governance'. *Urban India*, XIX(1). pp. 39–58.

Government of India. 1974. *Towards Equality*. Report of the Committee on the Status of Women in India. Delhi.

Hernes, H. 1982. *The State—Women No Entrance?* Oslo: Universitatforlaget.

Kishwar, M. 1996. 'Women and Politics: Beyond Quotas'. *Economic and Political Weekly*. 26 October. pp. 2867–74.

———. 2000. 'Equality of Opportunities *vs* Equality of Results'. *Economic and Political Weekly*. 19 November. pp. 4151–56.

Laufer, J. 1995. 'Introduction: l'égalité et la difference en débat' in EPHESIA, *La place des femmes. Les enjeux de l'identité et de l'égalité au regard des sciences socials*. Paris: La Découverte.

MARG. 2000. *Daughters of the 74th Amendment. A Study of Women Elected to the Municipal Bodies in Karnal and Delhi*. New Delhi.

Mathur, M.P. 1999. 'The Constitution (74th) Amendment Act and Urban Local Governments: An Overview'. *Urban India*, XIX(1).

Mohanty, P.K. 1999. 'Municipal Decentralisation and Governance: Autonomy, Accountability and Participation' in *Decentralisation and Local Politics*.

eds. S.N. Jha & P.C. Mathur. New Delhi: Sage Publications.
Mukhopadhyay, A. 2000. 'Mayor-in-Council: The Calcutta Perspective' in *Mayor-in-Council System in a Comparative Perspective*. ed. A. Ghosh. New Delhi: Institute of Social Sciences.
Nandy, A. 1990. *At the Edge of Psychology: Essays in Politics and Culture*. Delhi: Oxford University Press.
Nanivadekar, M. 1997a. *Electoral Process in Corporation Election: A Gender Study*. Mumbai. Bharatiya Stree Shakti.
——. 1997b. *Empowering Women: Assessing the Policy of Reservations in Local Bodies—A Report*. Mumbai: Rambhau Mhalgi Prabodhini.
Pateman, C. 1989. *The Disorder of Women. Democracy, Feminism and Political Theory*. Cambridge: Polity Press.
Pinto, M. 2000. *Metropolitan City Governance in India*. New Delhi: Sage Publications.

Abridged from the original, published as 'Women in Calcutta Municipal Corporation: A study in the context of the debate on Women's Reservation Bill', Occasional Paper, (no. 2), 2001, Centre de Sciences Humanities, New Delhi. Publication of French Research Institute in India.

The Impact of Reservation in the Panchayati Raj

RAGHABENDRA CHATTOPADHYAY & ESTHER DUFLO

1. Introduction

The 73rd Amendment paved the way for a fundamental change in the way public goods are delivered in rural areas in India. Through the structure of the Panchayati Raj, local councils directly elected by the people are responsible for making decisions on an array of public goods decisions. Twice a year, the councils must also convene village meetings (gram sabhas), where the villagers must approve their plan and their budget. Eventually, the gram panchayats (GP) are supposed to be given control over an even broader array of social services, including basic education and primary health care. The hope is that decentralisation, by bringing decision-making closer to the people, may improve both the quality of social services delivery in India, which is in many ways disastrous (e.g., Probe Team 1999), and its adequacy to meet people's needs.

However, in a country with a heterogenous population, a danger is that decentralisation will make it more difficult to protect the interests of weaker segments of the population, notably women, the Scheduled Castes (SC), and the Scheduled Tribes (ST), and, in particular, to ensure that they get their fair share of public goods. To alleviate this concern, the 73rd Amendment required that a fraction of seats at all levels be reserved to women, SCs and STs. While reservations for SCs and STs are in place in other elected bodies (national and state legislative assemblies), the 73rd Amendment is the first one in India that mandated women's reservation, and this made it a landmark piece of legislation as well as, to some extent, a test case.[1] It also makes an objective and rigorous analysis of its effects particularly important.

A necessary condition for the efficacy of the reservation policy is that the elected representatives have independent power and autonomy, over and above not only the direct control of the villagers (exerted through voting or through the gram sabhas), but also above the control of the bureaucracy, the parties' hierarchies, and the local elites. Thus, by asking whether or not reservations make a difference for political outcomes we can start answering two important questions on the Panchayati Raj. First, do the panchayat leaders matter at all? Second, do they make decisions that better reflect the needs of their own groups?

This paper summarises some of the findings from our research project on local decentralisation (Chattopadhyay and Duflo 2003a, 2003b).[2] We answer these questions using two data sets we collected in two districts, Birbhum, in West Bengal, and Udaipur, in Rajasthan. In both places we conducted detailed village surveys, from which we learned both the types and the locations of the public goods provided on the ground since the last election. We also collected data on gram sabhas and complaints to the GP (by men and women), and we therefore know, in each place, what women and men seem to care most about.

A key feature of the reservation policy is that the seats to be reserved were randomly allocated, which ensures that the only difference between reserved and unreserved villages is that some of them were picked to be reserved, while some were not. With a large enough sample, this means that if we find any difference between the types of goods that are provided in GPs that are reserved for women pradhans and in those that are not, this must reflect the impact of the policy. We first show that women invest more in goods that are relevant to the needs of local women: water and roads in West Bengal; water in Rajasthan. They invest less in goods that are less relevant to the needs of women: non-formal education centres in West Bengal; roads in Rajasthan. In Birbhum, where we have data on investments in hamlets populated by SCs, STs and the general population within each village, we also show that SC pradhans invest a larger share of public goods in SC hamlets than do non-SC pradhans.

This research thus shows that some of the fears expressed regarding decentralisation are not founded. Local leaders seem to have some effective control over decisions, even when they are women or SCs. Moreover, it indicates that the oft-heard anecdotal evidence regarding women being entirely controlled by their husbands when in office should not be given too much weight. Correcting the imbalances in political agency leads to a correction of imbalance in other spheres as well (Sen 1999). Reservations of electoral seats may therefore be an effective tool to safeguard the interest of the weaker groups.

2. Institutions

2.1 The panchayat system

The panchayat is a system of village-level (gram panchayat), block-level (panchayat samiti), and district-level (zilla parishad) councils, members of which are elected by the people, and are responsible for the administration of local public goods. Each gram panchayat (GP) encompasses 10,000 people in several villages (between five and 15). The GPs do not have jurisdiction over urban areas, which are administered by separate municipalities. Voters elect a council, which then elects among its members a pradhan (chief) and an upa-pradhan (vice-chief).[3] Candidates are generally nominated by political parties, but have to be residents of the villages they represent. The council makes decisions by majority voting (the pradhan does not have veto power). The pradhan, however, is the only member of the council with a full-time appointment.

The panchayat system has existed formally in most of the major states of India since the early 1950s. However, in most states, the system was not an effective body of governance until the early 1990s. Elections were not held, and the panchayats did not assume any active role (Ghatak and Ghatak 1999). In 1992, the 73rd Amendment to the Constitution of India established the framework of a three-tiered panchayat system with regular elections throughout India. It gave the GP primary responsibility for implementing development programmes, as well as in identifying the needs of the villages under its jurisdiction. Between 1993 and 2003, all major states but two (Bihar and Punjab) had at least two elections. The major responsibilities of the GP are to administer local infrastructure (public buildings, water, roads) and identify targeted welfare recipients. The main source of financing is still the state, but most of the money that was previously earmarked for specific uses is now allocated through four broad schemes: The Jawahar Rozgar Yojna (JRY) for infrastructure (irrigation, drinking water, roads, repairs of community buildings, etc.); a small additional drinking water scheme; funds for welfare programmes (widows, old age, and maternity pensions, etc.); and a grant for GP functioning.[4] The GP has, in principle, complete flexibility in allocating these funds. At this point, the GP has no direct control over the appointments of government-paid teachers or health workers, but in some states (Tamil Nadu and West Bengal, for example) there are panchayat-run informal schools.

The panchayat is required to organise two meetings per year, called 'gram samsad'. These are meetings of villagers and village heads in which all voters may participate. The GP council submits the proposed budget to the gram samsad and reports on their activities in the previous six months. The GP leader also must set up regular office hours where villagers can lodge complaints or requests.

In West Bengal, the Left Front (communist) government gained power in 1977 on a platform of agrarian and political reform. The major political reform was to give life to a three-tiered panchayat electoral system. The first election took place in 1978 and elections have taken place at five-year intervals ever since. Thus, the system put into place by the 73rd Amendment all over India was already well established in West Bengal. Following the Amendment, the GP was given additional responsibilities in West Bengal. In particular, they were entrusted to establish and administer informal education centres (called SSK), an alternative form of education for children who do not attend school (an instructor who is not required to have any formal qualification teaches children three hours a day in a temporary building or outdoors).

In Rajasthan, unlike West Bengal, there was no regularly elected panchayat system in charge of distribution of state funds until 1995. The first election was held in 1995, followed by a second election in 2000. Since 1995, elections and gram samsads have been held regularly, and are well attended. The setting is thus very different, with a much shorter history of democratic government. As in West Bengal, the panchayat can spend money on local infrastructure, but unlike in West Bengal, they are not allowed to run their own schools.

2.2 Reservation for women, Scheduled Castes and Scheduled Tribes

In 1992, the 73rd Amendment provided that one-third of the seats in all panchayat councils, as well as one-third of the pradhan positions, must be reserved for women. Seats and pradhan positions were also reserved for the two disadvantaged minorities in India, Scheduled Castes and Scheduled Tribes, in the form of mandated representation proportional to each minority's population share in each district. Reservations for women have been implemented in all major states except Bihar and Uttar Pradesh (which has only reserved 25 per cent of the seats for women).

In West Bengal, the Panchayat Constitution Rule was modified in 1993 to reserve one-third of the councillor positions in each GP for women, and a share equal to their population for SCs and STs; in a third of the villages in each GP, only women could be candidates for the position of councillor for the area. The proportion of women elected to panchayat councils increased to 36 per cent after the 1993 election. The experience was considered a disappointment, however, because very few women (only 196 out of 3,324 GPs) advanced to the position of pradhan, which is the only one that yields effective power (Kanango 1998). To conform to the 73rd Amendment, the Panchayat Constitution Rule of West Bengal was again modified in April of 1998 (Government of West Bengal 1998) to introduce reservation of pradhan positions for women and

SCs/STs. In Rajasthan, the random rotation system was implemented in 1995 and in 2000 at both levels (council members and pradhans).

In both states, a specific set of rules ensures the random selection of GPs where the office of pradhan was to be reserved. All GPs in a district are ranked in consecutive order according to their serial legislative number (an administrative number pre-dating this reform). GPs that have less than five per cent SCs (or STs) are excluded from the list of possible SC (or ST) reservation. A table of random numbers (in the electoral law) is then used to determine the seats that are to be reserved for SCs and STs, according to the numbers that need to be reserved in these particular districts. They are then ranked in three separate lists, according to whether or not the seats had been reserved for a SC, for a ST, or are unreserved. Using these lists, every third GP starting with the first on the list is reserved for a woman pradhan in the first election.[5]

From discussions with government officials at the Panchayat Directorate who devised the system and district officials who implemented it in individual districts, it appears that these instructions were successfully implemented. More importantly, in the district we study in West Bengal, we could verify that the policy was strictly implemented. After sorting the GPs into those reserved for SC/ST and those not reserved, we could reconstruct the entire list of GPs reserved for women by sorting all GPs by their serial number (allocated several years before the law was passed), and selecting every third GP starting from the first in each list. This verifies that the allocation of GPs to the reserved list was indeed random, as intended.[6]

Table 1, panel A shows the number of female pradhans in reserved and unreserved GPs in the two districts we study. In both districts, all pradhans in GPs reserved for a woman are female. In West Bengal, only 6.5 per cent of the pradhans are female in unreserved GPs. In Rajasthan, only one woman was elected on an unreserved seat, despite the fact that this was the second cycle. Women elected once due to the reservation system were not re-elected.[7] Panel B shows the number of SC pradhans in Birbhum, in reserved and unreserved areas. Again, the policy dramatically increased the fraction of SC pradhans in reserved areas. In this paper, we will focus on reservation for SCs, rather than STs, because all GPs in Birbhum have more than five per cent SCs, so that no GP is excluded from being reserved. However, many GPs have less than five per cent STs, so that the number of GPs in our study would be too small.[8]

3. Data collection

We collected data in two locations: Birbhum in West Bengal and Udaipur in Rajasthan. In the summer of 2000, we conducted a survey of all GPs in the district of Birbhum, West Bengal. Birbhum is located in the western part of West Bengal, about 125 miles [200 kilometres] from the state capital, Calcutta. At the time of the 1991 census, it had a population of 2.56 million. Agriculture is the main economic activity, and rice is the main crop cultivated. The male and female literacy rates were 50 per cent and 37 per cent, respectively. The district is known to have a relatively well-functioning panchayat system.

There are 166 GPs in Birbhum, of which five were reserved for pre-testing, leaving 161 GPs in our study. Table 2 shows the means of the most relevant village variables collected by the 1991 census of India in GPs reserved for women and GPs that are not reserved, and their differences. As expected, given the random selection of GPs, there are no important differences between reserved and unreserved GPs.[9] Note that very few villages (three per cent among the unreserved GPs) have tap water, the most common sources of drinking water being hand-pumps and tubewells. Most villages are accessible only by a dirt road. Ninety-one per cent of villages have a primary school but very few have any other type of school. Irrigation is important; 43 per cent of the cultivated land is irrigated, with at least some land being irrigated in all villages. Very few villages (eight per cent) have any public health facilities.

We collected that data in two stages. First, we conducted an interview with the GP pradhan. We asked each one a set of questions about his or her family background, education, previous political experience, and political ambitions, as well as a set of questions about the activities of the GP since his or her election in May 1998 (with support from written records). We then completed a survey of three villages in the GP: two villages randomly selected in each GP, as well as the village in which the GP pradhan resides. During the village interview, we drew a resource map of the village with a group of 10 to 20 villagers. The map featured all the available infrastructure in the village, and we asked whether each of the available equipment items had been built or repaired since May 1998. Previous experience of one of the authors, as well as experimentation during the pre-testing period, suggested that this method yields extremely accurate information about the village. We then conducted an additional interview with the most active participants of the mapping exercise, in which we asked in more detail about investments in various public goods. We also collected the minutes of village meetings, and asked whether women and men of the village had expressed complaints or requests to the GP in the previous six months. For all outcomes for which it was possible, we collected the same information at the GP-level and at the village-level. The village-level information is likely to be more reliable, because it is not provided by the pradhan, and because it was easy for villagers to recall investments made in their village in the previous two years. However, the information given by the GP head refers to investment in the entire GP, and is thus free from sampling error. Therefore, when an outcome is available at both levels, we perform the analysis separately for both and compare the results.

Between August and December of 2002, we collected the same village-level data (there was no pradhan interview) in 100 hamlets in Udaipur, Rajasthan, chosen randomly in a subset of villages covered by a local NGO, Seva Mandir.[10] The reference period for asking about investment was also two years, 2000–2002. In Rajasthan, there was no regularly elected panchayat system until 1995. Table 2 displays the characteristics of villages reserved for women and unreserved in our sample.[11] Udaipur is a much poorer district than Birbhum. It is located in an extremely arid area with little irrigation and has male and female literacy rates of 27.5 per cent and 5.5 per cent respectively.

Because the villages are bigger, they are more likely to have a middle school, a health facility and a road connection, compared to villages in West Bengal. As in Rajasthan, we see no difference between the characteristics of reserved and unreserved villages before the reservation policy was implemented.

4. Findings

In the absence of reservation, if we found that different public goods investments are undertaken in GPs that elect women and SCs, compared to GPs that do not, it would be very difficult to interpret these results, since the few places that elect women or SCs are presumably very different from places that do not elect women. For example, places that are dominated by SCs may elect a SC pradhan and also invest more in the SC hamlet, but this would not imply that if we constrain random places to elect SC pradhans, the pradhan will have any power to implement the policy he chooses. By contrast, in this case, because the reserved seats were randomly assigned, we can now compare the outcome in GPs where the position of pradhan is reserved for a woman or a SC to those where it is not reserved, and be confident that any difference reflects only the impact of the reservation policy.

4.1 Reservation for women

4.1.1 Effects on the political participation of women

Table 3 displays the effect of having a woman pradhan on the political participation of women. Columns (1) and (2) display the average participation rates in reserved and unreserved GPs, respectively. Column (3) displays the difference. Differences that are significant at the 95 per cent confidence interval, using standard significance tests, are in bold. In West Bengal, the percentage of women among participants in the gram samsad is significantly higher when the pradhan is a woman (increasing from 6.9 per cent to 9.9 per cent). Since reservation does not affect the percentage of eligible voters attending the gram samsad, this corresponds to a net increase in the participation of women, and a decline in the participation of men. This is consistent with the idea that political communication is influenced by the fact that citizens and leaders are of the same sex. Women in villages with reserved pradhans are twice as likely to have addressed a request or a complaint to the GP pradhan in the previous six months, and this difference is significant.[12] The fact that the pradhan is a woman therefore significantly increases the involvement of women in the affairs of the GP in West Bengal.

In Rajasthan, the fact that the pradhan is a woman has no effect on women's participation at the gram samsad or the occurrence of women's complaints. Note that women participate more in the gram samsad in Rajasthan, most probably because the process is very recent, and the GP leaders are trained to mobilise women in public meetings.[13]

4.1.2 Requests of men and women

Table 4 shows the fraction of formal requests by type of goods made by villagers to the panchayat in the six months prior to the survey.[14]

In West Bengal, drinking water and roads were by far the issues most frequently raised by women. The next most important issue was welfare programmes, followed by housing and electricity. In Rajasthan, drinking water, welfare programmes, and roads were the issues most frequently raised by women. The issues most frequently raised by men in West Bengal were roads, irrigation, drinking water and education. With the exception of irrigation, men have the same priorities in Rajasthan. Note that these patterns of preferences are expected, in view of the activities of both men and women in these areas. Women are in charge of collecting drinking water, and they are the primary recipients of welfare programmes (maternity pension, widow's pension, and old age pension for the destitute, who tend to be women). In West Bengal, they are the main source of labour employed on the roads. In Rajasthan, both men and women work on roads, and the employment motive is therefore common to both. However, men travel very frequently out of the villages in search of work, while women do not travel long distances; accordingly, men have a stronger need for good roads.

4.1.3 Effects of the policy on public goods provision

Table 5 presents the effects of the pradhan's gender on all public goods investments made by the GP since the last election in West Bengal and Rajasthan. The first column presents the average number of investments (repair or new construction) in each category in reserved GPs, and the second presents the same number in unreserved GPs. The third column presents the difference between the two. In all cases, the number below the coefficient is the standard error of the estimate. Differences in bold are significantly different from 0 at the 95 per cent level of confidence, using standard significance tests.

In both West Bengal and Rajasthan, the gender of the pradhan affects the provision of public goods. In both places, there are significantly more investments in drinking water in GPs reserved for women. This is what we expected, since in both places, women complain more often than men about water. In West Bengal, GPs are less likely to have set up informal schools (in the village, this is significant only at the 10 per cent level) in GPs reserved for women. Interestingly, the effect of reservation on the quality of roads is opposite in Rajasthan and in West Bengal; in West Bengal, roads are significantly better in GPs reserved for women, but in Rajasthan, it is the opposite. This result is important since it corroborates expectations based on the complaint data for men and women. The only unexpected result is that we do not find a significant effect of reservation for women on irrigation in West Bengal. In West Bengal, we run the same regression for GP-level investments (instead of village-level). The results, presented in panel B, are entirely consistent, and the effect on informal schooling is significant at the five per cent level in the GP-level regression.

These results suggests that the reservation policy has important effects on policy decisions at the local level. These effects are consistent with the policy priorities expressed by women.

4.1.4 Robustness

Some doubt the effectiveness of the reservation policy, citing anecdotal evidence that women pradhans are observed to be subservient to their husbands or other powerful men. As Table 6 shows, 17 per cent of the spouses of the women leaders have previously been elected to the panchayat. Forty-three per cent of the female leaders acknowledge being helped by their spouse. The interviewers are more likely to find the women hesitant, they are more likely to acknowledge that they did not know how the GP functioned before being elected and that they do not intend to run again.

However, despite all this, what remains is that women do different things than men. This remains true even for women who say they are helped by their husbands or for women whose husbands were previously elected in the panchayat.[15] We also have good reasons to think that the effects of the policy are indeed due to the gender of the pradhan, rather than other aspects of the reservation policy. In Chattopadhyay and Duflo (2003a), we show that the difference between men and women remains identical when we restrict the comparison to other men who were elected recently, men who will not be able to be re-elected, or SC/ST pradhans.

The impression that women are not effective leaders thus seems to stem largely from the social perceptions of women that the policy precisely tries to address. What these results show is that, despite the handicaps they may face in terms of education and prior experience, and the preconception of weak leadership, women have a real impact on policy decisions. Using data collected by the Public Action Centre, matched with data on reservation, Tapalova (2003) finds illuminating results. Not only does she find that the quality of water provided is better in GPs that are reserved for women, and that women are somewhat less likely to demand bribes, but she also finds that villagers are *less* likely to be satisfied about the quality of the water when GPs are reserved for women, despite receiving objectively better service. This suggests that women tend to be considered as worse policy-makers even in cases where they are objectively better. This may explain the scepticism about the impact of the policy in the face of the evidence.

4.2 Reservation for Scheduled Castes

These results focus on West Bengal, where we have conducted the village survey for the entire village, and not only for one hamlet per village. Because there are at least five per cent of SCs in these villages, they also focus on reservation for SCs.

4.2.1 Effect on the type of public goods

The first question we can ask is whether SC pradhans, like women pradhans, choose to invest in different types of public goods than non-SC pradhans. In Table 7, we reproduce in column (1) the difference between GPs reserved for women and unreserved GPs shown in Table 5. In column (2), we show the same difference, but for GPs reserved for SCs. In contrast to the previous results, no difference is significant. We can see that, unlike women, SC pradhans do not radically change the types of investment they undertake.

4.2.2 Effect on the location of public goods

We might expect a larger impact, however, on the *location* of these investments. Specifically, do SC pradhans invest more in SC hamlets? The SC population may not need a different set of public goods than the non-SC population, but they may want these goods to be located in their hamlet, rather than in the other hamlets in the village. The reservation to a SC pradhan may ensure that this happens. When we collected the data in the PRA, we made sure to indicate the location of each public good: is it in the SC hamlet, the ST hamlet (if any), the general hamlet, or in common areas?

To verify that villages were indeed comparable before the reservation was put in place, Table 8 displays information about the location of public goods in these villages *before 1998*, when the reservation policy was first introduced. For each good, we construct the share of public goods that are located in the SC area, normalised by the share of the population that lives in the area. Therefore, an index smaller than one suggests that the SC hamlet has fewer goods than one would expect on the basis of the SC share in the population of the village, and an index higher than one suggests that the SC hamlet has more goods than one would expect on the basis of the SC share in the population of the village. In column (1), we display the normalised share in GPs that were not reserved for SCs between 1998 and 2003. In column (2), we display the normalised share in GPs that were reserved for SCs between 1998 and 2003. Because the reservation was randomly assigned, we do not expect any significant difference in the investment shares between GPs that are reserved for SCs and GPs that are not reserved for SCs. Three important facts emerge from this Table. SCs get a somewhat smaller share of public goods than non-SC on average (the index for the average is 0.93), but the index is not significantly different from one, and the extent of under-investment in SC hamlets depends on the types of goods. It seems that in SC hamlets there tends to be more public provision of goods for which there are private substitutes (drinking water wells, sanitation equipment) and less public provision for goods for which there are fewer private substitutes (schools, adult education). Second, there are much less privately provided equivalents of public goods in SC hamlets (we have information for water and irrigation equipment). Third, the indices are very similar in reserved and unreserved GPs, which is reassuring. Before 1998, SC hamlets were not treated differently in GPs that were reserved for SCs from 1998 to 2003.

Table 9 displays the normalised investment shares in SC and non-SC GPs, their differences and their ratio. Overall, across all goods, and controlling for the difference in population share, the SC hamlet received 14 per cent more investments in goods in GPs reserved for SCs, relative to GPs that were not reserved for SCs. Note that we have excluded the pradhan's village from this sample, which shows that the observed differences are not due to the direct effect of the pradhan putting more goods next to his own home. Instead, this seems to reflect a general tendency to favour the SC population when the pradhan position is reserved for SCs. This result is consistent with the results in Pande (2003), who finds that there are more transfers targeted to SCs in states where there are more reservations for SCs in Parliament, and of Besley, Pande, Rahman and Rao (2003), who find that SC households are more likely to receive public transfers if the pradhan is SC.

When we look at different goods separately (Table 9), we see that the increase in the share of public goods going to the SC hamlet in GPs reserved for SCs seems to reflect the existing imbalance across goods: Except for informal schools, where the share is smaller in GPs reserved for SCs, the share of goods going to the SC hamlet increases for all goods, and it increases more for goods where the share is already higher in non-reserved hamlets (sanitation, for example). It appears that when the SCs gain more power, they do not feel the need to radically change the types of goods that they are getting, but rather to get a little more of everything.

Conclusion

This paper has shown that reservation for SCs and women in the Panchayati Raj makes a difference: Both women and SCs invest more in what women and SCs seem to want (water for women, goods in SC hamlets for SCs). This underscores the power of the elected panchayat leaders and, by implication, the importance of the 73rd Amendment. In this regard, it is particularly important that the results are comparable in Rajasthan, where the 73rd Amendment was the first attempt to revive the panchayat structure, and in West Bengal, where it had been active since the late 1970s.

These results also suggest that, given the difficulty of targeting public transfers to specific groups in an otherwise decentralised system, reservation may be a tool to ensure not only adequate representation but also adequate delivery of local public goods to disadvantaged groups. They fly in the face of scepticism founded on anecdotes or prejudice that women or SCs are not capable of being independent leaders. These results show that, whatever the process underlying the effects may be, women and SC leaders make a difference on the ground. Correcting imbalance in political agency does result in correcting inequities in other spheres as well (Sen 1999).

In this light, recent developments that try to tag other objectives onto the reservation policy are troubling. Six states (Haryana, Rajasthan, Andhra Pradesh, Orissa, Madhya Pradesh, and Himachal Pradesh) now have laws mandating a two-child norm for members of the panchayat. As we can see in Table 6, women and men pradhans have the same number of children on average (around 2.5 in West Bengal). Since women do not necessarily control their fertility choices, and are unlikely to find it worthwhile to fight their family in order to be eligible for the panchayat, this policy is likely to discourage women, or members of the SCs and STs, from being candidates, even when there is reservation, thus encouraging the situations that critics of the reservation policy describe, where 'puppet candidates' will take the place of real candidates. De facto, it will thus reduce women's agency and, if anything, may result in an increase in fertility, rather than the opposite.[16]

This would be an unfortunate outcome, given the evidence that panchayat leaders make a difference and that bringing women and SCs into politics may help in improving their welfare. Reduced fertility may be achieved by increasing women's bargaining power in the family, and an effective democracy with adequate women's representation may be more effective at achieving it than regulation that takes away from women and SCs what the 73rd Amendment guarantees them.

Acknowledgements

Indian Institute of Management, Calcutta and the Massachusetts Institute of Technology. We thank Daron Acemoglu, Abhijit Banerjee, Timothy Besley, Anne Case, Mihir Ghosh Dastidar, Angus Deaton, Marie Lajus, Steve Levitt, Costas Meghir, Rohini Pande and Emmanuel Saez for discussions, Prasid Chakraborty and Mihir Ghosh Dastidar for organising and supervising the data collection in West Bengal, Callie Scott and Annie Duflo for organising the data collection in Rajasthan, and Lucia Breierova, Shawn Cole and Jonathan Robinson for excellent research assistance, and the National Institutes of Health (through grant RO1HD39922-01) and the

John D. and Catherine T. MacArthur Foundation for financial support. Chattopadhyay thanks the Institute for Economic Development at Boston University for its hospitality.

Notes

1. There are reservations for women in many other countries, however. Quotas for women in assemblies or on parties' candidate lists are in force in the legislation of over 30 countries (World Bank 2001), and in the internal rules of at least one party in 12 countries of the European Union (Norris 2001).
2. More details can be found in these papers.
3. In Rajasthan, the chief is called a sarpanch. In this paper, we will use the terminology pradhan for both states.
4. According to the balance sheets we could collect in 40 GPs in West Bengal, the JRY accounts for 30 per cent of total GP income, the drinking water scheme five per cent, the welfare programmes 15 per cent, the grant for GP functioning 33 per cent, and the GP's own revenue for eight per cent. GPs can also apply for some special schemes—a housing scheme for SC/STs, for example.
5. For the next election, every third GP starting with the second on the list was reserved for a woman, etc. The Panchayat Constitution Rule has actual tables indicating the ranks of the GPs to be reserved in each election.
6. We could not obtain the necessary information to perform the same exercise in Rajasthan. However, there too, the system appears to have been correctly implemented.
7. The one woman elected on an unreserved seat was not previously elected on a reserved seat.
8. In future work, we will address this question in Rajasthan.
9. The standard errors are omitted from the table for clarity, but none of the differences are significant at the 95 per cent confidence level.
10. Rajasthani villages are much more spread out than West Bengali villages (a Rajasthani village covers an area on average 10 times bigger than a West Bengali village) and are much less densely populated. They are made of a series of independent 'hamlets', which are not administrative entities but function as independent villages. Our sampling unit is the hamlet: We first sampled 100 villages (with probability of selection weighted by village size) and then one hamlet per village (again, the probability of selection was weighted by village size).
11. For Udaipur, we could not obtain the data necessary to match villages to panchayat in the entire district.
12. In the subsample of villages in which we conducted follow-up surveys, we also asked whether men had brought up any issue in the previous six months. In all cases but one (a reserved GP), they had.
13. Interestingly, women's participation is significantly higher when the position of council member *of the village* is reserved for a woman (results

not reported to conserve space). This difference is probably due to the very long distance between villages in Rajasthan.

[14] We recorded the exact complaint or request, for example, the need to repair a specific well. We classified them *ex post* into these categories. In West Bengal, we had initially not asked about issues raised by men. A random subset of 48 villages was subsequently resurveyed later.

[15] Results available from the authors on request.

[16] There is considerable evidence that higher bargaining power leads to a reduction in women's fertility.

References

Besley, Timothy, Rohini Pande, Lupin Rahman, and Vijayendra Rao. 2003. 'The politics of public goods provision: Evidence from Indian local government.' Mimeo. LSE. Forthcoming in Journal of the European Economic Association.

Chattopadhyay, Raghabendra, and Esther Duflo. 2003a. 'Efficiency and rent seeking in local governments: Evidence from randomized policy experiments in India.' Mimeo. MIT.

——.(2003b) 'Women as policy makers: Evidence from a randomized policy experiment in India'. Mimeo. MIT. Forthcoming in *Econometrica*.

Ghatak, Maitreya, and Maitreesh Ghatak. 1999. 'Grassroots democracy: A study of the panchayat system in West Bengal.' Mimeo. Development Research Group. Calcutta and University of Chicago.

Government of West Bengal. 1998. *The West Bengal Panchayat (Constitution) Rules, 1975*. Department of Panchayats and Rural Development.

Kanango, Sukla Deb. 1998. 'Panchayati Raj and emerging women leadership: An overview' in *People's Power and Panchayati Raj: Theory and Practice*. ed. Bansaku. Indian Social Institute. ch. 5. pp. 77–95.

Norris, Pippa. 2001. 'Breaking the barriers: Positive discrimination policies for women' in *Has Liberalism Failed Women: Parity, Quotas and Political Representation*. eds. Jyette Klausen and Charles Maier. St Martins Press. ch. 10.

Pande, Rohini. 2003. Can mandated political representation increase policy influence for disadvantaged minorities? Theory and evidence from India.' *American Economic Review* 93(4). pp. 1132–51.

Probe Team. 1999. 'The school environment' in *Public Report on Basic Education in India*. Delhi: Oxford University Press. ch. 4.

Sen, Amartya. 1999. *Development as Freedom*. 1 ed. Random House.

Topalova, Petia. 2003. 'Women are changing governance in India? The impact of female leadership on household satisfaction, quality of public goods and governance.' Mimeo. MIT.

World Bank. 2001. *Engendering Development: through Gender Equality in Rights, Resources, and Voice*. Oxford University Press and World Bank.

Table 1

	Reserved For Women (1)	Unreserved For Women (2)
A. WOMEN'S RESERVATION AND MEN'S REPRESENTATION		
WEST BENGAL		
Total number	54	107
Proportion of female pradhans	100%	6.5%
RAJASTHAN		
Total number	40	60
Proportion of female pradhans	100%	1.7%
B. SC RESERVATION AND SC REPRESENTATION	Reserved For SC	Non reserved For SC
WEST BENGAL		
Total number	55	106
% SC	100	7.5

Table 2

Dependent variables	West Bengal Mean, reserved GP (1)	West Bengal Mean, unreserved GP (2)	West Bengal Difference (3)	Rajasthan Mean, reserved GP (4)	Rajasthan Mean, unreserved GP (5)	Rajasthan Difference (6)
Total population	974	1022	-49	1249	1564	-315
Female literacy rate	0.35	0.34	0.01	0.05	0.05	0.00
Male literacy rate	0.57	0.58	-0.01	0.28	0.26	0.03
% cultivated land that is irrigated	0.45	0.43	0.02	0.05	0.07	-0.02
Dirt road	0.92	0.91	0.01	0.40	0.52	-0.11
Metal road	0.18	0.15	0.03	0.31	0.34	-0.04
Bus stop or train station	0.31	0.26	0.05	0.40	0.43	-0.03
Number of public health facilities	0.06	0.08	-0.02	0.29	0.19	0.10
Tubewell is available	0.05	0.07	-0.02	0.02	0.03	-0.01
Hand-pump is available	0.84	0.88	-0.04	0.90	0.97	-0.06
Wells	0.44	0.47	-0.02	0.93	0.91	0.01
Tap water	0.05	0.03	0.01	0.12	0.09	0.03
Number of primary schools	0.95	0.91	0.04	0.93	1.16	-0.23
Number of middle schools	0.05	0.05	0.00	0.43	0.33	0.10
Number of high schools	0.09	0.10	-0.01	0.14	0.07	0.07

Notes: There are 2,120 observations in the West Bengal regressions, and 100 in the Rajasthan regressions.

Table 3

Dependent variables	Mean, reserved GP (1)	Mean, unreserved GP (2)	Difference (3)
WEST BENGAL			
Fraction of women among participants in the gram samsad (in percentage)	9.80	6.88	2.92
Have women filed a complaint to the GP in the previous 6 months?	0.20	0.11	0.09
Have men filed a complaint to the GP in the previous 6 months?	0.94	1.00	0.06
Observation	54	107	
RAJASTHAN			
Fraction of women among participants in the gram samsad (in percentage)	20.41	24.49	-0.04
Have women filed a complaint to the GP in the previous 6 months?	0.64	0.62	0.02
Have men filed a complaint to the GP in the previous 6 months?	0.95	0.88	0.073
Observations	40	60	

Table 4

	Women All (1)	Men (2)	Women All (3)	Men (4)
ALL PROGRAMMES				
Public works	0.84	0.85	0.62	0.87
Welfare programmes	0.10	0.04	0.19	0.03
Child care	0.01	0.01	0.07	0.01
Health	0.04	0.02	0.07	0.04
Credit or employment	0.01	0.09	0.05	0.04
BREAKDOWN OF PUBLIC WORKS ISSUES				
Drinking water	0.31	0.17	0.54	0.43
Road improvement	0.31	0.25	0.13	0.23
Housing	0.11	0.05	0.03	0.04
Electricity	0.08	0.10	0.03	0.02
Irrigation and ponds	0.04	0.20	0.02	0.04
Education	0.06	0.12	0.05	0.13
Adult education	0.00	0.01	0.00	0.00
Other	0.10	0.09	0.20	0.12

Notes: 1. Each cell lists the number of times an issue was mentioned, divided by the total number of issues in each panel.
2. The data for men in West Bengal comes from a subsample of 48 villages.

Table 5

Dependent variables	West Bengal Mean, reserved GP (1)	West Bengal Mean, unreserved GP (2)	West Bengal Difference (3)	Rajasthan Mean, reserved GP (4)	Rajasthan Mean, unreserved GP (5)	Rajasthan Difference (6)
A. VILLAGE LEVEL						
Number of drinking water facilities newly built or repaired	23.83 (5.00)	14.74 (1.44)	9.09 (4.02)	7.31 (.93)	4.69 (.44)	2.62 (.95)
Condition of roads (1 if in good condition)	0.41 (.05)	0.23 (.03)	0.18 (.06)	0.90 (.05)	0.98 (.02)	-0.08 (.04)
Number of panchayat-run education centres	0.06 (.02)	0.12 (.03)	-0.06 (.04)			
Number of irrigation facilities newly built or repaired	3.01 (.79)	3.39 (.8)	-0.38 (1.26)	0.88 (.05)	0.90 (.04)	-0.02 (.06)
Other public goods (ponds, biogas, sanitation, community buildings)	1.66 (.49)	1.34 (.23)	0.32 (.48)	0.19 (.07)	0.14 (.06)	0.05 (.09)
B. GP LEVEL						
1 if a new tubewell was built	1.00	0.93 (.02)	0.07 (.03)			
1 if a metal road was built or repaired	0.67 (.06)	0.48 (.05)	0.19 (.08)			
1 if there is an informal education centre in the GP	0.67 (.06)	0.82 (.04)	-0.16 (.07)			
1 if at least one irrigation pump was built	0.17 (.05)	0.09 (.03)	0.07 (.05)			

Notes: 1. Standard errors in parentheses.
2. In West Bengal, there are 322 observations in the village-level regressions, and 161 in the GP level regressions. There are 100 observations in the Rajasthan regressions.
3. Standard errors are corrected for clustering at the GP level in the village-level regressions for the West Bengal regressions, using the Moulton (1986) formula.

Table 6

	West Bengal		
Dependent variables	Mean, reserved GP (1)	Mean, unreserved GP (2)	Difference (3)
A. PRADHAN'S BACKGROUND			
Age	31.87	39.72	-7.85
Years of education	7.13	9.92	-2.79
Literacy	0.80	0.98	-0.19
Married	0.89	0.87	0.02
Number of children	2.45	2.50	-0.05
Below poverty line	0.46	0.28	0.18
Number of household assets	1.72	2.36	-0.64
Population of pradhan's own village	1554	2108	-554
Hesitates when answering the questions (interviewer's impression)	0.75	0.41	0.34
B. PRADHAN'S POLITICAL ASPIRATIONS AND EXPERIENCE			
Was elected to the GP council before 1998	0.11	0.43	-0.32
Was elected pradhan before 1998	0.00	0.12	-0.12
Took part in panchayat activities prior to being elected	0.28	0.78	-0.50
Knew how GP functioned	0.00	0.35	-0.35
Did not receive any formal training	0.06	0.00	0.06
Spouse ever elected to the panchayat	0.17	0.02	0.15
Spouse helps	0.43	0.13	0.30
Will not run again	0.33	0.21	0.13
C. PRADHAN'S POLITICAL PARTY			
Left Front	0.69	0.69	-0.01
Right (Trinamul or BJP)	0.19	0.18	0.01
Observations	54	107	

Table 7

Dependent variable	Difference Reserved-Unreserved	
	Women (1)	SC (2)
A. VILLAGE LEVEL		
Number of drinking water facilities newly built or repaired	**9.09** (4.02)	4.83 (4.66)
Number of irrigation facilities newly built or repaired	-0.36 (1.27)	0.85 (1.38)
Condition of roads (1 if in good condition)	**0.18** (.06)	-0.09 (.06)
Number of informal education centres	-0.06 (.04)	-0.02 (.05)
B. GP LEVEL		
1 if a new tubewell was built	**0.06** (.03)	0.03 (.04)
1 if at least one irrigation pump was built	0.08 (.05)	-0.09 (.06)
1 if a metal road was built or repaired	**0.18** (.08)	-0.11 (.08)
1 if there is an informal education centre in the GP	(-0.15) (.07)	(-010) (.07)

Table 8

	Share of goods available before 1998 in SC hamlets (normalised by SC share)		
	SC unreserved (1)	SC reserved (2)	Difference (3)
Private drinking water	0.399	0.460	0.061
Public drinking water	1.219	1.327	0.109
Private irrigation	0.478	0.213	-0.265
Public irrigation	0.959	0.589	-0.370
Sanitation	2.072	2.284	0.213
Informal education	1.067	0.470	-0.597
Adult education	0.804	1.588	0.784
Formal education	0.755	0.733	-0.022
Average all goods	0.809	0.820	0.011
Average all private goods	0.413	0.372	-0.040
Average all public goods	0.927	0.953	0.026

Table 9

	Normalised share			
	Not reserved for SC	Reserved for SC	Difference	Ratio
	(1)	(2)	(3)	(4)
Public goods built and repaired				
Public drinking water	1.049	1.540	**0.491**	1.468
Public irrigation	0.521	0.731	0.210	1.403
Sanitation	2.561	4.880	**2.319**	1.905
Informal education	1.061	0.818	-0.243	0.771
Adult education	0.697	1.048	0.350	1.502
Formal education	0.727	0.983	0.256	1.352
	Overall Difference (across all goods)		0.14	

Published as 'The Impact of Reservation in the Panchayati Raj: Evidence from a Nationwide Randomised Experiment' in *Economic and Political Weekly*, vol. 39, no. 9, November 2003, (pp. 979-86).

Panchayat Raj Institution (PRI) and Women's Reservation

R. GEETHA

The system of local governance in India is popularly known as Panchayat Raj (rule of five elders) on the traditional model of dispute resolution by five wise men. Though based on self-sufficiency and self-reliance, hierarchy of caste and patriarchy were present hence the Westminster model superceded [it]. But there has been a movement to evolve a decentralised participatory local government, especially after the publication of the Ashok Mehta Report in 1978.

The 73rd and 74th Amendments deal with the devolution of powers to local governments in three tiers know as PRI, apart from recognising the village voters' forum as the basis of democracy.

The PRI consists of three tiers. The first, the gram panchayat, is elected from and is responsive to the gram sabha or village assembly of which every adult male and female is a member. It is mainly in the nature of a deliberative body and is presided over by a pradhan (or village headman) who is directly elected. The panchayat is presided over by a sarpanch (head of the panchayat). The members are called the panches. The sarpanch can be directly or indirectly elected. This body has powers to decide both legal and developmental policies for the village. One panchayat may cover one or more villages, depending on the size of the population.

Taluq, mandal or block panchayats (also known as panchayat samitis or aanchal samitis in Arunachal Pradesh) are at the level of a cluster of villages and cover a plurality of panchayats, to coincide with the administrative divisions called blocks. The members may be directly or indirectly elected. It has a pramukh (the chief) and has representatives from all the panchayats. He or she may be indirectly elected.

At the district level is the zilla parishad (district board) which looks after the entire district. Its members may be directly or indirectly elected. Its chief (pramukh or president), is elected indirectly by the members.

There is a wide variation in the method of election and number of members, as the details are decided by the state legislatures and depend on the size and population of the states.

Structure: (a) The local government consists of three tiers except in the case of states with a population not exceeding 20 lakhs (1 lakh = 100,000).

(b) Membership in PRIs is by direct elections.

(c) There is a reservation membership (i) for women to the extent of not less than one-third of the seats; (ii) for Scheduled Castes and Scheduled Tribes in proportion to their share in the total population of the area; (iii) one-third of the SC and ST members will be women—this is a part of the total reservation for women members; and (iv) similarly not less than one-third of the total chairpersons at the three tiers of PRIs are reserved for women.

These representations are ensured by reserving territorial constituencies for the concerned groups. The reserved constituencies in turn are rotated in different constituencies of a panchayat or different panchayats of the samitis. In the case of the SCs and STs such a reservation will cease on the expiry of the period specified in Article 334 of the Constitution. By implication the reservation of seats for women both as members and chairpersons of all the three tiers will continue indefinitely. In Tamil Nadu, the Federation of Women Panchayat Presidents, represented for the rotation to be avoided and the government agreed to it.

Electoral outcome

The outcome of elections in terms of women's participation has been, however, one of tremendous enthusiasm. Elections in Karnataka, Orissa and West Bengal earlier had witnessed an appreciable turnout of women voters as well as candidates.

Not merely for the reserved constituencies, but even for the general constituencies, women had stood with great confidence. In many states, the percentage of women who had got into the PRIs exceeded the reserved positions.

In the elections to the Karnataka gram panchayats (December 1993), the percentage of women elected stood at 43.6 per cent.

It is, however, somewhat distressing to note that the Haryana Chief Minister should announce on the last day of nominations for the PRI elections—that the villages which arrived at a consensus regarding candidates for the gram panchayat and sarpanch (thereby assuring unanimity), will be rewarded with one lakh rupees. In essence this deprives the candidates of the possibility of contesting the elections and undermines the democratic process. May be that the vast transactions in buying and selling of potential candidates would ensure the success of the ruling party-sponsored candidates. The people themselves obviously saw other advantages in the unanimous elections, as it avoided controversies and fights, violence and expenses in campaigning and, above all, bad blood and division of the society. A few expressed the view that this would be better for future functioning as the sarpanch and members would not be identified with any particular faction. The final picture proved that this bait had been picked up by many panchayats, though the number of such panchayats elected unopposed was not a high proportion.

Experiences of elected women

Neither the reservation for women nor their actual presence in the panchayats have, however, made any immediate impact by way of sensitisation or attitudinal changes. The panchayats have not become any more sensitive to problems related to village women. The village level functionaries like school teachers, health workers and other government officials were merely performing their duties as before. They were indifferent to women panches. Complaints about unhealthy practices like the male teacher coming to class after consuming liquor or sexually harassing innocent schoolgirls were heard.

Further, the women who are elected are not always treated with due respect. Many elected women complained that their suggestions were not taken seriously nor were they consulted while decisions were being made. Some felt that their views were ignored only because they were women; sometimes they were pressurised by their men to approve the decisions made by the male-dominated panchayats.

The experience of changes in the family role of women was also widely varied. While a few women in Maharashtra had earlier opined that their membership had heightened their status in the family, some women in West Bengal had resented its interference in their domestic chores, resulting in the disruption of domestic life and neglect of family and home. In the absence of any income from panchayats as members many women have lost their jobs and wages.

Violence against women

While at the macro-level dissenting views were heard, at the local this dissent at times became more violent. By and large, the village men and families accepted the reservations silently, even if unhappily; and then sought how best it could be utilised in their own favour.

There were, however, instances of violent resentment. In Kachrauli village near Panipat in Haryana, an incumbent dalit woman member, Jindan Bai, was beaten up and abused by the police when she led an enquiry into a dubious land deal. In Madhya Pradesh, in the Harpura village of Bhind district, both the hands of a woman were broken; in another incident three sons of one Gutai Kori were brutally hacked to death in broad daylight.

Newspapers [carried] reports about Ms Tapati Sarkar, a Forward Bloc member of the Chandpara gram panchayat in the Gaighata Thana area in West Bengal, having been assaulted with an iron rod.

Earlier in Orissa, an up-sarpanch, Ms Basmati Bara of Kutra panchayat of Sundergarh district, had complained of sexual harassment by the Minister for Panchayats; the case had been taken up by the National Commission for Women.

In Uttar Pradesh, 60-year-old Llmon Devi, a woman pradhan, was murdered on 14 September. She was pradhan of Barauli village in Baghpat district. It is alleged that her independent way of working was not liked by the up-pradhan who wanted to misuse the powers of the gram panchayat. He figures as the main accused in the FIR lodged with the police according to whom about eight armed persons attacked the house of Llmon Devi at 8 am on 14 September 1999 and gunned her down. Her husband and son were also assaulted.

Daylight murder

On 29 March 2001, the president of Urappakkam panchayat in Tamil Nadu, Menaka was hacked to death by a four-member gang when she was attending to her work in the office at 11.30 am. Four members armed with long knives entered the office and before Menaka realised what was happening, they attacked her. She received cut injuries in the neck, head and face and died on the spot. The assailants also assaulted her brother Nehru who escaped. Two of the gangsters were identified and the brother said that one Kumar had planned to usurp a piece of vacant government land. But the plan was stalled by Menaka.

Soon after, the Tamil Nadu Federation of Dalit Panchayat Presidents held a meeting in Chingleput and passed a resolution to stop the torture of dalit panchayat chiefs. They highlighted the problems and voiced concern at the inability of successive governments to protect dalits and tribal panchayat chiefs. The meeting stated that dalits faced oppression when they organised auction of village resources including produce from tamarind trees and fishing rights in ponds.

All-women panchayats

In Muthupalli, Kurnool district of Andhra Pradesh, Varjara in Maharashtra in 1989, Sidghara in Madhya Pradesh, Rultika in West Bengal and Premkhara in Haryana there were all-women panchayats. The women had been elected unopposed. The reasons for this need to be analysed: whether the men not opposing them was an acknowledgement of their ability or a sign of not wanting to work with a woman chairperson. The earlier instance of Warangal district is a case of point; the gram panchayat presidentship had been reserved for a Scheduled Tribe candidate and since the high-caste males did not want to work under the leadership of a tribal and since the whole panchayat was to get an award if their choice was a unanimous one, they decided to elect a woman sarpanch. Then, since the men were reluctant to work under a woman, they turned it into an all-women panchayat.

However, this was not the case everywhere. In Bhende Khurd in Newasa taluq of Ahmednagar district in Maharashtra, an all-women panchayat was formed in December 1992. Nine members were elected unopposed. The local men in a village assembly meeting attended by 80 per cent of the total population, had decided to hand over charge of the panchayat to the women of the village.

Kerala—a model state

Kerala has had a very interesting experience in women's reservation in local bodies. Jalaja Chandran, [as] a case study as well as the experience of Muslim women are pointers and more basically people's plan and gender component have paved [the] way for the success of 33 per cent women's reservation.

Jalaja Chandran was 26 years old when she became president of the Mohamma gram panchayat in 1995.

Mohamma has been hailed as a model for women's participation in decentralised governance and planning. It has been singled out as a success story for its effective, full-scale utilisation of the public funds available for 'women's development' to benefit different aspects of women's lives. These funds have been used to not only improve the productivity and working conditions of enterprises in which local women are already engaged—such as agriculture, horticulture, fish and coir work and the processing of marine mollusc shells—but also to provide training and facilities to enable women to take up new forms of economic activity, often with financial and practical help from public institutions.

In an area where every available bit of waterfront land has been grabbed for tourism development the Mohamma panchayat has managed to secure approximately 50 per cent of land which provides the local community—especially women, who form the majority of fish and shell workers—with access to the water bodies they depend on for their livelihood. In addition, a new building has been constructed on another piece of land to house small industrial units newly set up by women's collectives. Funds have also been invested in the improvement of women's health, with particular attention being paid to occupational and mental health. A counselling centre attached to the primary health centre and a legal aid cell are two of the unusual community facilities provided by the panchayat that women are increasingly beginning to appreciate and use.

The panchayat president's initiative was obviously a key factor in many of these developments. Jalaja Chandran's story, in fact, highlights some of the peculiarities, pitfalls and potential of women's participation in local self-governance in Kerala. Insights gained from her experience may be useful in the context of ongoing attempts across the country to improve the effectiveness of women's political participation at the grass-roots.

But perhaps the most important advantage Jalaja enjoyed as the president of a gram panchayat in Kerala is the fact that decentralised governance in the state is not restricted to panchayat elections. Unlike her counterparts in most other states, she is vested with the power—and the responsibility—to make a real difference to the lives of her electorate. Thanks to a revolutionary step taken in 1996 by the Left Democratic Front (LDF) Government, 35-40 per cent of the state's outlay of funds from the Ninth Five Year Plan had been placed at the disposal of Panchayat Raj bodies. In addition, thanks to the People's Campaign for Decentralised Planning, launched in the same year to enable these institutions of local self-government to prepare plans in a transparent and participatory manner, elected representatives like Jalaja had ongoing, intensive, on-the-job training in mobilising citizens to participate in the planning process, identifying local needs, formulating plans to fulfil these, accessing and allocating available resources and, finally, ensuring the proper implementation of projects and programmes emerging from the plans.

Jalaja herself believes that if decentralised governance is working in Kerala—to the extent that it is—it is because planning and financial decision-making have also been substantially decentralised. She says she became conscious of how unique and critical a factor this is during the exchange visits of women members of village panchayats in Kerala and Karnataka organised by the Centre for Rural Management (CRM), Kottayam, with the cooperation of the Institute of Social Science, Bangalore.

While most GPs in Karnataka have no more than Rs 2.4 lakhs at their disposal annually—and even that relatively small amount is often not completely under their control—she was able to preside over the allocation and utilisation of a staggering Rs 70 lakhs in the very first year of her term—the sum of Plan funds and resources made available for specific projects and programmes by other public finance institutions. On the other hand, of course, Karnataka boasts nearly 10 times the number of elected women at the GP level (35,187 after the elections earlier this year, comprising nearly 45 per cent of the total number of GP members, compared to Kerala's 3878 and 36.2 per cent). It also has had a longer history of women's participation in the political process at the local level.

Another unique feature of Kerala's decentralised planning process, which has undoubtedly enhanced Jalaja's effectiveness as a panchayat president, is the earmarking of 10 per cent of the grant-in-aid funds available to each panchayat for what is known as the Women's Component Plan (WCP). Meant to be used for projects that will directly benefit women, the standard amount annually available for the WCP in each panchayat is approximately Rs 7.5 lakhs.

It is Jalaja's imaginative and insightful deployment of WCP funds that has earned Mohamma its reputation as a women friendly panchayat. In the current year she has managed to raise the WCP budget to 13 per cent of the available funds. A number of other panchayats have also apparently exceeded the stipulated 10 per cent allocation.

The WCP factor has also spawned village-level women's collectives in the form of neighbourhood and self-help groups.

In the past most such groups were essentially savings and micro-credit units, generally initiated and nurtured by non-government organisations and operating outside the political and economic 'mainstream'. However, in the wake of the PPC [People's Plan Campaign], both existing groups and newly formed ones have been registered by panchayats in order to make them eligible for WCP funds and presumably, to encourage their active participation in the decentralisation process. This development is obviously not free of pitfalls but it clearly has some positive potential.

For instance, the groups can not only encourage women's participation in the processes of local planning and governance but also provide women panchayat members and leaders with a prospective support base. Further, they can become platforms that enable women to articulate and find solutions for gender-related problems. According to Jalaja, the self-help groups in her panchayat do not restrict themselves to savings credit and income-generation activities alone but also use the forum to discuss a wide range of issues relating to women's lives and rights. Female panchayat leaders who are sensitive to women's multiple concerns and needs and recognise the tremendous potential of village-level women's collectives can clearly nurture the development of these groups into a forum that serves local women in different but equally vital ways.

Another important outcome of the focus on women's needs through the WCP is the increased participation of women in gram sabhas, the essential foundation of decentralised governance, which has reportedly risen from 26 per cent in the initial stages to 60 per cent more recently. Women also constitute two-thirds of the beneficiaries under individual beneficiary oriented programmes. The existence of active women's collectives that aid an integral part of the development process at the village level has no doubt contributed to those positive trends.

Yet another factor that probably helps to facilitate women's participation in gram sabhas in Kerala is the fact that, unlike in many other states these fora are convened at the ward level and presided over by the elected representative of the ward.

As a result they are relatively more accessible and manageable—especially for women—than their more unwieldy impersonal and possibly intimidating equivalents in other parts of the country. In Jalaja's experience, women are now among the most active participants in the gram sabhas.

Muslim women's role in Kerala

Consider this: one-fourth of the 100 village panchayats in the district are headed by Muslim women; two of the five municipalities—Malappuram and Tirur—have Muslim women chairpersons: six of the 14 block panchayats have Muslim women presidents and there are seven Muslim women in the 30-member district panchayat council (which was presided over by a Muslim woman during 1995–2000). On average, there are three Muslim women members in each of the panchayats and over 300 across the district.

This is remarkable for a community which, not long ago, frowned upon women going to the fair-price shop to fetch their weekly rations of rice and kerosene. This is remarkable again for a district which is home to perhaps the most underprivileged section of Kerala women, handicapped as they are by lack of higher education, dowry, teenage marriage and adolescent childbirth.

Interestingly, the huge majority of the elected representatives belong to the Indian Union Muslim League (some 20 panchayat presidents are of the League), a party unfriendly to the Women's Bill that aims to provide one-third seat reservation for women in the Lok Sabha and the state assemblies. The Muslim League, the second largest partner in the current UDF Government, had not fielded a single woman in the May Assembly election in which it contested 23 seats.

Initially, these women had to be dragged into the realm of politics and electoral battle by the political parties to meet the reservation stipulation. But they learnt the ropes amazingly fast. In a short time, they have shown how women's reservation could be an engine of social change in a depressingly male-dominated society. Politically empowered, they are gaining confidence to challenge the social norms that target women.

How did the Muslim women in the district gain entry to the political domain? 'It's only because of the one-third reservation for women in the Panchayati Raj Institutions provided by the 73rd and 74th Constitutional Amendments,' Ms Qamarunnisa Anwar, president of the Kerala State Vanitha League, told *The Hindu*. Had there been no reservation, none of these Muslim women would have made it to the panchayats and municipalities, she said.

'But for the reservation, I would not have entered politics and contested elections,' affirms Ms K.P. Mariyamma, lawyer and Malappuram district general secretary of the Vanitha League, who headed the district panchayat for five years as the position was reserved for a woman in the last term.

Ms R.K. Hafsath, the young mother of two children, who had ended her education after SSLC when she was married off, never even dreamt of entering politics and heading the Thripprangot panchayat. 'If there was no reservation for women, I would still be leading the life of a housewife confined to the four walls of my home,' she says proudly. This view is reflected by Ms T. Kunji Beevi, Tirur municipal chairperson; Ms C.H. Jameela, Malappuram chairperson; Ms K. Raziya, Tuvvur panchayat president, and virtually every panchayat president, or member or municipal councillor.

The upsurge in women's education in the 1990s, which was triggered by the Gulf boom, as well as the spread of television have aided in women's political participation. In the wake of the Gulf boom, a large number of educational institutions has been set up in the district, giving a fillip to female education.

Ms Minu Mumtaz, the defeated LDF candidate in Ponnani in the 1996 Lok Sabha election, points out that the political participation since the 1995 panchayat elections has triggered a new awareness and awakening among the Muslim women. It was as if a full generation had passed in just five or six years.

Muslim women, even distantly related to political work, were becoming bold, assertive and ready to take on the injustice of their male-controlled world, said Ms Mumtaz, who divorced her absentee husband using 'Fasq'. (Fasq, the female version of 'talaq', allows the woman to unilaterally divorce her husband after giving proper notice. Though Fasq is sanctioned by Islamic personal law, it is not legal in India and hence has to be legally validated through complex procedures). In Ms Mumtaz' view, politics was a key component of women's empowerment.

'These women have proved that women could do a lot of things for society and for the country' notes Ms Qamarunnisa Anwar, former chairperson of the State Social Welfare Board and the defeated 1996 Assembly candidate from Kozhikode-II. 'I was surprised how easily they learnt things and gained confidence.' She said the elected women disproved the general belief that the uneducated Muslim women were good-for-nothing and could not measure up to the educated women representatives from other communities.

Muslim League and Muslim women

The biggest political beneficiary of the one-third seat reservation for women in the panchayats and municipalities in Malappuram has been the Muslim League, the dominant party in the district.

Its women activists head 20 of the panchayats and two municipalities apart from holding hundreds of positions on gram panchayats, municipal councils, block panchayats, and the district panchayat. The League holds immense potential to emancipate Muslim women, which is closely linked to their political participation.

But the same party, which made so much political capital out of the reservation in the Panchayati Raj Institutions (facilitated by the 73rd and 74th Constitutional Amendments), is opposed to the idea of one-third quota for women in the Lok Sabha and the state assemblies. When the much-delayed Women's Bill came up in Parliament last time, the League, along with some other parties, opposed its introduction. The League masked its hostility to the Bill by demanding 'reservation for minorities first'.

League sources revealed that the party bosses had taken a decision, prior to the election, that women should be fielded only if the Women's Bill came through and reservation in assemblies was made statutory. Had the one-third reservation been applied to the assemblies too, the League would have been compelled to field eight women.

Dress code for women

The Muslim League is the only party in the state to have insisted on a dress code for its elected women representatives in panchayats and municipalities. The women have been asked to don Islamic dress (which means a sari, long-sleeved blouse and the headgear, 'mafta'). They are restricted from attending meetings and public functions after sunset. They have been advised to pay extra attention to their households, husbands and children (so that family life is not affected by the public role). The women have even been told to take care of their husbands' egos, lest the wives' positions trigger an inferiority complex or jealousy among them!

A League functionary justified the restrictions saying they were aimed to ward off possible public ridicule and the clerics' possible wrath. However, despite the displeasure of a small but influential section of the clerics, the Muslim masses in the district have generally welcomed and encouraged their women's political participation. They are even proud that some of them have become panchayat presidents and municipal chairpersons.

People's planning process

Despite the commitment of the Leftists to decentralised governance, the introduction of people's planning by the Left Democratic Front in 1996 was necessitated by the severe development crisis (Isaac 2000). The only option before the state government to realise the investment targets envisaged for the Ninth Plan was the mobilisation of small savings and voluntary labour on a massive scale. As is well known, the difference in levels between social development and the growth of material production sectors in the state, the hallmark of the much-acclaimed Kerala model of development, has been exerting great pressure on the state exchequer. It was estimated that the revenue expenditure in the state was 14.5 per cent higher than revenue receipts, which is 6.2 percentage points higher than that of the average for other states (George 1999). As a result, more than 50 per cent of the borrowing intended for capital expenditure was being expended to meet the deficit in the revenue account.

Behind the achievements of the people's planning were the efforts made in the mobilisation of voluntary work, small savings and beneficiary contribution by ensuring mass participation. An important achievement of people's planning is the negation of the notion of the planning process as a highly technical one which has to be performed by specialised technocrats.

The people's planning movement has opened up several avenues for women to organise and come to the forefront of political and social life. Realising the relevance of neighbourhood groups and their thrift fund, but in variance with the line of the World Bank agenda in organising women through SHGs, micro-enterprises for women were envisaged making use of their thrift fund, and loans from financial institutions supplemented with the plan fund from LSGIs [Local Self-Government Institutions]. Given the industrial scenario of the state, the spread of micro-enterprises manufacturing various consumer articles based on locally available resources and local demand assumes special significance.

The assembly elections held in May 2001 led to a change of government from the Communist Party of India (Marxist)-led LDF to the Indian National Congress(I)-led UDF. During the election campaign, both UDF and LDF were vocal on the continuation of the people's planning programme. From the beginning of people's planning in 1997-98, there was concerted effort to paint the movement as a political gimmick to mobilise people in favour of the ruling front.

The budget presented for 2001-02 and the plan fund allotted to the LSGIs has been revised downward by 16.43 per cent. This outlay may be viewed against the yearly increases made by the LDF government from Rs 7,490 million in 1997-98 to Rs 10,450 million in 2000-01. It may also be noted that the last instalment due to the LSGIs from the plan fund earmarked for 2000-01, but withheld by the LDF government, has not been disbursed. Now it has been made clear that the instalment stands cancelled. In other words, the effective fund allotment for 2001-02 is only Rs 5,720 million, which is only 76 per cent of the plan fund to LSGIs allocated in 1997-98 (at current prices).

New guidelines for people's planning

According to the earlier guidelines, an LSGI could form 8-12 task forces, one each for a subject group such as agriculture, industry, infrastructure, and so on. The strength of each task force was suggested to be 10-12 members. The composition and defined functions of each task force were, therefore, of crucial importance. It has been stated in the new guidelines that the number of members in a task force should not be less than five, implying thereby that if any LSGI decides to reduce the strength of the force from 12 to 5, it is free to do so. Further, the task force, called 'karmasamithi' in Malayalam in the earlier guidelines, has been changed to 'sectoral committees', substituting an English word for the earlier plain Malayalam term.

Each task force in the earlier guidelines included, among others, an activist, a technical expert, a government official and an elected representative of the LSGI, and functioned with a chairman (elected representative to the LSGIs), a vice-chairman (technical expert in the concerned subject group, residing in the LSGI area, and usually a social activist), a convener (an official employed in the LSGI), and a joint convener (an activist, who in most cases happened to be a resource person at the district level but residing in the LSGI area). In the newly constituted sectoral committees, the positions of vice-chairman and joint conveners, the representatives other than the elected member to the LSGI, do not figure. As per earlier guidelines, the practice was for the draft proposal of the project to be presented in gram sabhas and development seminars either by the convener or vice-chairman or any member of the task force other than a government employee. The official in the task force (convener) was only a silent spectator of the discussion. In the new guidelines, a clear direction is given that the secretary of the sectoral committee (an official) should present the draft proposal of projects.

In the new guidelines, the fact that officials have been elevated to positions of high prominence is clear from the instruction that the secretary of the gram panchayat (an official, should be the convener of the general body) convened for the formation of the sectoral committees. As elected representatives, people were in prominence during the previous four years and no such power was vested in government officials. Further, in order to ensure that interests of the vulnerable sections of society, such as women, Scheduled Castes and Tribes, were protected it was suggested in the earlier guidelines that one-third of the task force members should be women and representation from Scheduled Castes and Tribes in the total strength of the task force should be proportional to their population. From the Scheduled Castes and Tribes members of the task force, one member had to be co-opted to other task forces such as agriculture and industry in order to ensure that their interest in other sectors was also duly protected. This procedure also helped sectoral integration of projects prepared by different task forces. The new guidelines have totally ignored the importance and relevance of such integration. During the past four years, about 100,000 people worked as task force members and their role in people's planning was crucial at various stages of plan formulation and implementation. Since the size of the task force has been reduced and the role of the people in the planning process has been transferred to the officials, the task force (sectoral committees) would virtually cease to exist and it will have serious implications on the participation and involvement of people in the decentralisation process.

Gender issues

In the earlier guidelines, one-third of the total members in the task force formed in any LSGI were required to be women. Further, sectors other than women's development had to co-opt one member for other sectoral committees to ensure that the interests of women were duly represented and protected in the formulation and implementation of projects. The new guidelines have dropped these two clauses. It may force women to confine their role to women's development projects with no say over the other 90 per cent of the plan fund.

Under-sizing the ombudsman

In order to check malfeasance in local governance while discharging developmental functions, the system of ombudsman consisting of seven members including one high court judge, two district judges, two secretaries to the government and two eminent public persons selected in consultation with the leader of the opposition was constituted with adequate powers to conduct judicial investigations and inquiry into any allegation pertaining to any matter of local governance. The system of ombudsman has been watered down by removing six out of the seven members in the committees.

Tamil Nadu Federation

In Tamil Nadu, a Federation of Women Presidents of Panchayat Government has been formed. The Federation has called upon the state government to take steps to persuade the Centre to withdraw the 87th Constitution Amendment Bill, since the amendment to Article 243(C) to ensure linkage between panchayat tiers would be a major setback to the cause of decentralisation and would prevent the emergence of leaders from among the women, dalits and other disadvantaged groups.

The Federation, in a convention, has demanded that the state government take urgent steps to guarantee an environment in which women and dalits will be able to function with dignity and freedom.

Another resolution wanted the government officials to be treated as staff of the local government, making them accountable to the panchayat government.

Restrictions by state and central governments should be done away with, another resolution pointed out.

Other resolutions included repealing Section 205 of the Tamil Nadu Panchayat Act, 1994, which dealt with the removal of a panchayat president by the district collector and strengthening district panchayats and district planning committees.

A voiceferous advocate and former member of the Rajya Sabha, Ms Jayanthi Natarajan writes about the state-level convention of elected women panchayat presidents.

> It is truly amazing how the problems of women all over the country seem to crystallise into the same basic core issues. First, a fundamental resistance from male-dominated feudal society, colleagues, and family to the idea of women in authority. Secondly, the arrogance and insensitivity of the district-level bureaucracy to elected women representatives, resulting in a total lack of information or training being given to them. And finally, the indiscriminate use of the infamous Sec. 203 of the Tamil Nadu Panchayat Act, which in complete defiance of all democratic norms, gives district collectors the power to dissolve democratically elected district panchayats.
>
> Imagine if you will, the uproar that will result if the Cabinet Secretary could dissolve Parliament or the state Chief Secretary, the state Assembly. It is no coincidence that out of 98 panchayat presidents removed till date, over 66 just happen to be women and dalits. All the women present strongly resented this extra constitutional power exercised by the bureaucracy, and some even related bizarre tales about how local clerks actually refused to even hand over office keys to elected panchayat presidents.
>
> Many women also complained that they were intimidated into signing cheques which they did not want to. From all that was said it was very clear, to me at least, that the state government which is so vocal on autonomy for states is strangely reluctant to devolve the same powers to its own local bodies. In a nutshell, these bodies have no financial powers at all and therefore find it impossible to function in a meaningful way.

Andhra Pradesh—Fatima Bi: success story of a woman sarpanch

Fatima Bi, sarpanch of Kalva village in Kurnool district in Andhra Pradesh, who received the United Nations

Development Programme's Race Against Poverty award for the Asia-Pacific region from the United Nations Secretary-General Kofi Annan in New York on 17 October, is an illiterate women. She would have remained confined to the four corners of her house but for the reservation for women in local bodies. She was married at 14 and with three children, was an ordinary housewife just three years ago. Then came the panchayat elections and the seat of sarpanch of her village was declared reserved for women. Her husband, who had earlier toyed with the idea of contesting for the post, decided to field Fatima Bi, who won handsomely.

However, even after being elected, the lifestyle of Fatima Bi remained unchanged for a year. Her husband played sarpanch and she went on putting her thumb impression on official papers. One day the district collector visited Kalva and insisted on meeting the sarpanch and not her husband. Fatima Bi recollects, 'I could manage with all my effort only to say Salam-alaikum'. It was UNDP Project Director Vijay Bharathi who inspired her to come out and start working. Soon thereafter Fatima Bi saw the Telugu blockbuster *Ramuluamma*, starring Vijay Shanthi in the role of an angry woman fighting for justice, and was overwhelmed. A new Fatima Bi thundered in the first session of training for panchayat women: 'Where are the village records? How can I work without them?' The Mandal officials promptly promised to provide her with all the records. Then she called a meeting of the village women and asked them to join hands with her to undertake development of the village.

That was the beginning of an inspired leadership. A metal road was laid, check dams were built, a new school building constructed and the old school building repaired. Under the Chief Minister's Janma Bhoomi development programme, the village women raised Rs 30,000. A Rs two-lakh scheme of digging a five km irrigation drain and clearing 500 acres of fallow land for paddy cultivation was taken up. Fatima Bi led the womenfolk to join the Podupu Lakshmi groups and urged them to save a small amount of money every month. Within a year, 40 thrift and self-help groups with 300 women members gave Rs two lakhs as an interest-free loan to the Village

Development Organisation—an umbrella organisation of Kalva. The organisation is now run by a 430-woman committee of representatives of self-help groups with Rs 20 lakhs at its disposal. The loans granted by it have helped many families to undertake small businesses and improve their living conditions. The enterprising women of Kalva have now started helping the neighbouring village with loans.

Once poor and backward, Kalva is now a completely transformed village with happy faces all around and modern amenities in almost all houses. Child marriages are a thing of the past. The women who have suffered injustice in social spheres all along are now standing by the side of their daughters. 'No more illiteracy and no more inaction' has become their motto. Credit goes to the hard-working woman sarpanch who won the title of Uttam Sarpanch and received the award on Independence Day two years back. Fatima Bi, 33 is now planning a hospital and a ring road around her village to connect it to the bus stand.

Madhya Pradesh—Basanti Bai: down but not out

The entire village of Barkhedi was busy discussing the imminent future. An unexpected event was about to takes place—a woman, and a dalit woman at that, was to become sarpanch of the village. Many said, 'This is Kalyug and the government has gone mad'. Others blamed it on 'the madness of Raja Sahib (Chief Minister Digvijay Singh), who does not understand that women cannot rule'. Barkhedi is dominated by upper castes and its traditional leaders were very unhappy over the fact that the post of sarpanch had been reserved for SC women. When they realised that they could do nothing to stop it, they conspired to turn the situation to the best of their advantage. Almost all influential groups fielded their own proxy candidates.

1994: Basanti Bai makes history

In the summer of 1994, Basanti Bai, a Scheduled Caste woman, made history by becoming the first woman sarpanch of Barkhedi gram panchayat in Sehore district in Madhya Pradesh. What led her to contest the panchayat election? Her husband used to discuss politics with her and these discussions helped her to choose a new future for herself. 'I learnt politics from my husband, who used to discuss his views and experiences with me,' she admitted candidly. However, the realisation came very soon that her job as a sarpanch was not an easy one: the Constitution may have undergone a radical change but it has not yet changed the mindset of influential people.

The first no-confidence motion against Basanti Bai came too early, that is, in 1995. She lost the motion but not her confidence. She fought and won the by-election, which was held to fill the vacancy caused by her removal. This time, she secured more votes than those she had got in the last panchayat election. She and her family members thought that after having proven popularity a second time, she would be allowed to work for the rest of her term. But the second no-confidence motion was waiting for her again. This time too, the upper-caste people succeeded in disposing what the ordinary voters had proposed. Consequently, she was forced to contest another election in 1997. Basanti Bai won the third election as well.

The entire family of Basanti Bai remembers those days of sarpanchi (sarpanchship) when they were repeatedly threatened and fake complaints were registered in police stations in order to pressurise her to accept the lordship of the influential people of the village. People stopped giving them work on the plea, 'How can we employ a sarpanch?' The landless family had to go to the adjoining villages for daily wages and find alternative employment.

2000: A complete reversal

The struggle faced by Basanti Bai taught her all the laws relating to panchayats and she no longer required anybody's kindness to tell her that she could contest the election even if the post of sarpanch was not reserved for SC women. In the second general panchayat elections held in January last year, only three candidates were in the fray and she came third. 'Arre Saab! We could not even save our security deposits this time', exclaims her husband. 'Who wants a woman as sarpanch, that too from the Scheduled Caste category?' he asks with bitterness and we are left speechless.

Basanti Bai's family members and other villagers agree that since the seat was not reserved this time, her chances of winning were very bleak. 'Last time, we had no option but to accept her as she was the only woman with leadership qualities', says Balkishan, justifying himself and others who voted for Basanti Bai. 'This time, people of the village thought that an upper caste male sarpanch could do much more for the village than a woman, and they voted accordingly,' he adds.

2001: Perception of the village community

Most of the community groups in Barkhedi now feel that they made a mistake in not voting for Basanti Bai. 'A powerful man as sarpanch is of little use to a common villager like me', says Raghu, a shopkeeper. 'He never comes to help us. Each time we need his help, we have to go to his house and wait outside like one waits outside a police station. It depends on his mood whether he will come along with you or not', concludes Raju.

'Basanti Bai was easily accessible to everyone and even if an opponent went to her, she would help him. We now realise she was much, much better as sarpanch', concur members of a group along the roadside of the village. Many people said that she was still active and helped them in many ways, 'Whenever there is a problem, she goes to see the concerned government officials and ensures that the work is done'.

How she and her family earn their bread is an issue nobody in the village wishes to comment on. One villager whispered, 'No one in the village would give work to an ex-sarpanch'. That means she and other members of her family continue to go outside the village in search of work. Her elder son has shifted to Narsingarh and is working as a driver. The younger son has discontinued his studies and is looking for a job.

2001: Perception of family members

'The government has done nothing for us in the last 50 years. What support system do we have? In the name of giving power to dalits, the post was reserved for us. But nobody from the government came over to help us in overcoming the hurdles and difficulties hurled on us. There are no institutions to help us. Only our work and relationship with the community came to our rescue', says a bitter husband. 'We are still on the job and try to do whatever we can', he says. When we were talking, Basanti Bai was not at home; she had gone to Sehore for getting a hand-pump installed in the village.

'Arre! I didn't expect that you will come after me and that too when I am not sarpanch', said Basanti Bai when she saw us. 'I may not be sarpanch now but my life remains the same. Now I give more time to help the villagers. All the officers know me well. So I am better placed then the present sarpanch', explains Basanti Bai when asked about her present engagements. She has recently forced the PHED [Public Health Engineering Department] to instal a hand-pump in the village, which is in the grip of drought this year [...]

Panchayat Elections in Bihar

Women and dalits assert themselves despite large-scale violence

Bihar recently witnessed violent panchayat elections after a gap of 22 years. At least 96 persons, including a magistrate and several candidates, were killed during the six-phase polling from 11 to 30 April. In fact, election-related violence got a push just after the panchayat elections were announced. More than 40 candidates were murdered in different districts during the period between notification of polling dates and filing of nomination papers. The police recovered a large number of arms and ammunitions, most of which were illegal, in different districts. There were many incidents of booth capturing and intimidation of voters despite heavy police patrolling and shoot-at-sight orders.

After the 73rd Amendment, it was the first panchayat election in the country, which denied reservation in panchayat posts to women, SCs and STs—an open violation of Article 243D(4) of the Constitution. Strangely the Patna High Court had held that reservation for presidents is not tenable and based on that judgement the state government went ahead with the panchayat election without reservation. Yet, the entire village landscape was buzzing with activities as the long-awaited opportunity to make a difference in the notoriously deteriorating conditions in the state had finally arrived. Against a rural electorate of about four crore (40 million or 400 lakhs), a total number of 4.36 lakh candidates jumped into the ring. Over 40,000 seats were reserved for women, for which more than 1.25 lakh candidates were in the fray. About 22,000 candidates, many of them women, were elected unopposed—roughly five per cent of the total candidates, but what is significant is that not less than 20 per cent of gram panchayat contestants had no rivals. This is a clear indication of the terror of the strong men and criminals in the village communities of the state. Although elections were held on a non-party basis, all political parties created election cells in their offices and backed their candidates openly. Violating the electoral norms fixed by the State Election Commission, the ruling RJD member of the Legislative Council and Laloo Prasad Yadav's brother-in-law Subhas Yadav and his supporters were making rounds in four vehicles to ensure the victory for Chief Minister Rabri Devi's father, who was a candidate for the post of mukhiya in Salar Kalan gram panchayat.

The spirit of the electorate can be gauged by the fact that more than 65 per cent of voters exercised their franchise.

Rays of hope

An outstanding feature of the panchayat elections was enthusiasm and courage of women, who not only contested for different panchayat posts but also came out to vote despite all odds. Women constituted about 50 per cent of all voters who polled their votes.

Thirty-five-year old Draupadi, a resident of Bucha village in Khagaria district, had been kidnapped by associates of her husband's landlord employer in August last year. When panchayat elections were announced, she decided to field herself 'to fight the feudal bigwigs who control the destiny of the poor' in the backward north Bihar. Poonam Devi of Hardia village in the same district contested for the post of panch against the wishes of her husband who himself wanted to file nomination papers for the post. 'He refused to bear my election campaign expenses which I pooled from my parents,' says a cheerful Poonam.

In Narihar village in Saharsa district, Nilam Prakash ventured out of her home to fight against Rajpur heavyweight Mahodeo Singh, a big landlord who has controlled the levers of power in the locality for the last 30 years.

In Patna district, Nazra Khatoon, 32, was elected unopposed to the Nauhasa gram panchayat. Influential people, even some elder feudal lords, were disarmed by her vociferous campaign for drinking water, roads and job opportunities for the poor. 'Villagers realised that only a woman like Nazra would be able to represent the area in the most suitable manner' a 60-year-old man in Nauhasa village asserted.

In some constituencies, dalit men and women polled their votes in the face of threats of 'dire consequences' and even braving actual violence, while a large number of dalits were prevented from exercising their franchise in many other constituencies.

Uttar Pradesh—responsibility without authority: the plight of women pradhans

How the women pradhans in the most populous state of India are being prevented from exercising their statutory functions by the bureaucrats and the male-dominated social set-up in the villages was eloquently brought out at an open forum for about 300 elected women representatives of Panchayat Raj Institution of three districts—Dehradun, Tehri and Hardwar—organised by Rural Litigation and Entitlement Kendra (RLEK).

The participants in the forum stated that the government orders on devolution of powers to PRIs were a mockery. They spoke about the blatant practice of 'commission' demanded by DRDA [District Rural Development Agency] and block-level staff and how the women pradhans, unwilling to accede to the demand, were being denied clearance of the proposals submitted by them. As a result, they were branded as incompetent in the eyes of the villagers and very often made to quit their office through no-confidence motions. In this game, the up-pradhan who generally is a high-caste male, acts as an accessory in expectation of the coveted position of the pradhan. The forum therefore, strongly felt that if a no-confidence motion is passed against a woman pradhan she must be replaced by a woman pradhan only.

The women pradhans also referred to the village patwari as the source of 'terror' since he controlled all the information about the panchayat lands and indulged in all sorts of manipulations for their illegal transfers. The engineers posted in the villages openly embezzled development funds allocated to the panchayats.

Widespread use of corrupt practices among the local bureaucrats and challenges faced by the illiterate and uneducated women panchayat representatives in a male-dominated society has also been emphasised by studies conducted by Dr Ranjana Sheel and Dr Ravi Srivastava. Dr Srivastava mentions the case of a Kol woman pradhan Premawati, who after two years of her election to the post, had been unable even to take over the charge precisely because of the efficient networking against her among the local upper-caste lobby and the bureaucrats. In another instance, Puspa, who like Premawati was also a Scheduled Caste woman sarpanch and was being opposed by the upper caste up-sarpanch, found it difficult to push through the developmental agenda. Some other studies on the status of women in gram panchayats of the state reveal the same picture.

Summing up

The experience of women's reservation in panchayats (local bodies) has created excitement as well as tensions in Indian society. This is the reason why the Women's Reservation Bill becomes most controversial.

The positive experiences of women in Kerala can not be seen separately from the state government's initiative for people's plan and awakening of women at the grass-root level.

Remarkable women leaders all over the country have come to light in this experience of devolution of powers to panchayats.

The violence unleashed on women, especially dalit women, factors such as domination of administration and provisions empowering a bureaucrat to dismiss elected presidents, need to be reversed.

The positive feature is the growing consciousness to strengthen the gram sabhas, voters assembly at the village level and formation of women's committees and self-help groups all over the country.

Acknowledgements

My sincere thanks to Ms Akhila Sivadas, Ms Veena Nayyar, Dr Mohini Giri, Dr Padma Seth and Dr Syeda Hameed at New Delhi and Com. A.K. Roy (Dhanbad) for the fruitful discussions; to Initiatives of Women in Development documentation centre at Chennai and Parliament Library for providing the materials; to Ms Parvathy, Dr Kamala and Ms Alli who helped with the manuscript; to Sri Saravanan who typed the manuscript.

References

George, K.K. 1999. *Limits to Kerala Model of Development: an analysis of fiscal crisis and its implications.* 2nd ed. Thiruvananthapuram: Centre for Development Studies.

Issac, T.M. Thomas and Richard W. Franke. 2000. *Local Democracy and Development: the Kerala people's campaign for decentralized planning.* New Delhi: Leftword Books.

Excerpt from *Women's Representation in Indian Parliament and Legislatures, INSAF Bulletin* (27), 1 July 2004, (pp. 22-30).

Section IV
Alternatives to the Women's Reservation Bill

Women and Politics: Beyond Quotas

MADHU KISHWAR

Women who have lobbied for the last few years for a constitutional amendment reserving a 33 per cent quota for women in the Lok Sabha and state assemblies responded angrily when the Bill didn't go through on the same day that it was presented and the matter was referred to a select committee of parliament. They interpreted the demand for a more thorough discussion on the proposal as an attempt to sabotage it, as proof that our men are still seeped in patriarchal anti-women values. While there is no doubt that some male politicians are feeling perturbed at the prospect of having to suddenly yield so much ground to women, what transpired on the last two days of the monsoon session of the Lok Sabha gives little cause for pessimism. It is a characteristic case of looking at a glass as half-full or half-empty.

It is noteworthy that the move to reserve one-third of seats for women has the formal endorsement of virtually every major political party in the country. The BJP, the Congress, the Janata Dal and the CPI(M) have each promised 33 per cent reservation for women in their election manifestos for 1996. Even though many of these parties' members are unhappy at being cornered into actually implementing their poll promise, they dare not oppose the move openly. During the parliamentary debate, very few male politicians opposed the principle of reservations for women and the few who did so were put down by their own male colleagues for their indiscretion. A few MPs pointed to technical flaws and limitations of the Bill. Not all of these objections were frivolous, although some indeed were trying to delay or sabotage it. Women members took the offensive and wanted the Bill passed the same day without any debate since this was the last day of the session.

The very same people who went berserk over the move to reserve 27 per cent of government jobs and seats in educational institutions for members of Other Backward Classes (OBCs) have accepted the 33 per cent reservation for women (not just in legislatures but also in government jobs) with apparent grace and enthusiasm. This is because our country has a well entrenched tradition whereby any party, politician or public figure who tries to bad-mouth women in public or oppose moves in favour of women's equality is strongly disapproved of. During the last Maharashtra assembly elections, Bal Thackeray made some disparaging comments about women. It produced such a widespread negative reaction that many attribute Shiv Sena's subsequent poor showing at the polls to this big indiscretion. Therefore, no politician likes to be seen opposing measures that claim to work for women's 'empowerment', no matter how opposed he personally may be to a particular measure. Hence, compared to many other parts of the world, it is relatively easy to get legislation favouring women passed in India.

No party from the Right or the Left has ever opposed pro-women laws. The right to maternity benefit, right to equal pay for equal work, right to abortion, all of which took decades of struggle by the women's movement in the West came to be enacted in India without a fight. The law to reserve one-third seats in all panchayats and zilla parishads has already been put into effect in all the states of India without evoking any hostility or opposition from male politicians or society at large.

However, the very politicians who pay lip service to women's causes on public platforms and help enact laws favouring women actually help sideline women in their own parties.

Congress(I), for instance, had committed to give 15 per cent of election tickets to women way back in 1957 but never implemented that resolve. Even after all the major parties had promised 33 per cent reservation for women in legislatures, they all reverted back to tokenism when it actually came to giving party tickets for the 1996 Lok Sabha elections. The Congress(I) fielded only 49 women out of a total of 530 candidates. The BJP gave tickets to 23 women out of a total of 477 candidates that it fielded. The CPI(M) gave five seats to women out of 77, while the CPI fielded four women out of 43 candidates. The Janata Dal fielded 11 women out of 220 candidates. Of the 477 women candidates for the 1996 elections, about two-thirds stood as independents and one-third were put up by various political parties, the total being 3.3 per cent (477 out of 14,274).

The oddest thing about the marginalisation of women in Indian politics is that it is happening despite widespread social opinion in favour of women's active political participation. The recent countrywide opinion survey conducted by the Centre for the Study of Developing Societies for *India Today* provides the most encouraging and definitive endorsement that there is no real gender divide in India on this issue. Seventy-five per cent of men and 79 per cent of women favour active participation of women in politics and 75 per cent of men and an equal percentage of women favour reservations for women in legislatures ('The Maturing of a Democracy', *India Today*, 31 August 1996). Our leaders, however, have so far only obstructed women's involvement in politics. In this area, the electorate is far ahead of its political 'leaders', as in most other respects.

By and large, Indian men do not seem to feel threatened by women reaching positions of power, including those who may not allow their own wives or daughters the opportunity of doing so. In our country women such as Kiran Bedi or Indira Gandhi who are perceived as stronger than men get to be venerated like virtual goddesses. They are almost never subjected to ridicule and hostility that are often displayed towards such women in western countries. Contrast the way in which the first woman prime minister of France was treated with the kind of love and respect Indira Gandhi undeservingly got in this country.

Premature for whom?

The sentiment in favour of women being active in politics is nothing new. Women's right to equal political participation, including their right to vote, was accepted very gracefully in India much earlier than most western societies conceded to this demand. Indian women did not even have to fight for this right, unlike their western counterparts.

The story of how women came to be first represented in legislatures in the 1920s is in itself quite instructive. In response to the Indian agitation for representative government, the British government set up a committee headed by Montagu and Chelmsford in 1919 to work out a proposal for constitutional reforms towards the inclusion of some Indians in government. Many groups presented their case for representation before the committee. Among the many delegations that met this committee, Sarojini Naidu and Margaret Cousins led a small delegation of women to demand that women be granted the same rights of representation in legislatures as men. The British government predictably thought this demand was quite preposterous because women in most western countries had still not been given the right to vote, despite a protracted struggle. The Southborough Committee stated that 'the extension of the vote to women would be premature in a society which continued to enforce purdah and prohibitions against female education'.[1] However, instead of taking on themselves the onus of rejecting the demand outright the British government simply skirted the issue by leaving it up to each of the individual provincial legislatures that they had just set up in India to grant or to refuse the franchise to women. Their assumption was that since Indians were so 'backward', they would never accept the idea of equal political rights for women. But despite the fact that at this time there was no mass-based women's suffrage movement in India, each of the Indian provincial legislatures voted to make it possible within a short span of time for women to be represented at par with men without much fuss.

The testimony of Margaret Cousins, an Irish feminist who played a major role in women's organisations in India as well as in Britian, brings out the contrast between the western and Indian response to women's political rights very clearly:

> Perhaps only women like myself who had suffered from the cruelties, the injustices of men politicians, the man-controlled press, the man in the street, in England and Ireland while we waged our militant campaign for eight years there after all peaceful and constitutional means had been tried for fifty previous years, could fully appreciate the wisdom, nobility and the passing of fundamental tests in self-government of these Indian legislators ... Between the Madras Legislative Council in 1921 and Bihar Council in 1929 all the legislative areas of India had conferred the symbol and instrument of equal citizenship with men on women who possessed equal qualifications—a certain amount of literacy, property, age, payment of taxes, length of residence.[2]

This is because the British were only prepared for limited suffrage for those who possessed a certain amount of property and education. They were not willing to consider universal adult suffrage. When a meeting of representative women's organisations in 1930 drafted a memorandum demanding immediate acceptance of adult franchise without gender discrimination, it was turned down by the British government. The same demand received a totally different response from the Indian leaders. The very next year, in 1931 the Karachi session of the Indian National Congress took the historic decision committing itself to the political equality of women, regardless of their status and qualifications. This proposal met with virtually no opposition.

Mahatma Gandhi played a crucial role in creating a favourable atmosphere for women's participation in the freedom struggle by insisting that the struggle for women's equality was an integral part of the movement for swaraj. His choice of non-violent satyagraha as the mode of struggle also allowed women to play a far more active and creative role than is possible in more masculine-oriented movements based on violence. This galvanised huge numbers of women into action. He worked consciously to feminise the freedom movement.

> My contribution to the great problem [of women's role in society] lies in my presenting for acceptance of truth and ahimsa in every walk of life, whether for individuals or nations. I have hugged the hope that in this, woman will be the unquestioned leader, and having thus found her place in human evolution, will shed her inferiority complex.[3]

The programmes of action undertaken as part of non-violent satyagraha were such that women would not feel limited or unequal to men, as they inevitably do when sheer muscle power or capacity for inflicting violence are to determine the outcome of a struggle. Thus women were not to compete with men in imbibing negative qualities such as propensity towards the use of force but by their presence in the movement humanise it and save it from destructive tendencies. It is significant that all of Bapu's symbols of struggle and protest were from the feminine realm. Spinning, for instance, has traditionally been a woman's activity. By exhorting men to spin he tried to inculcate feminine virtues in them. Similarly, picketing liquor shops related to the evil effect of liquor on women and the household. By picking on salt as a symbol of a countrywide satyagraha, he brought the movement into every home and kitchen. There are numerous testimonies acknowledging the energy and dynamism women brought into the movement. To quote Nehru:

> Our women came to the forefront and took charge of the struggle. Women had always been there, of course, but now there was an avalanche of them which took not only the British government but their own menfolk by surprise. There were these women, women of the upper and middle class, leading sheltered lives in their homes, peasant women, working class women, rich women—pouring out in their tens of thousands in defiance of government orders and police lathis. It was not only the display of courage and daring but what was even more surprising was the organisational power they showed.[4]

Annie Besant became Congress party president as early as 1919. Sarojini Naidu was Gandhi's choice for president of the Congress Party as early in 1925. Starting with that kind of a high profile role, women's participation in politics enhanced dramatically in the 1930s and 1940s. However, the decades following Independence witnessed a remarkable decline in women's involvement in politics. This began in the heyday of Nehru's era, even though most women leaders believed him to be an outstanding champion of women's rights.

For instance, in the 1952 elections the Congress party had only 14 women members elected to Parliament. In the first Lok Sabha women constituted no more than 4.4 per cent of the total strength. This was at a time when there were thousands of outstanding women all over the country with the experience of the freedom movement behind them. Their long years of involvement in social and political work, running educational institutions, and so on, would have given them the requisite training and experience to be effective parliamentarians. But they were systematically ignored and bypassed. Even within the Congress party women found very little room in decision-making bodies. The women's front of the party also began to decline in importance especially after the passing of 'reformed' Hindu laws in the mid-1950s. Today very few people outside the Congress party are aware that there is a body called the Mahila Congress.

Thus while societies which have less of a tradition of public acceptance of women's political mobilisation have witnessed an increasing participation of women in politics, India's history has taken a surprising turn. In the five decades after Independence women have become marginalised in politics as compared to the earlier decades. During the 1930s and 1940s there were more women leaders at all levels in the Congress party alone than are found today in all the parties put together.

This decline is especially worrisome because it is not in consonance with trends in other areas of life. During the same period, women have made their presence felt in every other field, including those considered male citadels. We have a rising percentage of women lawyers, doctors, architects, entrepreneurs, engineers, high-placed bureaucrats, diplomats, and so on, but the percentage of women in Parliament and state legislatures has remained extremely low. The highest ever representation of women in Parliament was 7.9 per cent in 1984. That this is not due to aversion of Indian women for politics becomes obvious when we consider the number of outstanding women activists that have emerged in the realm of transformative politics in recent years, while political parties are failing to attract and absorb the younger generation of women. Numerous young women have gravitated towards working in voluntary organisations, in NGOs in both rural and urban areas. Some are even leading radical movements, challenging established power structures, doing literacy and health work for disadvantaged communities, working in peasant movements, among the landless poor, among tribals. Yet very few of these women wish to or succeed in entering electoral politics.

Why has our democracy failed to include women in its purview even while the representation and involvement of various other disadvantaged groups, such as the Scheduled and Backward Castes, has grown substantially? Why was a whole generation of women leaders who were active at the forefront of our freedom struggle denied a substantial presence in Parliament and state assemblies, especially considering that the social opinion in India has been in favour of women's participation?

This, in part, seems to be due to the Gandhian legacy. While he wanted a vanguard role for women in the freedom movement, the Mahatma did not encourage women to compete for power but wanted them to enter public life as selfless, devoted social workers to undertake the crucial task of social reconstruction. He wanted women to cleanse politics, to feminise it by bringing in the spirit of selfless sacrifice rather than compete with men in power-grabbing and thus prove their moral superiority even in the realm of politics. In Gandhi's view, 'Woman is the embodiment of sacrifice and her advent to public life should, therefore, result in purifying it, in restraining unbridled ambition and accumulation of property'.[5] It was given to women 'to teach the art of peace to the warring world thirsting for that nectar'.[6] Just as he himself scrupulously kept away from occupying any position of power after Independence, he assumed women would prefer to serve society in a selfless spirit than go for power grabbing because that would be reversion to barbarity. He was confident he knew women's aspirations and temperament and so decided their role on their behalf. 'And you sisters, what would you do by going to Parliament? Do you aspire after collectorships, commissionerships or even the viceroyalty? I know that you would not care to, for the viceroy has got to order executions and hangings, a thing that you would heartily detest.'[7] It was not an accident that after Independence many women worked for organisations like Sewa Dal while withdrawing themselves from active involvement in the Congress party. However, even those who remained in the party (or in the women's front of the Congress) began to be systematically sidelined as the party was taken over by power-hungry politicians who actually behaved like gangsters.

How women get marginalised

The process of turning the Congress party into an instrument of authoritarian rule started during the heyday of the Nehru era. For all his democratic pretensions, Nehru did not let power devolve on the local institutions of governance. As a thoroughbred brown sahib, Nehru was afraid of the kind of ferment that Mahatma Gandhi had created among ordinary people of India, including those in remote villages. This had the potential to create an alternative form of people-centred politics. Nehru felt threatened that if such forces grew strong they would undermine the very authority and power of the state. Though he continued to use the rhetoric of social transformation, Nehru worked hard to ensure the continuity of the colonial state by keeping the colonial educational system intact as well as allowing the bureaucracy to maintain its stranglehold over society. The constructive programmes of the Congress party that evolved under Gandhi's leadership were transformed into the 'community development' programmes run and controlled by bureaucrats. This way the Nehru government severed the mass contact of Congress workers with their respective communities and thereby killed the Congress party. The marginalisation of women was part of this process of destruction of the Congress as a party of local leaders with grass-roots support and areas of influence. Instead it became a party of power-brokers within a colonial mode of governance.

In this scheme the sarkari panchayats had no real functions or powers. They were put under the supervision and control of bureaucrats who had the power to dismiss panchayats and sarpanches who did not fall in line with the vested interests of the bureaucracy. The panchayats had neither the authority to levy taxes nor to take decisions regarding village development programmes or appointing village functionaries. Hence they remained totally dependent on the goodwill of the sarkar. Panchayat office-bearers could survive only through servility and sycophancy. The sarkari 'gram sewak' often became the boss because he had direct links with officialdom. Thus government-controlled panchayats became an important instrument of manipulation of society rather than forums for local decision-making. The panchayats were used as tools for the party to mobilise votes for their candidates at election time and to thwart all local political initiative. Under this system the bureaucracy acquired even greater control than it had during colonial rule; elected representatives had to appear before it as grovelling supplicants. Only those survived who entered into a loot and plunder nexus with bureaucrats. Thus, the Nehru era set into motion widespread depoliticisation of our society by snatching away all power and initiative from local communities and providing bureaucrats and party politicians with several vicious levers of control and manipulation.

As Indira Gandhi and her sons came to power, the Congress party degenerated dramatically and saw a further decline in women's political participation. Even though women across the country related to Indira Gandhi as a symbol of inspiration and saw her as Durga incarnate, she did not care to channel that enthusiasm into facilitating the entry of more women into politics. She wrecked her own party's organisation by preventing party elections from taking place and introducing the practice of nominations by the 'High Command' to party posts as well as distribution of party tickets for elections. At the same time she systematically went about subverting fledgeling institutions of democracy at various levels. She obstructed panchayat and zilla parishad elections wherever the Congress was not sure of being able to maintain its stranglehold and subjected various states to president's rule whenever her control over regional politicians was challenged. She also introduced the unhealthy practice of the prime minister nominating chief ministers to Congress-ruled states so that she could use them as puppets rather than letting them be elected by regional legislators. Her authoritarian brand of politics led to an enormous concentration of unaccountable power at the centre, especially in her own office. The centre controlled (still does) the financial levers which made the chief ministers of even non-Congress ruled states dependent on the Delhi darbar's goodwill. With decision-making bodies getting more and more remote from people's lives due to over-centralisation of power, the few women who were active in the party were further marginalised. Getting a party ticket was no longer easy for credible, dedicated self-respecting women political workers in villages, districts, or cities. It became necessary to be close to power-brokers with influence in the Delhi darbar in order to qualify for any post in the party or an opportunity to enter electoral politics. Since these power-brokers came to be despised and mistrusted by all self respecting, decent politically active people, it is not surprising that most women turned away from politics. A woman would be seriously jeoparadising her reputation by being closely associated with the likes of Jagdish Tytler, H.K.L. Bhagat, Sajjan Kumar, Dumpy Ahmed, Satish Sharma and their various regional 'avatars' who grew all-important after the Nehru-Gandhi dynasty's advent to power.

Indira Gandhi also initiated a new era of corruption in contesting elections; exorbitant spending and violence soon become the norm. Before her regime, the party provided funds and other support to their candidates after selecting them on the strength of their work in the constituency. From the 1970s onward, candidates virtually began to buy party tickets by offering large sums of money to central leaders in charge of selection. Indira Gandhi went about destroying all party leaders who had an independent political base and instead went out of her way to patronise people who would be dependent and servile to her. This way, she appeared to be the charismatic leader who alone could bring victory to the Congress. She seemed particularly averse to sharing the limelight with other women politicians, especially those who had cultivated an independent political existence. Therefore, many women stalwarts like Tarkeshwari Sinha and Nandini Satpathi as well as women of Indira Gandhi's own family (barring the corrupt and sycophantish Sheila Kaul variety) were deliberately eclipsed during Indira Gandhi's regime. Thus India's celebrated woman prime minister played a leading role in pushing women out of the political arena by making the world of politics so unsavoury that few self-respecting women or even men would dare venture into it. Not surprisingly the few women who survived were either as tough and corrupt as the worst of the male politicians or were wives and other female relatives of powerful male politicians who provided the necessary protection. Hence the phenomenon of 'biwi-beti' brigades making their appearance during election time while during normal times the Congress party lost its claim to having the largest contingent of active women workers. Today the BJP attracts far more women workers than the Congress but the BJP and other parties also use their women's fronts as mere auxiliaries mobilised into action for demonstrations, mass protests and campaign work during elections.

When Rajiv Gandhi came to power in 1984, he tried to project a pro-woman image for his party. He fielded a slightly larger number of women candidates (40 out of 492). In the sympathy wave that followed Indira Gandhi's assassination, the Congress party won by a landslide benefiting even the newcomers among women and 37 of the 40 Congress(I) women candidates were elected to the eighth Lok Sabha. There were 44 women MPs during Rajiv's first tenure as prime minister, the highest ever in the Lok Sabha. Yet they constituted no more than 7.9 per cent of the total. However, barring a few exceptions, he attracted mostly glamorous socialite types of women into the party (counterpart to his Doon School brigade) because by then the Congress party had lost the ability to attract a new generation of dedicated women (or men) workers into the party.

The number of women MPs dropped slightly to 39 and 36 in the next two elections. As a counter measure 'The National Perspective Plan' (NPP) prepared during Rajiv Gandhi's prime ministership advocated 30 per cent reservation for women, but suggested that the reserved seats in all elected bodies—from gram panchayat to Parliament—be filled through co-option. This was firmly rejected by women's organisations since it was evident that the Congress wanted to use women's reservations to subvert the democratic process and co-opt its own members.

Even though I focus mostly on the Congress party's instrumental role in the decline in women's participation in politics the blame should be equally shouldered by other parties—whether of the Left or Right—because the Congress culture is emulated by virtually all of them. In fact, the track record of non-Congress parties is no better as far as women's participation is concerned. A majority of women contest from the Congress party even while the overall percentage of party tickets given to women remains shamefully low. In recent years, the BJP seems to be overtaking the Congress party in fielding relatively larger number of women and giving them a certain visibility. It is the only party with a woman (Sushma Swaraj) as its general secretary and chief spokesperson. The first Lok Sabha had 14 Congress women MPs out of a total of 23; in the second Lok Sabha it had 21 out of 27 women MPs, with CPI and Jan Sangh claiming two each. The third Lok Sabha had 28 Congress women MPs and four from the Swatantra Party. The ninth Lok Sabha had 19 Congress women MPs against four from BJP, six of the CPI and none from CPI(M) or JD. The 10th Lok Sabha again had 22 out of 37 women MPs from the Congress, 10 from the BJP, two from the JD, one each from the CPI, CPI(M) and SSP. The present Lok Sabha has 14 Congress women MPs, 12 from the BJP, three from JD, one from CPI, none from CPI(M) and two from SP.

It is ironic that the move to implement 33 per cent reservation for women in legislatures has been now initiated by the JD-led United Front government. The track record of the JD and various parties which constitute the UF is worse than that of the Congress in making space for women in politics. For instance, in the last election, only three women were elected to Parliament on the JD ticket.

The other influential ally in the UF government, the Samajwadi Party, does no better. For instance, of the 64 seats it contested from Uttar Pradesh, it gave tickets to only three women candidates in the 1996 Lok Sabha elections. Nor have the CPI and the CPI(M) thrown up more than one or two women parliamentarians in the last two to three decades. Despite N.T. Rama Rao's success in appealing to women voters, the Telugu Desam Party (TDP) has also promoted very few women politicians. The present state assembly in Andhra Pradesh has only nine women members out of 294. At the height of NTR's popularity with women, the figures were 12 for 1983-1985 and 10 for the 1985-90 Vidhan Sabha (that is, it hovered around three per cent). So with the parties like the DMK, AIADMK, Asom Gana Parishad and the Akalis in Punjab. Not surprisingly today the UF government has only one lacklustre, junior-level woman minister, Kanti Singh, in the cabinet. She is not even a Member of Parliament but was made minister of state only because she is backed by Laloo Prasad Yadav, the influential chief minister of Bihar. Even more significantly, none of these parties have allowed women to acquire influence in the party's decision-making processes and power centres. Would it not have been more logical for these leaders to have started correcting this exclusion of women at the party level first?

The JD for all its pro-women rhetoric does not have a single woman in its 15-member Political Affairs Committee, while its National Executive includes 11 women out of a total of 75. Similarly, no woman is included in the 17-member United Front Steering Committee. The Congress(I) Working Committee has two women and 18 men. The BJP has 10 women out of 147 total members in its National Executive Committee. CPI(M) has five women out of 72 in its Central Committee but not a single woman among the 15 men who make up the higher level Politburo. The nine-member CPI Secretariat does not include a single woman and its 31-member National Executive has only three women. There are only seven women in its 125-member National Council. Most important of all women are not an effective presence. Given that they only have token representation, they have hardly been able to influence party programmes or decisions.

All the parties of the UF claim to be vehicles of social equity. Yet these parties are unable to involve women in their crusades for social justice. This is not surprising because most of the backward castes and communities which constitute the political and social base of the JD and its allies have come to acquire a culture of crippling restrictions for women including the practices of purdah, seclusion and female infanticide. Women of backward castes are not allowed a presence in political spaces at the village level and their status is among the lowest in the country.

This gets reflected in the absence of women in various parties that draw sustenance from these castes; hardly any notable women political figures have emerged from among the various backward castes. In the JD, the few notable women leaders like Mrinal Gore and Pramila Dandavate come from the erstwhile Socialist Party and are from the Brahmin castes, which limits their mass appeal among the backward castes. Low female participation is even more true of Scheduled Castes and Scheduled Tribes parties. For example, the Jharkhand Mukti Morcha—a party of tribals from Chhotanagpur area—has not allowed even one woman leader of any note to emerge from its ranks since its inception. Many would cite Mayawati of the Bahujan Samaj Party (BSP) as an example of a successful female politician from the Scheduled Castes. But she is clearly an exception to the rule; there are no other noteworthy women in the BSP. In the 1996 Lok Sabha elections, the BSP with her at the helm of affairs in Uttar Pradesh did not field a single woman candidate from Uttar Pradesh, its stronghold area. Like Indira Gandhi, Mayawati seems rather averse to letting other women share the limelight with her. Even for herself, it was not her political genius but her personal proximity and equation with BSP supremo Kanshi Ram which seems to have played the most important role in catapulting her to power within her party.

Similarly, Baba Saheb Ambedkar's dalit-based party, the Republican Party of India (RPI) has not thrown up a single important woman leader in its entire history. One lone brahmin woman, Neelum Gohre, used to be a known figure in the party but left to join the Congress some years ago because she found the RPI inhospitable to her as a woman. Up until now, women politicians in India have emerged largely from among urban castes, especially among brahmins of all regions, khatris of Punjab, bhadraloks of Bengal, and kayasthas of North India because these castes had initiated powerful movements for internal social reform from the 19th century onward, especially with regard to women's rights and status within these communities. That is why these castes witnessed a substantial increase in women's education, employment and participation in literary, cultural and even political affairs.

Much of the energy of the 19th century upper caste social reform movements got channelled into and merged with the Congress party during the Independence struggle, especially after Mahatma Gandhi assumed leadership. Therefore, it is from among upper castes that most of our outstanding women politicians and public figures have emerged. Sarojini Naidu, Hansa Mehta, Sarladevi Chaudhrani, Sucheta Kriplani, Kamladevi Chattopadhyaya, Vijaylakshmi Pandit and Tarkeshwari Sinha—all came to exercise a great deal of influence in public life and symbolised the spirit of breaking through. However, no such comparable internal social reform focusing on the status of women in these communities has been undertaken among backward and dalit castes which have developed a tradition of excluding women from the decision-making processes within the community. Hence the absence of women from these groups in our social and political life. This is not due to any inherent lack in these communities but largely because their leaders have by and large tended to concentrate their efforts on the economic and political dimensions of upward mobility for these caste groups seeking social justice vis-à-vis upper castes but neglecting the gender dimension of social equity. In the few instances where attempts at social reform have been undertaken, the response has usually been enthusiastic even among men as the success of leaders like the late Shankar Guha Niyogi in Madhya Pradesh, Sharad Joshi in Maharashtra and Pandurang Shastri Athavle of Swadhyaya movement in Gujarat demonstrates. These castes and communities have responded with enthusiasm whenever serious and sensitive attempts have been made by their leaders to redress the power imbalance between men and women. I witnessed the most touching confirmation of this during my association with the Maharashtra-based farmers' movement, the Shetkari Sangathana.

The social base of the Sangathana is primarily among small and medium farmers belonging to varied backward castes. This organisation played a significant and leading role during the 1980s and early 1990s to bring about radical social reform including large-scale participation of women in the farmers' movement and to improve their status in family and society. As an offshoot of that effort, the Sangathana gave a call for electing all-women panels in village panchayats in 1989 followed by their putting up mainly women candidates in the zilla parishad elections. In a characteristically Gandhian way, the leadership projected this as part of their campaign to cleanse politics and reduce the role of goondas in villages. The most astounding and significant aspect of Shetkari Sangathana's experience was that there was great enthusiasm among most of the male cadres and supporters of the Sangathana for this unprecedented move. The male cadres of the Sangathana campaigned with even greater enthusiasm than the women to make a success of this effort even though, in effect, it meant men were being asked to hand over the positions of local power and influence to women. In a number of Sangathana stronghold villages, all-women panchayats were elected with much fanfare and celebration by men.[8] Even though in both the panchayat and zilla parishad elections, the Sangathana was unable to get many women elected because money and muscle power play a crucial role in determining the outcome of those elections (thanks to the Congress-Shiv Sena combine's goonda politics in Maharashtra), within their own organisation and following, the idea received graceful endorsement rather than provoke resentment.

However, such efforts have been confined to a few select groups and organisations outside the purview of mainstream backward and Scheduled Caste politics. To realistically prepare ground for women to emerge from among the backward castes, backward caste leaders and parties will have to initiate widespread social reform movements within their respective communities.

Starting from within

Parties who are sincerely interested in seeing women take an active part in politics ought to begin by activising their women's fronts at all levels, and by recruiting more women at the decision-making levels in their respective parties. So far they have shown no inclination or preparation to do so.

Similarly, women's organisations who have been the prime lobby for more seats for women in Parliament, legislative assemblies, etc., have to work to ensure that women join various political parties in large numbers and develop their own constituencies by building alliances with other sections of society rather than waiting for reservations to give them automatic entry. In recent years a number of women have emerged in the public arena at the state, district and national level through their work with NGOs. Many of them consider party politics as a contemptible game and therefore keep a deliberate distance from it but a large number have actively lobbied to get a reservation quota for women. However, there are only a handful among our NGO activists who have the capability to take on the challenge of electoral politics. The very nature of our NGO sector estranges it from electoral politics. Since most NGOs' survival depends on international aid agencies, most of them have no real roots in our society. They are more visible in the international conference network than in their own neighbourhoods, cities, or communities—all essential prerequisites for electoral politics. In addition, their dependence on the government bureaucracy rules out active involvement in electoral politics, especially if it goes against the ruling party. Many of those who have worked for years on women's issues, cannot claim to have succeeded in creating even a solid electoral constituency among women, not to mention larger segments of our population and could not win a corporation election, leave alone a parliamentary one.

It could well be due to lack of political experience in mainstream politics that women lobbyists from the NGO sector have opted for this rather mechanical and constricting approach to enhancing women's participation in legislatures. The proposed Reservation Bill has some serious flaws.

The reservations proposed are along the following lines:

(a) one-third of seats will be reserved for women in the Lok Sabha and state legislatures.
(b) These reservations are for an indefinite period, unlike reservations for SCs and STs which lapse unless extended after every 10 years.
(c) The reserved constituencies are to be determined through a draw of lots. For SCs and STs, constituencies are reserved on the basis of population proportion. Constituencies with a high SC/ST population are selected for a period of time and are supposed to be delimited after some years. But since the population of women is evenly spread throughout the country, this formula cannot be applied for them. The draw of lots system will mean every time a new set of constituencies will be declared as reserved for women.
(d) There is also a provision for parallel reservations for SCs and STs, which is to say women belonging to SCs and STs will be getting one-third of seats reserved for people of that category—i.e. reservations within reservations.

The magic number

There are several problems inherent in this particular scheme. To begin with, why a 33 per cent quota? What is the significance of this number? Why not 13 or 43 per cent or even 73 per cent? The reservation quota for all other groups such as the Scheduled Castes and Tribes has been determined on the basis of their numerical strength in the overall population. Not so for women. In India the proportion of women as compared to men is a little less than 50 per cent. So why not 49 per cent reservation for women? Does the magical figure of 33 per cent represent some near-future scenario of our declining sex ratio? Are our policy-makers anticipating the advent of all kinds of new technologies to bring down the already low sex ratio to one-third of the population?

This is not at all to suggest that 33 per cent is a small figure, especially when offered on a silver platter, as is happening in our case. Even in Sweden, a country considered the most advanced democracy with the highest percentage of women in positions of political power anywhere in the world, women occupied 40 per cent of elected parliamentary seats in 1994. This after nearly a century of effort and struggle. The figures for other 'leading' democracies are pretty dismal. According to a 1988 survey, in 1987 women occupied 6.3 per cent of seats in the UK, 5.3 per cent in the US, 6.4 per cent in France and 9.9 per cent in Canada. Since then there has only been a two per cent increase in women's representation. Only China shows a comparably high figure of 21.2 per cent for the same year, with India having 7.9 per cent. Thus by reserving one-third seats in legislatures, India will be sending 180 women to the Lok Sabha, thus ensuring a quantum leap.

However, accepting 33 per cent permanent reservation for women is like demanding that some seats be reserved in every bus for women or the equivalent of a 'zanana dabba' (ladies compartment) in every train. Men then come to expect women to remain confined to the ladies section and get very upset if women occupy seats not reserved for them. Delhi buses earmark roughly six to eight seats for women. If a woman goes and sits in an unreserved seat she is likely to be insolently told by some man or the other to get up and move to a ladies seat. In other words, they assume that all the rest of the seats in the bus are reserved for men.

The reservation of seats in state legislatures and Parliament will produce a similar situation. Even though there will be no bar on women standing from general constituencies, it is highly unlikely that women will be given tickets from outside the reserved constituencies. This has happened with SCs and STs who have been permanently ghettoised to reserved constituencies. At the panchayat and zilla parishad level, in most states women are not being allowed to contest from general constituencies which are assumed to be reserved for men. Only in Karnataka and West Bengal have women managed to go beyond 33 per cent. For our legislatures, it will be much harder for women to secure tickets beyond the stipulated quota because of the far more intense competition for these seats. Therefore, their representation is likely to be frozen permanently at 33 per cent unless the Constitution is amended again to enhance the quota or withdraw these reservations.

The present scheme of reservation will ensure that women will enter the electoral battle only against other women and never get an opportunity to contest against men, a sure way to perpetually ghettoise women's politics. As it is, women in India have deeply imbibed the notion that 'women are women's worst enemies' because of the way women are pitched against each other in the family structure. Their dependence on men estranges them from other women because men mediate women's relations with the outside world. Therefore, political solidarity among women is hard to build. If even in electoral politics women are constantly pitched only against other women, there will be far less possibility of their working together as a concerted lobby cutting across party lines, at least on some crucial women-related issues. It will strengthen the tendency to view other women as permanent rivals rather than possible allies.

The draw of lots system of gender-based reservations will mean that every time a new set of constituencies will be declared as reserved for women. There would be no way to predict whose turn will come next. In any functioning democracy, politicians are expected to develop and nurse a constituency. However, an unpredictable and rotating reservation policy has resulted in killing women's incentive to building their own constituencies even at the zilla parishad level, because they have no way of knowing which ones will be declared as reserved constituencies next. A similar set-up for legislatures will result in women candidates becoming even more dependent on their respective parties, rather than working among their own constituencies to help them win elections. Even after being elected by the support of a particular area, there will be no incentive to responsibly serve that constituency because if in the next draw of lots that constituency is de-reserved these women will have to shift elsewhere for the next election. This will lead to less responsible politics in general as also among women. For instance, a man may have worked hard in his constituency after being elected. But he will not be sure of being able to stand from the same if the draw of lots system is to decide that constituency is to be earmarked for women. This will inevitably produce a backlash from men and damage the legitimacy of women's participation in politics as is beginning to happen at the zilla parishad level.

The parallel reservation quota announced by the government whereby women belonging to SCs and STs will be getting one-third of the seats reserved for people of that category will mean that the women from the backward castes will not be covered by this. Within the backward caste-based parties, the few upper caste women that exist will be the automatic beneficiaries of reservation. But chances are that we will be saddled with more 'biwi-beti' brigades because OBC leaders are likely to resort to fielding their mothers or sisters or wives to ensure that the women's quota stays within their caste control and women legislators do not pose any challenge to their power. The current scheme of reservation makes this easy and may further encourage formation of caste-blocks in a party, making en bloc defections easier than today.

At the panchayat level, 'biwi' brigades can still serve the useful purpose of getting men used to including women in village debate and decision-making, even if the women are totally lacking in political experience and are used as puppets. The tasks expected of a panchayat or corporation member are relatively simple, often concerned with organising civic amenities in the locality with which most villagers have close familiarity. Therefore, someone who may initially enter village politics as someone's wife does not necessarily require much time to become a fully functioning panchayat leader, provided some of her family restrictions are removed. But the presence of such proxy figures in Parliament and state assemblies is not only counter-productive, but actually harmful. Political socialisation of such women legislators, required for being an effective member of state assemblies and Parliament, cannot take place smoothly when women members remain filially attached and politically dependent on the male party leaders. Reproduction of kinship-groups within existing caste-groups in the parties in Parliament and state legislatures is likely to further contribute to the breakdown of our party system and representative democracy.

There is nothing inherently wrong in women using family connections in politics to gain an advantage just as men do and as happens in other professions. In Chandrika Kumaratunge of Sri Lanka and Aung San Suu Kyi, we have two very outstanding examples of women who got a tremendous initial advantage due to their family name but then emerged out of their parental shadow and outshone their respective fathers in politics both in terms of vision as well as quality of political leadership. However, it could also be due to the fact that both of them had already lost their respective fathers before they plunged into politics. But most women do not manage to break the umbilical cord with the men of their family because their well-being in the family depends on the goodwill of men. Thus women who came on the strength of paternal connections tend to be used as proxies—a position which even the most untalented of men do not allow themselves to be forced among them.

Many argue that if such useless men, members of mafia and criminal groups, can be selected to represent us in Parliament and state assemblies, why do we put such high demand on women and expect them to mould themselves on the Aung San Suu Kyi model?

At the risk of sounding elitist, I would say it is time we began taking our legislatures seriously or they will never function effectively. Parliament ought to be a forum for the most seasoned, thoughtful and well-informed individuals among us. It is supposed to perform the awesome responsibility of legislating and policy-making at the macro level for nearly a billion people. It is no place for political novices to learn their first lessons in parliamentary democracy. Our Parliament and state assemblies are being treated like a chaotic bazaar contributing seriously to misgovernance. Most of those who get elected are simply ill-equipped for the required political task of forcing new equations among various perspectives and interests. Consequently our entire population becomes saddled with idiotic laws because many of our legislators don't have the elementary skills for hammering out sensible, implementable legislation.

Whenever serious laws are being debated and passed, both the treasury and opposition benches tend to get emptied out. Our legislators are more adept at coming to blows and staging walk-outs than actually debating issues of importance. We should try to bring about a qualitative change with women's participation in these fora, rather than bring them down further with women simply joining as puppets in this unholy enterprise.

Any polity in which violence and crime dominate, women as a group become automatically marginalised—partly out of choice but largely due to the fact that barring exceptions, women cannot effectively compete with men in gangsterism. Sooner or later they lose out and just as well. Where connections to powerful patriarchs is an important requirement for women in politics and where thugs dominate politics, only women like Benazir Bhutto, Indira Gandhi and Jayalalitha can survive to demonstrate that at least some women can be as ruthless, corrupt and vicious as the worst of male politicians.

Corrective measures

All this is not to deny that the peripheralisation of women in the politics of our country is a very bad sign. There is an urgent need for corrective measures to enhance women's participation in politics.

If we look around the world we find that women have found a respectable and enduring political foothold only in those societies which have genuinely functioning democracies. In such countries, political parties function with a measure of political and financial accountability. Society is organised around just and humane norms instead of valorising aggression. Of all the countries in the world, the Scandinavian countries seem to have evolved into well-functioning democracies. It is no coincidence that women have made enduring and substantial gains in these societies. In 1994, the proportion of women in the Swedish Parliament had already reached 40 per cent and is nearly half in the local institutions of governance such as the Country Councils. Swedish women constitute 43 per cent of all parliamentary committee members. In the more macho and violent US, women constitute a bare eight per cent of the US Senate, despite a vibrant women's movement in that country.

Given that the marginalisation of women is integrally linked to the marginalisation of all decent people from our party politics, we need broad-based electoral reforms to make our parties function in an accountable and transparent way. The proposed reservation might bring about a quantitative increase in women's representation, the quality of their participation will not improve if the over-all polity remains as filthy as it has become. For that we need wide-spectrum electoral reforms that will curb the role of muscle and money power in politics and democratise decision-making in the party by ensuring regular and fair elections at all levels, make it easy for people to fight elections without seeking patronage of political dons, and work out a sensible proportional representation system which facilitates representation of various marginalised groups without mechanical reservation quotas.

The following proposal put forward by Shetkari Sangathana of Maharashtra in its Aurangabad Conference of 1993 (after carrying out a review of the fall-out of one-third reservation quota at the panchayat and zilla parishad level) seems to be more promising than the mechanical rotating quota system being currently proposed.

The proposal involves the creation of multi-seat constituencies with one-third quota reserved for women. For instance, three constituencies could be clubbed together to make one—and each clubbed constituency can be represented by three people, one of whom must be a woman. This could be done either through a proportional representation system or even maintaining our current 'first-past-the-post system'. The first two seats would go to whichever candidates poll the highest number of votes—whether they are male or female. The third seat would go to the woman who polls the highest number of votes among the women candidates. This same principle could also be extended into a 50 per cent reservation for women in which each constituency is represented by one man and one woman.

There are several advantages of this system:

(a) Representation of women would not be frozen at a 33 per cent limit. Every constituency will be represented by at least one woman but it would not be limited to one if women candidates manage to win general seats as well.

(b) All the voters in every constituency would get a chance to vote for a woman candidate, if they so desire, as opposed to the presently proposed quota system in which voters of only one-third of all constituencies will get an opportunity to elect women candidates. There could also be a provision for cumulative voting so that if a voter chooses, she/he could give all three votes to one candidate

(c) The tendency to ignore one's constituency (due to the uncertainty that comes with rotating reserved constituencies) would be eliminated. Women would be able to opt for the constituency where they have built support, rather than be shunted around from one constituency to the other.

(d) Men would not feel forced out of their nursed constituencies, but simply be asked to share space with women. All candidates, regardless of sex, would have an opportunity to win the first two seats if they are able to garner enough votes.

(e) Women will not be fighting only against other women, but would compete with men as well. They would also get an opportunity to team up with two other colleagues to cover their joint constituency on behalf of their party, so they would not be confined to the zenana dabba.

(f) In multi-seat constituencies, voters will have the choice to elect leaders from more than one party. If the three winning candidates are from different parties, they are likely to act as a check on their colleagues and compete with each other in 'serving the constituency'.

It may well be argued that clubbing three constituencies together will make them unduly large and unwieldy. But then three people are required to campaign and serve it jointly. Perhaps it would help to promote a little more of team spirit in our politicians than currently exists.

If, in addition, we could put an end to the control over party tickets by the 'High Commands', we would have the possibility of better quality people emerging within party politics. To do this, we would have to ensure by law that inner party elections are held regularly in every party. Candidates for legislatures as well as at the panchayat and zilla parishad levels should be selected through primary elections at the appropriate levels by party members. If a party does not wish to field women candidates, it could choose to put up only two candidates. It would not have to draw a total blank in a constituency simply because it did not have eligible women or it did not want to put up women candidates.

These changes ought to be simultaneously accompanied by other electoral reforms which bring about financial transparency, effective and meaningful control over election expenditure, and well-defined rules that allow for public monitoring. However, the real cleansing of our politics will take place only when being in a position of power in the government (whether as a politician or a bureaucrat) does not provide a licence to loot people and the public exchequer as is presently the case. The licence-permit raj has to be thoroughly dismantled before democracy can work in this country and we can begin to live as free citizens.

Acknowledgements

I am grateful to my colleague D.L. Sheth for his useful comments and valuable suggestions on an earlier draft of this paper. My special thanks to Paige for her feedback and help in finalising this article.

Notes

1. *Report of the Committee for the Status of Women*, pp. 284–5.
2. Margaret Cousins, *Indian Womanhood Today*, Kitabistan Series, Allahabad, 1937, pp. 32–3.
3. *Harijan*, 24 February 1940, CW Vol LXXI, p. 208.
4. Jawahar Lal Nehru, *The Discovery of India*, p. 27.
5. *Young India*, 17 October 1929.
6. *Harijan*, 24 February 1940.
7. D.G. Tendulkar, *Mahatma*, Vol III, p. 61, Publications Division.
8. The functioning of each of these panchayats needs to be studied in detail to assess the differences, if any, they made in the political and social atmosphere of the village. I personally was able to look at just one of them in Vitner village, but for only a short period of time—nearly six to eight months after it was elected. The atmosphere in the village was one of euphoria and enthusiasm, especially among men. The Sangathana was unable to sustain this campaign as other priorities took over.

Published in *Economic and Political Weekly*, vol. 31, no. 43, 26 October 1996.

Women's Reservation and Democratisation: An Alternative Perspective

VASANTHI RAMAN

Indian society has been passing through a prolonged phase of social strife on account of ever new social communities and groups pressing their entitlements. Therefore, in a very substantial sense, the Women's Reservation Bill and the discussions around it mirror the current social turmoil in Indian society and the contestations for access to power and resources between the traditionally deprived and disadvantaged sections and those who have continued to be socially and economically dominant.

Women have for centuries been part of the traditionally deprived sections of society and attempts to open access to power and resources for them as part of a wider democratisation process are very much in order. However, having said this, it must be recognised that the task is difficult in view of age-old attitudes and structures which have been used to keep women in subjugation. Achieving any measure of success on this front calls for carefully negotiating the extremely complex, segmented and stratified hierarchical social order which has served as the source of denial to women of any kind of autonomy and power along with the other socially and economically deprived sections of Indian society.

At least two distinct and clearly articulated, though opposed, positions with regard to the Bill have emerged. The first position is that a blanket one-third reservation would assure representation to women in legislative bodies, particularly in the context of their progressively declining numbers in Parliament and state assemblies since Independence.

One assumption underlying this position is that women constitute a distinct social category and other discriminations which distinguish one group of women from another are hardly relevant for ensuring their empowerment so long as their overall representation is assured. As time passes, women belonging to deprived social communities and groups would see the social and political benefits of representation and would begin to make a bid for positions of power and authority. Whether this will indeed happen in view of the serious structural constraints within which the deprived and disadvantaged social communities, including the women within them, operate is something that this position does not address seriously.

The other position is one of opposition to the Bill in its present form on the ground that it is likely to exclude women from the OBCs [Other Backward Classes] and the minorities. Almost all the political parties except the CPI and the CPI(M) are deeply divided on this issue. The BJP leadership is in favour of the Bill in its present form, even though one of its women MPs had expressed reservations on the ground that OBC women were likely to get excluded. Needless to say, there is also a strong resistance on the part of a considerable number of political leaders to 'encroachments' into what has been a traditionally male preserve.

The protagonists of the Bill highlight the traditionally sanctioned exclusion of women from the public sphere as crucial. Emphasising the dimension of gender oppression at the expense of other oppressions (of caste, ethnicity, class, religion, etc.) glosses over the complex and intricate ways in which gender oppression is embedded in these categories. Historically, women's suppression has no doubt been very important in maintaining upper caste exclusivity and hegemony. Affirmative action for women would certainly play a role in undermining male and upper caste dominance. Even so, certain recent developments suggest the need for addressing gender oppression in more subtle and nuanced ways if access to power and resources to all categories of women is to be ensured.

One recent development relates to the increasing presence

and visibility of women, particularly in education and administration (and this in spite of the decreasing representation of women in Parliament). The stratum of women who have been the major beneficiaries of the development process have been women from the upper caste, middle classes. Even a cursory look at the educational institutions and government bureaucracy will confirm this.

This phenomenon has to be seen in the context of the overall performance and ensconcement of the upper caste, educated middle classes in the structures of government and administration. Conversely, women (and men) from the subaltern groups and classes have by and large been marginalised by the development process. That these groups are SCs, STs, OBCs and minority groups (particularly Muslim) needs to be emphasised. The liberalisation policies since the 1980s have only sharpened the polarising thrust of the development paradigm pursued so far with the cushion of the welfare state finally abandoned in the 1990s. The pursuit of the neo-liberal paradigm has heightened traditional social and economic differences of caste, class, religion and ethnicity, and women have only got more and not less embedded in their groups, leading to greater differentiation among them. This also accounts for the differential political articulation among women. The responses to the Mandal Commission recommendations and the Uniform Civil Code debate testify to this.

The Mandal issue in fact posed the question of democratisation of Indian society in a very sharp way. The response to Mandal, at one level hysterical opposition on the part of the upper castes (with women playing an active role) and at another level one of opportunistic support on the part of all political parties, is a significant pointer to the importance of the issue, particularly with regard to eroding upper caste hegemony over the administration. After all, it should not be overlooked that it is the OBCs and the Muslims (given their numerical strength and, more importantly, their social location) who can pose a real challenge to the hegemony of the upper castes and not the SCs and STs. That is why even the most reactionary proponents of upper caste dominance can be patronising with regard to the SCs and STs but become hysterical in their opposition to the demands of the OBCs and the minorities, particularly the Muslims.

The fact that the emancipatory slogans of the women's movement of the 1970s and the early 1980s have been hijacked by the Hindu Right to consolidate their hold over upper caste educated middle classes (with the latter actively participating in the conflagration of the 1990s), is evidence enough of the consolidation of the forces of the status quo. That there is some realisation of this is clear from the unease and even the retreat from an unequivocal support to the Uniform Civil Code on the part of many national level women's organisations. In fact, both the issue of women's reservation and the question of the Uniform Civil Code are good examples of how gender justice can be made a casualty precisely because it has been posed in terms whereby the specific social and historical roots of gender inequality both within and between communities have been ignored.

What is happening to Indian society is a criss-crossing of movements of various oppressed sections. Often these movements pull in different and even opposite directions, thus defeating the democratisation process in the short run. It is a challenging task both for the leaders of these movements and social analysts to unravel the myriad oppressions that characterise Indian society and to draw out the major strand which will strengthen and contribute to the overall process of democratisation of society. The levers of change have to be sought in an overall democratisation of society. In a plural society like ours, the political system has to ensure a modicum of equality between all the groups and communities if history's longest oppression is to be seriously tackled. This would imply that the struggle for gender justice and equality will have to be woven into the struggle for emancipation of each of the oppressed groups and communities.

The 81st Amendment Bill is a good example of how the aspirations of one group are pitted against those of another. The Bill in its present form will willy-nilly strengthen and shore up the interests of the dominant groups. On the other hand, women's representation from all sections will not only be more democratic, but will also contribute significantly to the democratisation process within communities.

Published in *Economic and Political Weekly*, Commentary, 11-17 December 1999.

Enhancing Women's Representation in Legislatures

JAYAPRAKASH NARAYAN, DHIRUBHAI SHETH,
YOGENDRA YADAV & MADHU KISHWAR
(Forum for Democratic Reforms)

The ugly scenes and stalemate over tabling the Women's Reservation Bill in Parliament have had a very beneficial effect. They have finally brought the grim truth into sharper focus that politics has proven to be very inhospitable for women in independent India. What we are witnessing today is a worrisome phenomenon of further decline in the participation of women, not only in our legislatures, but in many other of our political and public spaces.

Most countries in the world have failed to give due space and representation to women in their political life. Women are moving in the direction of near equal participation in only a handful of countries, such as Germany, Sweden, Norway, Denmark and Finland. In these societies women have begun to seriously alter the very nature of politics, making enduring, and substantial gains in every field. However, in all other countries, including the supposedly advanced democracies of western Europe and North America, where women exercise certain freedoms and have acquired the wherewithal for economic independence, female presence in legislatures remains small and relatively insignificant.

In India the problem for women is more serious for several reasons:

1. While in many other countries women are inching forward bit by bit, in India the participation of women in politics has actually declined since the days of the freedom movement, both in quantity and quality.
2. Government and politics are more important factors in the

economic, social, and power structures in India than in most other countries with stronger civil societies, and so, the effect of women's marginalisation in politics is even more detrimental here.
3. The increasing violence, sexual harassment and victimisation of women at the ground level in many of our political parties has made their participation extremely hazardous now.

There were many more outstanding women leaders and workers in the Congress Party at all levels during the freedom movement than are at present in all parties put together. In states like Maharashtra and Gujarat, virtually every neighbourhood and most villages could boast of at lease one effective woman leader, even into the 1950s. But as politics became more centralised as well as criminalised, thus undermining all other institutions of civil society, women were pushed out of leadership positions to function on the margins, at best relegated to the domain of social work at the local level. Even that tradition eroded from the 1970s onward.

The setback to women's participation is even more severe at the state level than in the Lok Sabha (See Tables 1 and 2). This is clearly evident in Bihar, which had 14 women elected to the Vidhan Sabha in 1952, 31 women in 1957, and 26 women in 1962. But in the 1967 elections, women won only 11 seats. Their number declined to four in 1969. Thereafter, it reached a plateau, leveling at a mere 13 during the last state assembly elections.

The representation of women in the Lok Sabha has basically remained stagnant. It reached a 'high' of eight per cent in 1984. This figure has not been crossed since then. Thereafter, it has showed some decline rather than register an increase. This despite the fact that every major national party in recent years has declared through their manifestos that they would implement a 33 per cent reservation for women in all legislatures.

One of the most puzzling features of this depressed level of women's political representation in our legislative bodies is that it seems to have no direct correlation with literacy and other seemingly related indicators. A comparison between the states of Kerala and Rajasthan, whose literacy rates are at opposite ends of the spectrum, demonstrates this clearly. In Kerala, the overall literacy rate is reportedly 90 per cent, with 86 per cent female literacy. By contrast, in Rajasthan, female literacy is a mere 20 per cent and only 12 per cent of females are literate in rural areas. Kerala has a matrilineal tradition in which women have a much larger measure of autonomy and freedom of movement. Kerala's women also tend to marry at a much later age compared to women in other states. Most women in Rajasthan live far more restricted lives in aggressively patriarchal communities that still practice purdah and perform child marriages. But the cultural and educational advantage that women in Kerala have, does not translate into higher political participation as compared to Rajasthan. The percentage of women in the legislative assemblies of both states is low. In Kerala it rose from less than one per cent in 1967 to six per cent in 1991. However, in Rajasthan, the representation of women was four per cent in 1967 and reached eight per cent in 1985-90, slightly more than in Kerala, but not significantly greater. Since then it has been going down.

Similarly, the state of Manipur, which has a tradition of women playing a dominant role in both the family and the community (again due to a matrilineal heritage), never produced a single woman legislator till 1990—when it elected its first. Nagaland and other North-eastern states which have less repressive cultures for women have similarly low levels of women's representation. By contrast, take the proportion of women in politics in UP, Bihar, and Madhya Pradesh. Though these states are known for their low education levels and repressive cultural norms for women, they have not only sent a relatively larger proportion of women to the Lok Sabha than those from the North-east, but have also elected relatively more female MLAs.

In independent India, pervasive gender discrimination has resulted in sidelining even veteran women politicians. It is difficult for women to establish a foothold without patronage from powerful men in the party—that too through close personal relations, as wives, daughters and sisters. This is indeed a matter for serious concern because the level of political participation among women in any society acts as a reliable barometer of the health of its democracy.

It is significant that stagnation and/or decline in women's political participation rates run contrary to trends in many other fields.

Women in India have made major inroads in various male-dominated professions, including the governmental bureaucracy. In the fields of business, medicine, engineering, law, art, and culture, women who were given opportunities to acquire the necessary skills and education have proven themselves capable of holding their own, without availing of any special measures to facilitate their entry. But they have failed to gain ground in the field of politics. Moreover, the agenda of women's empowerment seems to have lost the kind of moral and political legitimacy it enjoyed during the freedom movement, as was evident from the ugly scenes in the aftermath of tabling the Women's Reservation Bill in Parliament. Such a response would have been inconceivable in the India of the 1920s to the 1940s.

All those trends indicate that women's representation in politics requires special consideration, and cannot be left to the forces that presently dominate our parties and government. Today, even the best of our female parliamentarians feel sidelined and powerless within their respective parties. The few women in leadership positions have not been able to encourage the entry of greater numbers of women in electoral and party politics, and are an ineffective minority within their own respective political groupings.

The very same male party leaders who compete with each other in announcing their support of special reservations for women have shown little willingness to include women in party decision-making, or even to help create a conducive atmosphere for women's participation in their own organisations. In fact, women's marginalisation is even more pronounced in the day-to-day functioning of almost all political parties than in the Lok Sabha. Therefore, it is urgently required that we take special measures to enhance women's political participation in ways that help them influence decision-making at all levels of our society and polity. Our democracy will remain seriously flawed if it fails to yield adequate space to women.

Given this worrisome scenario, the national debate and efforts to provide constitutional and legal mechanisms to enhance women's participation in legislatures are welcome and long overdue.

Problems with the present Bill

The 85th Constitutional Amendment Bill, introduced in the Lok Sabha in December 1999, includes the following key provisions:

(i) One-third of all seats in Lok Sabha and Vidhan Sabhas shall be reserved for women.
(ii) Such reservation shall also apply in case of seats reserved for Scheduled Castes (SCs) and Scheduled Tribes (STs).
(iii) There shall be rotation of seats so reserved for women.
(iv) Such rotation shall be determined by draw of lots, in such a manner that a seat shall be reserved only once in a block of three general elections.

This Bill is seriously flawed, insofar as it mechanically provides for entry of women members to fill one-third of vacancies in the Lok Sabha and Vidhan Sabhas. Such mechanical reservation and rotation suffers from serious defects:

1. One-third seats are reserved, and such reserved seats are rotated in every general election. This rotation will automatically result in two-thirds of incumbent members being forcibly unseated in every general election; the remaining one-third will be left in limbo until the last moment, not knowing whether or not their constituency will form part of the one-third randomly reserved seats and thus require them to scramble at short notice to find another seat to contest.

2. There is already resentment about reserved seats for SCs and STs being frozen in the same constituencies over a long period of time. Inevitably, there will be vociferous and justified demands for rotation of seats reserved for Scheduled Castes, and in some cases Scheduled Tribes, where their population may not be very large. This will trigger off further instability in our polity.
3. The population of Scheduled Castes and Scheduled Tribes is now estimated to be around 16 per cent and eight per cent respectively, on an all-India basis. In certain states, their combined population is much higher, reaching 35 per cent or more. In the event of rotation of all reserved seats (women plus SCs, STs) with one-third seats reserved for women, every single seat will be rotated in every general election. This means that practically every member of a legislature will be unseated in every single general election (See Table 3).
4. Such compulsory unseating violates the very basic principles of democratic representation. It jeopardises the possibility of sensible planning to contest and nurture a political constituency for both male and female candidates.
5. As legislators do not have the incentive to seek re-election from the same constituency, plunder will increase, and politics will be even more predatory and unaccountable. This will contribute to a more unstable political process, and make it difficult for women to build their long-term credibility as effective representatives, since they will not be able to contest twice from the same constituency.
6. If seats are reserved exclusively for women in every election through territorial constituencies, voters in such reserved constituencies would have no choice but to elect women only, violating the basic principles of democratic representation.
7. In such a situation, there is likely to be greater resentment against women, undermining the very objective of the Bill. Those men who get pushed out of their constituencies or who see their allies sidelined will either sabotage female

contenders in revenge, or spend much of their political capital helping their own female relatives in cornering these reserved seats. Such proxies would be expected to keep the seat 'safe' for the men until the next election, when they would again try to reclaim their seats. Such women would lack legitimacy in the eyes of the voters.

8. Women elected in reserved constituencies will be contesting against other women only, and will lack the legitimacy and opportunity needed to prove their ability and acceptability. Leadership acquired in such a manner will be seen as unnatural, artificial and foisted.
9. Women legislators, when elected, will not be able to nurse their constituencies on a long-term basis, and thus will be deprived of a strong political base and will forever be regarded as lightweight politicians. This in effect will make their presence in legislatures ornamental, and will not lead to a more effective participation in politics.
10. This Bill does not address the more fundamental issue of inadequate participation of women in politics and their much greater marginalisation within the political parties.
11. The experience of fixed quotas in a few countries where it has been tried, such as Nepal, the Philippines, and the erstwhile Soviet Union, has not produced very successful results for women's political participation.
12. While this Bill provides for election of SC and ST women as legislators, it does not adequately address the issue of participation of backward castes (BCs) and minorities. As parties have no choice about the seats reserved for women, they will be unable to nominate women candidates from these under-represented sections in constituencies where they stand a reasonable chance of success.
13. Even though there will be no legal bar on women standing from general constituencies, it is highly unlikely that any women will obtain party tickets to run for office outside the reserved constituencies. This same pattern is evident with SCs and STs who have been permanently ghettoised to fixed reserved constituencies.

14. This Bill is completely silent about women's representation in the Rajya Sabha and Legislative Councils. Given these serious infirmities, it is necessary to design better models for enhancing women's representation in legislatures. Therefore, we present an alternate model which will address many of the flaws listed above.

The Proposed Alternative Women's Reservation Bill

The important provisions of the proposed Alternative Bill are as follows.

1. A law should be enacted amending the Representation of the People Act, 1950, to make it mandatory for every recognised political party to nominate women candidates for election in one-third of the constituencies.
2. Each party can choose where it wishes to nominate women candidates, duly taking local political and social factors into account.
3. Among seats reserved for SCs and STs also, one-third of the candidates nominated by recognised parties shall be women.
4. To prevent a party from nominating women candidates only in states or constituencies where the party's chances of winning election are weak, and to ensure an even spread of women candidates, the unit for consideration (the unit in which at least one out of three party candidates shall be a woman) for the Lok Sabha shall be a state or union territory; for the State Legislative Assembly, the unit shall be a cluster of three contiguous Lok Sabha constituencies.
5. In the event of any recognised party failing to nominate one-third women candidates, for the shortfall of every single woman candidate, two male candidates of the party shall lose the party symbol and affiliation and all the recognition-related advantages.
6. A law amending Articles 80 and 171 of the Constitution should be enacted providing for women's reservation of one-third of the seats, elected or nominated, to the Rajya

Sabha or Legislative Councils. Corresponding amendments need to be made in the Fourth Schedule of the Constitution and, the Representation of the People Act, 1950.

Advantages of this model

1. Parties will be free to choose their female candidates and constituencies depending on local political and social factors. Parties will nurture women candidates where they can offer a good fight rather than in pre-fixed lottery-based constituencies, where they may or may not have viable women candidates. Thus there is flexibility and promotion of natural leadership.
2. Though seats are not reserved, there will be a large pool of credible and serious women candidates in the fray. This is so because the real contest in elections is only among candidates nominated by recognised parties. Table 4 clearly shows that the role of Independents in our elections is marginal and declining. In Lok Sabha elections, as many as 99.7 per cent of Independents are in fact losing their caution deposits.
3. A woman candidate will be contesting both against female and/or male candidates of rival parties. Therefore, the democratic choice of voters is not restricted to compulsorily electing only women candidates.
4. As women members are elected in competition with other candidates—without reserving seats—they will be seen as legitimate representatives in the eyes of the public and not just beneficiaries of charitable measures.
5. A winning woman candidate will have been elected on her own strength, backed by party support. She will not be a mere proxy or political lightweight.
6. There will be no need for rotation of reservation. Therefore the elected women and men can nurture their constituencies and emerge as major political figures in their own right, with an independent power base.
7. At the same time, in the absence of reserved seats, there

will be healthy competition for nomination for a particular seat between male and female politicians.
8. Parties will be able to nominate women from BCs, minorities and other communities for elective office in areas where there is electoral advantage to them. This obviates the need for a quota within quotas—an issue which has blocked the existing Bill. Those who are concerned about BC representation need not settle merely for one-third quota for BC women within the 33 per cent women's quota as they are demanding now. They can field as many BC or minority women as they think appropriate.
9. This method is mostly likely to find favour with political parties and incumbent legislators, as there will be no fear of being uprooted at short notice by draw of lots. Both compulsory reservation and regular rotation are avoided.
10. Unlike with the lottery system of reserved constituencies, in which women's presence is likely to get ossified at 33 per cent since there would be resistance to letting women contest from non-reserved constituencies, this model allows for far greater flexibility in the number and proportion of women being elected to legislatures. If women are candidates for one-third of all seats contested by each party, theoretically they could even win the vast majority of seats—all on merit.
11. This model also provides for reservation of seats for women in the upper houses.

However, given the present state of affairs, it is likely that, to begin with, about one-third of the contested seats will be won by women. But this percentage is likely to grow over time as women gain more confidence and strength. It also ensures that their presence in legislatures more nearly reflects their actual electoral strength so that they are not seen as mere recipients of charitable measures.

Plugging possible loopholes

1. A party may be tempted to nominate women from constituencies where it is weak. However, by making the

unit of consideration the state or union territory for Lok Sabha, and a cluster of three Lok Sabha constituencies for the Legislative Assembly, this risk is avoided. Parties will be compelled to nominate women in all states and regions. No serious party seeking power can afford to deliberately undermine its own chances of election on such a large scale. It is also mandatory to nominate women in one-third constituencies because otherwise twice the number of male candidates of the party will lose party nomination.

2. In the absence of actual reservation of seats, there could be fears that women may not be elected in one-third constituencies, as the voters may prefer a male candidate over a female candidate on account of gender bias. However, evidence so far suggests that women candidates of parties have not suffered any gender discrimination at the hands of voters. In fact, very often, the percentage of success of women candidates is higher than that of male candidates. Table 5 shows that the success rate of women candidates in Lok Sabha elections has been uniformly higher than that of their male counterparts in every general election. It is possible to argue that a few women who contest are more often party candidates, and therefore, their success rate is exaggerated. However, Table 6 clearly shows that even among candidates of recognised political parties, the success rate of women candidates is higher than that of men. While 32.53 per cent of women candidates of recognised parties have been elected to the Lok Sabha since 1984, the success rate of male candidates is only 26.50 per cent. This trend is seen in all general elections since 1984, except in 1989. Therefore, it is reasonable to assume that women will be elected in large numbers, and that, in fact, their presence in the Lok Sabha will exceed one-third in many cases. In any case, past evidence suggests that in at least a quarter of the constituencies, women are likely to get elected if recognised parties nominate them in at least one-third constituencies.

It is noteworthy that women's participation has increased dramatically, to near equal or even higher than equal participation, only in countries like Sweden, Denmark, Finland, Germany and the Netherlands which have implemented party-based quotas of the kind we are proposing.

Other necessary measures for enhancing women's participation

While it is necessary to institute a system of reservation for women as spelt out above, this or any other system of ensuring women's presence in legislatures is not by itself sufficient if our objective is to make women equal partners in democratic politics. The problem is not just that women in the political arena are denied tickets by political parties. The fundamental problem is that given the nature of electoral politics today, the system itself creates insurmountable obstacles for women. Proposals for reservation for women must therefore be a part of a larger package of general reforms in electoral politics.

The following general measures of electoral reform would go a long way towards making politics less intimidating for women.

1. Measures to check criminalisation of politics

(a) The list of offences where a conviction leads to disqualification from contesting election should be expanded as per the recommendations of the Law Commission.

(b) Disqualification should not be conditional upon final conviction. It should come into operation as soon as the judge has framed charges with references to offences specified above.

(c) A candidate should be required to make a declaration of all the cases pending against him or her, involving charges of criminal conduct or corruption, at the time of filing nominations. This declaration should be made public. False declaration should be a ground for disqualification.

2. To bring about internal democracy within political parties

All the recognised (national or state) political parties should be required to include in their respective constitutions:

(a) Rules governing membership of the party and a Register of Current Members that is open for inspection by any member or the representatives of the Election Commission of India.

(b) Provisions for a periodic and democratic election of all the office bearers and the highest executive body by the members of the party.

(c) Procedures for selection of the party's candidates for elections to legislatures.

(d) Procedures for deciding upon various policy documents including the party's election manifesto.

(e) Internal mechanism for adjudicating any dispute, including those concerning the interpretation of the party constitution.

(f) The Election Commission shall review the party constitutions for their compliance with the above mentioned requirements, and also serve as a court of final appeal against any decision of the internal adjudicating authority in every party. The failure to comply with the Election Commission's instructions or decisions will invite de-recognition of the party.

3. Measures to curb the influence of black money in politics

(a) Every candidate shall make a declaration of his/her income and property at the time of nomination. False or incomplete declaration shall invite disqualification.

(b) All citizens and corporations shall be exempted, upto a certain limit, from paying income tax on donations made to registered political parties.

(c) The candidates and political parties shall be required, after the completion of election, to file a detailed statement of account. Non-disclosure or false declaration should result in disqualification for the candidate and de-registration for political parties.

(d) While the current ceiling on electoral expenses needs to be revised, certain items of expenditure (direct inducements in cash or kind to the voter, or expenditure to bribe officials or hire hoodlums) shall be considered illegal.

(e) Every candidate who secures two per cent or more of the valid votes polled in a constituency shall be reimbursed a reasonable sum of, say Rs 10 for each vote secured.

(f) It shall be compulsory for all registered political parties to get a statement of income and expenditure audited annually. The statement shall be a public document.

4. Measures to curb electoral malpractices

(a) The local post-office shall be in charge of maintaining and revising electoral rolls on a regular basis. At present most citizens have no access to electoral rolls, and the procedure for additions, deletions and corrections are ineffective in reality, though the law is eminently sensible. There is evidence to suggest that in urban areas the electoral rolls are flawed upto 40 per cent.

(b) It should be mandatory for the Election Commission to provide Identity Cards to every citizen who figures on the electoral rolls. Once this process is completed, the voter identity card or other means of identification should be made compulsory for voting.

(c) If the proportion of 'tendered' votes in a polling booth is greater than one per cent of the total electorate, a repoll shall be ordered in the booth. A tendered ballot is given to a voter in whose name a false vote was already cast, and who establishes identity. Therefore, a tendered vote is indisputable proof of personation and rigging. At present a tendered ballot is kept in a separate cover and is not counted, while the false vote cast is counted! If this repoll provision is incorporated and publicised, people will then avail the facility of tendered vote, and rigging will be self-limiting for fear of a repoll.

Provisions of the Alternative Bill
A Bill to amend the Representation of People's Act–1951
(New Section 34)

Notwithstanding anything contained in this Act, every recognised political party shall nominate women candidates on behalf of that party, as nearly as may be, in at least one-third of the constituencies in which the party is contesting, in every general election.

Provided that for an election to the Lok Sabha, the State shall be the unit for such nomination, and for an election to the Legislative Assembly, a cluster of three parliamentary constituencies shall be the unit as nearly as may be.

Provided that for Lok Sabha election, in case of States with less than three seats, a cluster of States to be defined by the Election Commission shall be treated as a unit.

(For removal of any doubt, these provisions will apply in all States and Union Territories for recognised national parties, and in the respective State or States for recognised state parties)

Provided that in respect of seats reserved for Scheduled Castes and Scheduled Tribes, the State shall be the unit for nomination of women for all general elections; and one-third of all candidates nominated for the reserved constituencies shall be women.

Provided that in case of by-elections, the party shall nominate as nearly as may be one-third women candidates for the Lok Sabha and Legislative Assembly, with the nation as unit for Lok Sabha and State as unit for Legislative Assembly. Provided further that, in respect of State parties, this provision will apply for State as unit for Lok Sabha.

In the event of a recognised political party not complying with these provisions, for the shortfall of every woman candidate while nominating candidates for elective office, two male candidates of the party in the State or cluster of parliament constituencies, as the case may be, as decided by the party shall be deemed to be Independent candidates for all purposes including allotment of symbols.

The Election Commission or the officials authorised by it at the State or Union Territory level shall determine the compliance or otherwise of these provisions after the completion of withdrawal of nominations.

Provided that the candidates so disqualified shall be from reserved vacancies in case the shortfall is in reserved vacancies.

Part B—Constitution Amendment Bill
(Amending Article 80 and 171)

In the Council of States, as nearly as maybe one-third of all seats, whether elected or nominated, shall be reserved for women.

In the States in which Legislative Councils exist, as nearly as maybe, one-third of all seats filled from each category, whether elected or nominated, shall be reserved for women;

Provided that in case of members elected by members of local authorities, graduates, and teachers, the seats reserved for women shall be rotated, and decided by draw of lots.

Table 1: Women's Representation in Parliament 1952–1998

Year	Lok Sabha			Rajya Sabha		
	Seats	Women MPs	% of Women MPs	Seats	Women MPs	% of Women MPs
1952	499	22	4.41	219	16	07.31
1957	500	27	5.40	237	18	07.59
1962	503	34	6.76	238	18	07.56
1967	523	31	5.93	240	20	08.33
1971	521	22	4.22	243	17	07.00
1977	544	19	3.49	244	25	10.25
1980	544	28	5.15	244	24	09.84
1984	544	44	8.09	244	28	11.48
1989	517	27	5.22	245	24	09.80
1991	544	39	7.17	245	38	15.51
1996	543	39	7.18	223	19	08.52
1998	543	43	7.92	245	15	06.12
Average	527	31	5.91	239	22	09.11

RESERVATIONS FOR WOMEN

Table 2: Declining Representation of Women in State Legislatures 1952–1997 (% of Women MLAs)

State	1952	1957	1960-65	1967-69	1970-75	1977-78	1979-83	1984-88	1989-92	1993-97	1998-99	State Avg.
Andhra Pradesh	2.9	3.7	3.3	3.8	9.1	3.4	4.1	3.4	3.7	2.7	9.5	4.6
Arunachal Pradesh						0.0	3.3	6.7	3.3	3.3	1.7	3.0
Assam	0.5	4.6	3.8	4.0	7.0	0.8	0.8	4.0	4.0	4.8		3.2
Bihar	3.6	9.4	7.9	2.2	3.8	4.0	3.7	4.6	2.8	3.4		4.3
Goa				6.7	3.3	3.3	0.0	0.0	5.0	10.0	5.0	4.4
Gujarat			8.4	4.8	3.2		2.7	8.8	2.2	1.1	2.2	4.0
Haryana				7.4*	6.2	4.4	7.8	5.6	6.7	4.4		6.2
Himachal Pradesh	0.0			0.0	5.9	1.5	4.4	4.4	5.9	4.4	8.8	4.2
Jammu & Kashmir			0.0	0.0	5.3	1.3	0.0	1.3		2.3		1.5
Karnataka	2.0	8.7	8.7	3.2	5.1	4.0	0.9	3.6	4.5	3.1	2.3	4.3
Kerala	0.0	4.8	3.9	0.8	1.5	0.7	3.2	5.7	5.7	9.3		3.6
Madhya Pradesh	2.1	10.8	4.9	3.4	5.4	3.1	5.6	9.7	3.4	3.8	8.1	5.4
Maharashtra	1.9	6.3	4.9	3.3	9.3	2.8	6.6	5.6	2.1	3.8	4.2	4.6
Manipur					0.0*		0.0	0.0	1.7	0.0		0.3
Meghalaya					1.7	1.7	0.0	3.3		1.7	5.0	2.2
Mizoram					0.0	3.3	3.3	2.5	0.0	0.0	0.0	1.2
Nagaland				0.0			0.0	1.7		0.0		0.5
Orissa	9.6	3.6	1.4	3.6	1.4*	4.8	3.4	6.1	4.8	5.4		4.0
Punjab	2.2	5.8	5.2	1.0*	5.8	2.6	5.1	3.4	5.1	6.0		4.0
Rajasthan	0.0	5.1	4.5	3.3	7.1	4.0	5.0	8.0	5.5	4.5	7.0	5.0
Sikkim							0.0	0.0	6.3	3.1	3.1	2.5
Tamil Nadu	0.3	5.9	3.9	1.7	2.1	0.9	2.1	3.4	9.0	3.8		3.6
Tripura				0.0	3.3	1.7	6.7	3.3		1.7		3.0
Uttar Pradesh	1.2	5.8	4.4	2.8*	5.9	2.6	5.6	7.3	3.3*	4.0*		4.1
West Bengal	0.8	3.6	4.8	2.9*	1.6*	1.4	2.4	4.4	7.1	6.8		3.4
Delhi	4.2				7.1	7.1	7.1			4.3	12.9	7.3
Pondicherry			6.7	3.3	0.0	0.0	3.3	3.3	1.7	3.3		2.6
Period Average	**1.8**	**6.3**	**4.9**	**2.9**	**4.4**	**2.8**	**3.8**	**5.3**	**4.5**	**4.0**	**6.0**	**4.1**

Table 3: Rotation of Seats

	Now (%)	From 2001 (%)
Reservation for SCs	15.0	16.0
Reservation for STs	07.5	08.0
	22.5	24.0
Balance Seats	77.5	76.0
Reservation for Women 33.30%	26.0	25.4
Open for Men	51.5	50.6

Table 4: Independents Elected to Lok Sabha in Successive General Elections

Year	No. of Seats Filled	No. of Independents Elected	% of Independents Who Lost Deposit
1952	489	38	66.6
1957	494	42	60.1
1962	494	20	79.0
1967	520	35	86.2
1971	518	14	94.0
1977	542	09	97.2
1980	529	09	98.9
1984	542	05	99.7
1989	529	12	98.9
1991	534	01	99.5
1996	542	09	99.7
1998	542	06	

RESERVATIONS FOR WOMEN

Table 5: The Gender Advantage
Though the number of women elected to Lok Sabha has not been very impressive, their success rate (% of contestants getting elected) has always been higher than the male aspirants

Year	No. of Seats Available	Total No. of Contestants	Male Contested	Male Elected	Male % Winning	Female Contested	Female Elected	Female % Winning
1952	489	1,874	-	-	-	-	-	-
1957	494	1,518	1,473	467	31.7	45	27	60.0
1962	494	1,985	1,915	459	24.0	70	35	50.0
1967	520	2,369	2,302	490	21.3	67	30	44.8
1971	520	2,784	2,698	499	18.5	86	21	24.4
1977	542	2,439	2,369	523	22.1	70	19	27.1
1980	542	4,620	4,478	514	11.5	142	28	19.7
1984	542	5,570	5,406	500	9.2	164	42	25.6
1989	529	6,160	5,962	502	8.5	198	27	13.6
1991	521	8,699	8,374	492	5.9	325	39	12.0
1996	543	13,952	13,353	504	3.8	599	39	6.7
1998	543	4,750	4,476	500	11.2	274	43	15.7
Total			52,806	5,450	10.32	2,040	350	17.16

- Gender-wise data for 1952 not available. *Source:* 14 September 1999, *Times of India*, New Delhi

Table 6: Performance of Candidates of Recognised Parties in Lok Sabha Elections—Gender-wise

Year	Total Party Candidates Contested	Elected	%age	Male Contested	Male Elected	Male % Winning	Female Contested	Female Elected	Female % Winning
1984	1,394	510	36.59	1,327	469	35.34	67	41	61.19
1989	1,523	498	32.70	1,437	474	32.99	86	24	27.91
1991	2,319	516	22.25	2,180	479	21.97	139	37	26.62
1996	2,269	530	23.36	2,153	493	22.90	116	37	31.90
1998	1,964	488	24.85	1,831	451	24.63	133	37	27.82
Total	9,469	2,542	26.85	8,928	2,366	25.50	541	176	32.53

Source: Compiled by *Lok Satta* from Statistical Reports on General Election, Election Commission of India, New Delhi

Issued as 'Enhancing Women's Representation in Legislatures: An Alternative to the Government Bill for Women's Reservation', by Forum for Democratic Reforms, http://www.freespeech.org/manushi/116/alterbill.html, 26 July 2004.

Women and PR

GAIL OMVEDT

PR, acronym for proportional representation, is new to the majority of Indian feminists—but one that deserves thinking about, now that another session of the Lok Sabha has ended without any significant change on the issue of quota for women. As an editorial in a Women's Studies network bulletin put out by the Tata Institute of Social Studies in Mumbai recently said, 'The stalling of the Bill will not be able to reverse the process of women's heightened awareness ... and their mobilisation ... The time before the legislation is finalised is, therefore, precious time for reflection and deliberation.'

It appears there have been some healthy aspects to the last 'round' on the Women's Bill issue. Some aspects were depressingly familiar. Once again, in spite of assurances from government spokesmen, no action was taken. Once again angry women party leaders raised an uproar; Opposition leaders such as Ms Sonia Gandhi accused the Government of 'dragging its feet' and vowed their support for the cause. Once again there seems to be a stalemate, with the only declared opponents (under the leadership of the Yadavs of Uttar Pradesh and Bihar) saying they would not allow the Bill in its present form, while few of the established women leaders of the Congress or the Left appear ready to rethink their refusal to consider any alternative to what is, after all, a very badly written Bill.

Nevertheless, some new things have emerged. First, the stark antagonism between OBC and feminist leaders, which surfaced during earlier discussions with each speaking of the other in terms of near-slander, is to some extent easing. Numerous women's groups are admitting the legitimacy of OBC concerns, some supporting the idea of 'quotas within quotas'; this recognition, in turn, is linked to an increasing awareness that patriarchy is differentially felt over caste, class, gender and national identities. This means the issue of representation for women is not so simple, that in India in particular it is linked to caste and must inevitably be considered in this context. Hopefully this trend will ease one of the more disturbing aspects of the whole debate on the Women's Bill, the way it seemed to set (mainly upper caste) feminists against (mainly male) OBC leaders.

The second encouraging aspect of the recent round of discussions on reservation for women is that, for the first time, some serious alternatives are being publicly discussed. One of these is the alternative, proposed by the Samajwadi Party leader, Mr Mulayam Singh Yadav in 1998, developed as a campaign by the Manushi group through the Forum for Democratic Reforms and endorsed by the Election Commissioner and many eminent citizens including an MP and Minister, Ms Maneka Gandhi. (Mr Yadav might very well have endorsed it had he not felt alienated by the approach of the 'alternative' group which also tended to demonise his opposition to the original Bill). This alternative Bill would require that parties reserve a proportion of their seats for women and is a major advance on the original proposal.

It is hard to understand the bitter opposition to this (or any other) alternative presented by the proponents of the rotation-linked official Women's Bill: about the only argument put forward by these is that requiring the parties to field women candidates 'would not guarantee' an exact 33 per cent representation. That is true—there may be fewer, there are likely to be more. But since when has 33 per cent been a sacred number? The question is a move towards real empowerment—and in a way that brings about the total welfare of society. Neither Ms Madhu Kishwar nor the articulate feminists of the Left parties nor myself have ever wanted women's interests served at the cost of men's interests or in a spirit opposed to democratic social transformation—however different our ideas on that transformation, we agree on this much. Then why can't the women party leaders think about the system of electoral politics they are clinging to so stubbornly?

(Since Ms Madhu Kishwar has challenged my crediting Mr Yadav with first proposing this alternative, I would simply refer to a report by Mr K. Balakrishnan and Mr G.V.K. Narsimha Rao in *The Times of India* of 19 July 1998. They note: 'Affirmative action in favour of increased representation of women (in Europe and elsewhere) has been in the form not of reservation of parliamentary seats ... but of requiring political parties to ensure a minimum level of representation (say one-third) among their electoral lists. Mulayam Singh Yadav had proposed this as a more logical and practical option than reserving parliamentary seats by rotation; but it was not considered seriously or discussed').

Another alternative within the framework of the present system is also being put forward. It has been most recently argued by Mr Sharad Joshi, whom Ms Madhu Kishwar credits (and I would agree) with the major initiative to forward the political participation of women at the grass-roots. Mr Joshi argues for multi-seat constituencies which would require that one MP elected out of three be a woman. This has promise (why not double-seat constituencies, many would immediately ask, which would give women 50 per cent?). It also moves in the direction of a proportional representation system, precisely because it requires multi-seat constituencies.

And that is perhaps the final alternative we have heard about, much more far-reaching than any other proposal because it means a change of the basic electoral system within which quotas are to be instituted. Various forms of PR are currently in existence in the democratic countries, barring the Anglo-Saxon ones. In particular they exist in European countries which have the highest representation for women in national legislatures—almost entirely without any legal quota either in the form of reserved seats or quotas for party tickets. A 25-40 per cent representation of women in Parliament is not 'parity', but it is clear that PR makes a difference.

The PR systems can exist either with or without quotas. Mr

Satinath Choudhary proposes PR with quotas. I would support continuing the quotas for SCs and STs within a PR system, but it is fairly clear that Muslims and the OBCs would not need any quota, and I don't think women would either. Let us give PR a try for 10 years without special quotas for women and after that if there is no dramatic improvement in their representation, we can talk about quotas for them.

Women are starting to make an impact in politics. They are not always women whose politics we agree with. They are women as diverse in style and political ideology as Ms Mayawati, Ms Mamata Banerjee, Ms Sushma Swaraj and Ms Uma Bharati. But they are women who are gaining power on their own though, of course, with male support and in this sense they represent what we would like to see as the main future trend.

A major Constitutional Amendment would certainly take more time to consider than any of the current proposals. PR is very little understood in India—it was not understood at the time of the original Constitution debates, when only minority members spoke for it and seemed to understand it solely in terms of the forms of PR existing in Britain. And it is hardly understood now. The debate will take time. But it is worth taking some time to do things right, to move towards genuine empowerment of minorities and a stable and healthy parliamentary system. Women should lead the debate in India on moving towards a system of proportional representation, just as they seem to be doing in the US and elsewhere.

Published in *The Hindu*, 12 September 2000.

Dual-Member Constituencies: Resolving Deadlock on Women's Reservation

MEDHA NANIVADEKAR

On 15 July 2003 the proposal for converting 181 Lok Sabha (lower house of Parliament of India) constituencies into double-member constituencies to elect one woman and one man and thus increasing the number of parliament seats by 181 appeared somewhat acceptable at the four-party meeting[1] convened by the Lok Sabha Speaker Manohar Joshi. After this the Speaker reportedly asked the government to draft a fresh Women's Reservation Bill.[2] Afterwards, on 19 July 2003 at the national executive meet at Raipur the BJP passed a resolution on the issue and called upon the government to bring a Constitutional Amendment to convert one-third of the Lok Sabha constituencies into dual-member constituencies.[3] As part of the new formula, two Members of Parliament a male and a female will be elected in 181 parliamentary constituencies out of the total 543. However, at the moment, the Congress(I) and the Left parties appear unwilling to support the dual-member constituencies on the grounds that it would dilute the cause.

This proposal is an improvement over the controversial Women's Reservation Bill insofar as the rectification of the serious drawback seen in the provision of reservation by rotation is concerned. Highlights of the Women's Reservation Bill pending in the Lok Sabha are:

(1) As nearly as may be one-third of all seats in the Lok Sabha and state legislative assemblies shall be reserved for women.
(2) Reservation shall apply in case of seats reserved for

Scheduled Castes (SCs) and Scheduled Tribes (STs) as well.
(3) Seats to be reserved in rotation will be determined by draw of lots in such a way that a seat shall be reserved only once in three consecutive general elections.

This Bill is seriously flawed, insofar as the rotational reservation of one-third seats is concerned. Rotation may not be as harmful at the local level as it would be at the state and national level. The pre-election nursing of a Lok Sabha or assembly constituency is a very demanding task that involves a very heavy investment on the part of the political parties and more so on the part of individual aspirants. Rotational reservation of one-third seats exclusively for women would lead to a grave uncertainty for sitting women and men MPs and other aspiring candidates alike, eroding their meticulously developed political base and leaving them no scope to pursue politics as a life-long mission or career. This is harmful for the political career of an individual politician as well as for the process of the development of national level leaders with towering personalities. This would dwarf the popularly elected political leadership and strengthen the bureaucracy. It would also generate a political culture conducive for making short-term gains and also making people's representatives totally unaccountable to the electorate and to their own party. Moreover, this draft also ignores an important recommendation of the Joint Parliamentary Committee on the 81st Amendment Bill about extending reservation to the Rajya Sabha and legislative councils that was incorporated in Clause 21 of its report.[4] When some women's organisations and political parties treat the Women's Reservation Bill as sacrosanct and insist on passing it in the present form they overlook these major drawbacks of that Bill.

The most noticeable intervention in the reservation discourse has come from Madhu Kishwar by her persevering campaign through *Manushi* and advocacy through a signature campaign over this issue. Her Alternate Bill advocated by the Forum for Democratic Reforms[5] got the status of a Private Member's Bill promoted by Krishna Bose, Trinamul Congress member of the Lok Sabha and came into the limelight with the even more high-profile support from the Chief Election Commissioner himself. The distinctive provisions of the Alternate Bill (*Manushi* no. 116) are:

(1) Instead of reserving constituencies exclusively for women, Representation of the People Act 1951 should be amended to make it mandatory for every recognised political party to nominate women candidates for election in one-third of the constituencies.
(2) For the shortfall of every single woman candidate, two male candidates of the party shall lose the party symbol and affiliation and all the recognition-related advantages.

The second point that provides for a penalty cause is the most problematic provision in the Alternate Bill. Almost all party organisations in India are highly oligarchic in nature. The candidates seldom exercise any control over the parliamentary boards that decide upon the nomination of candidates in any election. This particular suggestion, if implemented, would penalise the male candidates for the lapse on the part of the party oligarchy. Moreover, the lack of clarity in determining as to which two male candidates should lose party affiliation, may further lead to more manipulative and exploitative practices. The candidates losing party affiliation would most certainly be the marginal ones who do not have any say in the matter. Furthermore, this proposal ignores the fact that mere candidature does not automatically amount to representation.

Madhu Kishwar also recommends the list system as it prevails in many countries. However, the Indian political parties are not the best examples of intra-party democracy. Party organisations are highly centralised and at times even authoritarian. The perennial tension between the legislative wing and the organisational wing is manifested in their struggle towards overpowering each other. In India, the only party organisations with true internal democracy were the old socialist parties of various hues, which, through their frequent fragmentations, only conveyed an unfortunate message that party organisations with internal democracy are self-destructive.

We have many examples of independent candidates getting elected as members of legislative assemblies and an exceptional few as MPs. Though the independents are often blamed for eroding the ethical base of elected representatives by shifting their loyalties, they also have the potential for defying party oligarchy and preserving plurality. The Alternate Bill provides a model that would strengthen the Goliath of party oligarchy at the cost of an individual party activist. This would leave no scope for plurality or even the potential for protesting against injustice inflicted by the party oligarchy, rendering an individual activist totally powerless.

Two other proposals were by Rami Chhabra (2000) and Mukesh Dalal (2000). Rami Chhabra tried to link women's reservation with the issue of delimitation of constituencies and suggested the conversion of all constituencies into dual-member constituencies, thus facilitating greater representation of people without disrupting the present balance among different states.

All these proposals are silent over the controversial OBC reservation. Parliament secretariat should release authentic statistics about current OBC representation in the Lok Sabha. This may reveal that the OBCs although socially and educationally backward, do enjoy considerable political clout and help settle the OBC issue once and for all.

The latest proposal is the July 2003 proposal for 181 dual-member constituencies that has just made its entry into the discourse. It is yet not so well known and therefore is not widely debated. But it deserves serious consideration and threadbare discussion. Just like any other proposal, even the proposal for 181 dual-member constituencies is not a perfect solution. But we need not insist on a perfect solution as long as the one available is sufficiently satisfactory. We have been coping with so many imperfect systems and processes for all these years, be it our method of election based on the principle of 'first past the post' that elects or defeats the candidate with the margin of just one vote over her/his nearest rival, our undemocratic party structures, criminalisation of politics, fragmented polity leading to unstable governments—all these issues easily qualify as red hot targets for perfectionism. If we really want perfection, let us not begin and end our perfectionism with the issue of women's reservation alone.

But the new proposal though workable, should not be implemented before overcoming these serious drawbacks:

- Although it provides for women's reservation in one-third constituencies, in real terms, it brings down the quota to 25 per cent (181 out of 724) as against the original commitment to 33 per cent that constitutes the 'critical mass', as Drude Dahlerup (1986: 275–98) calls it, necessary for making a dent on the system. This would be a setback to the seven years struggle and would also demoralise the champions of the 33 per cent quota.
- If parties nominate a man and a woman even from the constituencies of the sitting women MPs, it would amount to a reservation for men in a hitherto woman-held constituency. It would shatter the political base of the sitting woman MP at its very root, owing to her systemically disadvantageous position as against the highly privileged position of a male MP that gets accentuated even further by his membership of Parliament. This will make competition very uneven and would turn the scales in his favour at the subsequent election. This serious drawback undermines the whole process of women's empowerment by scuttling it at its very base.

I propose the following six changes to offset these drawbacks and to reach a win-win situation:

(1) The reduction from 33 per cent to 25 per cent can be compensated by way of women's reservation in the Rajya Sabha and legislative councils, as was proposed in Clause 21 of the Report of the Joint Parliamentary Committee on the 81st Constitution Amendment Bill in December 1996.[6] This new proposal is completely silent about women's representation in the Rajya Sabha and legislative councils. The memorandum submitted by Rambhau Mhalgi Prabodhini[7] to the Joint Committee on the 81st Constitution Amendment Bill had suggested that the reservation of seats for women be extended to the Rajya

Sabha and legislative assemblies as well (Nanivadekar 1997). This suggestion was accepted by the Committee and was included in its Report as Clause 21, but did not get incorporated in the 84th Amendment Bill and its subsequent versions. Sushma Swaraj, an esteemed member of the Joint Committee, had said that the Committee agreed with this in principle but needs suggestions about the modality for implementing this.[8] I propose a method (Table 1) for implementation of reservation in the Rajya Sabha and the legislative councils.[9]

Table 1: Proposed Modality for Implementing Women's Reservation in Rajya Sabha

	State Quota	Women's Quota	State Quota	Women's Quota	State Quota	Women's Quota	State Quota	Women's Quota
Total	18	6	14	5	13	4	1	1/3
After 2 years	6	2	5	2	5	2	-	Two terms open
After 4 years	6	2	5	2	4	1	-	Third reserved women
After 6 years	6	2	4	1	4	1	1	

Notes: A similar modality can be worked out for the legislative councils.
(1) Different ballot papers for women reserved seats.
(2) Method of proportional representation by single transferable vote to be retained

Each state elects one-third of its Rajya Sabha quota after every two years. In case of large states even the third is more than three so one seat can be reserved for women and the remaining two may remain open and separate ballot papers can be used for electing candidates to these seats based on proportional representation by single transferable vote. If this number is less than three then women's quota can be worked out as displayed in Table 1. In the first two biennial elections out of two seats one will be reserved for women and the other would remain open and in the third election both seats would remain open. Thus in a block of six years two seats would remain reserved for women. A similar model can be developed for the legislative councils that provide functional representation for groups as varied as teachers, graduates, local self-government institutions and the like. Reservation should apply to nominated MPs as well.

(2) The risk of shattering the base of sitting women MPs can be covered by treating their constituencies as dual women-member constituencies. The constituencies of sitting women members out of the first lot of 181 constituencies marked as dual-member constituencies should elect both women members to the Parliament. If these constituencies are treated as all-women constituencies, it will open up several possibilities like senior women politicians mentoring other women activists, teamwork among women or healthy competition among the equals. At the next election all constituencies from the first lot would become single-member constituencies and the women MPs would compete with each other as well as with new aspirant male candidates in the subsequent election. In the block of 181 dual-member constituencies dual-woman-membership would also be extended to the SC/ST constituencies with sitting women MPs. From these constituencies one woman from SC/ST category will be nominated and the other seat will be treated as reserved for women in general (Table 2).

(3) In the constituencies reserved for SC/ST from the block of 181 dual-member constituencies of former male MPs, one woman from SC/ST category be nominated while the other seat would be treated open for all men and women including SC/ST. Suggestions about lifting the 50-year old permanent reservation in case of SC/ST constituencies and introducing rotation instead are being made frequently (Kumar 2003). This would partly offer a solution to the issue of the permanent reservation in these constituencies that has sealed the fate of open category aspirants for over 50 years and which, in all probability, may continue forever. There is no threat of eroding the political base of SC/ST as the constituency would continue to remain reserved for SC/ST alone even after the expiry of that term. Presently there are 120 Lok Sabha constituencies

reserved for SC/ST, which can be evenly divided into three proposed lots (Table 2).
(4) Reservations need not be an eternal phenomenon. We can have 15 years time limit for the provision of the dual-member constituencies.
(5) Women's reservation in political party organisations, from the grass-roots level enrolment of party members, right up to the national executives and parliamentary boards would increase the pool of eligible women candidates, reduce the element of proxies and would eventually lead to a much higher representation of women even from open constituencies. Women's quota within the party structure should be implemented simultaneously with the reservation in dual-member constituencies, but should continue forever. There need not be any time limit for party quota. This would ensure a sustained pool of promising women candidates and also leave scope for open competition in constituencies. The Scandinavian countries have succeeded in increasing women's participation by providing electoral party quotas. We can experiment with the organisational quotas to increase the efficacy of representatives from reserved constituencies. Surprisingly, the CPI(M) leader Somnath Chatterjee had summarily rejected the idea of reservation[10] within the party organisation on the ground that oganisational posts should be filled on the basis of merit alone. This is a strange discrepancy in the official CPI(M) position that supports reservation in the Lok Sabha and legislative assemblies but curtly rejects it when it comes to reservation in the party organisation. Madhu Kishwar (1996) had rightly pointed out this tendency on the part of the political parties way back in 1996.
(6) Women's reservation should be extended to parliamentary committees as well for ensuring ample opportunity to women MPs for acquiring first-hand experience of all the intricacies of legislative affairs.

The composition of Lok Sabha committees reveals certain facts that may well be an eye-opener. Though there are 48 women

Table 2: Scenario in the First Election

Type of Constituency	Lot A-181 Dual-Member	Lot B-181 Single-Member	Lot C-181 Single-Member	Total
Sitting women MPs' constituencies	To be converted into dual-women-member constituencies	Open constituencies	Open constituencies	
SC/ST constituencies with sitting male MP	One seat reserved for SC/ST woman and other seat open for men/women including SC/ST men/women	Reserved for SC/ST men and women	Reserved for SC/ST men and women	
SC/ST constituencies with sitting woman MP	One seat reserved for SC/ST woman and other seat reserved for all women including SC/ST women	Reserved for SC/ST men and women	Reserved for SC/ST men and women	
Remaining constituencies	One man and one woman MP	Open constituencies	Open constituencies	
Total	362	181	181	724

Note: At present there are 48 sitting women MPs in Lok Sabha. If approximately 16 fall in the first lot, it would mean 181 + 16 = 197 seats to be reserved for women, that comes to nearly 27.20 per cent.

members in the Lok Sabha, they are severely under-represented in these committees. There are as many as eight all-male committees of the Lok Sabha. The history of the Estimates Committees dates back to pre-Independence days. From 1921 to 2002, as many as 86 persons have got the opportunity to chair this Committee, of which, there is not even a single woman. The Committee on Public Undertakings had so far had only one woman as the chairperson out of the total 20.

Women are over-represented on the Joint Parliamentary Committee on Women's Empowerment. The next highest representation of women, five out of 11, is on the committee dealing with as mundane a matter as the provision of computers for members. The need for such reservation becomes evident from the statistics pertaining to women's representation on these committees displayed in Tables 3a and 3b.

Table 3a: Women's Representation in Committees of Lok Sabha

Sr No	Committee	Lok Sabha Male	Lok Sabha Female
1	Committee on absence of members from the sittings of the House	13	2
2	Business Advisory Committee	14	1
3	Committee on Estimates	29	1
4	Fellowship Committee	5	0
5	General Purposes Committee	34	4
6	Committee on Government Assurances	13	2
7	House Committee	12	1
8	Committee on Members of Parliament Local Area Development Scheme (MPLADS)	25	0
9	Committee on Petitions	15	0
10	Committee on Private Members' Bill's and Resolutions	15	0
11	Committee on Provision of Computers for Members of Parliament, Offices of Political Parties and Officers of LSS	11	5
12	Rules Committee	15	0
13	Committee on Subordinate Legislation	16	0
14	Committee of Privileges	15	0
15	Committee on Papers Laid on the Table	15	0
	Total no. of members	247	16

Table 3b: Joint Committee on Empowerment of Women

Sr No	Committee	Lok Sabha Male	Lok Sabha Female	Rajya Sabha Male	Rajya Sabha Female
1	Committee on Empowerment of Women	7	13	0	10

Source: Compiled by Medha Nanivadekar from the lists of Lok Sabha Committees available on the official website of Parliament of India on 31 July 2003. Department related Committees and other JPCs not included.

The Parliamentary Committee on Women's Empowerment needs to be reconstituted in such a way that one-third of the seats would be reserved for men and two-thirds for women. This is very essential in order to forge a healthy partnership of men and women in gender mainstreaming. The present composition of the Joint Committee on Women's Empowerment shows that all 10 members from Rajya Sabha are women. Though higher representation of women is welcome, it should not send a wrong signal that men don't like to be on 'unimportant' committees like Committee on Women's Empowerment or that 'women's issues are the concern of women alone'. In collaboration with experts and activists in the field, this Committee should work out the implications of various governmental policies for women.

Chhaya Datar (1993: 40-1) had observed that there had been a bewildered response from political parties and women's organisations to the proposition of reservation of 33 per cent seats in local bodies for women. She had also warned then about not exaggerating the effect of this measure and had anticipated the possibility that these women would remain subject to patriarchal control and would be susceptible to manipulation by their male relatives. She also expresses concern over the way in which this change was brought about from above with a top-down approach. It would have had an altogether different ethos had it been the product of the movement itself. This is evident from the fact that even after 10 years of the implementation of the 73rd and 74th Amendments and an entry of over one million women into elective offices we have not yet succeeded in integrating gender perspective in the structures, processes and the agenda of rural and urban local self-government institutions.

However, some supplementary measures like special recruitment and training drives by political parties for improving the efficacy of their women activists, gender sensitisation of male and female activists to reduce the backlash against women's reservation, evolving minimum common agenda for women representatives, would be necessary to make the policy of reservation deliver the goods (Nanivadekar 1998).

We are discussing this whole issue at a juncture where the demands for extending women's reservation in legislatures to OBC women, reservation within reservation for more under-privileged subgroups from SC/ST categories, reservation in jobs for economically backward non-SC/ST and reservation for the minorities are being made forcefully. This has overloaded the reservation discourse to such an extent that it may get crushed under its own weight. This overloading of the discourse is bound to have some negative impact on the issue of women's political empowerment with the pretext that the survival issues like availability of adequate safe drinking water, fuel and fodder, health care and employment are far more crucial than reservation in the Lok Sabha. Even the women's organisations find it difficult to mobilise grass-roots women for what Caroline Moser (1993) calls the strategic gender needs like reservation as compared to the above-mentioned practical gender needs.

The National Commission for Women had a joint consultation with the Parliamentary Committee on Empowerment of Women on 21 August 2003 that was also attended by representatives of mass women's organisations and NGOs. Consensus eluded even this consultation. Some women's organisations and NGOs were staunch supporters of the Women's Reservation Bill and insisted on passing a one-line resolution demanding its passage in the present form. But some activists and academics expressed grave concern over the issue of rotation. Finally Poornima Advani, chairperson of the National Commission for Women succeeded in passing a resolution, 'Women's Reservation Bill in the present form be debated and voted in the Parliament'. It must be noted that in a day-long discussion, the supporters of the Women's Reservation Bill could not come up with any solution to the problem of rotational reservation which, in addition to depriving the sitting members of their meticulously nurtured constituencies, is also bound to result in rupturing the process of leadership development at the national level. Some of them insisted that the MPs need not treat their constituency as their own private property and that nobody is indispensable. Ironically, some of these high profile NGO activists supporting rotational reservation of Lok Sabha constituencies are having an almost dynastic life-long rule in their centralised, rigidly hierarchical and 'corporatised' NGOs that leave no scope for the internal circulation of elite. If we have to have the model of rotational power sharing, it should be ingrained in the whole system and not be confined to the election of political executives alone.

The failure to enact the Women's Reservation Bill in spite of the seven-year-old commitment of all major political parties combined with their undue insistence on forging a consensus despite the required numeric strength has reduced the discourse on women's empowerment to a mere farce. I am on record of the Joint Committee on the 81st Constitution Amendment Bill for my support to the Women's Reservation Bill. But after closely observing the recent history of the Bill and the experience of rotational reservation in local bodies I feel that we must now reconcile to the fact that the Women's Reservation Bill with the principle of reservation by rotation is not the best alternative available. We cannot afford to rupture the process of the development of national leadership by unseating Members of Parliament at every second election. On a practical level, as the repeated debacle of the Bill in Parliament has now made plain, the chances of its passage through Parliament are remote. Moreover, we need not adopt a fundamentalist posture to insist on the passage of the same Bill in its present form. It is necessary to discuss the issue of rotation dispassionately and be open to some viable alternatives.

The new proposal for converting one-third Lok Sabha constituencies into dual-member constituencies assuring men their existing share of the pie seemingly holds a much-needed promise for resolving the deadlock over women's reservation. Converting all constituencies into dual-member constituencies would have been a logical option, albeit with severe financial implications. The new proposal has yet another advantage: that of increasing the number of representatives without lifting the freeze on delimitation. The increase in the number of seats by way of dual-membership would also partly answer the objection to increasing the number of seats in each state on the basis of increased population on the grounds that it would reward the states like Uttar Pradesh, Madhya Pradesh and Rajasthan that have failed to implement the population policy and penalise Tamil Nadu and Kerala who have successfully implemented it.

Some women's organisations and political parties have objected to the new proposal on the grounds that it would create a hierarchy among women representatives from open constituencies and those from the reserved ones, it would unwittingly reduce the status of women representatives to the 'also ran' category of a symbolic nature thus defeating the very notion of empowerment. But this objection is baseless because we already have multi-member constituencies in Rajya Sabha elections, in the local self-government institutions in Maharashtra as well as in the election to cooperative bodies. Women representatives can make their mark by judiciously utilising their own development fund for the constituency.

The new proposal of dual-member constituencies may not be perfect but it is feasible and it can be further improved by incorporating the six changes discussed earlier at length. If discussed and advocated effectively, it would muster support from various quarters. One prominent objection against the proposal for increasing the number of seats would be about the increased expenditure. But democracy will take its toll. Otherwise, if we were so much concerned with economy alone, even at the cost of democracy, gender equality and social justice, the best economic models would only be tyrannical ones.

Women's organisations and political parties would do well to lobby for its enactment instead of sticking to rigid positions, be it treating the older draft as sacrosanct or the insistence on reducing the quota to 20 per cent, or insisting on reservation for the OBCs although they are politically quite powerful. We also need to set a deadline on consensus-building measures or else we would end up with the annual feature of having more and more new proposals every year demanding an altogether new debate starting afresh with a new light, thus stalling the passage of the Bill forever. Fifteen years of dual-member constituencies in addition to reservation within the party organisation, if implemented simultaneously, should give a stimulus enough for sustaining the level of women's representation even after the expiry of reservation of constituencies after 15 years. Now instead of waiting infinitely for forging the so-called consensus, a Bill about dual-member constituencies incorporating the six changes proposed here should be drafted and be allowed to take the litmus test on the floor of the House.

Notes

[1] The parties present were the Bharatiya Janata Party, Indian National Congress (I), the Communist Party of India (Marxist) and the Samajwadi Party.
[2] PTI news service, New Delhi, 15 July 2003.
[3] NDTV news, 19 July 2003.
[4] Report of the Joint Committee on 81st Constitution Amendment Bill, Lok Sabha Secretariat, December 1996, p. vii.
[5] The other authors of this Bill are Jayaprakash Narayan, Yogendra Yadav and Dhirubhai Sheth. Shetkari Sangathana leader Sharad Joshi is a staunch supporter.
[6] The Rambhau Mhalgi Prabodhini delegation consisted of two more members, Vinay Sahasrabuddhe and Sharayu Anantram.
[7] Report of the Joint Committee on 81st Constitution Amendment Bill, Lok Sabha Secretariat, December 1996, p. vii.
[8] Evidence submitted to the Joint Committee on 81st Constitution Amendment Bill, Lok Sabha Secretariat, December 1996, pp. 34–42.
[9] I gratefully acknowledge the brief discussion with Jayawantiben Mehta, the Minister of State for Power, and then esteemed member of this Joint Committee.
[10] Interview in *'Subah Sabere'* on DD1, 26 October 1998.

References

Chhabra, Rami. 2000. 'Baking a Bigger Pie: Linking Women's Reservation with Delimitation.' *Manushi*. no 121. November-December. pp. 32-35.

Dahlerup, Drude. 1986. 'From a Small Minority to a Large Minority: Women in Scandinavian Politics' in *Scandinavian Political Studies*. vol. 11. no. 2.

Dalal, Mukesh. 2000. 'Women's Reservation: Another Approach'. *Manushi*. no. 120. September-October.

Datar, Chhaya. 1993. 'The Women's Movement in Maharashtra: An Overview' in *Struggle Against Violence*. ed. Chhaya Datar. Calcutta: Stree.

Kishwar Madhu. 1996. 'Out of the Zenana Dabba: Strategies for Enhancing Women's Political Representation'. *Manushi*. no. 96. September-October.

Kumar, Sanjay. 2003. 'Delimitation on Basis of 2001 Census: Damage Control Exercise'. *Economic and Political Weekly*. 10 May.

Moser, Caroline. 1993. *Gender, Planning and Development: Theory, Practice and Training*. London: Routledge.

Nanivadekar, Medha. 1997. *Empowering Women: Assessing the Policy of Reservation in Local Bodies*. Mumbai: Rambhau Mhalgi Prabodhini.

———.1998. 'Reservation for Women: Challenge of Tackling Counterproductive Trends'. *Economic and Political Weekly*. vol. xxxiii. no. 28, 11-17 July. pp. 1815-19.

Narayan, Jayaprakash, Madhu Kishwar et al. 2000. 'Enhancing Women's Representation in the Legislatures: An Alternative to the Government Bill for Women's Reservation'. *Manushi*. no. 116. January-February.

Published in *Economic and Political Weekly*, Commentary, 25 October 2003.

Appendix I

The Constitution (Eighty-First Amendment) Bill, 1996

A Bill further to amend the Constitution of India.

Be it enacted by Parliament in the Forty-seventh Year of the Republic of India as follows:-

1. (1) This Act may be called the Constitution (Eighty-first Amendment) Act, 1996.
   (2) It shall come into force on such date as the Central Government may by notification in the Official Gazette, appoint.

2. After article 330 of the Constitution, the following article shall be inserted, namely:-
   '330A (1) Seats shall be reserved for women in the House of the People.
   (2) Not less than one-third of the total number of seats reserved under clause (2) of the article 330 shall be reserved for women belonging to the Scheduled Castes or as the case may be, the Scheduled Tribes.
   Provided that nothing in this clause shall apply in relation to a State or Union territory so long as the number of seats reserved for Scheduled Castes or Scheduled Tribes, as the case may be, in that State or Union territory, is less than three.
   (3) Not less than one-third (including the number of seats reserved for women belonging to the Scheduled Castes and the Scheduled Tribes) of the total number of seats to be filled by direct election to the House of the People in a State or Union territory shall be reserved for women and such seats may be allotted by rotation to different constituencies in that State or Union territory:

Provided that nothing in this clause shall apply in relation to a State or Union territory so long as the number of seats allotted to such State or Union territory is less than three'.

3. After article 332 of the Constitution, the following article shall be inserted, namely:-

'332A (1) Seats shall be reserved for women in the Legislative Assembly of every State.

(2) Not less than one-third of the total number of seats reserved under clause (3) of article 332 shall be reserved for women belonging to the Scheduled Castes or as the case may be, the Scheduled Tribes.

Provided that nothing in this clause shall apply in relation to a State or Union territory so long as the number of seats reserved for Scheduled Castes or Scheduled Tribes, as the case may be, in that State, is less than three.

(3) Not less than one-third (including the number of seats reserved for women belonging to the Scheduled Castes and the Scheduled Tribes) of the total number of seats to be filled by direct election in the Legislative Assembly of every State shall be reserved for women and such seats may be allotted by rotation to different constituencies in that State:

Provided that nothing in this clause shall apply in relation to a State so long as the number of seats allotted to such State is less than three.'

4. The Amendments made to the Constitution, by this Act, shall not affect any representation in the House of the People or in the Legislative Assembly of a State until the dissolution of the House or the Assembly, as the case may be, in existence at the commencement of this Act.

Statement of Objects and Reasons

Article 243D and 243T inserted by the Constitution (Seventy-third Amendment) Act, 1992 and the Constitution (Seventy-fourth Amendment) Act, 1992 respectively provide that not less than one-third of the seats shall be reserved for women in every Panchayat and every Municipality. Further, the said articles provide that, from amongst the seats reserved for the Scheduled Castes and the Scheduled Tribes not less than one-third seats shall be reserved for women belonging to the Scheduled Castes or, as the case may be, the Scheduled Tribes. The said articles also provide that such seats reserved for women may be allotted by rotation to different constituencies.

2. Having provided reservation for women in Panchayats and Municipalities, it is now proposed to provide reservation for women on the same lines in the House of the People and the Legislative Assemblies of the States by amending the Constitution. The major political parties are in favour of making such reservation for women.

3. The Bill seeks to achieve the aforesaid object.

New Delhi
The 4th September, 1996   *Ramakant D. Khalap*

Published in *Indian Journal of Gender Studies*, 6:1, 1999.

Appendix 2a

Women in National Parliaments as of 31 January 2007

The data in the tables below has been compiled by the Inter-Parliamentary Union on the basis of information provided by National Parliaments by 31 January 2007. The percentages do not take into account the case of Parliaments for which no data was available at that date.

World Average

Both Houses Combined
Total MPs	43,882
Gender breakdown known for	43,882
Men	36,446
Women	7,436
Percentage of women	16.9%

Single House or Lower House
Total MPs	37,174
Gender breakdown known for	37,174
Men	30,812
Women	6,362
Percentage of women	17.1%

Upper House or Senate
Total MPs	6,708
Gender breakdown known for	6,708
Men	5,634
Women	1,074
Percentage of women	16.0%

Regional Averages

	Single House or Lower House	Upper House or Senate	Both Houses combined
Nordic countries	40.8%		40.8%
Americas	20.0%	19.3%	19.9%
Europe—OSCE member countries including Nordic countries	19.7%	17.5%	19.2%
Europe—OSCE member countries excluding Nordic countries	17.6%	17.5%	17.6%
Sub-Saharan Africa	16.6%	18.5%	16.8%
Asia	16.5%	15.7%	16.4%
Pacific	12.4%	31.8%	14.5%
Arab States	9.5%	6.3%	8.8%

Regions are classified by descending order of the percentage of women in the Lower or Single House.

Appendix 2b

Women in National Parliaments as of 31 January 2007

The data in the table below has been compiled by the Inter-Parliamentary Union on the basis of information provided by National Parliaments by 31 January 2007. 189 countries are classified by descending order of the percentage of women in the Lower or Single House.

World Classification

Rank	Country	Lower or Single House				Upper House or Senate			
		Elections	Seats*	Women	%W	Elections	Seats*	Women	%W
1	Rwanda	09 2003	80	39	48.8	09 2003	26	9	34.6
2	Sweden	09 2006	349	165	47.3	-	-	-	-
3	Costa Rica	02 2006	57	22	38.6	-	-	-	-
4	Finland	03 2003	200	76	38.0	-	-	-	-
5	Norway	09 2005	169	64	37.9	-	-	-	-
6	Denmark	02 2005	179	66	36.9	-	-	-	-
7	Netherlands	11 2006	150	55	36.7	06 2003	75	22	29.3
8	Cuba	01 2003	609	219	36.0	-	-	-	-
"	Spain	03 2004	350	126	36.0	03 2004	259	60	23.2
9	Argentina	10 2005	257	90	35.0	10 2005	72	31	43.1
10	Mozambique	12 2004	250	87	34.8	-	-	-	-
11	Belgium	05 2003	150	52	34.7	05 2003	71	27	38.0
12	Iceland	05 2003	63	21	33.3	-	-	-	-
13	South Africa[1]	04 2004	400	131	32.8	04 2004	54	18	33.3
14	Austria	10 2006	183	59	32.2	N.A.	62	17	27.4
"	New Zealand	09 2005	121	39	32.2	-	-	-	-
15	Germany	09 2005	614	194	31.6	N.A.	69	15	21.7
16	Burundi	07 2005	118	36	30.5	07 2005	49	17	34.7

APPENDIX 2B

Rank	Country	Lower or Single House				Upper House or Senate			
		Elections	Seats*	Women	%W	Elections	Seats*	Women	%W
17	United Rep. Of Tanzania	12 2005	319	97	30.4	-	-	-	-
18	Uganda	02 2006	332	99	29.8	-	-	-	-
19	Seychelles	12 2002	34	10	29.4	-	-	-	-
20	Peru	04 2006	120	35	29.2	-	-	-	-
21	Belarus	10 2004	110	32	29.1	11 2004	58	18	31.0
22	Guyana	08 2006	69	20	29.0	-	-	-	-
23	Andorra	04 2005	28	8	28.6	-	-	-	-
24	The F.Y.R. of Macedonia	07 2006	120	34	28.3	-	-	-	-
25	Afghanistan	09 2005	249	68	27.3	09 2005	102	23	22.5
"	Vietnam	05 2002	498	136	27.3	-	-	-	-
26	Namibia	11 2004	78	21	26.9	11 2004	26	7	26.9
27	Grenada	11 2003	15	4	26.7	11 2003	13	4	30.8
28	Iraq	12 2005	275	70	25.5	-	-	-	-
"	Suriname	05 2005	51	13	25.5	-	-	-	-
29	Timor-Leste	08 2001	87	22	25.3	-	-	-	-
30	Lao People's Democratic Rep.	04 2006	115	29	25.2	-	-	-	-
31	Ecuador	10 2006	100	25	25.0	-	-	-	-
"	Switzerland	10 2003	200	50	25.0	10 2003	46	11	23.9
32	Lithuania	10 2004	141	35	24.8	-	-	-	-
33	Australia	10 2004	150	37	24.7	10 2004	76	27	35.5
34	Singapore	05 2006	94	23	24.5	-	-	-	-
35	Liechtenstein	03 2005	25	6	24.0	-	-	-	-
36	Honduras	11 2005	128	30	23.4	-	-	-	-
37	Luxembourg	06 2004	60	14	23.3	-	-	-	-
38	Tunisia	10 2004	189	43	22.8	07 2005	112	15	13.4
39	Mexico	07 2006	500	113	22.6	07 2006	128	22	17.2
40	United Arab Emirates	12 2006	40	9	22.5	-	-	-	-
41	Bulgaria	06 2005	240	53	22.1	-	-	-	-
42	Eritrea	02 1994	150	33	22.0	-	-	-	-
43	Ethiopia	05 2005	529	116	21.9	10 2005	112	21	18.8
44	Republic of Moldova	03 2005	101	22	21.8	-	-	-	-
45	Croatia	11 2003	152	33	21.7	-	-	-	-
46	Pakistan	10 2002	342	73	21.3	03 2006	100	17	17.0
"	Portugal	02 2005	230	49	21.3	-	-	-	-

APPENDIX 2B

Rank	Country	Lower or Single House				Upper House or Senate			
		Elections	Seats*	Women	%W	Elections	Seats*	Women	%W
47	Canada	01 2006	308	64	20.8	N.A.	100	35	35.0
"	Monaco	02 2003	24	5	20.8	-	-	-	-
48	Poland	09 2005	460	94	20.4	09 2005	100	13	13.0
"	Serbia	01 2007	250	51	20.4	-	-	-	-
49	China	02 2003	2980	604	20.3	-	-	-	-
50	Dem. People's Rep. of Korea	08 2003	687	138	20.1	-	-	-	-
51	Bahamas	05 2002	40	8	20.0	05 2002	16	7	43.8
"	Slovakia	06 2006	150	30	20.0	-	-	-	-
52	Dominican Republic	05 2006	178	35	19.7	05 2006	32	1	3.1
"	United Kingdom	05 2005	646	127	19.7	05 2006	32	1	3.1
53	Trinidad and Tobago	10 2002	36	7	19.4	10 2002	31	10	32.3
54	Guinea	06 2002	114	22	19.3	-	-	-	-
55	Senegal	04 2001	120	23	19.2	-	-	-	-
56	Latvia	10 2006	100	19	19.0	-	-	-	-
57	Estonia	03 2003	101	19	18.8	-	-	-	-
58	Saint Vincent & the Grenadines	12 2005	22	4	18.2	-	-	-	-
59	Equatorial Guinea	04 2004	100	18	18.0	-	-	-	-
"	Venezuela	12 2005	167	30	18.0	-	-	-	-
60	Mauritania	11 2006	95	17	17.9	01 2007	38	9	23.7
61	Sudan	08 2005	450	80	17.8	08 2005	50	2	4.0
62	Tajikistan	02 2005	63	11	17.5	03 2005	34	8	23.5
"	Uzbekistan	12 2004	120	21	17.5	01 2005	100	15	15.0
63	Italy	04 2006	630	109	17.3	04 2006	322	44	13.7
"	Nepal	01 2007	329	57	17.3	-	-	-	-
64	Mauritius	07 2005	70	12	17.1	-	-	-	-
65	Bolivia	12 2005	130	22	16.9	12 2005	27	1	3.7
66	El Salvador	03 2006	84	14	16.7	-	-	-	-
"	Panama	05 2004	78	13	16.7	-	-	-	-
"	Zimbabwe	03 2005	150	25	16.7	11 2005	66	23	34.8
67	United States of America	11 2006	435	71	16.3	11 2006	100	16	16.0
68	Turkmenistan	12 2004	50	8	16.0	-	-	-	-
69	Czech Republic	06 2006	200	31	15.5	10 2006	81	12	14.8
70	Cape Verde	01 2006	72	11	15.3	-	-	-	-
"	Philippines	05 2004	236	36	15.3	05 2004	24	4	16.7

APPENDIX 2B

Rank	Country	Lower or Single House Elections	Seats*	Women	%W	Upper House or Senate Elections	Seats*	Women	%W
71	Nicaragua	11 2006	92	14	15.2	-	-	-	-
72	Bangladesh[2]	10 2001	345	52	15.1	-	-	-	-
73	Angola	09 1992	220	33	15.0	-	-	-	-
"	Chile	12 2005	120	18	15.0	12 2005	38	2	5.3
74	Zambia	09 2006	157	23	14.6	-	-	-	-
75	Sierra Leone	05 2002	124	18	14.5	-	-	-	-
76	Bosnia and Herzegovina	10 2006	42	6	14.3	10 2002	15	1	6.7
"	Cyprus	05 2006	56	8	14.3	-	-	-	-
77	Israel	03 2006	120	17	14.2	-	-	-	-
78	Guinea-Bissau	03 2004	100	14	14.0	-	-	-	-
79	Malawi	04 2004	191	26	13.6	-	-	-	-
80	Republic of Korea	04 2004	299	40	13.4	-	-	-	-
81	Barbados	05 2003	30	4	13.3	05 2003	21	5	23.8
"	Ireland	05 2002	166	22	13.3	07 2002	60	10	16.7
82	Greece	03 2004	300	39	13.0	-	-	-	-
83	Dominica	05 2005	31	4	12.9	-	-	-	-
84	Gabon	12 2006	120	15	12.5	02 2003	91	14	15.4
"	Liberia	10 2005	64	8	12.5	10 2005	30	5	16.7
85	Niger	11 2004	113	14	12.4	-	-	-	-
86	France	06 2002	574	70	12.2	09 2004	331	56	16.9
"	Slovenia	10 2004	90	11	12.2	12 2002	40	3	7.5
87	Maldives	01 2005	50	6	12.0	-	-	-	-
"	Syrian Arab Rep.	03 2003	250	30	12.0	-	-	-	-
88	Burkina Faso	05 2002	111	13	11.7	-	-	-	-
"	Jamaica	10 2002	60	7	11.7	10 2002	21	4	19.0
"	Lesotho	05 2002	120	14	11.7	N.A.	33	12	36.4
"	San Marino	06 2006	60	7	11.7	-	-	-	-
89	Azerbaijan	11 2005	124	14	11.3	-	-	-	-
"	Indonesia	04 2004	550	62	11.3	-	-	-	-
90	Romania	11 2004	331	37	11.2	11 2004	137	13	9.5
91	Botswana	10 2004	63	7	11.1	-	-	-	-
"	Uruguay	10 2004	99	11	11.1	10 2004	31	3	9.7
92	Ghana	12 2004	230	25	10.9	-	-	-	-
93	Djibouti	01 2003	65	7	10.8	-	-	-	-
"	Morocco	09 2002	325	35	10.8	09 2006	270	3	1.1
"	Swaziland	10 2003	65	7	10.8	10 2003	30	9	30.0

APPENDIX 2B

Rank	Country	Lower or Single House				Upper House or Senate			
		Elections	Seats*	Women	%W	Elections	Seats*	Women	%W
94	Antigua and Barbuda	03 2004	19	2	10.5	03 2004	17	3	17.6
"	Central African Republic	05 2005	105	11	10.5	-	-	-	-
95	Hungary	04 2006	386	40	10.4	-	-	-	-
"	Kazakhstan	09 2004	77	8	10.4	09 2004	39	2	5.1
96	Mali	07 2002	147	15	10.2	-	-	-	-
97	Paraguay	04 2003	80	8	10.0	04 2003	45	4	8.9
98	Cambodia	07 2003	123	12	9.8	01 2006	61	9	14.8
"	Russian Federation	12 2003	447	44	9.8	N.A.	178	6	3.4
99	Gambia	01 2007	53	5	9.4	-	-	-	-
"	Georgia	03 2004	235	22	9.4	-	-	-	-
"	Japan	09 2005	480	45	9.4	07 2004	242	35	14.5
100	Malta	04 2003	65	6	9.2	-	-	-	-
101	Malaysia	03 2004	219	20	9.1	03 2004	70	18	25.7
102	Cameroon	06 2002	180	16	8.9	-	-	-	-
103	Brazil	10 2006	513	45	8.8	10 2006	81	10	12.3
104	Thailand	10 2006	242	21	8.7	-	-	-	-
"	Ukraine	03 2006	450	39	8.7	-	-	-	-
105	Montenegro	09 2006	81	7	8.6	-	-	-	-
"	Togo	10 2002	81	7	8.6	-	-	-	-
106	Congo	05 2002	129	11	8.5	10 2005	60	8	13.3
"	Cote d'Ivoire	12 2000	223	19	8.5	-	-	-	-
107	Colombia	03 2006	166	14	8.4	03 2006	102	12	11.8
"	Dem. Republic of the Congo	07 2006	500	42	8.4	01 2007	108	5	4.6
108	India	04 2004	545	45	8.3	07 2006	242	26	10.7
109	Guatemala	11 2003	158	13	8.2	-	-	-	-
110	Somalia	08 2004	269	21	7.8	-	-	-	-
111	Libyan Arab Jamahiriya	03 2006	468	36	7.7	-	-	-	-
112	Kenya	12 2002	219	16	7.3	-	-	-	-
"	Sao Tome and Principe	03 2006	55	4	7.3	-	-	-	-

APPENDIX 2B

Rank	Country	Lower or Single House				Upper House or Senate			
		Elections	Seats*	Women	%W	Elections	Seats*	Women	%W
113	Benin	03 2003	83	6	7.2	-	-	-	-
114	Albania	07 2005	140	10	7.1	-	-	-	-
"	Kiribati	05 2003	42	3	7.1	-	-	-	-
115	Madagascar	12 2002	160	11	6.9	03 2001	90	10	11.1
116	Belize	03 2003	30	2	6.7	03 2003	12	3	25.0
117	Mongolia	06 2004	76	5	6.6	-	-	-	-
118	Chad	04 2002	155	10	6.5	-	-	-	-
119	Algeria	05 2002	389	24	6.2	12 2006	144	4	2.8
120	Nigeria	04 2003	360	22	6.1	04 2003	109	4	3.7
"	Samoa	03 2006	49	3	6.1	-	-	-	-
121	Saint Lucia[3]	12 2006	18	1	5.6	01 2007	11	2	18.2
122	Jordan	06 2003	110	6	5.5	11 2005	55	7	12.7
123	Armenia	05 2003	131	7	5.3	-	-	-	-
124	Sri Lanka	04 2004	225	11	4.9	-	-	-	-
125	Lebanon	05 2005	128	6	4.7	-	-	-	-
126	Turkey	11 2002	550	24	4.4	-	-	-	-
127	Haiti	02 2006	98	4	4.1	02 2006	30	4	13.3
"	Iran (Islamic Rep. of)	02 2004	290	12	4.1	-	-	-	-
128	Vanuatu	07 2004	52	2	3.8	-	-	-	-
129	Tonga	03 2005	30	1	3.3	-	-	-	-
130	Comoros	04 2004	33	1	3.0	-	-	-	-
"	Marshall Islands	11 2003	33	1	3.0	-	-	-	-
131	Bhutan	N.A.	150	4	2.7	-	-	-	-
132	Bahrain	11 2006	40	1	2.5	12 2006	40	10	25.0
133	Oman	10 2003	83	2	2.4	N.A.	58	9	15.5
134	Egypt	11 2005	442	9	2.0	05 2004	264	18	6.8
135	Kuwait[4]	06 2006	65	1	1.5	-	-	-	-
136	Papua New Guinea	06 2002	109	1	0.9	-	-	-	-
137	Yemen	04 2003	301	1	0.3	04 2001	111	2	1.8

APPENDIX 2B

Rank	Country	Lower or Single House				Upper House or Senate			
		Elections	Seats*	Women	%W	Elections	Seats*	Women	%W
138	Kyrgyzstan	02 2005	72	0	0.0	-	-	-	-
"	Micronesia (Fed. States Of)	03 2005	14	0	0.0	-	-	-	-
"	Nauru	10 2004	18	0	0.0	-	-	-	-
"	Palau	11 2004	16	0	0.0	11 2004	9	0	0.0
"	Qatar	06 2005	35	0	0.0	-	-	-	-
"	Saint Kitts and Nevis	10 2004	15	0	0.0	-	-	-	-
"	Saudi Arabia	04 2005	150	0	0.0	-	-	-	-
"	Solomon Islands	04 2006	50	0	0.0	-	-	-	-
"	Tuvalu	08 2006	15	0	0.0	-	-	-	-

Notes: * Figures correspond to the number of seats currently filled in Parliament

1. South Africa: The figures on the distribution of seats do not include the 36 special rotating delegates appointed on an ad hoc basis, and all percentages given are therefore calculated on the basis of the 54 permanent seats.

2. Bangladesh: In 2004, the number of seats in Parliament was raised from 300 to 345, with the addition of 45 reserved seats for women. These reserved seats were filled in September and October 2005, being allocated to political parties in proportion to their share of the national vote received in the 2001 election.

3. Saint Lucia: No woman was elected in the 2006 elections. However one woman was appointed Speaker of the House and therefore became a member of the House.

4. Kuwait: No woman candidate was elected in the 2006 elections. One woman was appointed to the 16-member cabinet. As cabinet ministers also sit in Parliament, there is therefore one woman out of a total of 65 members.

Contributors

RAGHABENDRA CHATTOPADHYAY is Professor of Business Environment and Member of Faculty in the Public Policy and Management Group, Indian Institute of Management Calcutta since 1987. At present he is conducting a joint research on gender inequalities and quality of life in Indian villages with Professor Esther Duflo, Rohini Pande, Petia Topalova and Lori Beaman. He is also working on research projects on Rajasthan Police Reform, and the impact of micro-financing on the rural poor in India, with Professors Abhijit Banerjee and E. Duflo, both of MIT, USA.

MEENA DHANDA is head of Philosophy at the University of Wolverhampton, where she has taught since 1992. She did her DPhil in Philosophy at Oxford on 'The Negotiation of Personal Identity' and was a member of the editorial board of *Women's Philosophy Review* for several years. Her publications include: 'L'eveil des intouchables en Inde' (1993), 'Openness, Identity and Acknowledgement of Persons' (1994), 'Theorising with a Practical Intent: Philosophy, Politics and Communication', an interview with Professor Iris Marion Young (2000), 'Bringing us into Twenty-first Century Feminism, with Joy and Wit', an interview with Professor Michéle Le Doeuff (2002), 'The invisible power of piety wearing stilettos' (2006), 'What does the veil make me, and her?' (forthcoming). She is currently working on a project on dalit identity.

ESTHER DUFLO is the Abdul Latif Jameel Professor of Poverty Alleviation and Development Economics in the Department of Economics at the Massachusetts Institute of Technology. She is a co-founder and director of the Abdul Latif Jameel Poverty Action Lab and on the board of directors of the Bureau for Research and Economic Analysis of Development (BREAD). She is the director of the development economics programme at the Centre of Economic Policy Research. She is the recipient of the American Economic Association's Elaine Bennett Prize for Research (2003) and Le Monde's Cercle des économistes Best Young French Economist Prize (2005). She is currently the inaugural editor of the American economic journal: *Applied Economics*.

NANDITA GANDHI is Co-Director and Managing Trustee of *Akshara*, a women's resource centre in Mumbai and has been active in the women's movement. Her publications include 'Let A Thousand Flowers Bloom: Creating Alternative Classification Systems' and 'Quilting The Net: An Experiment With Online Learning' (2003). Dr Gandhi is the author of *When the Rolling Pins Hit the Streets: Women in the Anti Price Rise Movement in Maharashtra* (1996), and also co-author, with Nandita Shah, of *Issues at Stake: Theory and Practice in the Contemporary Women's Movement in India* (1992), and 'Inter Movement Dialogues: Breaking Barriers, Building Bridges' (2006).

R. GEETHA is a social and political activist. Based in Chennai, she is the South Regional Coordinator, National Campaign Committee for Unorganised Sector Workers.

MARY E. JOHN, Director of the Centre for Women's Development Studies, New Delhi, has been active in the fields of women's studies and feminist politics. She was Associate Professor and Deputy Director of the Women's Studies Programme at Jawaharlal Nehru University, New Delhi from 2001-2006. Her publications include *Discrepant Dislocations: Feminism, Theory and Post-colonial Histories*, (1996), *A Question of Silence? The Sexual Economies of Modern India* (co-edited with Janaki Nair, 2000), *French Feminism: An Indian Anthology* (co-edited with Danielle Haas-Dubosc et al., 2002), *Contested Transformations: Changing Economies and Identities in Contemporary India*, (co-edited with Praveen Kumar Jha and Surinder S. Jodhka, 2006), *Women's Studies in India: A Reader* (forthcoming, 2008).

MADHU PURNIMA KISHWAR is Senior Fellow at the Centre for the Study of Developing Societies (CSDS) in Delhi and Director of its Indic Studies Project. She is the founder editor of *Manushi—a Journal about Women and Society* published since 1979. In recent years her work has centred on issues relating to laws, liberty and livelihoods as well as activist interventions for policy reform for street vendors and cycle rickshaw pullers. Her numerous publications include *Religion at the Service of Nationalism and Other Essays* (1998), *Off the Beaten Track: Rethinking Gender Justice for Indian Women* (1999), *Rashtriyata ki Chakri Mein Dharm* (Hindi, 2005) and *Deepening Democracy: Challenges of Governance and Globalization in India* (2005). Kishwar has also conceptualised and anchored several television programmes and made documentaries dealing with current political issues.

STÉPHANIE TAWA LAMA-REWAL is Research Fellow at the Centre for the Study of India and South Asia (CNRS-EHESS, Paris), presently detached to the Centre de Sciences Humaines de New Delhi. She works on the political representation of groups (more particularly women) in India and Nepal. Her publications include, 'The Hindu Goddess and Women's Political Representation in South Asia: Symbolic Resource or Feminine Mystique?' in *Revue Internationale de Sociologie* (2001), *Femmes et politique en Inde et au Népal: Image et présence*, (2004), and *Democratization in Progress: Women and Local Politics in Urban India* (with Archana Ghosh, 2005).

VINA MAZUMDAR taught Political Science at the Universities of Patna and Berhampur. She was Director, Programme of Women's Studies, Indian Council of Social Science Research for five years (1975-80) and also Fellow of the Indian Institute of Advanced Studies, Shimla. As Member Secretary of the Committee on the Status of Women in India in 1974, she drafted the *Towards Equality* report, which has been the turning point, both for women's studies and the women's movement in India. As co-founder of the Centre for Women's Development Studies in Delhi, she was its Director for many years and is currently its Senior Fellow.

NIVEDITA MENON is a feminist scholar and political theorist who has published widely in Indian and international academic journals. She is currently Reader in the Department of Political Science, University of Delhi. Menon has been involved in a wide range of political and social movements, especially against the rise of sectarian politics and the mass displacement of workers. She is the author of *Recovering Subversion: Feminist Politics beyond the Law* (2004), and the editor of *Gender and Politics in India* (1999), and *Sexualities* (2007).

SAROJINI NAIDU (1879-1949) born Sarojini Chattopadhyay, was educated in Chennai, King's College, London, and Cambridge. In 1898, breaking the bonds of caste, she married Dr M.G. Naidu. Her poetry published in three volumes—*The Golden Threshold* (1905), *The Bird of Time* (1912), and *The Broken Wing* (1915)—was written in English but deals, in a romantic vein, with Indian themes. She was active in the Indian National Congress and in 1925 became its first woman president. She was a close associate of Mahatma Gandhi, and served as governor of the United Provinces (1947-49).

MEDHA NANIVADEKAR is Director, Centre for Women's Studies at Shivaji University Kolhapur, India and a professional lecturer at the Women and Politics Institute, USA. She has conducted research with the Institute comparing women's political empowerment in the US and India, focusing on the role of women's organisations and the impact of women serving in the national legislatures. In 2003 she was appointed on the National Women's Commission's panel of experts on Women's Political Empowerment in India. Her publications include: *Electoral Process in Corporation Election: A Gender Study* (1997), and *Empowering Women: Assessing the Policy of Reservations in Local Bodies—A Report* (1997).

CONTRIBUTORS

JAYAPRAKASH NARAYAN, a physician by training, joined the Indian Administrative Service (IAS) in 1980 and had a distinguished career. In 1996, he resigned as Secretary to the government and formed Lok Satta to work for fundamental political changes. He is currently its Campaign Coordinator and has also served on several panels constituted by the Government of India, including the National Advisory Council (NAC) for the implementation of the National Common Minimum Programme; Vigilance Advisory Council and the Second Administrative Reforms Commission.

GAIL OMVEDT is currently Visiting Professor and Coordinator, School of Social Justice, University of Pune, India. Born in the USA, she became an Indian citizen in 1983. As a scholar-activist, she has been actively involved with movements for women's empowerment such as benefits for abandoned women, women's land rights and anti-caste and environmental campaigns. Among her numerous books are: *We Shall Smash this Prison: Indian Women in Struggle* (1979), *Reinventing Revolution: New Social Movements in India* (1993), *Gender and Technology: Emerging Asian Visions* (1994), *Dalit Visions* (1994), *Buddhism in India: Challenging Brahmanism and Caste* (2003), *Ambedkar: Towards an Enlightened India* (2005) and *Seeking Begumpura: The Social Vision of Anti-caste Intellectuals* (forthcoming). She has been a consultant on gender, environment and rural development for UNDP, NOVIB and other institutions.

ANNE PHILLIPS is Professor of Political and Gender Theory, and holds a joint appointment at the Gender Institute and Department of Government at the London School of Economics. She has written widely on themes in feminist political theory, ranging through equality and difference, democracy and representation to human rights and multiculturalism. Her publications include *Engendering Democracy* (1991), *The Politics of Presence: the Political Representation of Gender, Ethnicity and Race* (1995), *Which Equalities Matter?* (1999), *Multiculturalism without Culture* (2007), and a recently co-edited book, with

John Dryzek and Bonnie Honig, the *Oxford Handbook of Political Theory* (2006).

SHIRIN RAI is Professor in the Department of Politics and International Studies at the University of Warwick, UK and is currently Director of a Leverhulme Trust-funded Programme on 'Ceremony and Ritual in Parliament'. Her other research foci are gender and representation in the Indian Parliament, global governance and gender politics of development. Her publications include *Chinese Politics and Society: An Introduction* (with co-author Flemming Christiansen, 1996), *International Perspectives on Gender and Democratisation* (ed., 2000) and *Gender and Political Economy of Development: From Nationalism to Globalisation* (2002).

VASANTHI RAMAN is Fellow at the Indian Institute of Advanced Study, Shimla. She has been Senior Fellow at the Centre for Women's Development Studies, New Delhi and was it Deputy Director from 2005-2007. Important articles include: 'Understanding Hindu-Muslim Relations: The Banaras Story' (2002), 'The Implementation of Quotas for Women: The Indian Experience' (2003), 'The Diverse Life-Worlds of Indian Childhood' (2003), 'The Surang (Tunnel) of Madanpura: Partition Motif in Banaras' (2007), 'The Women's Question in Contemporary Indian Politics' (republished 2007). Her forthcoming book is titled, *The Warp and the Weft: Understanding Community and Gender in the Tana Bana of Banaras Weavers*.

LOTIKA SARKAR is Senior Fellow at the Centre for Women's Development Studies, New Delhi and earlier taught criminal law, at the Faculty of Law, University of Delhi. With Vina Mazumdar, she wrote the Report for the Government of India Committee on the Status of Women in India, published as *Towards Equality* (1974). Professor Sarkar has played a central role in important legal debates, including public interest litigation. Her recent publications include *Women and Law: Contemporary Problems* (edited with B. Sivaramayya, 1994), and *Between Tradition, Counter tradition and Heresy: Contributions in Honour of Vina Mazumdar* (with Leela Kasturi and Kumud Sharma, 2002).

NANDITA SHAH is Co-Director and Managing Trustee of *Akshara*, a women's resource centre in Mumbai, where she introduced the Yuvati Mela, a popular, interactive communications model for young women. Dr Shah is a professional social worker, activist of the women's movement and a gender trainer. She has co-authored a number of books and articles, including *Issues at Stake: Theory and Practice in the Contemporary Women's Movement in India* (with Nandita Gandhi, 1992) and 'Women Workers and Industrial Restructuring in Two Industries in Mumbai' (2005).

BEGUM JEHAN ARA SHAH NAWAZ (1896-1979) was educated at Queen Mary College, Lahore. As vice-president of the Central Committee of the All India Muslim Women's Conference she succeeded in having a resolution passed against polygamy in 1918. She was one of two women delegates to the Round Table Conference. In 1935, she founded the Punjab Provincial Women's Muslim League. In 1946, she was sent to the USA to explain the Muslim League's point of view. Her publications include *Father and Daughter: A Political Biography* (1971).

D.L. SHETH is Honorary Senior Fellow at the Centre for the Study of Developing Societies (CSDS) and was its director from 1984-1987. He is Editor of the journal *Alternatives: Global, Local, Political*, was founder director of Lokayan, a project on development, decentralisation and democracy (1980-82), a member of the National Commission for Backward Classes (1993-96), and president of Delhi Peoples' Union for Civil Liberties (PUCL). He has contributed to the 2004 Human Development Report, is the editor of *Minority Identities and the Nation State* (with Gurpreet Mahajan), and of *The Multiverse of Democracy* (with Ashis Nandy, 1996). He has written numerous papers on caste, poverty and development.

CONTRIBUTORS

RAJESWARI SUNDER RAJAN is Global Distinguished Professor of English at New York University. She is the author of *The Scandal of the State: Women, Law and Citizenship in Postcolonial India* (2003); *Real and Imagined Women: Gender, Culture and Postcolonialism* (1993); and has edited a collection of essays, *Signposts: Gender Issues in Post-Independence India* (1999) and most recently, co-edited *The Crisis of Secularism in India* (2006).

YOGENDRA YADAV is Co-Director of Lokniti and Senior Fellow at the Centre for the Study of Developing Societies, CSDS. He has designed and co-ordinated the National Election Studies from 1996 to 2004. He is one of the General Editors of *Lokchintan* and *Lokchintak Granthamala*, a series of social science anthologies in Hindi, is on the International Advisory Board of the *European Journal of Political Research*, and currently Executive Editor of *Samayik Varta*. He is a psephologist and political commentator analysing elections on several TV channels. Amongst his writings are: 'Understanding the Second Democratic Upsurge: Trends of Bahujan Participation in Electoral Politics in the 1990s' (2000), 'A Radical Agenda for Political Reforms' (2001), and 'Predicting the 1998 Indian Parliamentary Elections' (with Rajeeva L. Karandikar and Clive Payne, 2002).